In the Classroom

- Read all of the directions. Make sure you understand them. When you see ▨, be sure to follow the safety rule.

- Listen to your teacher for special safety directions. If you don't understand something, ask for help.

- Wear safety goggles when your teacher tells you to wear them and whenever you see 👓.

- Wear a safety apron if you work with anything messy or anything that might spill.

- If you spill something, wipe it up right away or ask your teacher for help.

- Tell your teacher if something breaks. If glass breaks do not clean it up yourself.

- Keep your hair and clothes away from open flames. Tie back long hair and roll up long sleeves.

- Be careful around a hot plate. Know when it is on and when it is off. Remember that the plate stays hot for a few minutes after you turn it off.

- Keep your hands dry around electrical equipment.

- Don't eat or drink anything during an experiment.

- Put equipment back the way your teacher tells you.

- Dispose of things the way your teacher tells you.

- Clean up your work area and wash your hands.

In the Field

- Always be accompanied by a trusted adult—like your teacher or a parent or guardian.

- Never touch animals or plants without the adult's approval. The animal might bite. The plant may be poison ivy or another dangerous plant.

Responsibility

- Treat living things, the environment, and each other with respect.

McGRAW-HILL
SCIENCE

MACMILLAN/McGRAW-HILL EDITION

RICHARD MOYER ■ LUCY DANIEL ■ JAY HACKETT
PRENTICE BAPTISTE ■ PAMELA STRYKER ■ JOANNE VASQUEZ

NATIONAL
GEOGRAPHIC
SOCIETY

McGraw-Hill
School Division

New York   Farmington

PROGRAM AUTHORS

Dr. Lucy H. Daniel
Teacher, Consultant
Rutherford County Schools,
North Carolina

Dr. Jay Hackett
Emeritus Professor of Earth
Sciences
University of Northern
Colorado

Dr. Richard H. Moyer
Professor of Science
Education
University of Michigan-
Dearborn

Dr. H. Prentice Baptiste
Professor of Curriculum and
Instruction
New Mexico State
University

Pamela Stryker, M.Ed.
Elementary Educator and
Science Consultant
Eanes Independent School
District
Austin, Texas

JoAnne Vasquez, M.Ed.
Elementary Science
Education Specialist
Mesa Public Schools,
Arizona
NSTA President 1996–1997

NATIONAL
GEOGRAPHIC
SOCIETY

Washington, D.C.

CONTRIBUTING AUTHORS

Dr. Thomas Custer
Dr. James Flood
Dr. Diane Lapp
Doug Llewellyn
Dorothy Reid
Dr. Donald M. Silver

CONSULTANTS

Dr. Danny J. Ballard
Dr. Carol Baskin
Dr. Bonnie Buratti
Dr. Suellen Cabe
Dr. Shawn Carlson
Dr. Thomas A. Davies
Dr. Marie DiBerardino
Dr. R. E. Duhrkopf
Dr. Ed Geary
Dr. Susan C. Giarratano-Russell
Dr. Karen Kwitter
Dr. Donna Lloyd-Kolkin
Ericka Lochner, RN
Donna Harrell Lubcker
Dr. Dennis L. Nelson
Dr. Fred S. Sack
Dr. Martin VanDyke
Dr. E. Peter Volpe
Dr. Josephine Davis Wallace
Dr. Joe Yelderman

McGraw-Hill School Division

A Division of The McGraw-Hill Companies

Copyright © 2000 McGraw-Hill School Division,
a Division of the Educational and Professional
Publishing Group of The McGraw-Hill Companies, Inc.

McGraw-Hill School Division
Two Penn Plaza
New York, New York 10121

Printed in the United States of America

ISBN 0-02-277436-X / 4

4 5 6 7 8 9 071/046 05 04 03 02 01 00 99

CONTENTS

UNIT 1

CLASSIFYING LIVING THINGS

UNIT 2 MATTER ON THE MOVE

UNIT 3

LEARNING ABOUT EARTH'S HISTORY

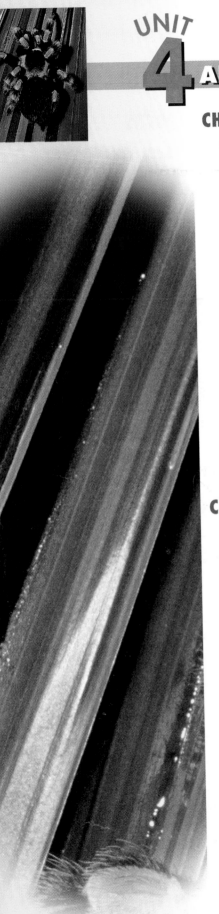

UNIT 4 ANIMALS

UNIT 5 ELECTRICITY AND MAGNETISM

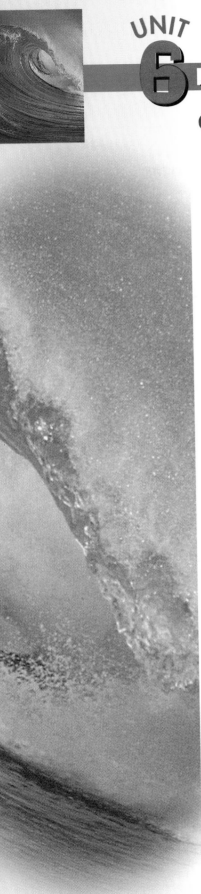

UNIT 6 EARTH'S WATER

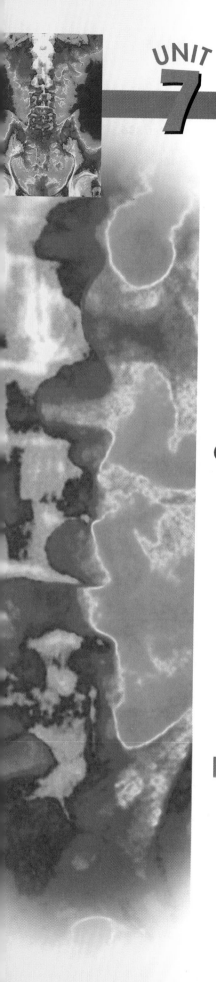

UNIT 7

HUMAN BODY: A BODY IN MOTION

EXPLORE ACTIVITIES

READING CHARTS

READING GRAPHS

READING MAPS

READING TABLES

READING DIAGRAMS

FACTS PROBLEMS PUZZLES

NATIONAL GEOGRAPHIC FUNtastic FACTS

DID YOU KNOW?

PROBLEMS AND PUZZLES

YOUR TEXTBOOK at a Glance

Begin each topic with an **Explore** question. Investigate further by doing an **Explore Activity**.

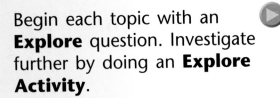

SCIENCE MAGAZINE

Flips, Slides, and Turns

Let's create geometric patterns by moving figures around. Try these three ways.

Flip it!
Flip a figure over a line, and the second figure looks like a mirror image of the first! Hold out your hands in front of you, palms up. Spread out your fingers. The shape of your right hand is like a mirror image of your left. Check it out. Flip your left hand over onto your right, palms facing each other. Then open your hands!

Slide it!
Slide a figure across a line. The second figure looks the same, but it's in a different place!

Turn it!
Turn a figure around a point on a line. Imagine holding one end of the figure and moving the other end in a circle!

One of those patterns is made inside an electric motor! There's a metal coil sitting between the poles of a magnet. Electric current flows through the coil and magnetizes it. Because it's between the magnet's poles, the coil spins as its magnetic field interacts with the magnet's magnetic field. That movement keeps the motor running. The spin follows one of the geometric patterns. Which one do you think it is?

DISCUSSION STARTER
1. Why does the coil in an electric motor spin?
2. Which of the geometric patterns do you think a coil in an electric motor represents? Why?

To learn more about geometric patterns, visit www.mhschool.com/science and enter the keyword FLIPS.

interNET CONNECTION

Math Link

NATIONAL GEOGRAPHIC **World of SCIENCE**

A Closer Look

Discuss an exciting **Science Magazine** after each topic. Find a **National Geographic World of Science** in each unit.

Topic 4 PHYSICAL SCIENCE

WHY IT MATTERS

Electricity and Magnets

Did you know that a compass needle always points north? That is how a compass helps you find your way in unfamiliar places.

When Jenna's toy crane lifted a bar magnet, the magnet always pointed in the same direction. When the crane lifted a nonmagnet, it pointed in any direction. Jenna wondered if a hanging magnet is like a compass. Do you think so?

EXPLORE

HYPOTHESIZE How does a bar magnet compare with a compass? Write a hypothesis in your *Science Journal*. How could you find out?

DID YOU KNOW?

There are more microorganisms ___ il than there ___ mong ___ acteria that ___ ycin

___ ti-

___ and cure certain types of infections

NATIONAL GEOGRAPHIC

FUNtastic Facts

It looks like a cross between a horse and a salad, but it's a fish. This foot-long animal—the leafy sea dragon—lives off the coast of Australia. Its wavy spines and leaflike appearance help conceal it on the seabed where it feeds. How might the fish's appearance help it survive?

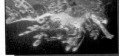

Brain Power

How can switches and one power source control more than one light in a parallel circuit? Where would you put switches to control each light in this circuit?

Flex your brain with questions about real-world facts.

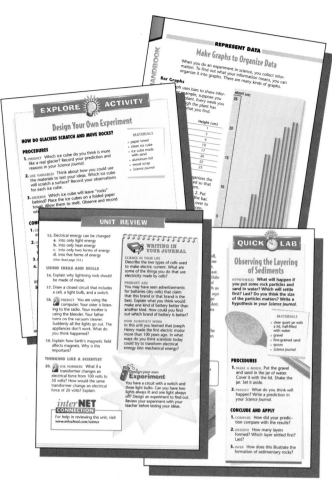

EXPLORE ACTIVITY

Investigate How a Bar Magnet Is Like a Compass

Play around with magnets to test how they compare with a compass.

MATERIALS
- 2 bar magnets
- 1 m of string
- compass
- ruler
- tape
- heavy book
- *Science Journal*

PROCEDURES

1. **OBSERVE** How do the bar magnets interact when you place them next to each other in different positions?

2. **PREDICT** Which way will the bar magnet point if you hang it as shown? Record your prediction in your *Science Journal*.

3. **OBSERVE** Test your prediction. Record the results.

4. **COMPARE** Place the compass on a flat surface away from the magnets. Compare the directions in which the compass and magnet point.

5. **OBSERVE** Hold the compass near the hanging magnet. What happens?

CONCLUDE AND APPLY

1. **COMMUNICATE** How do the two magnets interact with each other?

2. **COMPARE** How did your hanging magnet compare with other students' magnets?

3. **COMMUNICATE** What happened when you brought the compass near the hanging magnet?

4. **INFER** Of what must a compass be made?

GOING FURTHER: Problem Solving

5. **INFER** What do you think was pulling the magnet and compass?

Design Your Own Experiments, do **Quick Labs**, use **Internet Connections**, and try **Writing in Your Journal**. Use the **Handbook** for help.

Reading Graphs, Diagrams, Maps, and **Charts** help you learn by using what you see.

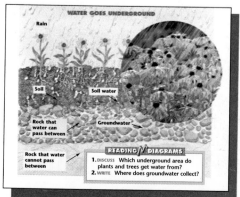

WATER GOES UNDERGROUND

Rain

Soil

Soil water

Rock that water can pass between

Groundwater

Rock that water cannot pass between

READING DIAGRAMS
1. DISCUSS Which underground area do plants and trees get water from?
2. WRITE Where does groundwater collect?

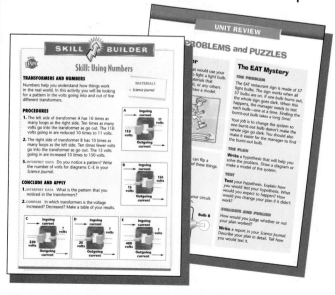

Build your skills with **Skill Builders** and **Problems and Puzzles**.

INVITATION TO SCIENCE

Goodall quietly observes
a group of chimps.

Even as a little
girl, Goodall
loved animals!

Jane Goodall

From the time Jane Goodall was very small, she was fascinated by animals. By the age of eight or nine, she was dreaming of going to Africa.

At 23 she traveled to Africa. Soon she began a study of wild chimpanzees there. She thought that her research might take three years. However, it has lasted more than three decades. It has become the world's longest study of animals in the wild.

Goodall's work depends on careful observation. She watches the chimps for hours, recording everything she sees. She stays as quiet as she can. "It's important not to disturb what the chimpanzees are doing," she explains, "because then you won't see them as they really are."

Goodall has discovered many things about chimps that no one knew before. For example, she discovered that chimps use tools.

Goodall still has many questions about chimps, so her research is likely to go on and on!

Protected by mosquito netting, Goodall writes up her notes.

Goodall enjoys sharing what she's learned.

BE A SCIENTIST

Have you ever seen fish swim in a tank or aquarium? If you have you probably noticed how easily they move through the water. They don't float on top. They don't sink to the bottom. Most objects either float or sink when you drop them in a bathtub or sink full of water. Fish can move themselves up or down with ease. How can fish swim at different depths?

EXPLORE

Why do some things float and some things sink? How can some things float lower than others? Write a possible explanation in your *Science Journal*. How might you test your explanation?

Investigate Why Things Sink or Float

Think of a sentence about sinking and floating that you can test, like: Heavier things sink, and lighter things float.

MATERIALS

- plastic film canister
- empty plastic soda bottle (with top)
- ball of modeling clay
- large metal lid for mayonnaise, jam, or pickle jar
- tub or bucket of water
- balance
- sand or salt
- ruler
- *Science Journal*

PROCEDURES

1. Fill the sink or tub with water.

2. Put the tops tightly on the empty canister and soda bottle.

3. **PREDICT** Weigh the canister, soda bottle, lid, and ball of modeling clay, and measure the lengths and widths. Discuss which ones you think will sink and which will float. Why? Write ideas in your *Science Journal*.

4. **OBSERVE** Place the objects in the water one by one. Record whether they sink or float.

5. **EXPERIMENT** Now try to change the results any way you can. Make just one change at a time. Test the canister and bottle when they are filled with water, sand, or salt. Change the shape of the modeling clay. Each time you make a change, weigh and measure the items. Record the results.

CONCLUDE AND APPLY

1. **DRAW CONCLUSIONS** Did the heavier items always sink? Why?

2. **DRAW CONCLUSIONS** Did the height and width of the objects make a difference? If so, how?

3. Could you make the modeling clay float by changing its shape?

S5

What Makes Things Sink or Float?

The Explore Activity showed how something that's floating can be made to sink. It also showed how things that sink can be made to float.

Water can actually push something upward. A push or pull is called a **force** (fôrs). The upward force of water or air is called **buoyancy** (boi′ən sē). This force gives an object the ability to float. Early sailors needed to know how to build boats that would not sink. They studied objects and their ability to float in water. They also studied fish. Fish offer some important clues about buoyancy.

Over time, people made boats in different shapes to serve different purposes.

How Do Scientists Begin?

One scientist who studies fish is Dr. Eugenie Clark. When Eugenie Clark was nine years old, her mother let her go to the aquarium. She had many questions about the fish.

She studied fish at the aquarium almost every Saturday. When she grew up, she became a scientist who studies fish. She has discovered 11 new types of fish!

Scientists begin by being curious and asking a lot of questions. They think of ways to answer their questions and test their ideas. Finding answers and testing them can be exciting. It can also be a long process. One question often leads to another.

Why do things float or sink? The answer is partly because of an object's **weight** (wāt), or the amount of force with which an object is pulled down toward Earth. The more **matter** (mat′ər) an object has, the greater its weight. Matter is what everything is made of. All solids, liquids, and gases are matter.

The answer to why things float is also partly because of the **density** (den′si tē) of the object. Density is the amount of matter in a given space. Density measures how much matter an object has *for its size*. If an object is more dense than water, it sinks. If it is less dense than water, it floats.

Dr. Eugenie Clark studies fish and other animals, such as snakes.

What Can Affect Density?

The size and shape of an object can affect its density. The shape of an object controls the amount of water that it pushes out of the way. This is called **displacement** (dis plās′mənt). Even a dense material can be made to float if it can be shaped to displace enough water. If the amount of water that is displaced weighs more than the object, it will float. This is how a large ship can float. Even though the ship is heavy, it still weighs less than the large amount of water it displaces. If the displaced water weighs less than the object, the object will sink.

An important thing Dr. Clark had to learn was how to be a deep-sea diver. She learned that the right amount of metal weights strapped to her body gave her body the same density as water. Changing the weights made it easier to sink or float underwater.

She also learned that as a diver descends into the sea, the weight of the water above presses down on the diver. The force water puts on objects that are in the water is **water pressure** (wô′tər presh′ər). The deeper the diver goes, the more the water pressure increases. Divers need to give their bodies time to adjust to changing water pressure, especially when returning to the surface. If divers surface too fast, they can die!

This diver uses metal weights to sink far below the ocean surface.

How Do Scientists Use Others' Work?

Dr. Clark studied what other scientists had learned about fish. It helped her answer some of her questions.

Her first question was: Why don't fish sink or float? She learned that many types of fish have pockets of air inside them called swim bladders. Because air is less dense than water, swim bladders help keep fish from sinking. When you hold air in your lungs, it helps you float in the water, too.

Engineers copied the idea of swim bladders when they designed modern submarines. Submarines have built-in tanks that can be filled with water to make the submarine go down. The submarine can also shoot air into the tanks. This pushes out the water and makes the submarine rise to the surface.

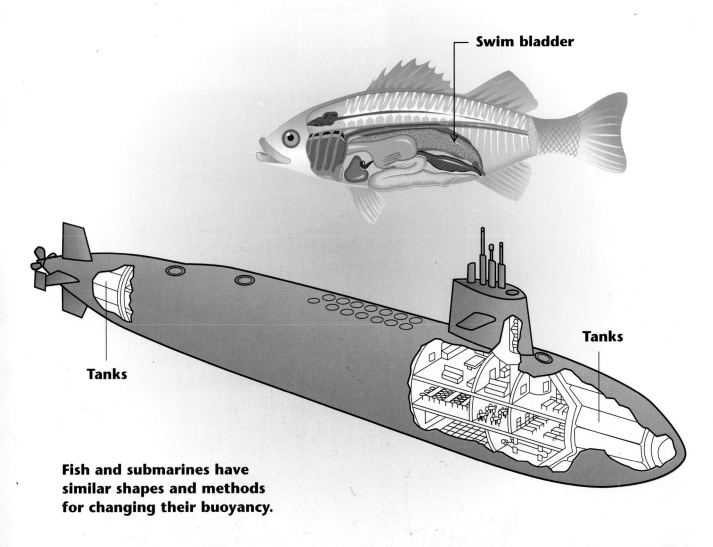

Fish and submarines have similar shapes and methods for changing their buoyancy.

Can Scientists Find More than One Answer?

Dr. Clark discovered that sharks don't have swim bladders. How do they keep from sinking? She learned that many types of sharks have large amounts of oil in their livers. Oil is less dense than water. This is one way sharks keep from sinking. Some sharks gulp air at the surface and hold it in their stomachs when they want to swim at shallow depths.

While investigating sharks Dr. Clark discovered that the most important thing that keeps them from sinking is their shape. Even though a shark's body is heavier than seawater, its fins keep it from sinking. Its long side fins are called pectoral fins. When the shark moves, the fins work like the wings of an airplane. If a shark stops moving, it sinks to the bottom. When it swims it can adjust the flow of water around its fins to help it go up or down in the water.

Long fins help sharks move through water the same way that wings help airplanes fly in the air.

How Do Scientists Get Their Ideas?

Scientists study books and articles to find out facts. They also ask questions. They always try to test their ideas for themselves.

Dr. Clark heard things about sharks that didn't seem right to her. People warned her that all sharks are dangerous. Most people fear sharks because sharks can eat just about anything they choose in the sea. Some have called sharks the masters of the sea.

Dr. Clark learned that there are around 370 types of sharks. When she studied them closely, she found that each type behaves differently.

During her investigations she learned that most sharks are shy and swim away from people. Fewer than 30 types of sharks have ever attacked humans. She learned that more people die from bee stings than shark attacks!

People generally fear big sharks the most. The biggest shark of all is the giant whale shark. It can grow to over 15 meters (50 feet) long. By studying it carefully, Dr. Clark learned that the whale shark is one of the most harmless type of shark. She even rode on one to celebrate her birthday!

Dr. Clark studied many different types of sharks and found that not all of them are dangerous to people.

How Do Scientists Test Their Ideas?

The more Dr. Clark learned about sharks, the more curious she became. She asked scientists who studied animal behavior if people could teach sharks to do things. Some scientists didn't think sharks were smart enough to learn. She wanted to find out for sure.

Dr. Clark did many experiments in big tanks to see what sharks could learn. With her students she built a white wooden square target and placed it underwater in the shark pen.

Could a shark learn that if it pressed its nose against the target, it would get food as a reward? The sharks learned very quickly to press the target when they wanted food.

Dr. Clark repeated the experiment by changing one of the **variables** (vâr′ē ə bəlz). A variable is one of the things in an experiment that can be changed or controlled. To make it harder for the sharks, she gave the reward only to sharks that pressed the target and then swam to the other end of the pool. They soon learned this, too.

She showed that sharks can learn many things. In her experiments she proved that some types of sharks can tell light from dark. Some can even tell the difference between simple patterns.

This shark learned to press the correct target to get a food reward.

One day in winter, Dr. Clark set up her experiment as usual, but the sharks didn't press the target. She wondered if they had forgotten everything she had taught them.

By springtime she had the answer. She learned that sharks lose interest in food when the water gets colder. When the water warmed up in the spring, the sharks began to press the target for food again. She discovered that sharks could learn and had a good memory as well.

How Can I Be Like a Scientist?

Scientists start with curiosity! They look carefully at things around them. How can huge steel boats in the harbor weigh many tons but still float in the water? How do fish swim so easily at different depths? How do fish learn things? You may have observed things around you that made you wonder. Being a scientist means trying to find answers to questions like these.

Scientists do experiments so they can test their ideas. Each time they repeat an experiment, they try to change just one variable. By changing one variable at a time, they can follow a trail that leads toward an answer to their question.

Now let's go back and look at how you changed variables in the Explore Activity to test your ideas about floating and sinking.

Ocean scientists study many kinds of fish and boats to learn more about buoyancy.

You Asked Questions and Investigated

A scientist begins an experiment by observing. Before the Explore Activity, you saw fish swim without sinking or floating. You saw a pebble sink and a big ship float.

Seeing these things helped you ask well-defined, or clear, questions: Which of these objects will sink and which will float? Will the heaviest one sink to the bottom? Does the size and shape of the object make a difference?

When you ask questions, think about how you could test your ideas to answer the questions.

When you wrote down your possible explanation at the beginning of the Explore Activity, you were stating a **hypothesis** (hī poth′ə sis). A hypothesis is a statement in answer to a question; you must be able to test the statement. You then planned your investigation by choosing the objects to test.

You measured and weighed the objects and observed what happened when you placed them in the water. You recorded and organized the information to help you understand it better. Then you changed one variable at a time and observed the results. You gathered the information you needed.

Scientists set up experiments to find answers to their questions.

You Used Results to Answer Questions

A scientist analyzes the information he or she gathers in an experiment. You thought about the measurements you made and what they meant. From this you formed answers to your hypothesis. You learned that the weight of an object alone does not determine whether it will sink or float.

To change the buoyancy of these objects, you filled them with different materials to make them more or less dense. You also changed their shape. Different types of fish use both these techniques. Some use swim bladders to change their density. Some, like sharks, use the shape of their fins to keep from sinking.

Dr. Clark records her findings in her journal.

Your investigation helped you test your ideas about floating and sinking. This knowledge helped you understand how fish control their depth in water.

Scientists share the results of their experiments with others. During the Explore Activity, you shared your findings with your classmates. You recorded the results in your *Science Journal*. A chart or table could be used to make the information easier to understand.

You can work like a scientist by following the same careful methods.

S15

Repeating Your Experiment

Sharing the results of your experiment helps you decide how strong or weak your hypothesis is. Scientists often repeat their experiments to be sure their results are correct. They may also think of new experiments to help them learn more about the answers to their questions.

Now try the Explore Activity again. Each time you do a step, think of how a scientist works. See if you can label each step with what a scientist does.

In this book you will be doing many Explore Activities. Complete all the steps you just learned each time. It's called using scientific methods. It's what makes you a real scientist! Answers are important, but it's also important *how* you found the answers.

Dr. Clark's questions about the Moses sole led to even more experiments.

On one research trip in the Red Sea, Dr. Clark observed that the Moses sole fish oozed a milky liquid onto her hand when she held it. She wondered if it might be some kind of poison the fish used to protect itself!

To test her hypothesis, Dr. Clark put the Moses sole and other small fish in a plastic bag filled with water. Through the plastic she squeezed the Moses sole until a few drops of the liquid came out. The other small fish in the bag all died quickly. They had been killed by the poison of the Moses sole.

What would this poison do to bigger, more dangerous fish, such as sharks? She tested her hypothesis and learned that even hungry sharks avoided the Moses sole. Her research led to the development of the strongest shark repellent ever found. It could keep sharks away from divers for up to 18 hours!

Dr. Clark's work is an example of how important scientific research can be. The information gathered in research can be used to make things that help us. Many of these discoveries even save lives!

Shark repellent helps to keep divers safe while they study sharks.

REVIEW

1. What makes something float?

2. How do scientists like Dr. Eugenie Clark learn about fish?

3. What did Dr. Clark learn about the different types of sharks?

4. How did Dr. Clark use variables to test her ideas?

BE A SCIENTIST Glossary

These words describe how scientists do their work. You can use them when you conduct experiments in this book and on your own.

analyze to separate anything into its parts to find out what it is made of and how it is put together

ask questions to ask about what you don't know based on what you see around you

classify to group objects according to characteristics

collect data to put together all useful information

communicate to share information

compare to find out or show how things are the same

define to make up a description based on observations and experience

draw conclusions to decide what is correct from all the facts you have learned

experiment a test that is used to discover or prove something

explain to tell the meaning of or tell how to do something

infer to form an idea from facts or observations

interpret data to explain the meaning of all the information that has been gathered

make decisions to make up your mind from many choices

measure to find the size, volume, area, mass, weight, or temperature of an object or how long an event occurs

model something that represents an object or event

observe to use one or more of the senses to identify or learn about an object or event

plan to think out ahead of time how something is to be done or made, including methods and materials

predict to state possible results of an event or experiment

repeat to do something again the same way to see if the results are the same

test the examination of a substance or event to see what it is or why it happens

theory an explanation based on observation and reasoning

use numbers to explain data by ordering, counting, adding, subtracting, multiplying, and dividing

These are words you can use to think about ideas when you read or study.

cause and effect something (cause) that brings about a change in something else (effect)

compare and contrast to find out how things are the same (compare) and how they are different (contrast)

identify to name or recognize

sequence a series of things that are related in some way

These are the new Science Words that you learned in Be a Scientist.

buoyancy the upward force of water or air

density the amount of matter in a given space

displacement the amount of water an object pushes out of its way

force a push or a pull

hypothesis a statement in answer to a question; you must be able to test the statement

matter what everything is made of; all solids, liquids, and gases

variables things in an experiment that can be changed or controlled

water pressure the force water puts on an object that is in it

weight the amount of force with which an object is pulled down toward Earth

METHODS OF SCIENCE

Here is a chart that shows the steps to follow when solving a problem in science.

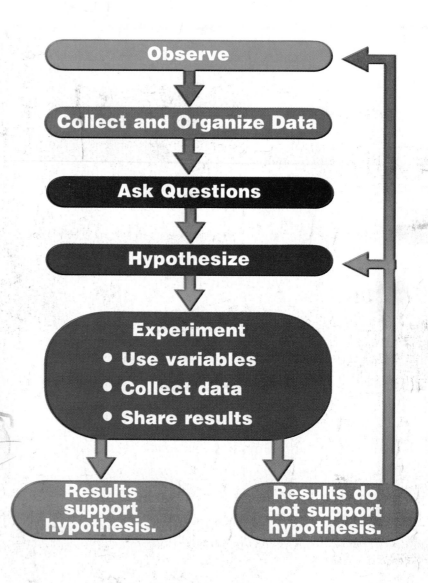

Observe

Collect and Organize Data

Ask Questions

Hypothesize

Experiment
- Use variables
- Collect data
- Share results

Results support hypothesis.

Results do not support hypothesis.

READING N' CHARTS

WRITE How would you solve a problem in science? Write a paragraph based on the chart.

CHAPTER 1

HOW LIVING THINGS ARE PUT TOGETHER

How can you tell something is a living thing? Do you see living things here? How can you tell? What do living things do that nonliving things don't do? What are living things made up of?

In Chapter 1 look for and read lists. A list is a helpful way to put information together. You may have used a shopping list.

1

Topic
LIFE SCIENCE
1

WHY IT MATTERS

You can identify living and nonliving things by observing their characteristics.

SCIENCE WORDS

oxygen part of air; needed by most plants and animals to live

organism a living thing that carries out basic life functions on its own

cell the smallest unit of living matter

tissue a group of similar cells that work together to carry out a job

organ a group of tissues that work together to do a certain job

organ system a group of organs that work together to carry on life functions

Identifying Living Things

How do you know if something is living or not?

MEOW! A kitten runs by chasing a toy. The toy seems to try to escape from the kitten as it zips by. Both things seem to be similar. They both are made of parts. These parts work together to do jobs, like moving. However, they are not the same. One is living. One is nonliving. How can you tell?

EXPLORE

HYPOTHESIZE Sometimes it is hard to tell if an object is living or nonliving. However, living things have certain parts in common. What might they be? Write a hypothesis in your *Science Journal.*

Investigate What Living Things Are Made Of

Observe parts of an onion plant with a microscope and a hand lens.

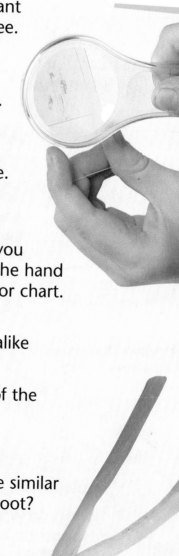

MATERIALS

- onion plant
- prepared slides of onion skin and leaf
- hand lens
- microscope
- *Science Journal*

PROCEDURES

1. OBSERVE In your *Science Journal*, draw the whole onion plant. Label its parts. Write down how each part might help the plant live.

2. OBSERVE Ask your teacher to cut the plant lengthwise. Draw and label what you see.

3. OBSERVE Observe a small section of onion skin and a thin piece of a leaf with the hand lens. Draw what you see.

4. OBSERVE Use the microscope to look at the onion skin and the leaf section. Use high and low power. Draw what you see.

CONCLUDE AND APPLY

1. COMMUNICATE What did you see when you examined the onion skin and leaf with the hand lens and the microscope? Make a table or chart.

2. COMPARE AND CONTRAST How are your observations of the onion skin and leaf alike and different?

3. DRAW CONCLUSIONS What do the parts of the onion plant seem to be made of?

GOING FURTHER: Problem Solving

4. EXPERIMENT Do you think you would see similar structures if you observed a part of the root? How could you find out?

3

What Are Living Things?

Do you think you have anything in common with the onion plant shown in the Explore Activity? Although you aren't green and don't have leaves growing out the top of your head, you have more in common with an onion than you might imagine!

The one thing you have in common is that you are both living things. Most living things share certain characteristics. Among them are the basic needs for food, water, a place to live, and oxygen (ok'sə jən). Most living things use oxygen to turn food into energy. Plants need oxygen to use the food they make. Another characteristic of living things is that they are made of parts. Each part has a specific job to keep a living thing alive.

Plants, people, and other animals are all organisms (ôr'gə niz'əmz). An organism is a living thing that carries out five basic life functions on its own.

Organisms come in all shapes and sizes. Tiny flies, onion plants, great blue whales—even you—are all organisms. It doesn't matter if an organism lives in the water, on the ground, or in the tops of the tallest trees. All organisms carry out five basic life functions.

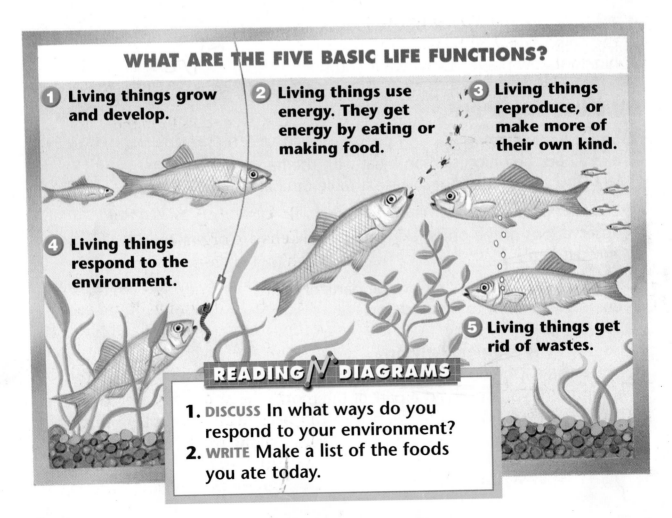

WHAT ARE THE FIVE BASIC LIFE FUNCTIONS?

1. Living things grow and develop.
2. Living things use energy. They get energy by eating or making food.
3. Living things reproduce, or make more of their own kind.
4. Living things respond to the environment.
5. Living things get rid of wastes.

READING DIAGRAMS

1. DISCUSS In what ways do you respond to your environment?
2. WRITE Make a list of the foods you ate today.

What Are Living Things Made Of?

The small, boxlike structures making up the onion plant in the Explore Activity are called **cells** (selz). A cell is the smallest unit of living matter. In other words cells are the "building blocks" of living things. All living things are made of cells—even you.

Although all living things are made of cells, all cells are not the same. The plant cells in the Explore Activity had a boxlike shape. Some even contained a green material, called *chlorophyll* (klôr'ə fil'). When sunlight strikes chlorophyll, the cell can make food for the plant. Animal cells don't contain chlorophyll and are not box shaped. You will learn more about plant and animal cells in Topic 2.

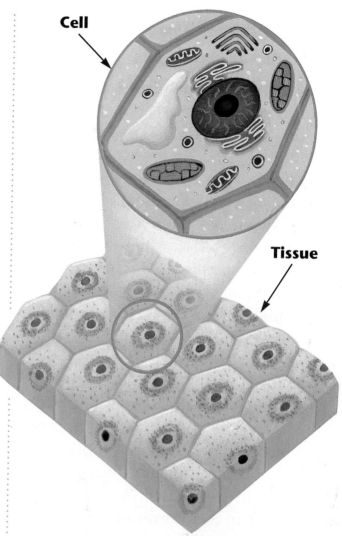

Cell

Tissue

Groups of cells form the tissues that make up an onion plant's leaves.

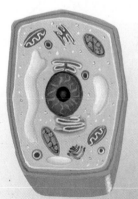

Plant cell

How are these two cells similar and different?

Animal cell

Cells Working Together

Cells are organized into **tissues** (tish'üz). A tissue is a group of similar cells that work together to carry out a job. In the onion plant, each layer of onion skin you observed is a tissue. Bones, muscles, and nerves are tissues in your body.

Each tissue has its own job, or function. In an onion plant, the tissues making up the roots absorb water. In your body, muscle and bone tissues work together to move you.

How Do Tissues Work Together?

Groups of tissues form **organs** (ôr′gənz). Organs are tissues that work together to do a certain job. Your brain and heart are two of the organs in your body. Your heart's job is to pump blood to all body tissues. What jobs does your brain do?

Roots, stems, and leaves are organs of an onion plant. A leaf is an organ that makes the food for the onion plant. What do the roots and stem do?

A group of parts that works together forms a *system*. An **organ system** (ôr′gən sis′təm) is a group of organs that work together to carry on life functions. A plant's roots, stem, and leaves are one organ system. In your body the digestive system is one example of an organ system. It breaks down food and absorbs the nutrients you need to live.

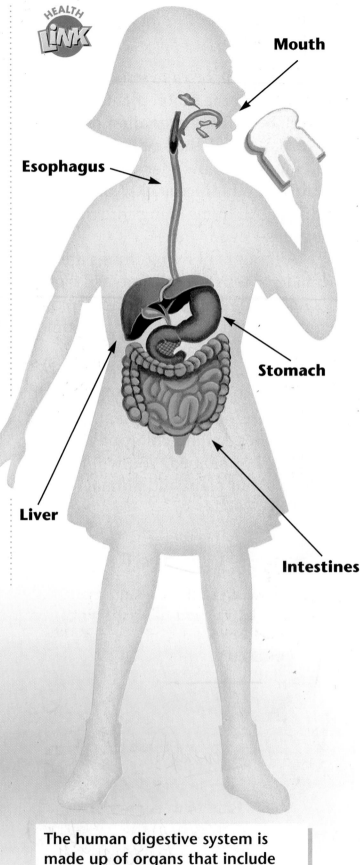

The human digestive system is made up of organs that include the liver, stomach, and intestines.

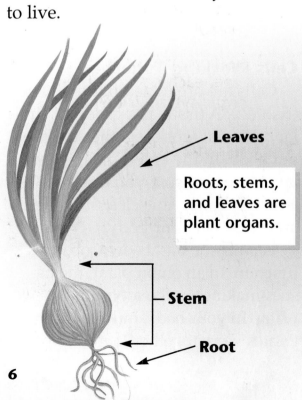

Roots, stems, and leaves are plant organs.

6

Are There One-Celled Organisms?

In this topic you learned that an organism is a living thing that carries out five basic life functions. To review, these basic life functions include:

- growing and developing
- using energy
- reproducing
- responding to the environment
- getting rid of wastes

An onion plant is made up of cells, tissues, organs, and organ systems. It uses these parts to carry out basic life functions.

Do you think that something that is made of only one cell and has no tissues, organs, or organ systems can be an organism? Why or why not?

Brain Power

Tell which of these is an organism. Explain why you think so. Hint: Which carries out all five basic life functions?

Putting It All Together

HYPOTHESIZE What body parts work together to allow you to perform a simple task like writing? Write a hypothesis in your *Science Journal.*

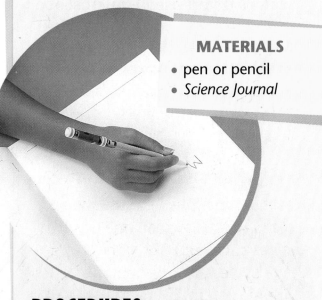

MATERIALS
- pen or pencil
- *Science Journal*

PROCEDURES

1. Write your name in your *Science Journal.*

2. INFER As you write think about what each body part, organ, and organ system is doing.

CONCLUDE AND APPLY

1. COMMUNICATE Write a paragraph that tells what organs you were using. Consider the organs you use to see, touch, breathe, and think.

2. DRAW CONCLUSIONS How did your body parts and organs work together to allow you to write?

What Kinds of Organisms Live in Pond Water?

Believe it or not, many different one-celled organisms live on Earth. You can even find many of them in a single drop of pond water.

What kinds of organisms are small enough to live in a drop of water? If you used a microscope to examine some pond water, you might see organisms like these.

Organisms that are so small you need a microscope to see them are called *microorganisms*.

Do any of these microorganisms have parts that might be helpful for living in water? What are they?

Many microorganisms are helpful. Many, like these, are a food source for other animals. Many feed on dead organisms in the water. Some can be harmful. They cause disease and illness in humans and other animals.

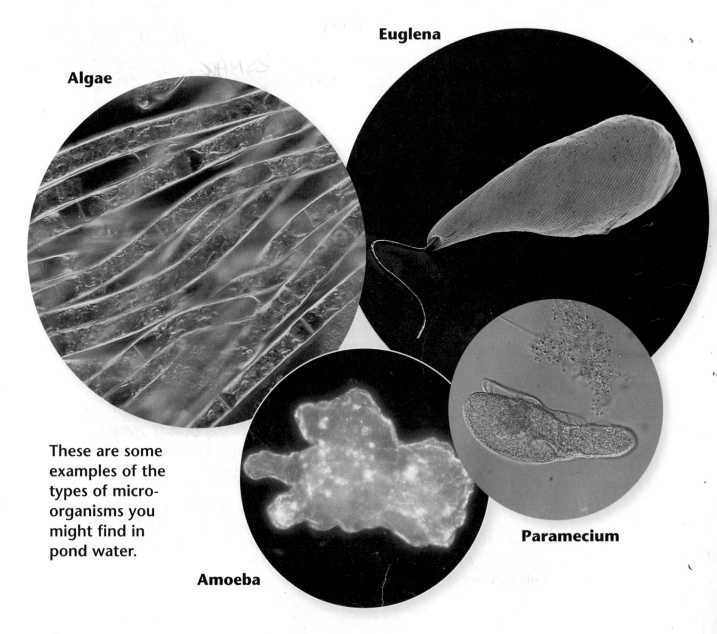

Euglena

Algae

Amoeba

Paramecium

These are some examples of the types of micro-organisms you might find in pond water.

All living things have certain characteristics. Being able to recognize these characteristics lets you identify something as living or nonliving. Identifying something as a living thing helps you decide how to treat it. You would treat a doll very differently from a living baby!

A doll is not a living thing. What does a baby need that a doll does not?

1. How can you identify a living thing?

2. Name three living things. Explain how you know each is living. Be sure to include the five basic life functions.

3. What is an organ?

4. **COMMUNICATE** Give an example of an organ system. What does this system do?

5. **CRITICAL THINKING** *Apply* In what ways are microorganisms different from you? How are they similar to you?

WHY IT MATTERS THINK ABOUT IT
A doll cries, moves its arms and legs, drinks a bottle, and wets a diaper. How do you know it is not an organism?

WHY IT MATTERS WRITE ABOUT IT
What if your younger sister thinks her doll is a living thing? How would you explain to her that it is not a living thing?

READING SKILL Give an example of a list that you found in this topic. What was the list about?

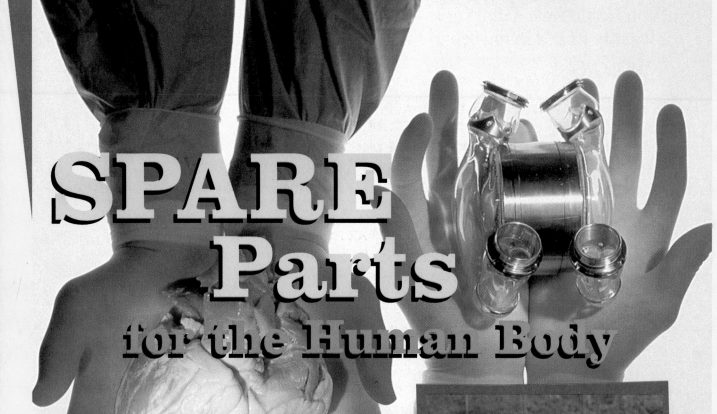

SPARE Parts
for the Human Body

Do you think this artificial heart (above right) looks like a real heart?

This athlete can run, thanks to an artificial leg that bends.

Science, Technology, and Society

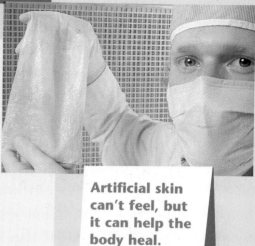

Ever see a peg-legged pirate in a movie? Long ago using wood to replace missing body parts was common. Today we can do better.

People still lose body parts in accidents or because of diseases. These people are given artificial, or manufactured, body parts. Lost teeth can be replaced by implants made with plastic or porcelain. The implants look like real teeth. Arms or legs can be replaced by artificial limbs made of plastic or special metals. These limbs bend and work much like natural ones.

Most organs are harder to replace. Doctors have implanted artificial hearts to replace diseased ones. Since the main function of a heart is to move blood, a small pump was chosen for the job.

However, no pump works as well as a real heart. An artificial heart can't be used for long because it damages cells. After a few days, doctors must transplant a healthy heart into the person's body.

Scientists have also developed artificial skin. It's used mostly for people who've been badly burned. Like an artificial heart, artificial skin isn't meant for permanent use. However, it helps keep germs outside and fluids inside the body while the body heals.

Artificial skin can't feel, but it can help the body heal.

Discussion
Starter

1 Why are bones and teeth easier to replace than organs such as hearts, livers, and lungs?

2 What is the main purpose of using artificial skin?

*inter*NET CONNECTION To learn more about artificial body parts, visit www.mhschool.com/science and enter the keyword **SPARE.**

11

WHY IT MATTERS

Knowing the basic structures of cells helps you tell the difference between plant and animal cells.

SCIENCE WORDS

chloroplast a plant cell's food factory

cell wall a thick, stiff structure that protects and supports a plant cell

vacuole a holding bin for food, water, and wastes

nucleus cell's control center

cell membrane a cell's thin outer covering; found beneath the cell wall in plants

cytoplasm a jellylike substance that fills the cell

chromosome a threadlike structure that controls an organism's traits

Looking at Cells

Have you ever tossed a ball against a wall? It is a fun way to pass the time on a sunny summer afternoon. However, did you ever think about the things around you? What is the wall made of? What are the plants made of? What are YOU made of?

This wall is made up of bricks. The tree and other living things are made up of cells. Compare the person and the tree. How are they alike and different?

EXPLORE

HYPOTHESIZE How could you find out how plant and animal cells are different? Write a hypothesis in your *Science Journal*.

Investigate How Plant and Animal Cells Are Different

Use a microscope to look at plant and animal cells to find out if they are different. The plant cells are from a freshwater plant called *Elodea* (i lō'dē ə). The animal cells are cheek cells that line the inside of a person's mouth.

MATERIALS

- prepared slide of *Elodea* leaf
- prepared slide of human cheek cells
- microscope
- *Science Journal*

PROCEDURES

1. Place the slide of *Elodea* on the microscope stage.

2. OBSERVE Focus through the top layers of cells using low power. Focus on one plant cell. Draw it in your *Science Journal*.

3. OBSERVE Place the prepared slide of cheek cells on the microscope stage. Focus on one cheek cell using low power. Draw it.

4. COMMUNICATE Draw a table like this one. Record your observations.

Characteristics of Plant and Animal Cells			
	Shape	Color	Cell Structures Present
Plant cell			
Animal cell			

CONCLUDE AND APPLY

1. OBSERVE What did you see when you observed the *Elodea* cells?

2. OBSERVE What did you see when you observed the cheek cells?

3. COMPARE AND CONTRAST How are the *Elodea* and cheek cells similar and different?

4. COMPARE AND CONTRAST How does the *Elodea* cell compare with the onion skin cell you observed in Topic 1?

GOING FURTHER: Apply

5. INFER How do you think scientists use cell structure in classifying organisms?

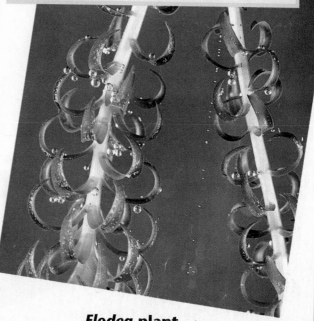

Elodea **plant**

How Are Plant and Animal Cells Different?

Most cells have everything they need to carry out the five basic life functions. However, as the Explore Activity showed, plant and animal cells are not made up of all the same parts. The diagram on this page shows the major parts of a typical plant cell. The diagram on the next page shows the major parts of a typical animal cell.

Cells also contain some other parts that have specific jobs. One part is like the cell's power plant. Food is burned here to give the cell energy.

Another part of the cell is like a chemical factory. It helps make the cell's building materials.

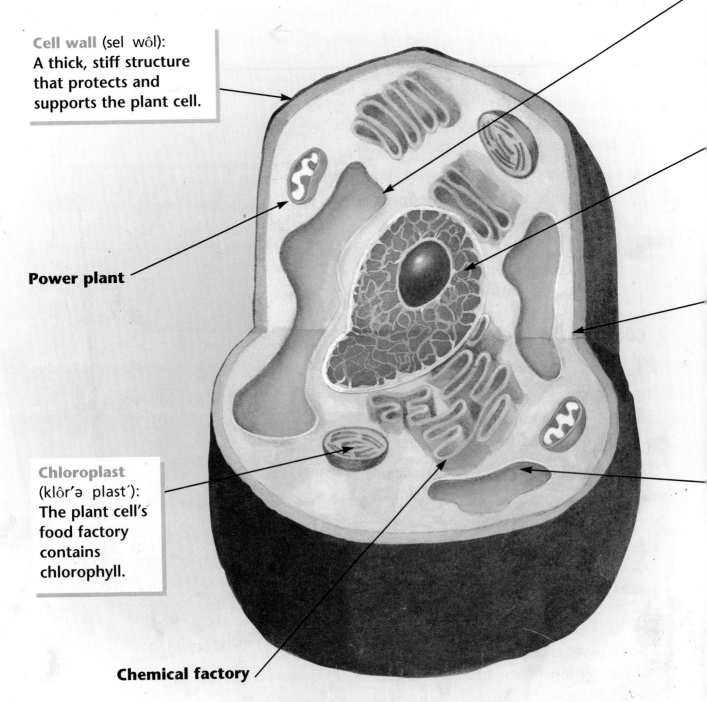

Cell wall (sel wôl):
A thick, stiff structure that protects and supports the plant cell.

Power plant

Chloroplast (klôr′ə plast′):
The plant cell's food factory contains chlorophyll.

Chemical factory

Vacuole (vak′ū ōl′):
A holding bin for food, water, and wastes. Plant cells have one or two vacuoles. Vacuoles are small in animal cells. Animal cells have more vacuoles than plant cells.

Power plant

Nucleus
(nü′klē əs):
The nucleus is one of the largest parts of the cell. It controls cell activities.

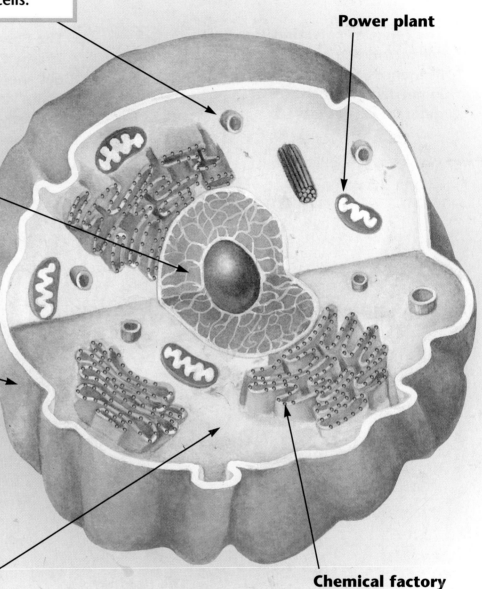

Cell membrane
(sel mem′brān):
An animal cell's thin outer covering. In plants it is found beneath the cell wall.

Chemical factory

Cytoplasm
(sī′tə plaz′əm):
The jellylike substance that fills the cell. It is mostly water but contains many important chemicals.

READING ∿ DIAGRAMS

1. **DISCUSS** How are the cell wall and cell membrane similar and different?
2. **WRITE** List the two cell parts that a plant cell has that an animal cell doesn't.

What Do Cell Parts Do?

Different cell parts help carry out the five basic life functions. Each part can be compared with something in the real world.

① The Fences: Protection The cell membrane and cell wall are like fences. Gates, or holes, let in needed materials. Other gates let wastes leave the cell.

② The Food Factory: Making Food Chloroplasts are a plant cell's food factories. They contain chlorophyll and use energy from the Sun to make food. Animals get energy from foods they eat.

③ The Power Plant: Produces Energy Plant and animal cells get energy in the "power plant." It works like an engine to break down fuel, which is food, and releases energy.

⑤ The Copy Shop: Reproduction The nucleus has the master plans for all cell activities. It contains chromosomes (krō′mə sōmz′). Chromosomes are threadlike structures that control an organism's traits. To reproduce, a cell makes a copy of its chromosomes. It splits to form two cells. Each new cell gets a copy of the chromosomes.

④ The Chemical Factory: Growth and Change "Chemical factories" in a cell make building materials. Other parts put the materials together to help the cell grow and change.

⑥ The Holding Bin: Storage A vacuole stores food, water, and wastes.

Brain Power

Is this a model of a plant cell or animal cell? Why do you think so?

Skill: Making a Model

MODELING PLANT AND ANIMAL CELLS

Most cells are too small for you to see without a microscope, but you can build models of cells. Models are three-dimensional copies or drawings of real things. A model can help you see how something looks or behaves.

SAFETY: Do not eat any of the activity materials!

1. **PLAN** In your *Science Journal*, make a list of parts of an animal cell. Name a material to stand for each part.

2. **MAKE A MODEL** Build an animal cell using the materials you named for each part.

3. **REPEAT** Follow the same process for a plant-cell model. How will it be different from your animal-cell model?

4. **COMMUNICATE** Compare your cell models. Record your observations.

MATERIALS

- small plastic bags with twist ties
- prepared, light-colored gelatin
- beads or marbles
- green jelly beans or olives
- lima beans
- marshmallows
- clear plastic box
- tape
- scissors
- *Science Journal*

CONCLUDE AND APPLY

1. **EXPLAIN** How did building a model help you understand the shape of each type of cell?

2. **OBSERVE** What cell structures do your models have?

3. **COMPARE AND CONTRAST** What structures do both of your models share? What structures don't they share?

4. **INFER** In what ways do you think your cell models are similar to real cells? In what ways are they different?

How Can You Compare Plant and Animal Cells?

As the Explore and Skill Builder activities showed, plant and animal cells are different. The basic differences between most plant and animal cells include their covering, color, and shape. Cells also differ depending on the types of jobs they do and the tissues they make up.

What observations did you make of the *Elodea* and human cheek cells? They are alike in some ways. Both are small. Both are filled with a jelly-like substance. Both have outer coverings with small structures inside.

Elodea and human cheek cells are also different in some ways. These are the basic differences between most plant and animal cells:

- **Covering** A plant cell has a thick wall. An animal cell has a thin covering.
- **Color** Most plant cells have green coloring. An animal cell does not.
- **Shape** Most plant cells have a boxy shape. Animal cells have a wide variety of shapes.

As you continue this topic, you will learn more about plant and animal cells. You will also learn about the jobs cell parts have.

THE SHAPE OF A CELL TELLS A LOT ABOUT ITS JOB

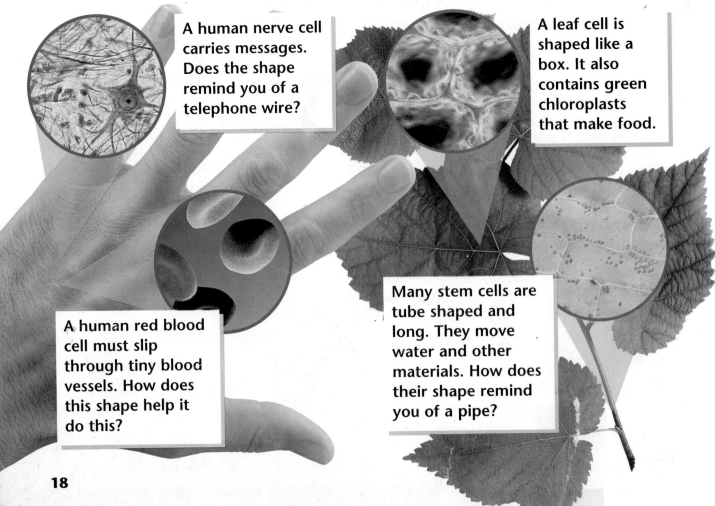

A human nerve cell carries messages. Does the shape remind you of a telephone wire?

A leaf cell is shaped like a box. It also contains green chloroplasts that make food.

A human red blood cell must slip through tiny blood vessels. How does this shape help it do this?

Many stem cells are tube shaped and long. They move water and other materials. How does their shape remind you of a pipe?

Are There Other Types of Cells?

The one-celled microorganisms that live in pond water are called *protists* (prō′tists). Here are some other types of cells and organisms.

Bacteria (bak tîr′ē ə) are one-celled organisms. A bacterium (singular) has a cell wall but no nucleus. The chromosomes are scattered through the cell. Bacteria do not have many cell structures. Bacteria are much smaller than most plant, animal, or protist cells.

A great variety of these microorganisms live on Earth. Some cause illnesses, like strep throat. Many bacteria are helpful. Some are used to make foods like cheese and buttermilk. Some break down waste materials, such as dead plants and animals.

Have you ever eaten a mushroom or used yeast to make bread? These are two examples of *fungi* (fun′jī). Yeast is a one-celled organism. A mushroom is made of many cells. Fungi cells have a cell wall and a nucleus, like plant cells. Some cells even have more than one nucleus.

Fungi do not have green chloroplasts or make food. Some fungi, like mushrooms, absorb nutrients from dead organisms. Have you ever seen a fungus growing on a log in the forest? Along with bacteria, it is breaking down the log and absorbing nutrients from it.

How are fungi cells like animals cells? How are they like plant cells?

These are examples of three typical bacteria cells as seen through a microscope.

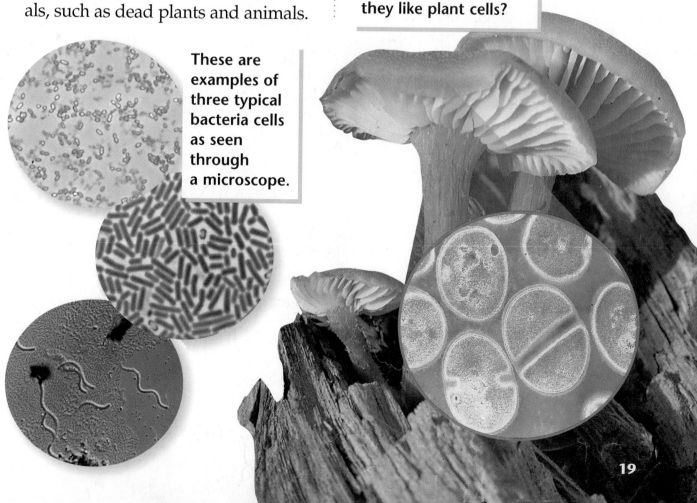

Is It Living?

Viruses (vī′rəs ez) are described as particles. They are much smaller than cells. They can't be seen with a microscope like the one you use. They can be seen only with a very powerful microscope.

A virus is not a cell. A virus is not living. It does not have a nucleus or other cell parts. The only thing a virus contains is a set of plans for invading living cells.

A virus does not make or use food. It does not grow, change, or respond to its environment. The only life function a virus seems to perform is being able to reproduce.

If a virus is not living, how can it reproduce? It cannot reproduce on its own but must use a living cell, as shown here.

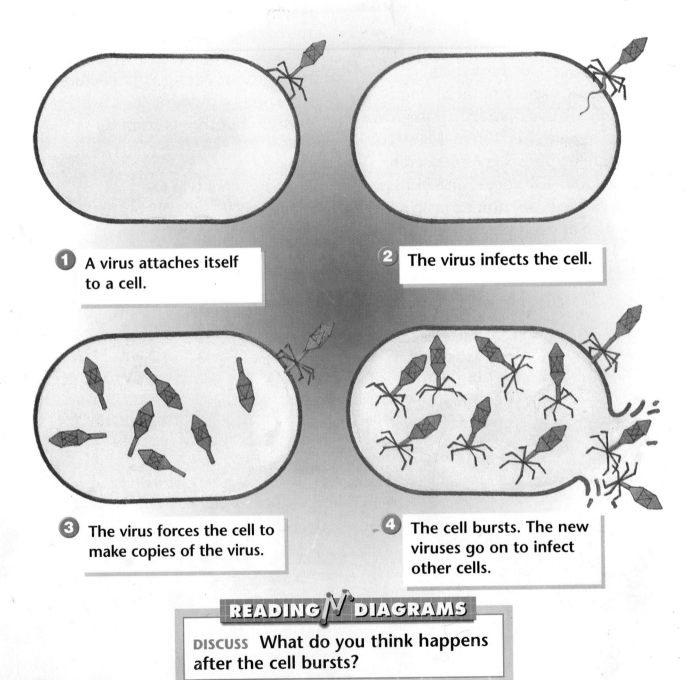

1. A virus attaches itself to a cell.

2. The virus infects the cell.

3. The virus forces the cell to make copies of the virus.

4. The cell bursts. The new viruses go on to infect other cells.

READING ⚡ DIAGRAMS

DISCUSS **What do you think happens after the cell bursts?**

20

FUNtastic Facts

Nerve cells can be very long. A nerve cell connecting your big toe or your thumb to your spine may be 1 meter long. The longest animal nerve cells are found in a giraffe's leg. They can measure up to 2 meters in length. Why is it important for nerve cells to be so long?

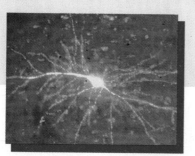

WHY IT MATTERS

There are many different types of cells, and there are many types of organisms in the world. Now that you know what a cell looks like and how its parts work, you can identify types of cells. It will also help you understand how organisms are different. For example, plants are different from animals in many ways. That is why plant cells have parts different from animal cells. You will use this knowledge as you learn more about how organisms are classified.

REVIEW

1. How are cells and organisms similar to bricks and buildings?

2. How are plant and animal cells alike and different?

3. Describe the functions of the cell membrane, nucleus, and cytoplasm.

4. MAKE A MODEL What if you made models of bacteria and fungi cells? How would they be different from your model of a plant cell?

5. CRITICAL THINKING *Apply*
A cell has green structures inside. How do you know what kind of cell it is? What kind of outer covering do you think it has?

WHY IT MATTERS THINK ABOUT IT
What if plant cells did not have cell walls? How do you think this would affect a plant?

WHY IT MATTERS WRITE ABOUT IT
What if animal cells had a cell wall? How would this affect them?

LARGER THAN LIFE

What lets you see things up close and personal? A microscope! It helps you view a tiny world that has a big effect on our lives. If it weren't for the microscope, we wouldn't know about cells, bacteria, or viruses.

A microscope lens is thick in the middle and thin at the edges. When light rays from an object go into the lens, they bend. When the rays reach your eyes, the object looks much larger than it is.

The first microscopes had one lens. They were called simple microscopes. English scientist Robert Hooke looked at cork through a microscope in 1665. What he saw looked like boxes, so he named them cells!

Today we use compound microscopes with two or more lenses. One is near the object. Another is near your eye. The bottom lens makes an object look bigger than it is. The top lens makes it look even bigger!

Physical Science Link

The electron microscope doesn't shine light on an object, and you don't look through lenses to see the object. This microscope hits an object with tiny electric particles. The magnetic lenses pull together a detailed picture of the object!

Scientists use microscopes to search for cures for diseases. They also study plant cells to find out which grow well where it seldom rains—or rains too much!

Microscopes are used for many other tasks. Robert Hooke would be very impressed!

DISCUSSION STARTER

What's the difference between a simple and a compound microscope?

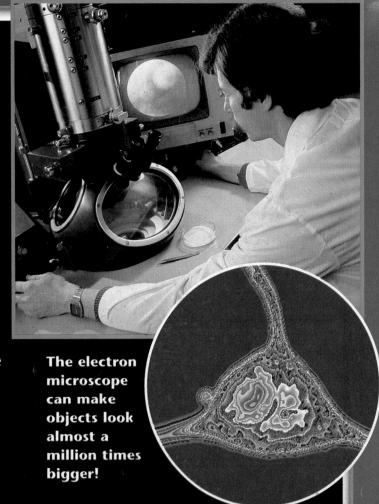

The electron microscope can make objects look almost a million times bigger!

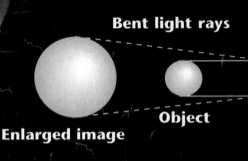

Bent light rays

Lens

Enlarged image

Object

Light rays

Eye

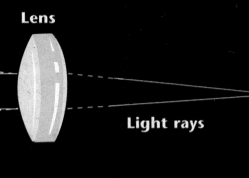

To learn more about microscopes, visit *www.mhschool.com/science* and enter the keyword UPCLOSE.

*inter*NET
CONNECTION

SCIENCE WORDS

cell p. 5

cell membrane p. 15

cell wall p. 14

chloroplast p. 14

chromosome p. 16

cytoplasm p. 15

nucleus p. 15

organ p. 6

organism p. 4

organ system p. 6

oxygen p. 4

tissue p. 5

vacuole p. 15

USING SCIENCE WORDS

Number a paper from 1 to 10. Fill in 1 to 5 with words from the list above.

1. The cell structure that holds water, food, and wastes is the __?__.

2. The thin, outer covering found both in plant and animal cells is the __?__.

3. A structure in a plant cell that makes food is a(n) __?__.

4. A group of similar cells that work together to carry out a job form a(n) __?__.

5. Groups of tissues form a(n) __?__.

6-10. Pick five words from the list above that were not used in 1 to 5, and use each in a sentence.

UNDERSTANDING SCIENCE IDEAS

11. How is a virus not like an organism that lives in pond water?

12. Why don't animal cells have chloroplasts?

USING IDEAS AND SKILLS

13. **READING SKILL: RECOGNIZE A LIST** Define an organ system and give an example. Make a list of what the organ system would be made of, starting with the cell.

14. **MAKE A MODEL** Draw and label both a plant cell and an animal cell. In your plant cell drawing, circle in red the parts not found in an animal cell.

15. **THINKING LIKE A SCIENTIST** What do you know about how a virus works? How could you use this information to stop a virus that makes people sick?

PROBLEMS and PUZZLES

Living or Nonliving How can you tell if a white spot on a tomato is a living thing? Describe a safe way you could test it to find out.

Are All Plants Alike? Have an adult take you to a nearby park. Use a hand lens to study the plants there. How are the flowers, leaves, and stems alike? Different?

CHAPTER 2
HOW ORGANISMS ARE CLASSIFIED

Can you tell a plant from an animal just by looking? Do you see a plant and an animal here? How can you tell one from the other? Are all living things either an animal or a plant? Is an ant an animal? Is a mushroom a plant? As you read this chapter, you will be able to answer these questions.

In Chapter 2 you will compare and contrast many things. When you compare things, you see how they are alike. When you contrast things, you see how they are different.

WHY IT MATTERS

Classifying organisms helps people to study and learn about living things.

SCIENCE WORDS

kingdom the largest group into which an organism is classified

trait a characteristic of an organism

genus a group made up of two or more very similar species

species the smallest group into which an organism is classified

Classification

Have you ever had to sort, or classify, a group of items? What were they? How did you do it?

Things like toys can be organized into groups. First you have to decide what characteristic to use to define the groups. For example, it could be soft toys or hard toys.

Do you think living things can be organized into groups, too? Why or why not?

EXPLORE

HYPOTHESIZE **What characteristics do you think scientists use to classify living things? Write a hypothesis in your** *Science Journal.*

Design Your Own Experiment

HOW ARE ORGANISMS CLASSIFIED?

PROCEDURES

1. **OBSERVE** Choose eight very different organisms that you would like to classify and learn more about. You may choose the ones you see here. Record their names in your *Science Journal.*

2. **COLLECT DATA** What would you like to know about your organisms? Where would you look to find the information? Design a table to record the information.

3. **CLASSIFY** Try to place all of the organisms into groups. What characteristics did you use to help you make your choices?

CONCLUDE AND APPLY

1. **IDENTIFY** How many groups were formed? What were the major characteristics of the organisms in each group?

2. **EXPLAIN** What organisms were placed in each group?

3. **COMMUNICATE** Make a list of the characteristics of the organisms in each group.

GOING FURTHER: Apply

4. **REPEAT** Test your classification system by adding a new organism. Does it fit in a group? Why or why not? If not, what changes could you make to your system so that it would fit?

MATERIALS

- reference books
- *Science Journal*

CLASSIFYING ORGANISMS

Kingdom	Number of Cells	Nucleus	Food	Move from Place to Place
Ancient Bacteria Kingdom	one	no	make	some move
True Bacteria Kingdom	one	no	make or obtain	some move
Protist Kingdom	one	yes	make or obtain	some move
Fungus Kingdom	one or many	yes	absorb	no
Plant Kingdom	many	yes	make	no
Animal Kingdom	many	yes	eat	yes

READING CHARTS

1. WRITE What organisms can make food? Make a list.
2. DISCUSS Why do you think plants and fungi don't need to move?

How Are Organisms Classified?

The Explore Activity shows that one way to classify organisms is by their physical characteristics.

To classify organisms into large groups, scientists also study many other characteristics. They look at body form and how an organism gets food. They observe if it moves from place to place. They also study the number of cells, if the cells have a nucleus, and cell parts. Even an organism's blood and how it grows and develops before it is born are studied.

For many years scientists could not settle on a single classification system. People often used different names to describe the same organism. This often led to confusion. With time a worldwide classification system was developed. It divides organisms into large groups, called **kingdoms** (king'dəmz). Organisms in each kingdom share basic **traits** (trāts). A trait is a characteristic of a living thing. Organisms within a kingdom are similar to one another but are different from organisms in other kingdoms. The chart above shows the basic traits of organisms in each kingdom.

To Which Kingdom Does an Organism Belong?

A chart can help you organize a lot of information. This chart can help you determine what types of organisms belong in each kingdom. Simply ask the following questions.

Brain Power

An organism is made of many cells, and each cell has a nucleus. It eats food and moves. To which kingdom does it belong?

DOES THE ORGANISM . . .	IF YES, . . .	IF NO, . . .
. . . have a nucleus?	. . . it can be an animal, plant, fungus, or protist.	. . . it can be a true bacterium or ancient bacterium.
. . . have many cells?	. . . it can be an animal, plant, or fungus.	. . . it can be a true bacterium, ancient bacterium, fungus, or protist.
. . . eat or obtain food?	. . . it can be an animal, fungus, or true bacterium.	. . . it can be a true bacterium, ancient bacterium, plant, or protist.
. . . move?	. . . it can be an animal, protist, true bacterium, or ancient bacterium.	. . . it can be a plant or fungus.

How Can Organisms Be Classified Further?

Mountain lions and houseflies belong to the animal kingdom even though they are very different. That is why scientists use smaller and smaller groups to further classify organisms. The smaller the group, the more similar the organisms in it are to each other.

There are seven groups into which an organism can be classified. This chart shows the groups from largest to smallest. There are fewer different kinds of organisms in each group as you move down from the kingdom level.

Kingdom
Members of the animal kingdom move in some way, eat food, and reproduce.

Phylum
A *phylum* is a large group within a kingdom. Members share at least one major characteristic, like having a backbone.

Class
A phylum is broken down into smaller groups, called *classes.* Members of this class all produce milk for their young.

Order
A class is made up of smaller groups, called *orders.* Members of this order are meat eaters.

Family
An order is made up of still smaller groups of similar organisms. These groups are called *families.* Dogs, wolves, and coyotes belong to the same family.

Genus
A family is made up of organisms belonging to similar, even smaller groups. Each group is called a genus. Dogs and wolves belong to the same genus.

Species
The smallest classification group is a species. A species is made up of only one type of organism that can reproduce only with another organism of the same species. All dogs belong to the same species.

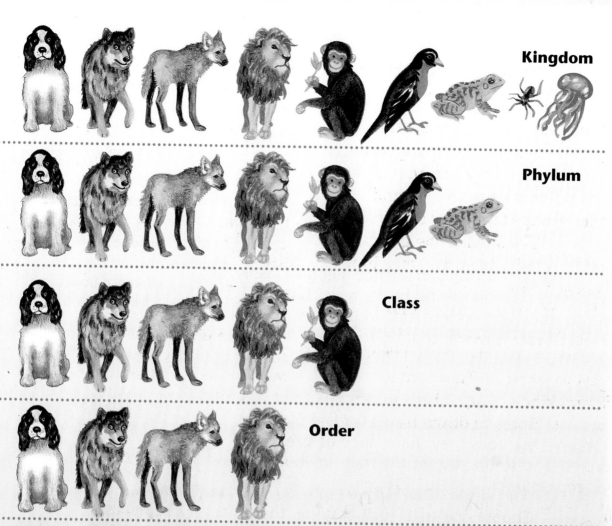

Kingdom

Phylum

Class

Order

Family

Genus

Species

READING /\/ CHARTS

1. **DISCUSS** Are there more organisms in a class or a family? How can you tell?
2. **REPRESENT** Design another chart that shows how the groups are organized. How is it different?

SKILL BUILDER

Skill: Classifying

CLASSIFYING LEAVES

When you organize toys or living things into groups, you are classifying. When you classify, you organize things into smaller groups based on their traits. This skill is important not only in science. People classify things every day. Classifying helps make things easier to study and understand. To practice this skill, you will classify leaves according to different traits.

MATERIALS

- 10 leaves or leaf pictures
- ruler
- reference books
- *Science Journal*

PROCEDURES

1. OBSERVE Spread out the leaves (or leaf pictures). Observe the traits they share, such as size, color, shape, and so on. Record the traits in your *Science Journal*.

2. CLASSIFY Choose one trait, such as color, that you recorded in your *Science Journal*. Organize all ten leaves based on that trait. Draw the way your leaves are organized. You may use a table.

3. REPEAT Follow the same procedure for two other traits you recorded.

CONCLUDE AND APPLY

1. IDENTIFY In how many different ways were you able to classify the leaves?

2. COMPARE AND CONTRAST How did your classification system differ from other students' systems? In what ways were they similar?

3. CLASSIFY Give some examples of how other things are classified. Use a kitchen, bedroom, closet, or supermarket.

4. DRAW CONCLUSIONS How do you think using a worldwide classification system might help scientists identify and understand organisms?

How Are Organisms Named?

The classification system helps classify organisms into smaller and smaller groups. It also plays a part in how each organism is named. The naming system that we use today was developed in the 1700s by a Swedish scientist, Carolus Linnaeus.

The first part of an organism's name uses that organism's **genus** (jē′nəs) name. Remember, a genus is a group made up of two or more very similar species. The second part of its name uses its **species** (spē′shēz) name. Remember, a species is the smallest classification group. It is made up of only one type of organism that can reproduce only with another organism of the same species.

For example, the genus name for a lion is *Panthera*. A number of large cats share this genus name. However, only the lion has the full name *Panthera leo*.

Yipes!

Using both the genus and species names lets scientists identify specific organisms. For example, the table shows two members of the small cat genus, *Felis*. Which would you rather have curl up in your lap?

Common Name	Genus Name	Species Name
Jaguar	*Panthera*	onca
Tiger	*Panthera*	tigris
Lion	*Panthera*	leo
Mountain lion	*Felis*	concolor
House cat	*Felis*	catus

Are There Organisms That Have Never Been Classified?

Scientists have named and described about 1.75 million species on Earth so far. However, scientists are always looking for organisms that have never been described or classified. Some scientists estimate that we may be sharing the world with 5 million to 15 million species. Many of these species live in tropical rain forests.

Rain Forest Organisms

Scientists are working to find and classify rain forest organisms never seen before. Who knows what interesting and helpful organisms are just waiting to be discovered!

There are many reasons to study rain forest organisms, such as finding new types of medicines. Unfortunately more than 50 acres of rain forest are being cleared every minute for farming and timber.

Red-Eyed Green Tree Frog

Emerald Tree Boa

Red-Breasted Toucan

These are just a few of the thousands of different organisms that live in the rain forest.

These changes affect organisms. If plants that an animal depends on for food or shelter are destroyed, the animal may die. If this continues for a long time, a species may die. That is why scientists are trying to gather information about rain forest organisms as quickly as they can.

There are more than 300,000 different beetles on Earth. Imagine trying to tell one beetle from another without a classification system!

Classifying organisms helps people in three ways. First, it allows them to keep track of organisms. Second, classification helps people communicate by using one naming system. Finally, classification helps to organize information about organisms for further studies. Studying groups helps people see the "big picture" of how life is organized.

REVIEW

1. Name the different kingdoms. What are the key traits of organisms in each kingdom?

2. Describe how a kingdom is divided into smaller groups.

3. What do scientific names provide that common names do not provide?

4. **CLASSIFY** List and classify ten organisms. What traits did you use? How many groups did you create? Did any organisms not fit into one of the groups? Explain.

5. **CRITICAL THINKING** *Evaluate* How might the extinction of one organism affect others?

WHY IT MATTERS THINK ABOUT IT Prairie dogs are not dogs. Jellyfish are not fish. How do you think using scientific names instead of common names helps prevent misconceptions?

WHY IT MATTERS WRITE ABOUT IT List at least three things that have different names in different parts of the country, for example, soda and pop.

35

HELPING ONE ANOTHER

Could there be life on Earth without plants? Without animals? Even if there could, how would one survive without the other?

Plants provide most of the food animals eat. Animals also use plants and trees for shelter. Humans also make medicines from plant parts.

The colorings of some animals blend in with the plants around them. Some animals use plants to hide and store food. Plants even produce oxygen for animals to breathe!

Plants do a lot for animals, but plants need animals, too. When bees eat nectar from flowers, they pollinate flowers. Pollen is a dustlike material needed to grow new plants. As a bee feeds, pollen grains stick to its body. Then when the bee flies to another flower, it deposits some pollen there.

The pollen helps form new seeds so new flowers can grow!

Some animals eat fruit plants but can't digest the seeds. These are later passed through the body and deposited somewhere else. Other seeds cling to an animal's fur and fall off later in some other area. If plant seeds just fall, a garden becomes too crowded for every plant to grow. Animals help put seeds where they'll have a chance to grow.

Some plants need animals as food! The leaves of a Venus's-flytrap snap shut to catch insects that land. The bladderwort traps insects in pouches on its underground roots!

DISCUSSION STARTER

1. Why do you think some plants need insects for food?

2. How do humans help plants spread their seeds around?

To learn more about the relationships of plants and animals, visit **www.mhschool.com/science** and enter the keyword HELP.

*inter*NET
CONNECTION

WHY IT MATTERS

Learning about the past helps us learn about the present.

SCIENCE WORDS

fossil any evidence of an organism that lived in the past

embryo an undeveloped animal or plant

extinct describes an organism that is no longer alive on Earth

Classifying Organisms of the Past

How much do we know about the great meat-eating dinosaur *Tyrannosaurus rex*? It was 14 meters (46 feet) long and 6 meters (20 feet) tall, and it weighed 8 tons (17,600 pounds). It walked upright on two powerful legs. Its tiny arms were really too short even to reach its mouth. How do we know so much about *T. rex*? The evidence it left behind tells us.

EXPLORE

HYPOTHESIZE Does this dinosaur skeleton remind you of any animals alive today? What might be learned from comparing the bones of past and present-day animals? Write a hypothesis in your *Science Journal*.

Investigate Using Skeletons to Compare Organisms

Carefully observe and compare the three skeletons.

PROCEDURES

1. COMPARE AND CONTRAST Compare the picture of the dinosaur skeleton on page 38 with the skeletons on this page.

2. COMMUNICATE Make a chart in your *Science Journal* that lists the similarities and differences. Use the computer if you like.

CONCLUDE AND APPLY

1. IDENTIFY Write a paragraph about the similarities and differences you noticed among the skeletons.

GOING FURTHER: Apply

2. DRAW CONCLUSIONS What types of things can be learned by comparing the skeletons of present-day animals with the skeletons of animals of the past?

MATERIALS

- ruler, pencil, and paper, or computer with charting program
- *Science Journal*

This is a skeleton of a bird.

This is a skeleton of a reptile.

How Are Skeletons Used to Compare Organisms?

A **fossil** (fos'əl) is any evidence of an organism that lived in the past. Fossils are often skeletons preserved in rock. When someone discovers a new fossil, he or she might wonder, "How would the organism that made this fit into today's classification system?" As in the Explore Activity, he or she might compare the fossil with bones of similar animals living today.

Many people are interested in the history of organisms that lived in the past. They might also study an organism of today and wonder what its ancestors were like. Finding this type of information is something like filling in a family tree.

As scientists try to learn more about an organism's past, they must consider that organisms change over time. Change in living things over time is called *evolution* (ev'ə lü'shən).

For example, using fossils of skulls, teeth, and leg bones, scientists have traced the ancestors of the modern horse back about 60 million years. At right are only some of the ancestors of the horse. The first ancestor was about the size of a small dog. How do the leg bones of today's horse compare with its ancestor's bones?

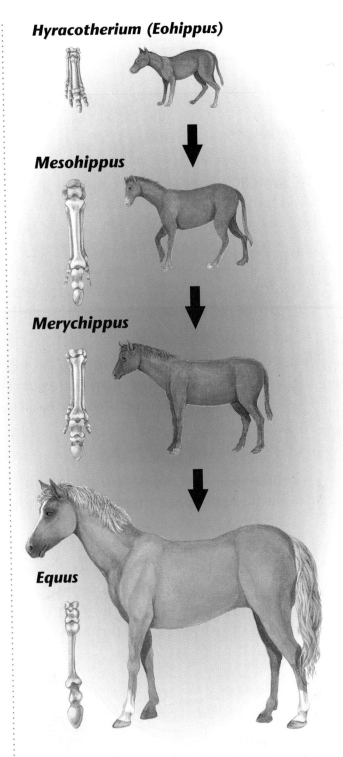

Hyracotherium (Eohippus)

Mesohippus

Merychippus

Equus

Based on fossil evidence, scientists think Hyracotherium (Eohippus) is the ancestor of all horses. What similarities and differences do you see? How did the animals' appearance and leg structure change?

What Does Other Fossil Evidence Tell You?

Another thing that we can learn is the age of a fossil compared with other fossils. This can be done by studying the rock layer in which a fossil is found.

How do you think studying rock layers tells you about a fossil's age? Looking at other fossils found in the same rock layer tells that the organisms lived at about the same time. The oldest fossils are in the oldest rock layers, which are at the bottom. Younger fossils are found in later, upper rock layers. These fossils are younger than fossils in lower layers.

Fossils found in layer A are younger than fossils found in layer B. Which rock layer contains fossils older than layer C?

QUICK LAB

Older and Younger

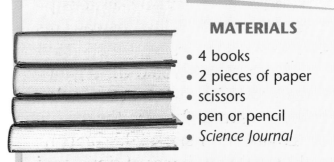

MATERIALS

- 4 books
- 2 pieces of paper
- scissors
- pen or pencil
- *Science Journal*

HYPOTHESIZE Relative dating is placing things in order from oldest to youngest. What do you look for to help you decide which is older and younger? Write a hypothesis in your *Science Journal*.

PROCEDURES

1. **OBSERVE** Cut a piece of paper into four pieces. Draw a "fossil" on each piece. Place one fossil inside the front cover of each book. Stack the books.

2. **INTERPRET DATA** Challenge your partner to find the fossils and arrange them in order of which is "oldest" and "youngest." Record any observations you make in your *Science Journal*.

3. **REPEAT** Switch roles and repeat the activity.

CONCLUDE AND APPLY

1. **EXPLAIN** What did the books represent?

2. **IDENTIFY** Which fossil was oldest? Youngest? What evidence helped you decide?

Can Organisms That Seem Different Be Related?

What do you think the organisms on this page have in common? Do their limb bones seem similar to you in any ways?

Even though each animal uses these bones differently, the bones are arranged in similar ways. Scientists compare limbs to understand what is similar and different about organisms. They can see which have similar features and might be related. Related organisms have a common ancestor. For example, a common ancestor had bones similiar to the bones of these animals.

Think about related organisms and common ancestors like this. Two cousins are related. A great-grandmother would be one of their common ancestors.

Scientists look for evidence of common ancestors when they classify organisms. Some of their findings are surprising. For example, whales are more closely related to humans than to sharks! You can see this by looking at whale flipper bones. They are much more like human arm bones than shark fins.

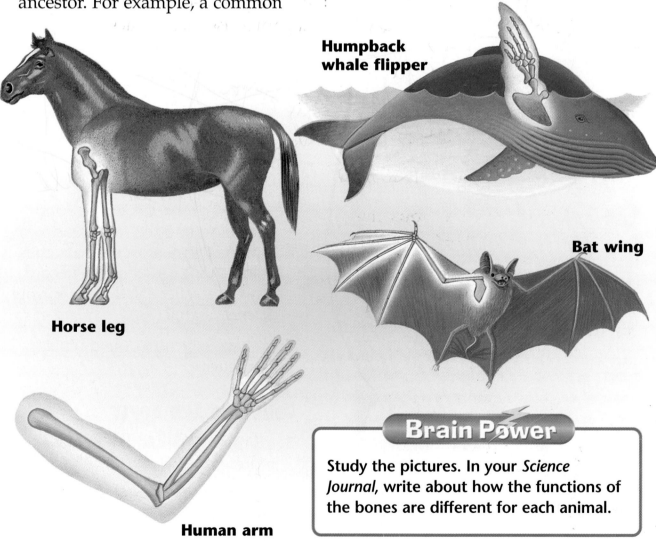

Humpback whale flipper

Horse leg

Bat wing

Human arm

Brain Power

Study the pictures. In your *Science Journal*, write about how the functions of the bones are different for each animal.

What Are Some Other Clues?

Another clue to finding similarities among organisms comes from before they were even born. An undeveloped animal or plant is called an **embryo** (em'brē ō').

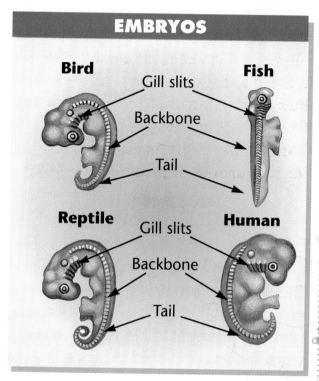

EMBRYOS

Bird

Gill slits

Backbone

Tail

Fish

Reptile

Gill slits

Backbone

Tail

Human

What do you notice as you compare these four embryos? Each has a backbone, or a spine. They all have gill slits and a tail. These features suggest that the organisms have a common ancestor.

An embryo changes before it is ready for the world. Some features are lost in certain animals as the embryo grows. Humans do not have gill slits or a tail when they are born.

Many organisms are **extinct** (ek stingkt'), or no longer alive on Earth. To help classify them, scien-tists can compare fossil embryos with each other and with modern embryos.

Still another clue that organisms might be related can be found in "leftover" structures. Humans don't need a tail, but a human adult has a tailbone at the end of the spine. Some snakes have tiny hip and limb bones. A baleen whale has small, useless hip bones. These bones are inherited, or passed along, from ancestors.

These useless bones are clues that help classify organisms into groups that probably have a common ancestor. That means they are probably related to organisms that have and use those bones

This blind salamander lives in deep, dark caves. Yet it has useless eyes that don't see. What conclusions can you draw about this salamander's ancestors?

These animals are extinct.

Woolly mammoth

Dusty seaside sparrow

Dodo bird

Why Do Organisms Become Extinct?

Many organisms are extinct. Some scientists believe that 99 out of every 100 species that have ever lived on Earth are extinct.

Judging from fossils, there have been many *mass extinctions*. A mass extinction is when many different species die out at about the same time. The best-known mass extinction is that of the dinosaurs. They died out 65 million years ago, along with more than half of all other animal and plant species.

Some scientists believe that a giant comet hit Earth and caused the extinction of the dinosaurs. Walter Alvarez, along with his father, Dr. Luis Alvarez, found evidence to support the comet theory. The comet would have created great clouds of dust that blocked sunlight. This would have caused dark and cold periods.

Without sunlight, plants could not have made the food they needed to survive. Without plants, plant-eating dinosaurs would have died. Without them, meat-eating dinosaurs would have died.

Other scientists believe that many huge volcanoes erupted, creating great clouds of dust. Still others think that dinosaurs spread deadly diseases as they moved about Earth. Dinosaurs may also have eaten plants that other species depended on, causing them to starve and die. Maybe many events together caused the dinosaur's extinction.

Can People Cause Extinction?

Do you think people can cause extinction? As a matter of fact, people play a big role in extinction. People use pesticides and chemicals, destroy places where animals live, and use up resources. They also hunt and fish. This causes many species to become endangered, or in danger of becoming extinct.

Condors are an endangered species.

In a way, learning about the past helps us learn about the present. Knowing how organisms have changed over time and who their ancestors were helps us to better understand the history of life on Earth. It also helps us classify living and extinct organisms.

People today are often interested in their past. They research family history and learn about ancestors. This helps them learn about where their families came from and how they changed over time.

REVIEW

1. What kinds of clues do fossils give about organisms of the past?

2. Is a fossil older or younger than another fossil in a lower rock layer? Explain.

3. How do embryos help identify a common ancestor of different organisms?

4. COMMUNICATE Explain some possible causes of dinosaur extinction. What are some causes of extinction today?

5. CRITICAL THINKING *Analyze* Some snakes have tiny hip and limb bones. What does this tell you about their ancestors? What traits might you find in the group they once belonged to?

WHY IT MATTERS THINK ABOUT IT
Why do you think it is interesting for people to learn about their ancestors?

WHY IT MATTERS WRITE ABOUT IT
What types of questions would you ask if you could talk to one of your ancestors? Why?

READING SKILL Write about how you can compare and contrast organisms of today with organisms of the past.

Helping Endangered Species

Ever wish that you could help endangered animals and plants? Some kids in Hawaii did, so they found a way to help! Students at the Enchanted Lake Elementary School wanted to help as many endangered species as they could—in Hawaii and elsewhere around the world. The kids started Project Lokahi. *Lokahi* is Hawaiian for "harmony."

With help from the students of Enchanted Lake, some organisms might not end up as "things of the past!"

Many species in Hawaii had no natural enemies. Without enemies they lost their defenses over time. For example, the Hawaiian raspberry lost its thorns, and some birds lost the ability to fly.

People brought predators to Hawaii from other parts of the world, such as mongooses, rats, Argentine ants, and wild pigs. These predators greatly harmed the bird and plant populations of the islands. Foreign plants were also harmful. The South American banana poka (pō'kə) and the miconia (mī cō'nē ə) are two vines that suffocated native plants.

To help endangered species, the kids set up a Web page on the Internet. There they explain which animals are in trouble and where the animals live. For example, the Web page lists the green sea turtle. At one time people hunted these turtles for their eggs,

Hawaiian Islands

Kauai

Niihau

Oahu

PACIFIC OCEAN

Molokai

Lani

Maui

Kahoolawe

Hawaii

meat, and shells. Green sea turtles lay their eggs on beaches in North Carolina and other warm places.

After learning about the turtles, people might help to protect them. People might put signs on the beaches or post fliers to warn people when the turtles are laying their eggs.

DISCUSSION STARTER

1. What kinds of information would convince people to protect endangered species?

2. Why do you think the kids chose the name Lokahi for the project?

Sea turtles need a safe place to lay their eggs.

To learn more about endangered species, visit *www.mhschool.com/science* and enter the keyword ATRISK.

*inter*NET
CONNECTION

Topic
LIFE SCIENCE
5

It is important for people to understand how living and nonliving things depend on one another.

SCIENCE WORDS

ecosystem living and non-living things in an environment and how they interact

community the living part of an ecosystem

population one type of organism living in an area

habitat an organism's home

producer an organism that makes food

consumer an organism that eats food

decomposer an organism that breaks down wastes and the remains of other organisms

Organisms and Where They Live

What types of organisms live in deserts? Deserts are the driest places on Earth. In some deserts the amount of rain in a year would make a puddle only the thickness of a few pages in this book. During the day some deserts sizzle at temperatures above 45°C (113°F). Surprisingly some animals and plants make their homes in deserts. How do they survive? In fact how do living things in any environment survive?

EXPLORE

HYPOTHESIZE The key to an organism's survival is how it interacts with other living and nonliving things. What might these interactions be? Write a hypothesis in your *Science Journal*. Test it.

Investigate How Living and Nonliving Things Interact

Build a terrarium as a model of an environment. Observe it to see how living things interact with each other and their surroundings.

PROCEDURES

1. MAKE A MODEL Landscape your terrarium. Put taller plants in the back. Spread grass seed and any rocks, twigs, or other things you like.

2. If you add small animals, such as earthworms, sow bugs, and snails, add a water dish.

3. MEASURE In your *Science Journal*, make a data table. Record the height of each plant. Measure the plants in two weeks, and record the data. Make a bar graph.

4. Place the terrarium in a lighted area. Avoid direct sunlight.

5. COMMUNICATE Draw a diagram of your terrarium. Draw arrows to show how the organisms depend on each other.

CONCLUDE AND APPLY

1. CLASSIFY What are the living and nonliving things in the terrarium?

2. INFER Why should the terrarium not be placed in direct sunlight?

GOING FURTHER: Apply

3. OBSERVE Continue to maintain and observe your terrarium. Did anything unusual happen? Why do you think this happened?

MATERIALS

- prepared terrarium container
- small plants and animals
- plastic spoon
- ruler
- water mister
- grass seeds, rocks, twigs, sticks, bark, dried grass
- *Science Journal*

49

How Do Living and Nonliving Things Interact?

The terrarium in the Explore Activity is a model of an **ecosystem** (ek'ō sis'təm). Ecosystems include both living and nonliving things. The nonliving part of your ecosystem included water, pebbles, air, light, and soil. The living part of the ecosystem included the plants and animals. The study of how living and nonliving things interact is called *ecology* (ē kol'ə jē).

The living part of an ecosystem forms a **community** (kə mū'ni tē). Each ecosystem has its own community. The terrarium community had small plants and animals. A desert community includes beautiful cacti and deadly scorpions.

Do you think the members of a community can be grouped further? Communities can be divided into different **populations** (pop'yə lā'shənz). A population is made of only one type of organism. Your terrarium ecosystem had populations of organisms such as snails and earthworms.

Each organism's home is called its **habitat** (hab'i tat'). An earthworm lives in a soil habitat. A whale's habitat is the ocean. A termite's habitat is a termite nest.

What makes up the community in this ecosystem?

This diagram will help you understand the different parts of an ecosystem.

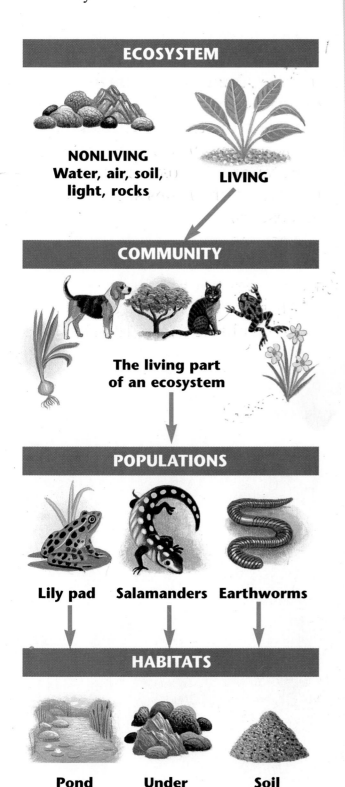

ECOSYSTEM

NONLIVING
Water, air, soil, light, rocks

LIVING

COMMUNITY

The living part of an ecosystem

POPULATIONS

Lily pad   Salamanders   Earthworms

HABITATS

Pond   Under rocks   Soil

A Misty Experiment

HYPOTHESIZE What kinds of habitats do different organisms prefer? Form a hypothesis. Use your terrarium to find out.

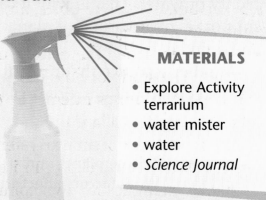

MATERIALS
- Explore Activity terrarium
- water mister
- water
- *Science Journal*

PROCEDURES

1. Lightly spray one side of your terrarium each day for one week. Leave the other side dry.

2. **OBSERVE** In your *Science Journal*, record your observations of how the organisms react each day.

CONCLUDE AND APPLY

1. **PREDICT** Which organisms preferred the wet side of the terrarium? Where would you expect these organisms to live in the wild? Explain.

2. **PREDICT** Which organisms preferred the dry side of the terrarium? Where would you expect these organisms to live in the wild? Explain.

How Are Ecosystems Different?

What makes one ecosystem different from another? In many cases water is the key. A desert is very dry. Only a small number of species of plants and animals can survive with little water. A rain forest has plenty of water. That is why it can support a great variety of plants and animals.

Another resource that can affect ecosystems is sunlight. Some plants, like cacti, grow where there is little water but plenty of sunlight. These types of plants could not grow in an area where there is little sunlight, even if there is plenty of water.

Still another resource is soil. Areas with soil that has many nutrients can support many plants. Few plants grow in areas with soil that does not have many nutrients.

How are all these plants similar and different? What factors affect the types of plants that grow in these ecosystems?

These plants grow in a desert.

The types of plants and animals that live in a particular ecosystem depend on a combination of these things. For example, a woodland forest has enough water and rich enough soil for grasses to grow. However, it does not have enough sunshine for most types of grasses. Too much of the Sun's light is blocked by the trees. The forest floor is so dark that most kinds of grasses can't grow there.

These plants grow in a rain forest.

What Types of Roles Do Organisms Play?

A community works like a team. Each member of the team has its own job to do. There are three different types of team members.

Producers (prə dü'sərz) make food. Consumers (kən sü'mərz) use the food that producers make or eat other organisms. Decomposers (dē'kəm pō'zərz) break down wastes and the remains of other organisms.

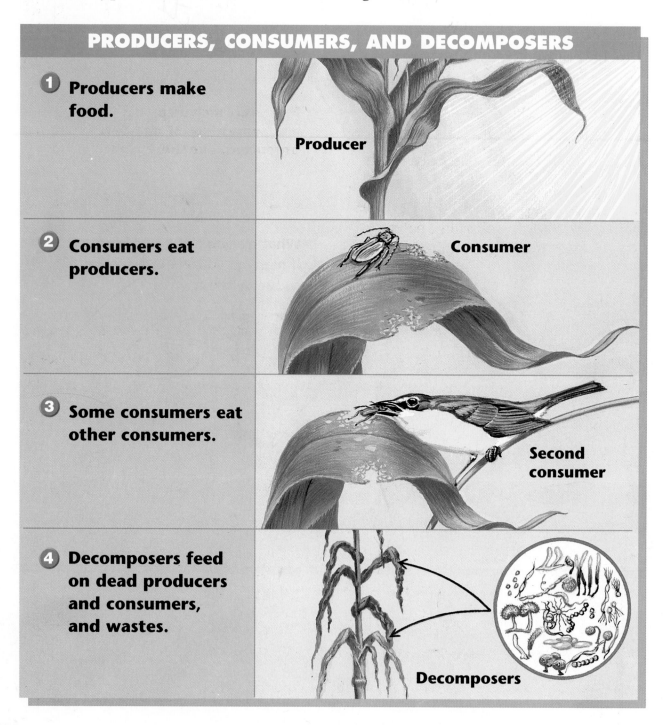

PRODUCERS, CONSUMERS, AND DECOMPOSERS

1. **Producers make food.**

   Producer

2. **Consumers eat producers.**

   Consumer

3. **Some consumers eat other consumers.**

   Second consumer

4. **Decomposers feed on dead producers and consumers, and wastes.**

   Decomposers

What Are Producers?

How do you think you can identify a producer? You can tell most producers by their green color. The color shows that their cells have chloroplasts. Chloroplasts are the cell's "food factories" you learned about in Topic 2. To make food, producers use water, air, simple chemicals, and the Sun's energy.

Producers are the "energy capturers" of the world. They capture light energy from the Sun and transform it into food. Producers use only some of the food they make for themselves. Most of the food goes to other members of the community that eat producers, and organisms that eat them.

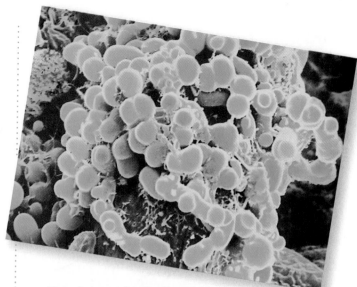

Producers include plants and some kinds of one-celled organisms, like these algae.

Brain Power

What do you think would happen if many producers in a community suddenly died?

What Are Consumers and Decomposers?

Food passes along from producers to consumers.

Consumers

Which organisms do you think were consumers in the terrarium? Organisms that eat food are consumers. Consumers include animals and some kinds of one-celled organisms. Consumers in the terrarium may have included insects and frogs.

To stay alive, consumers must get food from other organisms. There are three types of consumers. Some eat plants. A second type eats only animals. A third type of animal consumer eats both plants and animals. Which type of consumer are you?

Decomposers

Decomposers in the terrarium may have included microorganisms such as bacteria and some kinds of fungi. They may also have included larger organisms such as worms and snails. Decomposers break down living and dead matter into simple chemicals that they use for food. The chemicals left behind by decomposers are recycled, or used over and over again. Producers use these chemicals for making food.

Have you ever seen mold? Molds are a type of decomposer that often spoils food. Where do molds grow?

Some consumers eat other consumers, but all consumers depend on producers for food. Why is this so?

56

DID YOU KNOW?

The largest animals on Earth, blue whales, are toothless consumers. Their jaws are lined with hundreds of thin plates that strain out from ocean water tiny living things such as algae and tiny sea animals. If there were no algae, could the whales survive? Why or why not?

QUICK LAB

Observe a Decomposer

HYPOTHESIZE What do you think molds need to grow? Write a hypothesis.

MATERIALS
- 5 sealable plastic bags
- 4 food samples
- piece of cardboard
- warm water
- hand lens
- marking pen
- *Science Journal*

PROCEDURES

SAFETY: Do not open the bags after you seal them.

1. Moisten the food samples. Place each in a labeled plastic bag. Put a piece of cardboard in a bag.

2. Seal the bags, and place them in a warm, dark place.

3. **OBSERVE** In your *Science Journal*, record your daily observations.

CONCLUDE AND APPLY

1. **OBSERVE** On which samples did mold grow?

2. **INFER** Will molds grow on any type of material? Explain how the cardboard helped you answer this question.

3. **OBSERVE** How did the molds change the foods?

57

How Can You Spoil the Spoilers?

Where do you think the decomposers in the activity came from? Decomposers live almost everywhere. When they find moisture and food, they begin to grow. Soon, one organism reproduces to become billions. You saw this growth on the foods.

Why don't all foods spoil quickly? This diagram shows five ways to stop decomposers from spoiling foods.

The Deep Freeze
Low temperatures completely stop some decomposers from growing and slow the growth of others. Then they cannot multiply. This allows frozen foods to keep for months without spoiling.

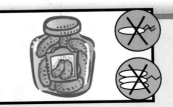

Pickling
Decomposers can't survive in vinegar, but you can eat foods with vinegar. Pickling foods in vinegar and other chemicals kills decomposers and keeps them from multiplying.

Can It
Canned foods can last for years. Canning uses two steps to preserve foods. First, the cans are sealed so no new decomposers can enter the can. Then, the food is boiled to kill decomposers.

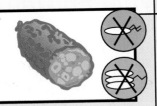

Salting
Decomposers are just like you. They need fresh water. If you give them salty water, they can't survive. Salting can keep foods from spoiling for months.

Drying
Decomposers need water. If you dry foods well, decomposers stop growing. This keeps dried foods from spoiling.

 Kill decomposers

 Stop decomposers from multiplying

 Keep decomposers from entering

READING CHARTS

1. **WRITE** What are three ways to stop decomposers from spoiling food?
2. **REPRESENT** Make a table that gives one example of each way.

An ecosystem is made of many parts, including you! All parts must work together to support the ecosystem. When parts don't work together, ecosystems are disturbed. It is important for people to understand ecosystems and how living and nonliving parts of the natural world depend on one another. They can work together to keep the ecosystems healthy.

How are these people helping preserve an ecosystem?

REVIEW

1. Describe how the living organisms in the terrarium interacted with the nonliving things and each other.

2. Explain the relationships among an ecosystem, community, population, and habitat.

3. Draw a diagram of an ecosystem. Include the terms *community, population, habitat, producers, consumers,* and *decomposers.*

4. **INFER** Two batches of beans were canned. Batch 1 spoils. What might have gone wrong?

5. **CRITICAL THINKING** *Evaluate* Could an ecosystem exist without (a) producers, (b) consumers, (c) decomposers? Explain.

WHY IT MATTERS THINK ABOUT IT
Ecosystems can be found almost anywhere you look—even in your schoolyard! What are some things you can do to preserve an ecosystem?

WHY IT MATTERS WRITE ABOUT IT
Describe one ecosystem that you observed. What living and nonliving things did it include? How did they interact?

SAVED BY THE SUN

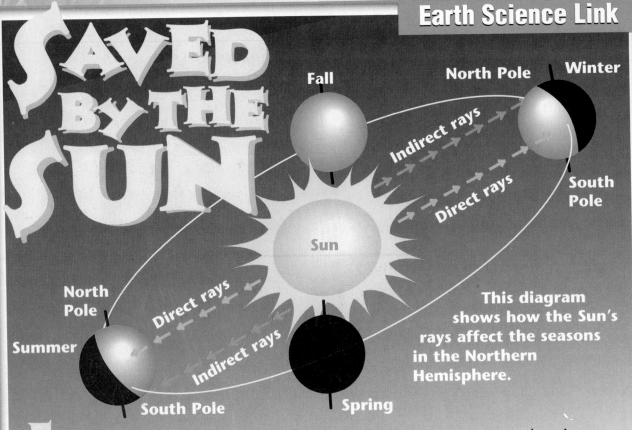

Fall

North Pole

Winter

Indirect rays

Direct rays

South Pole

Sun

North Pole

Direct rays

Summer

Indirect rays

South Pole

Spring

This diagram shows how the Sun's rays affect the seasons in the Northern Hemisphere.

Everything on Earth depends on the Sun. Without it producers couldn't grow. Consumers would starve. Without producers and consumers, decomposers would starve, too.

Earth is saved by the Sun's energy. At any one time, different parts of Earth receive different amounts of solar energy. Places facing the Sun receive its direct rays. Other places get indirect rays that provide less energy. How warm a place is depends on how much solar energy reaches it.

People can collect solar energy and use it to heat their homes. Using solar energy helps save natural resources such as coal, oil, and wood.

DISCUSSION STARTER

How might Earth be different if it weren't tilted on its axis?

To learn more about solar energy, visit *www.mhschool.com/science* and enter the keyword SUNNY.

interNET CONNECTION

SCIENCE WORDS

community p. 50
consumer p. 54
decomposer p. 54
ecosystem p. 50
embryo p. 43
extinct p. 43
fossil p. 40

genus p. 33
habitat p. 50
kingdom p. 28
population p. 50
producer p. 54
species p. 33
trait p. 28

USING SCIENCE WORDS

Number a paper from 1 to 10. Fill in 1 to 5 with words from the list above.

1. All the organisms in an ecosystem form a(n) __?__.

2. The first part of an organism's scientific name comes from its __?__ name.

3. The largest group into which an organism is classified is the __?__.

4. A characteristic of a living thing is known as a(n) __?__.

5. An organism that makes its own food is known as a(n) __?__.

6–10. Pick five words from the list above that were not used in 1 to 5, and use each in a sentence.

UNDERSTANDING SCIENCE IDEAS

11. Which classification group would have the most members? The least?

12. How can fossils help classify an extinct organism?

USING IDEAS AND SKILLS

13. **READING SKILL: COMPARE AND CONTRAST** Draw a diagram or chart that describes the relationships among producers, decomposers, and consumers.

14. **CLASSIFY** Classify the terms *habitat, population,* and *community* by completing this table. The table shows the living and nonliving parts of an ecosystem. Give examples to illustrate each term.

Ecosystem
Living things include:
Nonliving things include:

15. **THINKING LIKE A SCIENTIST** How could scientific names be important in daily life?

PROBLEMS and PUZZLES

Sandy or Moist Would a houseplant grow best in sandy soil or moist potting soil? How could you test to find out? How could you be sure you are testing only the soil?

Field Test Look for plants growing in your neighborhood. Are some growing better than others? If so, try to determine why.

SCIENCE WORDS

cell wall p. 14   habitat p. 50
cytoplasm p. 15   nucleus p. 15
ecosystem p. 50   organ p. 6
extinct p. 43   oxygen p. 4
fossil p. 40   species p. 33
genus p. 33   vacuole p. 15

USING SCIENCE WORDS

Number a paper from 1 to 10. Beside each number write the word or words that best completes the sentence.

1. Groups of tissues form a(n) ___?___.

2. A holding bin for food, water, and wastes is called a(n) ___?___.

3. The jellylike substance that fills a cell is called ___?___.

4. The basic needs of most living things are food, water, a place to live, and ___?___.

5. Evidence of an organism that lived in the past is called a(n) ___?___.

6. If an organism is no longer alive on Earth, it is ___?___.

7. A cell's control center is the ___?___.

8. An organism's home is called its ___?___.

9. An environment of living and non-living things is called a(n) ___?___.

10. A group made up of two or more very similar species is called a(n) ___?___.

UNDERSTANDING SCIENCE IDEAS

Write 11 to 15. For each number write the letter for the best answer. You may wish to use the hints provided.

11. The scientific naming system uses
    a. kingdom and phylum
    b. class and order
    c. genus and species
    d. family and kingdom
    (Hint: Read page 33, left column.)

12. Organisms that make food are
    a. consumers
    b. second consumers
    c. decomposers
    d. producers
    (Hint: Read page 54, right column.)

13. The main factor that makes one ecosystem differ from another is
    a. sunlight
    b. water
    c. soil
    d. people
    (Hint: Read page 52, left column.)

14. Humans would be considered
    a. producers
    b. consumers
    c. decomposers
    d. spoilers
    (Hint: Read pages 54–57.)

15. Which is an opinion supported by this unit?

  a. Humans can't control the destruction of Earth's ecosystems.

  b. Scientists have discovered most of the species on Earth.

  c. All parts of an ecosystem support one another.

  d. Only a few of the species that have ever lived are extinct.

  (Hint: Read page 59, left column.)

USING IDEAS AND SKILLS

16. Discuss how an animal performs the five life functions.

17. Name three plant and three human organs. How are their jobs similar? Different?

18. How do people affect extinction? What do you think should be done about this?

19. **CLASSIFY** Classify 20 things in your school as living or nonliving.

THINKING LIKE A SCIENTIST

20. **MAKE A MODEL** What materials would you use to make a model of *Tyrannosaurus rex*?

inter**NET** CONNECTION

For help in reviewing this unit, visit **www.mhschool.com/science**

WRITING IN YOUR JOURNAL

GROWING UP
One of the basic life functions of living things is to grow and develop. You may not notice it, but you grow and develop every day. Make a list of things you can do now that you could not do when you were younger.

SEEING SCIENCE AROUND YOU
Have you ever traveled to somewhere very different from your home? How was it different? Was the weather different? Were there different animals and plants? If you lived there all the time, how would your life be different?

MAKING A DIFFERENCE
Every year in April, the world observes Earth Day. On Earth Day students do things to help keep Earth a healthy place to live. What could you and your friends do this Earth Day to help?

Design your own Experiment

Plants need water, sunlight, and air to survive, but which do they need most? Form a hypothesis. Design an experiment that tests which is most important.

PROBLEMS and PUZZLES

Organism Trading Cards

Make trading cards of your favorite organisms. On the front draw or paste a picture of the organism. On the back include information about its ecosystem, habitat, and genus and species name. Also include whether it is a producer, consumer, or decomposer. Use encyclopedias or other sources to find information. Challenge your friends to identify the organisms and to tell you anything else they may know about them. Trade them with your friends. It's a fun way to learn about organisms!

Ecosystem: my home
Habitat: under my blanket
Genus: Felis
Species: catus
Consumer

Brad's Birthday-Bread Baking Problem

THE PROBLEM

Brad's Birthday Bread won't rise. Brad's problem is that someone smeared dough on his recipe. He can't read whether to grow his yeast in cold, warm, or hot water. Yeast is a tiny fungus that makes bread rise. Yeast feeds on sugar and grows best at a certain temperature. Brad doesn't know what this temperature is.

THE PLAN

Write a hypothesis of how to make Brad's yeast grow. Think of a plan that will help you test your hypothesis.

TEST

Test Your Hypothesis Obtain yeast, sugar, and water. Your teacher will tell you how much of each ingredient to add. Then test your hypothesis. You can tell that the yeast is growing when it looks bubbly. At what water temperature does yeast grow best?

EVALUATE AND PUBLISH

Was your hypothesis correct? If not, how did you change it to find the best temperature for growing yeast?

Write a report that tells what you did.

CHAPTER 3

DESCRIBING MATTER

Everything you can see and touch is made of matter. In fact, even some things that you can't see or touch are made of matter, too. How do you know if something is made of matter? In this chapter you will learn about the characteristics of matter. You will also learn about ways matter can be measured and what matter is made of.

In this chapter you will read for sequence of events. As an example you will read about the steps in making a shirt from plastic.

WHY IT MATTERS

Matter can be described and classified by its characteristics.

SCIENCE WORDS

matter anything that takes up space, has mass, and has properties that you can observe and describe

buoyancy the upward force of water or air on an object

mass the amount of matter making up an object

solid a form of matter that has a definite shape and takes up a definite amount of space

liquid a form of matter that takes up a definite amount of space and has no definite shape

gas a form of matter that does not take up a definite amount of space and has no definite shape

Matter

What do you think would be in the Museum That Matters—the world's biggest museum? "Everything that matters," said the museum guide. "It's all here, from bananas to basketballs, from icicles to bicycles, from clouds to whales to mountaintops."

"What *don't* you have?" asked a visitor. How would you answer the visitor?

EXPLORE

HYPOTHESIZE How could you investigate a "mystery substance" to determine if it belongs in the museum? Write a hypothesis in your *Science Journal*. Test your ideas.

Investigate How You Can Describe It

Observe, test, and describe a "mystery substance" in as much detail as you can.

MATERIALS

- mystery substance
- assorted tools
- small bowl
- water
- *Science Journal*

PROCEDURES

Safety: Do not taste the mystery substance.

1. **OBSERVE** Record as many observations of the mystery substance as you can in your *Science Journal*. Here are some ideas.

   - How does it look, feel, and smell? Will anything stick to it? Can you use it like glue? Does it work like a magnet?

   - Use tools to test it. Is it strong, brittle, or flexible? Can you mold it? Does it shatter or bend?

   - What happens if you put some in water?

   - Will it copy pictures from the comics?

CONCLUDE AND APPLY

1. **COMMUNICATE** List five words or phrases that you would use to describe the mystery substance.

2. **EXPLAIN** Do you think the mystery substance belongs in the Museum That Matters? Why or why not?

GOING FURTHER: Apply

3. **COMPARE** List five words or phrases that you would use to describe your shoe. How are the words like those you used to describe the substance?

How Can You Describe It?

Study the words and phrases used to describe the mystery substance in the Explore Activity. Can you classify them into groups such as hardness, color, texture, shape, and size?

The words and phrases described some of the *properties* (prop′ər tēz) of the substance. A property is a characteristic of something that you can observe.

What Things Are Made Of

Do you think the mystery substance belongs in the Museum That Matters? It would belong because it is made of **matter** (mat′ər). Matter is anything that takes up space. Matter also has properties that you can observe and describe. Some of these properties include color, texture, shape, size, and hardness.

Many things in the world are made of matter. However, not *all* things in the world are matter. Think about the color yellow, the month of October, and the number 46. They are not matter but ideas. They do not take up space. They cannot be described by properties. For example, the color yellow is used to *describe* matter. Yellow can't *be* hard, big, or cold.

Brain Power

Copy this table into your *Science Journal*. Complete the table for the listed items. Then add three other examples of nonmatter.

Investigate How You Can Describe It

Observations of the mystery substance

1. Feels smooth
2. Is soft, and stretches like taffy when it is warm
3. When it's cold, it is hard and breaks into pieces when pulled

What types of words are used to describe the mystery substance?

Matter or Nonmatter

Item	Matter	Nonmatter	Reason
Yellow		X	
Birthday			
Car			
Dog			
Light			
Mirror			
		X	
		X	
		X	

What Are Some Other Properties of Matter?

On page 68 you learned that some of the properties used to describe matter include color, texture, shape, size, and hardness. Some other properties include smell, temperature, magnetic attraction, and **buoyancy** (boi'ən sē).

You are probably familiar with most of these properties, but what is buoyancy? Buoyancy is the upward force of water, another liquid, or air that keeps things afloat. What examples of buoyancy can you find in this drawing?

Properties help people choose the right types of matter for different jobs. What properties does glass have that make it good for classroom windows but bad for gym windows? Based on their properties, where might you use iron instead of wood? Where might you use wood instead of iron?

Examples of buoyancy

This table shows some souvenirs made by the Utterly Useless Souvenir Company. It also shows the properties that make each item useless. Complete the table. Then make up some useless souvenirs of your own.

Utterly Useless Souvenirs	
Utterly Useless Item	**Properties That Make It Useless**
Glass baseball bat	too brittle, not strong enough
Rubber mirror	
Wooden bicycle tires	
Aluminum foil tissues	

Is It Matter?

How else can you tell if something is matter? All matter has **mass** (mas). Mass is the amount of matter making up an object. For example, a dictionary has more mass than a marble.

Mass is measured in units called *kilograms* (kil'ə gramz'). Small objects are measured in units called grams (g). There are 1,000 grams in 1 kilogram (kg).

An instrument called a *balance* (bal'əns) is used to measure mass. As you can see, it looks a little like a seesaw. To use this pan balance, the object you want to measure is placed in one pan. Known masses are placed in the other pan until the balance is even. The mass of the object is equal to the sum of all the known masses.

This book you are reading, the water you drink, and helium filling a balloon are three examples of *states* (stāts), or forms, of matter.

A textbook is an example of a **solid** (sol'id). Solid matter has a definite shape. It takes up a definite amount of space. The particles of matter making up a solid are packed together tightly.

The mass of the object is equal to the sum of all the masses needed to balance the instrument.

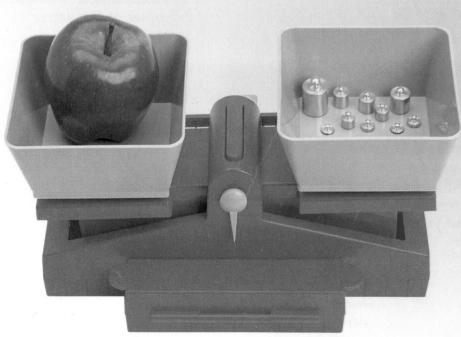

How would you describe the water you drink? Water is an example of a **liquid** (lik'wid). In a liquid the particles of matter move more than they do in a solid. They can change position and move past one another.

Liquid matter does not have a definite shape. However, it does take up a definite amount of space. For example, one cup of milk is one cup of milk. It doesn't matter whether it is in a measuring cup or spilled on a table.

The helium in a balloon is an example of a **gas** (gas). In a gas the particles of matter can move freely. They can move farther apart from one another than in a solid or liquid.

A gas does not have a definite shape. It does not take up a definite amount of space. The helium in a balloon takes the shape of the balloon. If the balloon bursts, the particles of helium spread out into the air.

This shows the arrangement of particles making up a liquid.

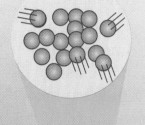

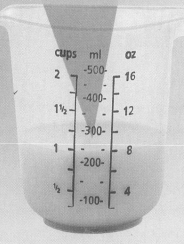

This shows the arrangement of particles making up a gas.

This table shows differences between solids, liquids, and gases.

	Definite Shape?	Size
States of Matter		
Solid	yes	fixed size
Liquid	takes shape of container	fixed size
Gas	takes shape of container	no fixed size

QUICK LAB

Identifying Matter

HYPOTHESIZE Is air matter? Write a hypothesis in your *Science Journal*. Use what you know about matter to design an experiment to find out.

MATERIALS

- 2 balloons
- meterstick
- string
- scissors
- *Science Journal*

PROCEDURES

Safety: Use the scissors carefully!

1. **EXPERIMENT** Using the materials, design an experiment to determine whether air has mass. Record your setup in your *Science Journal*.

2. **USE VARIABLES** Test the experiment. Record each step, all your observations, and your results.

CONCLUDE AND APPLY

1. **DRAW CONCLUSIONS** Is air matter? What evidence do you have to support your conclusion?

2. **INFER** Dan blew up a balloon until it burst. Does the broken balloon support the idea that air is matter or the idea that air is nonmatter? Explain.

What Are Matter's Characteristics?

These four points will help you review the characteristics of matter.

- **Matter has mass.** Mass is a measure of how much matter an object contains. Mass can be measured using a balance. The standard unit of mass is the kilogram.

- **Matter takes up space.** The balloon in the activity expanded as it was filled with air. Air is a type of matter.

- **Matter has properties.** Different types of matter have different properties. Diamonds are hard and shiny. Cotton is soft and fluffy. Glass is hard and can shatter.

- **Matter can exist as a solid, a liquid, or a gas.** Some types of matter, like water, can exist in all three states. You will learn more about this in Topic 4.

NATIONAL GEOGRAPHIC

FUNtastic Facts

Air has mass because it is made up of tiny particles, and each particle has mass. The air in a box 1 meter long, 1 meter tall, and 1 meter deep has a mass of 1300 grams. That's about the mass of this book. What's the mass of the air in your classroom?

MATH LINK

What Happens to the Matter We Use?

What do you think we do with all the trash we create? The most common solutions are to bury garbage in a landfill, burn it, or dump it in the ocean. Each solution has a problem. We can run out of places to bury garbage. Burning it pollutes the air. Dumping it in the ocean pollutes the water. What are some other solutions? Try the "three Rs."

1 **Reduce**
Reduce the amount of things you use that become garbage.

The package is much larger than the toy. Try to buy things that don't have a lot of extra packaging.

2 **Reuse**
Try to use something again instead of throwing it away.

Can you think of another use for a plastic milk container?

3 **Recycle**
Many things can be made into something else. Check if your community has a recycling program. Find out what types of materials are accepted. Then try to contribute to it.

This bottle was made from recycled glass.

These boxes were made from recycled paper.

Can Recycled Materials Be Made into Clothing?

Did you ever think you could wear recycled plastics? This shirt, and others like it, are made in part from recycled plastics. Up to 150 pieces of clothing can be made from 3,700 two-liter bottles!

Some of the fibers in this shirt were made from recycled plastics.

FABRIC FROM PLASTIC

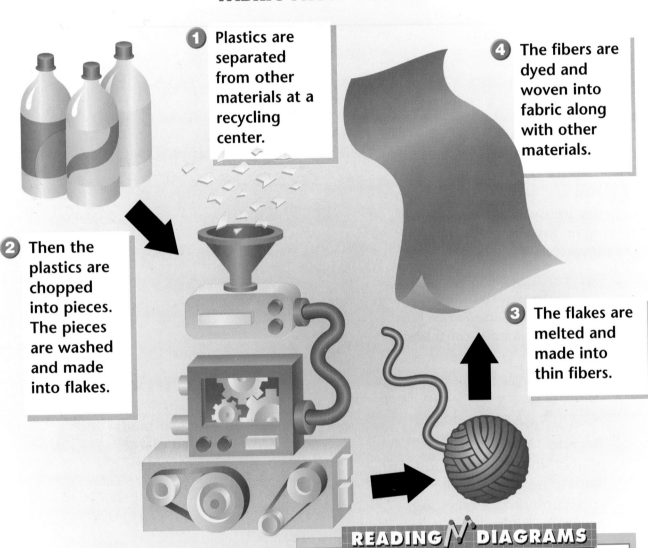

1 Plastics are separated from other materials at a recycling center.

2 Then the plastics are chopped into pieces. The pieces are washed and made into flakes.

3 The flakes are melted and made into thin fibers.

4 The fibers are dyed and woven into fabric along with other materials.

READING DIAGRAMS

1. DISCUSS How are plastics turned into a shirt?
2. WRITE Make a list of the steps.

Colors, numbers, and ideas are *not* matter. You and everything you touch *are* made of matter. Why does this matter? The more you know about what something is made of and its properties, the better choices you can make about how to use it. For example, knowing about the properties of certain types of plastics allows people to recycle them into other useful things. This helps reduce pollution and gives new life to old things!

What can *you* do to help reduce garbage and pollution?

REVIEW

1. Choose two items that would belong in the Museum That Matters. List all the properties you can to describe each one.

2. What is mass?

3. How can the three Rs help you reduce pollution?

4. **COMPARE** What are the three states of matter? How are they different from one another?

5. **CRITICAL THINKING** *Analyze* Why is the number 12 not matter, but 12 marbles are matter?

WHY IT MATTERS THINK ABOUT IT
If you could invent a way to reuse a material or recycle it into something else, what would it be?

WHY IT MATTERS WRITE ABOUT IT
Write a brochure advertising your new product. What is it made of? How can it be used?

MOUNTAINS of Matter

A garbologist digs into a pile of trash at a landfill.

A Closer Look

The average American throws away about 1.8 kilograms (4 pounds) of trash a day. That's over half a ton a year! What do we do with that much matter?

For years it was put into landfills, another name for dumps. There garbage is heaped higher than houses! Then the heaps are covered with dirt or plastic.

The original idea for landfills was good. People thought that the covered trash would rot, or break down organically by the action of bacteria. Then the organic matter would make the soil richer!

What was really happening? To find out, garbologists from the University of Arizona dug into old landfills. Dr. Bill Rathje and his crew found 30-year-old newspapers that were still easy to read. They also found corn on the cob, green grass clippings, and a hot dog that still looked like a hot dog!

No one had ever before dug into a real landfill. People just assumed the stuff was decaying. It wasn't! Landfills don't let enough moisture and air get into the buried garbage. Now our landfills are overflowing, and we're running out of space for new ones.

Do you recycle? Do you buy things made from recycled materials? Do you avoid products with too much packaging? It matters to all of us. It's our Earth!

This newspaper was still readable after being buried for 12 years!

Discussion
Starter

1 If everyone creates 4 pounds of trash a day, how much is created each year by your class? Your school?

2 What did garbologists find to help them date when things had been buried?

*inter*NET
CONNECTION To learn more about garbology, visit
www.mhschool.com/science and enter the keyword **TRASH.**

77

WHY IT MATTERS

Matter can be measured in different ways.

SCIENCE WORDS

metric system a system of measurement based on units of 10

length the number of units that fit along one edge of something

area the number of unit squares that fit inside a surface

volume how much space an object takes up

weight the measure of the pull of gravity between an object and Earth

density the amount of matter in a given space

Measuring Matter

Have you ever bought something? How much did you pay? Vic and Vickie sell grapes at the farmer's market. Vickie uses measurements that everyone knows and agrees on what they mean. What about Vic's measurements? How much is a *nice price*? You're not sure. Who would you rather buy grapes from? Why?

EXPLORE

HYPOTHESIZE **What if you are buying or selling items in a marketplace where everyone measures things in his or her own way? How could you solve the problems this causes? Write a hypothesis in your *Science Journal*.**

"Good sized— bunch" Nice Price!

4 lbs for $3.25

Design Your Own Experiment

HOW CAN YOU MEASURE MATTER?

PROCEDURES

MATERIALS
- variety of objects that can be "sold"
- play money
- *Science Journal*

1. **PLAN** Decide who will be the merchant and who will be the customer. As the merchant set up goods and determine their prices. As the customer decide on the types and quantities of things you want to buy.

2. **COMMUNICATE** Pretend to buy and sell things. Compare your ideas of what each quantity should be. Who is at an advantage and who is at a disadvantage each time? Record your "measurements" and observations in your *Science Journal.*

3. **USE NUMBERS** Calculate the price for each purchase. Record the calculations and prices.

4. **COMMUNICATE** Work together to agree on how to measure items.

CONCLUDE AND APPLY

1. **COMMUNICATE** In the first part of the activity, you did not have a system of set measurements. How did you know if you were selling your things too cheaply? How did you know if you were paying a fair price or not?

2. **EXPLAIN** Do you think it is important to agree on how to measure things? Why or why not?

GOING FURTHER: Problem Solving

3. **INFER** How would having set measurements help you as a merchant? How would it *not* help you?

How Can You Measure Matter?

The Explore Activity showed what can happen if people all measure things their own way. That is why systems of *standard units* have been developed. A standard unit is a unit of measure that people agree to use.

Standard units of the English system include pounds, yards, and gallons. This is the system mostly used in the United States.

Most other countries and all scientists use standard units of the **metric system** (met′rik sis′təm). The metric system is based on units of 10. For example, 1 meter (m) is divided into 100 centimeters (cm). A meter is a bit longer than a yard. One centimeter is about the width of your little finger's nail. The table at the bottom left shows you how different units of the metric system relate to one another.

Using Standard Units

Standard units are used to measure things in several ways. **Length** (lengkth) tells you the number of units that fit along one edge of something.

Length can be measured using different units. In the metric system, units of length are based on the meter. Lengths in the English system are based on the yard. One yard equals 36 inches, or 3 feet.

Which units you use depends on what you are measuring. You wouldn't measure the length of a butterfly wing in meters. You wouldn't measure the floor of your room in inches. The system you choose probably depends on where you live.

Comparing Metric Units

Metric Unit	Equal To
1 centimeter	$\frac{1}{100}$ meter
1 decimeter	10 centimeters
1 meter	10 decimeters
	100 centimeters
1 decameter	10 meters
1 hectometer	100 meters
1 kilometer	1,000 meters

Some Examples of Lengths

Matter	Length
Fourth grader	54 inches
Python snake	31 feet
Football field	100 yards
Butterfly wing	$2\frac{1}{2}$ centimeters
Giant squid	17 meters
Blue whale	30 meters
Cleveland to Miami	1,710 kilometers

READING TABLES

DISCUSS **How many centimeters are in one meter? One decimeter?**

Area (âr'ē ə) is a measurement that describes the number of unit squares that fit inside a surface. Area is measured in units such as square centimeters or square inches. An easy way to find the area of a rectangular object is to multiply its length by its width.

How can you find the area of an irregular shape? First, divide it into smaller shapes. Then, find the area of each shape. You might need to estimate parts of shapes. Add the area of each shape to find the total area.

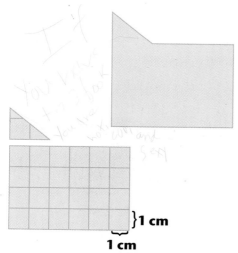

}1 cm

1 cm

What is the area of this shape?

Volume (vol'ūm) describes how much space an object takes up. It measures the number of cubes that can fit in an object. Solids are mea-

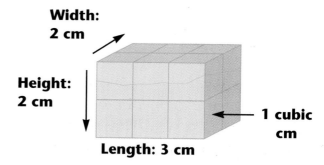

Width: 2 cm

Height: 2 cm

1 cubic cm

Length: 3 cm

Volume: 3 cm x 2 cm x 2 cm = 12 cubic cm

sured in units such as cubic centimeters or cubic inches. To find the volume of a solid rectangle, multiply its length by its width and its height.

You can also measure the volume of a liquid. In the metric system, it is measured in units called liters (L). One liter is made up of 1,000 milliliters (mL). One mL of a liquid takes up the same amount of space as a 1-cm cube.

You can use water to measure the volume of a solid. First, measure some water. Then, completely submerge the object. Subtract the original water level from the new water level. The water level rises by the exact volume of the object.

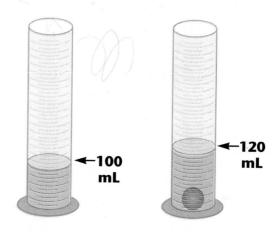

←100 mL

←120 mL

120 mL – 100 mL = 20 mL
20 mL = 20 cubic cm = volume of the ball

Brain Power

A square has sides that measure 6 cm each. A rectangle has two sides measuring 5 cm each and two sides measuring 7 cm each. Which has a greater area? Use a diagram to explain your answer.

SKILL BUILDER

MATH LINK

Skill: Inferring

EXAMINE IF SHAPE AFFECTS VOLUME

Does the volume of an object change if its shape changes? In this activity you will use water to help you find the volume of clay molded into different shapes. You will use your observations and measurements to infer the answer to the question. When you infer, you use observations to figure something out.

MATERIALS

- clay
- graduated cylinder
- water
- string
- paper towels
- *Science Journal*

PROCEDURES

1. Fill the graduated cylinder with 50 mL of water.

2. Make a solid figure out of the clay. Press the string into it.

3. **OBSERVE** Hold the string. Lower the clay into the water until it is completely covered. Carefully observe and record the new water level in your *Science Journal*.

4. Remove the figure. Rearrange it to make a different shape. Do not add or take away any clay.

5. **REPEAT** Repeat step 3.

CONCLUDE AND APPLY

1. **USE NUMBERS** What was the volume of each figure? How did you find out?

2. **INFER** Does an object's volume change when you change its shape? How do you know?

3. **REPEAT** Repeat the procedure with a third shape of clay to verify your results.

4. **INFER** Toy A raised the water level in a tank 1 cm. Toy B raised the water level 2 cm. What can you infer about their volumes?

What Other Ways Can Matter Be Measured?

A third way matter can be measured is by **weight** (wāt). Mass and weight may seem similar, but they are *not* the same. Weight is the measure of the pull of gravity between an object and Earth. Gravity is an attracting force between objects. This force depends on the mass of the objects and the distance between them.

Weight can be measured using an instrument called a *scale*. The metric unit for weight is the *newton* (nü'tən).

An object has the same mass anywhere, on Earth and on the Moon. However, the keys would weigh less on the Moon than on Earth. Why? The pull of gravity on the Moon is less than on Earth. As a result, the weight of an object on the Moon is only about 1/6 of its weight on Earth.

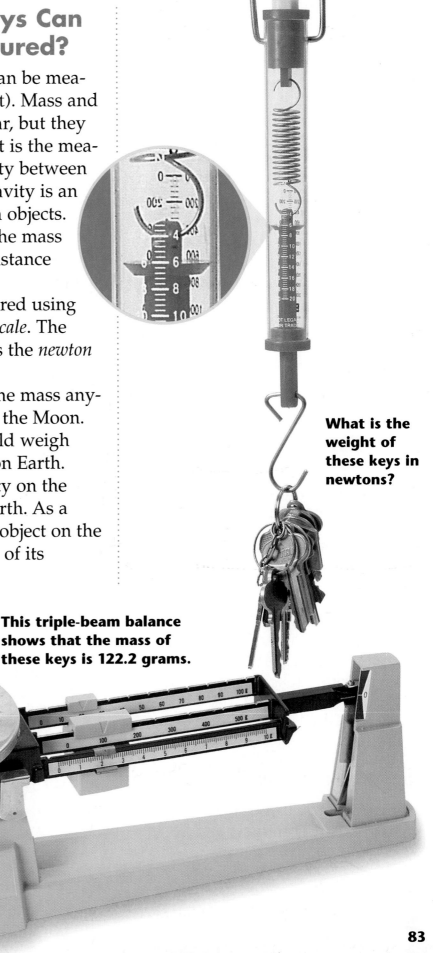

What is the weight of these keys in newtons?

This triple-beam balance shows that the mass of these keys is 122.2 grams.

Comparing Densities

HYPOTHESIZE How can you compare densities of different items? Write a hypothesis in your *Science Journal.*

MATERIALS
- equal-sized samples of a wooden block, clay, and foam
- pan balance
- metric ruler
- *Science Journal*

PROCEDURES

1. **OBSERVE** Does each sample have the same volume? How can you tell?

2. **PREDICT** Which sample do you think has the greatest density? The least?

3. **COMPARE** Use the balance to compare the masses of the samples. Record the data in a table in your *Science Journal.*

CONCLUDE AND APPLY

1. **COMPARE** Rank the items from greatest to least density.

2. **INFER** Why would you need information about both mass and volume to compare density?

What Is Density?

Do a kilogram of foam and a kilogram of rocks have the same size? Were you fooled? They both have the same mass, yet they are very different in volume. One kilogram of foam would take up more space than 1 kilogram of rocks. That is because the **density** (den′si tē) of foam is less than the density of rocks.

Density is the amount of matter in a given space. It describes how tightly packed matter is. It is the mass in a given unit of volume.

The density of an object is given in grams per cubic centimeter. One cubic centimeter is written as 1 cm^3. The amount of matter does not affect its density. The densities of a large piece and a small piece of the same matter are the same.

How can you find an object's density? First, use a balance to find the object's mass in grams (g). Then, find its volume in cubic centimeters. Write the fraction as $\frac{\text{g}}{\text{cm}^3}$.

These samples have the same volume. The denser sample is the one with more mass—lead.

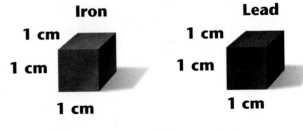

Real-World Density

Why does a hot-air balloon float? Adding heat energy causes the air particles inside the balloon to move about quickly. This makes them spread out. Therefore, they are less dense than the cooler air particles outside the balloon. The force of gravity pulls down the cooler, more dense air. This forces up the warmer, less dense air.

What about matter that is out of this world? One type of star is known as a red giant. When a red giant becomes very massive, it can lose its outer layers in a huge explosion. When the star blows itself apart, it becomes known as a supernova. All the matter making up a supernova becomes tightly pressed together. It occupies a very small volume. This very dense star is called a *neutron* (nü'tron) star.

How dense is a neutron star? One cubic centimeter of matter from a neutron star would have a mass of 1,000,000,000,000,000 kilograms! Now that's dense!

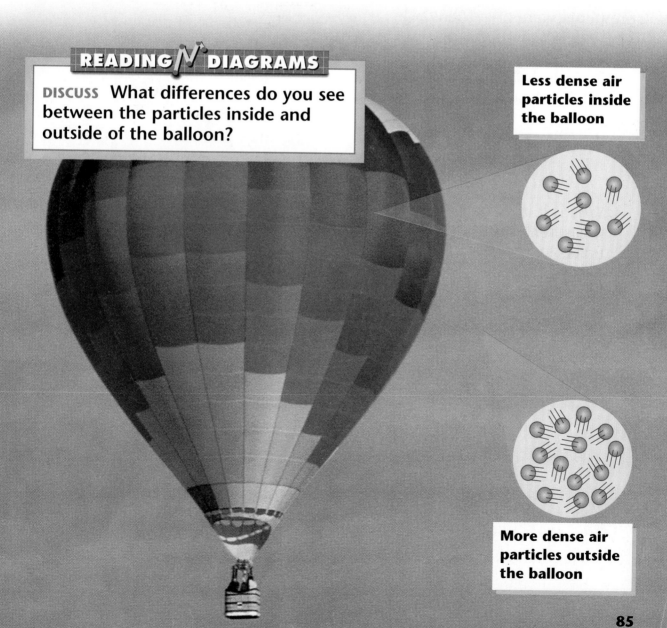

READING N DIAGRAMS

DISCUSS What differences do you see between the particles inside and outside of the balloon?

Less dense air particles inside the balloon

More dense air particles outside the balloon

Imagine trying to buy clothes, take medicine, bake cookies, or read a map without standard units of measure. What would happen if people tried to build a house without agreeing on units? Nothing would fit. They couldn't find accurate distances. No one would agree on size or position.

Just think of how many measurements go into a project like a space launch. If just a few of those measurements were off—the whole project could be in trouble! In a sense our whole world is like a space launch. We depend on standard units of measure every day, in countless ways. Even for something as simple as buying grapes!

How many ways could you measure these grapes?

1. Why is it important to make measurements using standard units?

2. What is the difference between mass and weight?

3. Explain how you would find the area of this shape.

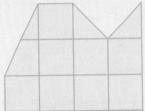

1 cm

4. **INFER** What should a hot-air balloonist do to go higher? What should she do to make her balloon come down?

5. **CRITICAL THINKING** *Analyze* Two cubes have the same mass. Cube A has twice the length, width, and depth of cube B. What can you say about their densities?

WHY IT MATTERS **THINK ABOUT IT** Did you do anything recently that might have been different if standard units didn't exist? What was it? How would it have been different?

WHY IT MATTERS **WRITE ABOUT IT** Describe at least three ways you depended on standard units of measure this week.

History of Science

WHO SET THE STANDARDS?

The platinum-iridium standard kilogram in Sevres, France

About 5,000 years ago, people began using standard weights. The earliest weights, the shekel (shek'əl) and the mina (mi'nə), were developed in what is now Iraq.

The shekel was about 8 grams. The mina was made up of 60 shekels. It was about $\frac{1}{2}$ kilogram. A common weight about the size of a mina was used in Europe. It was the pound. *Pound* means "weight" in Latin.

The metric system was developed in the 1790s. The original standard mass was the gram—the mass of a cubic centimeter of pure water at 4°C. This was later replaced by a simpler standard—a metal mass of 1 kilogram. Today the standard kilogram is still a piece of metal. It's kept in a safe place near Paris, France.

DISCUSSION STARTER

1. What were two of the earliest standard units?

2. Why do you think the standard kilogram is kept in one place?

To learn more about measurement, visit **www.mhschool.com/science** and enter the keyword DIMENSIONS.

inter**NET** CONNECTION

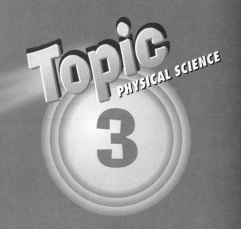

WHY IT MATTERS

Matter is made of tiny particles that can be classified, mixed, and combined.

SCIENCE WORDS

element a substance made up of only one type of matter

mixture two or more types of matter that are mixed together; each keeping its own chemical properties

filter a tool used to separate things by size

evaporation the change of a liquid to a gas

compound a substance made when two or more elements are joined; each losing its own properties

What Matter Is Made Of

How do you classify things? You sort them into groups according to characteristics that vary from case to case. Here is one way to classify the following items—a white chicken, a black cat, a white poodle, a yellow pencil, and a maple tree. How would you classify them?

EXPLORE

HYPOTHESIZE How would you design a classification system for ten items? Write a hypothesis in your *Science Journal.* How can you test your ideas?

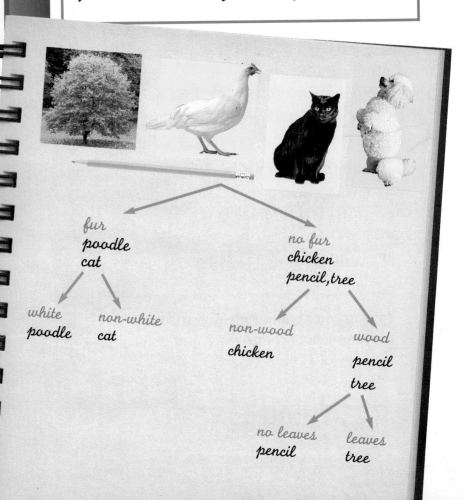

Investigate How You Can Classify Matter

Design and test a classification system for a group of ten items.

MATERIALS

- 10 assorted items
- index cards
- *Science Journal*

PROCEDURES

1. COMMUNICATE Write the name of each item on an index card.

2. CLASSIFY Sort the items into groups based on properties you can observe. Record the properties in your *Science Journal*. Try to use a system like the one on page 88.

CONCLUDE AND APPLY

1. COMMUNICATE What properties did you use to classify the items?

2. COMMUNICATE Were you able to place all the items into the groups? Why or why not? Explain in your *Science Journal*.

GOING FURTHER: Problem Solving

3. CLASSIFY Can you classify each object in its own group? Why or why not? Would changing your system allow you to do so? How?

How Is Matter Classified?

As the Explore Activity showed, you can classify things by their properties. How do you think classifying helps you learn what matter is made of?

People once thought that everything was made up of different combinations of four "ingredients"— water, air, earth, and fire. We now know that the building blocks of matter are the 112 known **elements** (el′ə mənts). An element is a substance that is made up of only one type of matter. Gold, silver, and oxygen are elements.

An element cannot be broken down into other simpler materials with different properties. The properties of a large or small piece of an element are the same.

A Table of Elements

All known elements are classified according to their properties. They are classified in a table called the periodic table of the elements. Here you see a part of this table. The name for each element is in a box. The boxes are arranged according to some of the elements' properties. Here the elements that are gases are shaded blue. Liquids are shaded yellow. Solids are shaded white.

Periodic means "repeating in a pattern." The elements in the periodic table are arranged in columns called groups. The elements in a group have similar properties. All the elements in group 18 are gases that do not combine easily with other elements. How are the elements in group 11 similar?

This is part of the periodic table.

10	11	12	13	14	15	16	17	18
								He Helium
			B Boron	**C** Carbon	**N** Nitrogen	**O** Oxygen	**F** Fluorine	**Ne** Neon
			Al Aluminum	**Si** Silicon	**P** Phosphorus	**S** Sulfur	**Cl** Chlorine	**Ar** Argon
Ni Nickel	**Cu** Copper	**Zn** Zinc	**Ga** Gallium	**Ge** Germanium	**As** Arsenic	**Se** Selenium	**Br** Bromine	**Kr** Krypton
Pd Palladium	**Ag** Silver	**Cd** Cadmium	**In** Indium	**Sn** Tin	**Sb** Antimony	**Te** Tellurium	**I** Iodine	**Xe** Xenon
Pt Platinum	**Au** Gold	**Hg** Mercury	**Tl** Thallium	**Pb** Lead	**Bi** Bismuth	**Po** Polonium	**At** Astatine	**Rn** Radon

Gases   Solids   Liquids

How Are Elements Named?

As you study the elements, you might notice that many have interesting or unusual names. Some names come from Latin words that describe a property of the element. For example, the Latin name for lead is *plumbum*. The names *oxygen* and *nitrogen* come from Greek words.

Some elements are named to honor scientists, like mendelevium. This element is named after the Russian scientist Dmitry Mendeleyev (də mē′trē men′də lā′əf). He developed the first periodic table.

Other elements are named after the place in which they were discovered. Where do you think californium was discovered?

Each element has a standard shorthand symbol for its name. Some elements just use the first letter of their name, like C for carbon. Calcium also starts with a C. To avoid confusing it with carbon, its chemical symbol uses the first two letters of its name, Ca. Some elements' symbols come from their Latin name, such as Pb for lead.

When writing chemical symbols, remember that the first letter is always uppercase. The second letter, if there is one, is always lowercase.

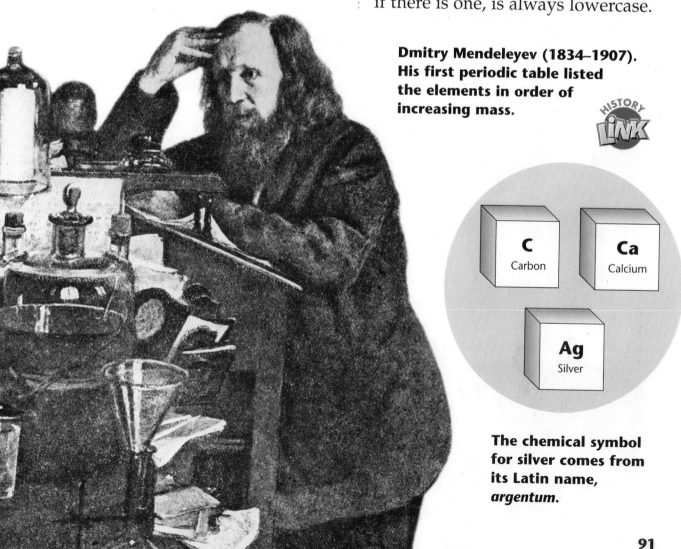

Dmitry Mendeleyev (1834–1907). His first periodic table listed the elements in order of increasing mass.

HISTORY LINK

The chemical symbol for silver comes from its Latin name, *argentum*.

What Happens if You Mix Elements?

Have you ever heard the story of King Midas? Everything he touched turned to gold, a valuable metal. In the Middle Ages, people tried to make gold out of other substances. They tried everything—boiling, burning, mixing, and melting matter from one form to another. They learned a lot about the properties of matter, but they never got close to making gold.

Gold is an element. An element can't easily be changed into another element. However, elements can be combined to form a **mixture** (miks'chər). In a mixture two or more types of matter are combined, but each type keeps its original chemical properties.

Brain Power

Why do you think people failed to make gold out of something else?

Have you ever eaten a mixture of peas and carrots? The peas are still peas, and the carrots are still carrots. The ingredients of a mixture do not change their chemical properties.

In a mixture each element keeps its own chemical properties.

Peas + carrots = a mixture of peas and carrots

How Can Mixtures Be Separated?

The parts of a mixture can be separated using their physical properties. These properties include size, shape, color, volume, density, and state. One way to separate a mixture is simply to pick out each different type of matter. In a mixture of peas and carrots, you can easily pick out the carrots or the peas, based on physical properties such as size, shape, and color.

You can also separate some mixtures by using a **filter** (fil'tər). A filter separates things by size. Items smaller than the holes in the filter pass through it. Larger pieces are left behind.

Filters come in a variety of sizes. The type of filter you use depends on the size of the particles you want to separate. For example, a colander separates water from cooked pasta. The water passes through the holes, and the noodles stay behind.

How might you separate a mixture of salt and water? The salt particles dissolved in the water are very small. They would pass through most filters.

One way to separate this mixture is by **evaporation** (i vap'ə rā'shən). Evaporation is the change of a liquid to a gas. When liquid water evaporates, it becomes a gas. It goes into the air. The salt is left behind. Another example is the solids that are left behind as a ring after bathwater evaporates.

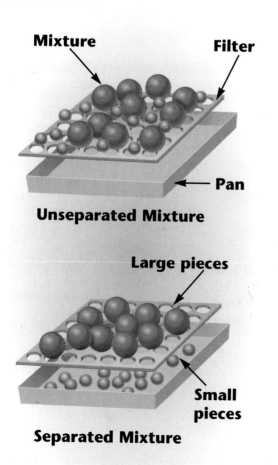

Mixture **Filter**

Pan

Unseparated Mixture

Large pieces

Small pieces

Separated Mixture

Water evaporates

Water is gone

Solid mixed in water **Solid left behind**

93

QUICK LAB

Mix and Unmix

HYPOTHESIZE How can you use physical properties to separate the parts of a mixture? Write a hypothesis in your *Science Journal.*

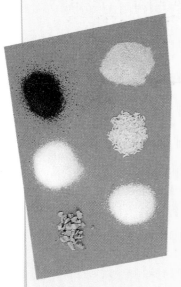

MATERIALS

- goggles
- mixture from your teacher
- piece of dark paper
- magnet
- filter paper
- plastic funnel
- tweezers or forceps
- container
- water
- *Science Journal*

PROCEDURES

 Safety: Wear goggles.

1. **OBSERVE** Design an experiment to separate the mixture. Hint: You may need to use more than one method or to repeat some methods more than once. Record your observations and the results in your *Science Journal.*

CONCLUDE AND APPLY

1. **OBSERVE** Were you able to completely separate the mixture? How do you know?

2. **HYPOTHESIZE** How could you separate a mixture of white sand and salt? Test your ideas.

Is Every Combination of Elements a Mixture?

Do you think all combinations of elements can be separated physically into their parts? No, they cannot. For example, no amount of crushing, grinding, or bending can separate sugar into its components. That is because sugar is a **compound** (kom′pound). A compound forms when two or more elements are combined chemically.

The properties of a compound are different from the properties of the elements it is made of. Each element loses its properties when elements are combined chemically. A compound can only be separated by chemical means, not physical properties.

Comparing Mixtures and Compounds

	Mixture	Compound
How are the parts combined?	Two or more components or elements are mixed together.	Two or more elements are combined chemically.
Do the elements keep their own properties?	Yes	No
How can it be separated?	By physical properties	By chemical means

What Are Some Real-World Compounds?

Water, table salt, sugar, and rust are examples of common compounds.

Each is made up of a combination of elements.

COMMON COMPOUNDS

1 Oxygen and hydrogen are gases. If you simply mix them, they keep their properties. Under certain conditions they can combine to form the compound water.

2 Sodium is a shiny metal. Chlorine is a poisonous, yellowish green gas. Together they combine to form the compound sodium chloride—common table salt.

Oxygen   Hydrogen   Water

Sodium   Chlorine   Salt

3 Sugar is a compound. It is formed when carbon, a black solid, and two gases, oxygen and hydrogen, are combined and changed chemically.

4 Rust is a compound that results when iron is exposed to oxygen. How is it unlike both elements it is made of? What different properties does it have?

Carbon   Oxygen   Hydrogen   Sugar   Oxygen   Iron   Rust

READING [N] DIAGRAMS

1. **WRITE** What do all compounds have in common?
2. **REPRESENT** Using different symbols, draw another diagram showing the elements that make up sugar.

What Are Some Real-Life Uses of Mixtures?

Some elements can't be put to good use in their pure form. Pure gold is too soft for jewelry. Pure aluminum is too light and weak for pots and pans. Pure iron is too brittle and rusts too easily for use in cars. How then do people make gold jewelry, aluminum pans, and cars made of iron?

The answer is in *alloys* (al'oiz). An alloy is a mixture of two or more metals. A mixture of gold and a little copper is stronger than pure gold. A mixture of aluminum and carbon is stronger that pure aluminum. A mixture of iron, chromium, nickel, and carbon is called steel.

Making alloys is a little like cooking. Different recipes give alloys different properties. For example, low-carbon steel is strong but flexible. High-carbon steel is strong but brittle. Medium-carbon steel is somewhat strong and somewhat flexible.

Many common items are made of alloys.

96

Knowing the properties of elements and compounds has helped scientists develop the science of chemistry. Chemistry affects almost everything in your world. Scientists use chemical knowledge to change, improve, or invent such things as foods, medicines, and materials of all kinds. They also use chemistry to understand the world of living things around us and how the universe itself functions.

Understanding how rust forms has allowed scientists to develop special paints. Once applied to an item, the paint helps prevent rust from forming.

REVIEW

1. What is an element?

2. How are elements named?

3. How does a compound differ from a mixture?

4. **INFER** Why are alloys used to make certain products?

5. **CRITICAL THINKING** *Analyze* You can breathe oxygen when it is mixed with other gases. You can't breathe oxygen when it is combined with iron to form rust. Why not?

WHY IT MATTERS THINK ABOUT IT
Do you think you would like to be a chemist? Why or why not?

WHY IT MATTERS WRITE ABOUT IT
Write a short paragraph describing the types of things you would like to learn about elements if you were a chemist.

READING SKILL Sequence the events of the steps you followed to separate the mixture in the Quick Lab.

A Chemist Who MATTER-ed

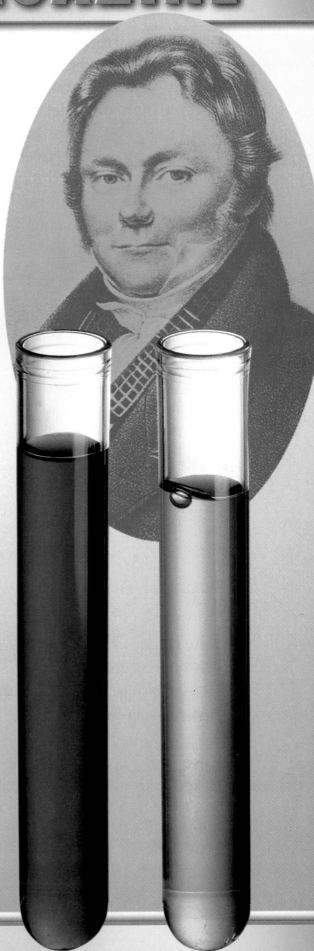

Jöns Jacob Berzelius (1779–1848) was born in Sweden. He became a doctor but had many ideas about the nature of matter. Therefore, he became a chemist. He tested his ideas by doing experiments and keeping careful records.

Berzelius helped to organize the field of chemistry. He wasn't always right. Some of his ideas later proved to be wrong, but his work led to many discoveries. He coined new words to name his discoveries. Berzelius was the first to use rubber tubing, filter paper, and other equipment that's now used in most labs.

History of Science

DISCUSSION STARTER

1. How do we know Jöns Jacob Berzelius did many experiments?

2. How do we know he was organized?

Berzelius's work led to many achievements in science. Here are just a few.

- Berzelius set up a quick way to write the names of the elements. Each element is written as one or two letters. For example, oxygen is O, gold is Au, silver is Ag, and carbon is C.

- He discovered three elements—cerium, selenium, and thorium.

- He figured out the weight of each element.

- He studied many compounds and discovered which elements were in them.

- He was the first to isolate the elements calcium and silicon.

- He gave protein its name.

- He made valuable contributions to the atomic theory.

To learn more about Berzelius, visit *www.mhschool.com/science* and enter the keyword CHEMIST.

inter**NET** CONNECTION

99

SCIENCE WORDS

area p. 81
compound p. 94
density p. 84
evaporation p. 93
filter p. 93
gas p. 71
liquid p. 71

mass p. 70
matter p. 68
metric
  system p. 80
mixture p. 92
weight p. 83

USING SCIENCE WORDS

Number a paper from 1 to 10. Fill in 1 to 5 with words from the list above.

1. The particles making up a(n) __?__ can move about freely, take up a definite amount of space, but do not have a definite shape.

2. The __?__ is the system of measurement used by all scientists.

3. In a(n) __?__ two or more types of matter are combined, and each type keeps its chemical properties.

4. The particles making up a(n) __?__ can move about freely. They do not take up a definite amount of space and do not have a definite shape.

5. In a(n) __?__ two or more elements are combined, and each does not keep its original properties.

6–10. Pick five words from the list above that were not used in 1 to 5, and use each in a sentence.

UNDERSTANDING SCIENCE IDEAS

11. Choose an object. Describe as many of its properties as you can.

12. Why do you think people might easily confuse mass and weight?

USING IDEAS AND SKILLS

13. **READING SKILL: SEQUENCE OF EVENTS** List the steps in finding the area of an irregular shape.

14. **INFER** Why is it important to use standard units of measure?

15. **THINKING LIKE A SCIENTIST** You want to separate a mixture of balls with 1-inch and 3-inch diameters. Filters come with $\frac{1}{2}$-, $1\frac{1}{2}$-, $2\frac{1}{2}$-, and $3\frac{1}{2}$-inch holes. Which could you use to separate the mixture? Which could you not use?

PROBLEMS and PUZZLES

Dog Gone Think about the properties of a dog and a car. How many ways are they different? Can you think of a way in which they are the same?

Buoyancy Test Bigger things sink, while smaller things float. True or false? How would you prove your answer? Demonstrate your answer. Ask others to share their ideas with you.

CHAPTER 4
ENERGY AND CHANGE

If you can tell how to make a pizza from start to finish, you can tell many ways matter changes. Make dough by mixing ground-up flour with water. Shape it into pie crust. Make a sauce by crushing some tomatoes and stirring in spices. Shred some cheese. What's left to do? How does each ingredient change?

 In this chapter you will read for cause and effect, to find out why things happen.

WHY IT MATTERS

Matter can be changed in two basic ways.

SCIENCE WORDS

chemical change
a change that produces new matter with different properties from the original matter

physical change
a change that begins and ends with the same type of matter

Types of Changes

What is the Statue of Liberty made of? The Statue of Liberty is perhaps the best-known symbol of freedom in all the world. It was a gift to the United States from France. The shiny copper statue was erected in New York Harbor and unveiled at a festive ceremony on October 28, 1886. However, after more than 100 years of being outdoors, the copper statue has turned green. Why do you think this happened?

EXPLORE

HYPOTHESIZE Compare the statue with clean copper. What do you think caused the statue to turn green? Write a hypothesis in your *Science Journal.* How could you test your ideas?

GEOGRAPHY LINK

Investigate What Causes the Change

Investigate the conditions that cause a penny to change.

PROCEDURES

 Safety: Wear goggles.

1. Put a small wad of modeling clay on the bottom of the petri dish or plastic glass.

2. Wedge the penny in the clay so that it is vertical.

3. Add 1 tsp. of vinegar to the petri dish or glass. Cover the petri dish with the plastic glass. If you put the penny in the glass, cover the glass tightly with plastic wrap.

4. **PREDICT** What do you think will happen to the penny? Record your prediction in your *Science Journal.*

CONCLUDE AND APPLY

1. **OBSERVE** What happens to the penny after one hour? After three hours? Overnight? Record your observations in your *Science Journal.*

2. **COMPARE** How is this penny different from the penny that your teacher soaked in vinegar overnight?

3. **HYPOTHESIZE** What do you think caused the changes to your penny but not the soaked penny?

GOING FURTHER: Problem Solving

4. **EXPERIMENT** Do you think other materials would change also? Repeat the activity using a paper clip.

MATERIALS

- goggles
- petri dish or 10-oz clear-plastic glass
- modeling clay
- shiny penny
- 1 tsp. vinegar
- 10-oz clear-plastic glass or plastic wrap
- *Science Journal*

What Causes the Change?

The penny in the Explore Activity turned green. The green material was the result of a **chemical change** (kem'i kəl chānj). Chemical changes are changes in matter itself. In a chemical change, you start with one kind of matter and end with another. The new matter has properties different from the matter you started with.

Copper in the penny reacted with the vinegar vapors. This created a compound called copper acetate. Copper acetate has properties different from copper and vinegar. It is not hard and shiny like copper. It is not a liquid like vinegar.

You can find evidence of chemical changes all around you if you know where to look! Does table salt look like the shiny metal sodium and the yellowish green, poisonous gas chlorine? No! However, it is the result of a chemical change between those elements.

Does sugar look like the black element carbon? No! However, it is the result of a chemical change between carbon and the gases oxygen and hydrogen.

Tarnish is a compound that forms on silver when it is exposed to air. Although tarnish is not harmful, it can be annoying. It coats pretty silver with a dull black finish.

Tarnish

A compound has properties that are different from the elements it is made of.

Salt

Copper acetate

What Are the Products of Chemical Changes?

In a chemical change, the product has properties different from the matter you started with. Sometimes the product is a compound. Sometimes the product is the elements making up a compound.

These diagrams show how elements combine to form the compound sugar and how sugar can be broken down into its elements.

MAKING AND BREAKING DOWN SUGAR

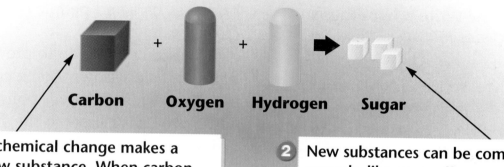

Carbon   +   Oxygen   +   Hydrogen   →   Sugar

1 A chemical change makes a new substance. When carbon, oxygen, and hydrogen are combined in the right amounts, they form sugar.

2 New substances can be compounds, like sugar. A compound does not look like the elements that make it up and has different properties.

3 A chemical change can break compounds apart. What is left behind are the elements it was made of. For example, the compound sugar can be broken apart into its elements. Hydrogen and oxygen are given off as water. Carbon is left behind.

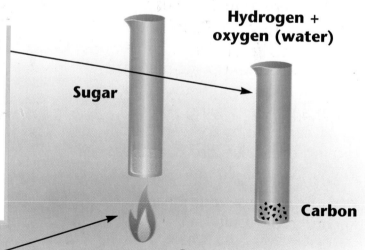

Sugar

Hydrogen + oxygen (water)

Carbon

4 This type of chemical change needs energy to take place. Energy is always involved in a chemical change. Some changes need energy. Others give off energy.

READING 𝒩 DIAGRAMS

1. **WRITE** List the elements that make up the compound sugar.
2. **DISCUSS** How is a compound different from the elements it is made of?

105

QUICK LAB

Preventing Chemical Change

HYPOTHESIZE Why do you think most pennies you use every day aren't green? Write a hypothesis in your *Science Journal*.

MATERIALS
- goggles
- petri dish or 10-oz clear-plastic glass
- modeling clay
- 3 shiny pennies
- 1 tsp. vinegar
- 10-oz clear-plastic glass or plastic wrap
- other materials as needed
- *Science Journal*

PROCEDURES

 Safety: Wear goggles.

1. **HYPOTHESIZE** Set up the materials as in the Explore Activity. Think about a different thing you can do to each penny to keep it from turning green. Record your ideas in your *Science Journal*.

2. **EXPERIMENT** Test your ideas. Record your results.

CONCLUDE AND APPLY

1. **COMPARE** Make a class table of the results for each test. What kept the pennies from turning green?

2. **INFER** What do you think prevents the pennies you use every day from turning green?

Are Chemical Changes Beneficial or Harmful?

As you just learned, some chemical changes can form compounds. Some compounds, like sugar, are beneficial. Some, like tarnish, are only annoying. Others, like rust, can be harmful. Rust can weaken a bridge so cars and people cannot cross it safely.

What can people do to prevent, or at least slow down, some chemical changes? Some silver polishes add a protective layer to the silver as it is being cleaned. Some bridges are being built so that a small amount of electricity can be run through the metal supporting structure. This helps slow the formation of rust.

Rust has weakened this bridge.

Are There Other Types of Changes?

You have just seen one way matter can change—through chemical changes. Matter can also change in another way—through **physical changes** (fiz'i kəl chānj'əz). A physical change begins and ends with the same type of matter.

How can you tell the difference between a chemical change and a physical change? Sometimes it isn't easy, but these guidelines should help. Here are a few examples of different kinds of physical changes.

PHYSICAL CHANGE → **MIXTURE:** Each element keeps its original chemical properties.

CHEMICAL CHANGE → **COMPOUND:** The product has properties that are different from those of the original elements.

PHYSICAL CHANGE

A CHANGE IN SIZE OR SHAPE The original properties of the matter do not change even if it is cut, folded, or stretched.

B CHANGE IN POSITION OR TEXTURE The original properties of the matter do not change even if it is moved, rearranged, or crumpled.

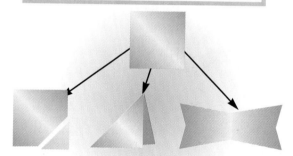

Cutting   Folding   Stretching

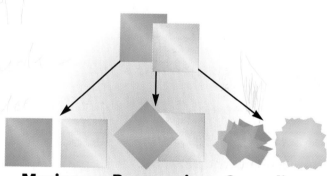

Moving   Rearranging   Crumpling

C CHANGE IN STATE The original properties of the matter do not change even if it is melted, frozen, or heated.

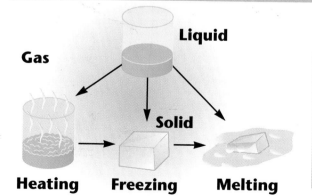

Gas   Liquid   Solid

Heating   Freezing   Melting

READING DIAGRAMS

1. **WRITE** Make a list of three ways matter can change physically.
2. **DISCUSS** Why is a change in state a physical change?

What Makes Matter Change State?

In Topic 1 you learned that matter can exist in three states. Your science book is a solid. It will remain a solid no matter what you do to it. However, some types of matter can exist in more than one state. For example, water can exist as a solid, a liquid, or a gas.

What makes matter change from solid, to liquid, to gas? The answer is heat energy. Heat energy makes the particles of matter move. The more heat energy matter has, the faster its particles move. Taking away heat energy slows particles down.

Solids The particles of a solid are fixed. They move only a little. They vibrate more rapidly when heat energy is added to them. If enough heat energy is added, a solid may melt and form a liquid.

Liquids Particles of a liquid form groups that move past one another. Adding more heat energy causes the particles to move so fast that the liquid breaks up. Some particles may escape as a gas.

Gases Adding still more heat energy breaks up groups completely.

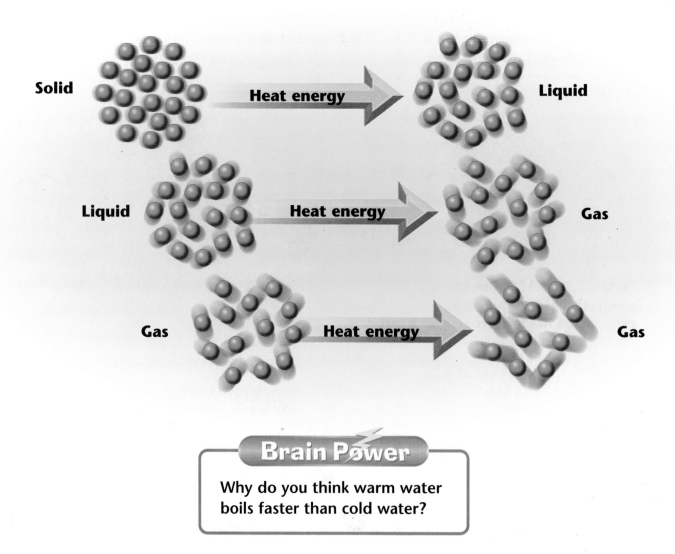

Solid → Heat energy → Liquid

Liquid → Heat energy → Gas

Gas → Heat energy → Gas

Brain Power

Why do you think warm water boils faster than cold water?

Skill: Experimenting

HOW HEAT ENERGY AFFECTS EVAPORATION

Sometimes the only way to answer a question is to perform an experiment. In an experiment you first form a hypothesis. Then you set up conditions to test your hypothesis. Follow the steps below to test how heat energy affects evaporation.

MATERIALS

- 3 paper-towel pieces
- 3 rubber bands
- three 10-oz clear-plastic glasses
- thermometer
- clock or watch
- desk lamp
- container of water
- *Science Journal*

PROCEDURES

1. Place a wet paper towel across the top of each plastic glass. Secure each with a rubber band.

2. PREDICT Place one glass where you think the paper towel will dry fastest. Place another where you think it will dry slower. Place the third where you think it will dry slowest.

3. MEASURE Use the thermometer to measure the temperature near each glass. Record the temperatures in your *Science Journal*.

4. Record the time you start timing. Then touch each paper towel every two minutes. Record the time the first paper towel is dry.

5. REPEAT Repeat step 4 until another towel is dry.

CONCLUDE AND APPLY

1. INTERPRET In which place did a paper towel dry the fastest? What was the temperature?

2. INTERPRET In which place did a paper towel dry the slowest? What was the temperature?

3. INFER Would water evaporate from a paper towel as fast if you put another inverted glass on top of it? Try it.

What Are Some Real-World Changes?

What kinds of chemical and physical changes take place in the real world? Here are some examples. Can you think of any others? Keep track of changes you notice during the day. Decide if they are physical or chemical changes.

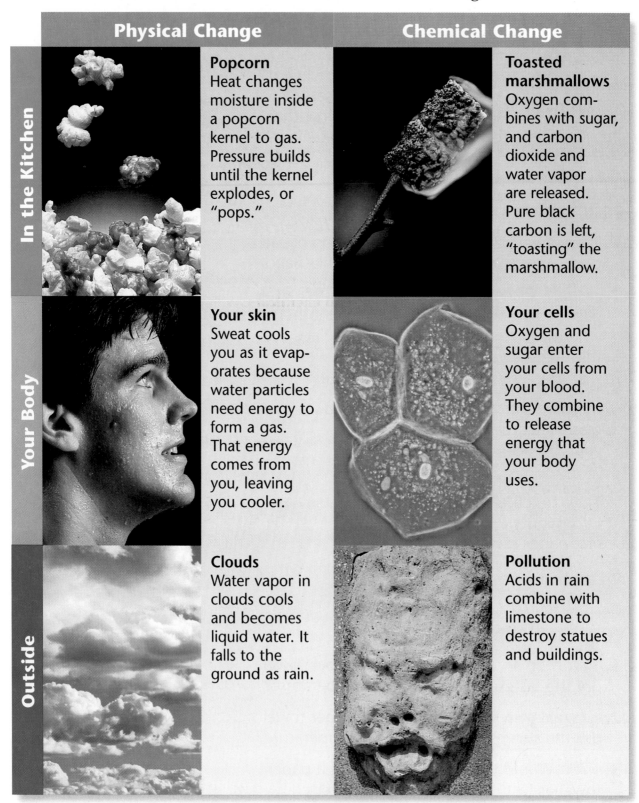

	Physical Change	Chemical Change
In the Kitchen	**Popcorn** Heat changes moisture inside a popcorn kernel to gas. Pressure builds until the kernel explodes, or "pops."	**Toasted marshmallows** Oxygen combines with sugar, and carbon dioxide and water vapor are released. Pure black carbon is left, "toasting" the marshmallow.
Your Body	**Your skin** Sweat cools you as it evaporates because water particles need energy to form a gas. That energy comes from you, leaving you cooler.	**Your cells** Oxygen and sugar enter your cells from your blood. They combine to release energy that your body uses.
Outside	**Clouds** Water vapor in clouds cools and becomes liquid water. It falls to the ground as rain.	**Pollution** Acids in rain combine with limestone to destroy statues and buildings.

People have learned a lot about matter in our world. They have learned how matter can be changed. Physical changes let us use water as solid ice cubes to cool off. As water vapor it helps heat our homes. Chemical changes make the food we eat into energy for our cells. Even something as simple as baking bread involves many physical and chemical changes.

Baking is all about physical and chemical changes!

REVIEW

1. What is the difference between a physical and a chemical change?

2. What can cause a solid to change into a liquid? A liquid to change into a gas? Explain what happens.

3. Describe and explain some types of changes you can see every day.

4. **EXPERIMENT** Is salt dissolving in water a physical or a chemical change? How could you design an experiment to test your answer?

5. **CRITICAL THINKING** *Apply* Would pond water evaporate faster in winter or summer? Explain.

WHY IT MATTERS THINK ABOUT IT The flesh of a cut apple turns brown after a little while. Do you think this is an example of a chemical or a physical change? Why?

WHY IT MATTERS WRITE ABOUT IT Write a short paragraph or create a chart, list, or table explaining the differences between physical and chemical changes.

READING SKILL Explain what is happening on page 105 in terms of cause and effect.

Everything Changes

Look around you. You already know a lot of physical and chemical changes that take place. Weathering and erosion are two more.

Weathering causes both physical and chemical changes. Did you ever trip over a crack in a sidewalk? It was probably caused by a physical change.

First, rainwater filled a tiny crack in the sidewalk. Then, it froze and expanded. The ice pushed the crack farther open. In time the crack was big enough to trip you!

Erosion is a physical change. It can be caused by water, wind, or gravity.

Moving water can carry away tiny bits of soil and rock. During storms water moves faster and carries away more soil. As the water slows down, it drops the soil in a new place.

Earth Science Link

Strong winds can pick up bits of soil and drop them somewhere else. Plant roots help hold soil in place. The roots slow down both water and wind erosion.

Gravity can also cause a sudden physical change. If freezing rain cracks rocks on a hillside, gravity can pull the hill down in a landslide!

DISCUSSION STARTER

1. Which changes would happen even if no people lived on Earth?

2. Which kinds of changes have you seen in your community?

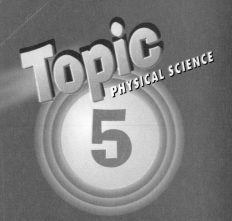

WHY IT MATTERS

Heat travels and affects matter in different ways.

SCIENCE WORDS

heat the movement of energy from warmer to cooler objects

insulator a material that does not transfer heat very well

conductor a material that transfers heat well

convection the transfer of energy by the flow of liquids and gases

conduction the transfer of energy caused by one particle bumping into another

radiation the transfer of heat through space

Heat

What could allow whales to survive in freezing-cold water? People and whales are both mammals. However, they each can live in very different places. Blue whales spend much of their time in the freezing-cold waters around the South Pole. People can survive only a short time in freezing temperatures without protection.

EXPLORE

HYPOTHESIZE Whales have a thick layer of body fat beneath their skin. Do you think it keeps them warm in the freezing waters? Write a hypothesis in your *Science Journal.* How can you test your ideas?

Investigate How Fat Keeps Mammals Warm

Test if a layer of fat can help keep your hand warm in cold water.

MATERIALS

- plastic bag containing lard or solid vegetable shortening
- 2 vinyl surgical gloves
- bucket or pan of ice water
- timer or watch with second hand
- paper towels
- *Science Journal*

PROCEDURES

1. **COLLECT DATA** Put on one glove. Ask your partner to time how long you can comfortably keep your hand in the ice water. Record the results in your *Science Journal*.

2. Move your gloved hand around in the bag of lard to coat it well. Be sure to spread the lard over your entire hand and between your fingers.

3. **COLLECT DATA** Ask your partner to time how long you can keep your lard-coated hand in the ice water. Record the results.

4. **COLLECT DATA** Trade places and let your partner repeat the procedure.

5. **USE NUMBERS** Take an average of both of your results.

CONCLUDE AND APPLY

1. **COMMUNICATE** How long on average were you able to keep your hand in the ice water in step 1? In step 3?

2. **INFER** What role do you think the lard played in keeping your hands warm?

GOING FURTHER: Problem Solving

3. **INFER** If the lard represents a whale's blubber, how might it help the whale survive?

How Does Fat Keep Mammals Warm?

The Explore Activity showed that you can keep your hand in cold water for a long time when it is coated with a layer of lard or vegetable shortening. Why do you think a layer of fat can keep your hand warm?

In Topic 1 you learned that matter is made of particles that are always moving and have energy. **Heat** (hēt) is the movement of this energy from one material to another. Energy moves from warmer to cooler objects.

When you are cold, you wrap yourself in a blanket to get warm. Whales have a built-in "blanket" of fat, or blubber. Why does a blanket keep you warm? Do you think a blanket or blubber creates heat?

A blanket and a whale's blubber are examples of **insulators** (in'sə lā'tərz). An insulator is a material that does not transfer heat very well. A glove also is an insulator. When you first put on a glove, it doesn't feel warm. Slowly your hand warms it up. The glove does not transfer the heat from your hand to the air very well. The heat builds up inside the glove. Your hand stays warm.

The opposite of an insulator is a **conductor** (kən duk'tər). A metal frying pan is an example of a conductor. It transfers heat quickly from a burner to the food.

Brain Power

Why do two blankets keep you warmer than one? Does an electric blanket need to be a good insulator to keep you warm? Explain.

Wood also is a good insulator. Why do you think it is often used to make handles for pots and pans?

What Makes Energy Move from One Object to Another?

When warm and cool objects touch, energy is transferred from the warmer object to the cooler object. Remember, the more energy an object has, the faster its particles move. The particles of a warm object cause the particles of a cool object touching it to move faster. The particles of the warm object slow down as they transfer their energy. Eventually the particles making up both objects are moving at the same speed.

The fat of a whale does not easily transfer energy from the whale to the water touching its skin. That is how an insulator helps keep something warm.

More energy: high-speed vibration

Direction of energy flow

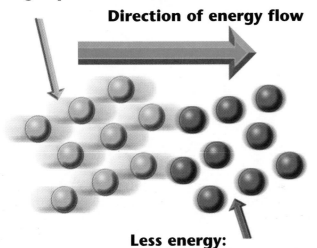

Less energy: low-speed vibration

Heat always flows from the object with more energy to the object with less energy.

Bag in a Bag

HYPOTHESIZE What happens when objects of different temperatures touch? Write a hypothesis in your *Science Journal.*

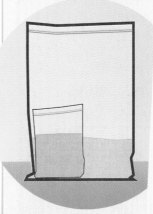

MATERIALS

- small sealable plastic bag containing 1 c of ice water
- large sealable plastic bag containing 1 c of hot water
- paper towels
- thermometer
- watch or timer
- *Science Journal*

PROCEDURES

1. COLLECT DATA Record the temperature of the ice water and the hot water in your *Science Journal.*

2. PREDICT Seal the small bag. Place it in the large bag, then seal it. Predict how the water temperatures will change with time.

3. COLLECT DATA Wait two minutes, then take the temperature of the water in each bag. Repeat this several times. Record the data.

CONCLUDE AND APPLY

1. OBSERVE What was the final temperature of the water in each bag?

2. INFER How can you explain your findings?

How Is Heat Transferred?

Heat can be transferred by the flow of a liquid or gas. This is called **convection** (kən vek'shən). One example is warm air from a heater.

Heat is also transferred by **conduction** (kən duk'shən). This can occur between two objects, like in the "Bag in a Bag" activity. It can also occur within an object, like a pot.

HEAT TRANSFER

1 Heated particles in a gas or liquid move faster, become less dense, and rise.

2 These particles bump into other particles and continue the process.

CONVECTION

CONDUCTION

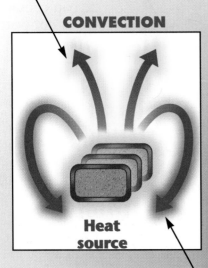

Heat source

2 Cooler, more dense air or liquid is pulled down by gravity.

1 Fast-moving particles bump into other particles and transfer some of their energy.

READING ⁄ DIAGRAMS

1. **WRITE** Make a list of the ways heat can be transferred through matter.
2. **DISCUSS** By what method does heat travel through liquids or gases? Through matter that is touching?

How do you think heat from the Sun reaches Earth? It must travel through space, where there is no matter. **Radiation** (ra′dē ā′shən) is the transfer of heat through space.

RADIATION

1 Heat from the Sun travels through space in light waves that move in all directions.

Sun

2 When the light waves reach matter on Earth, some of their energy is absorbed.

Skin

3 This causes particles of matter to move faster. You feel the energy as heat.

QUICK LAB

Matter and Heat

HYPOTHESIZE What happens to air when it is heated? Write a hypothesis in your *Science Journal.*

MATERIALS

- goggles
- inflated balloon
- blow dryer
- string
- ruler
- marking pen
- timer or watch with second hand
- *Science Journal*

PROCEDURES

Safety: Wear goggles.

1. MEASURE Use the string and ruler to measure the balloon. Mark the spot where you measured it. Record the data in your *Science Journal.*

2. MEASURE Heat the balloon with the blow dryer for one minute. Measure the distance around the balloon at the marked spot. Record the data.

CONCLUDE AND APPLY

1. How did heat affect the size of the balloon?

2. EXPLAIN What happens to the air particles in the balloon when it is heated?

119

How Does Heat Affect Size?

What the Quick Lab showed is true for most matter. Most types of matter *expand* (ek spand'), or get larger, when they are heated. When cooled, most matter *contracts* (kən trakts'), or shrinks. Why do you think this happens?

Remember that the particles making up matter are constantly colliding and bouncing off one another. Adding energy makes the particles move faster. Faster-moving particles bounce off one another with more energy. Therefore they take up more space. This makes matter expand. The opposite happens when energy is taken away.

You can see examples of matter expanding and contracting in your own life.

EXAMPLES OF MATTER EXPANDING AND CONTRACTING

Your bicycle tire seems flat on a bitter-cold day. It didn't lose any air. The cold simply caused the air inside the tire to contract.

Tennis balls and basketballs bounce much higher on hot days. When heated the air inside them expands, making them harder.

To open a jar, you run hot water over the lid. The heat makes the metal jar lid expand faster than the glass. That is because metal is a better conductor of heat. This loosens the lid.

READING DIAGRAMS

1. **REPRESENT** Draw a diagram showing how the particles of air in the tire might be arranged on a warm day and a very cold day.
2. **WRITE** In your own words, write a description of why running a metal jar lid under hot water helps loosen the lid.

What Is the Difference Between Heat and Temperature?

As you learned in this topic, heat is the flow of energy from warmer objects to cooler objects. Heat is not the same as *temperature* (tem′pər ə chər). Temperature is a measure of how hot or cold something is.

Temperature is measured with an instrument called a *thermometer* (thər mom′i tər). A thermometer is filled with a liquid—usually mercury or alcohol. When the temperature rises, the particles of the liquid begin to move about and expand. The expanding liquid climbs the glass thermometer tube. When the temperature decreases, the particles of the liquid slow down. The liquid contracts and falls back down the tube.

A liquid climbing and falling inside an unmarked tube can only tell you that one thing is warmer than another. To know by how much, a scale must be used. Two commonly used scales for measuring temperature are the Fahrenheit scale and the Celsius scale.

How are these two scales different? Water freezes on the Fahrenheit scale at 32° (32 degrees) and boils at 212°. On the Celsius scale, water freezes at 0° and boils at 100°.

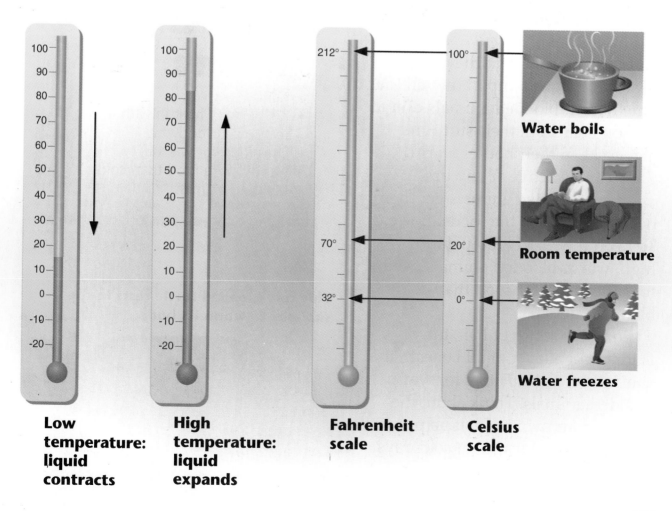

Low temperature: liquid contracts

High temperature: liquid expands

Fahrenheit scale

Celsius scale

Water boils

Room temperature

Water freezes

How Do Animals Use Heat?

All animals need heat to stay warm and alive. However, some animals need less heat than others. Animals that depend on heat from their environment are classified as *cold-blooded* animals. They include fish, reptiles, and insects.

Cold-blooded animals don't have much control over their body temperature. It changes with the temperature of their surroundings. When it is warm, cold-blooded animals absorb heat from their surroundings, and they are active. When it is cool, they absorb less heat and move slowly or not at all.

All birds and mammals, including humans, are *warm-blooded* animals. This means that they keep nearly the same temperature all the time. Warm-blooded animals don't rely on heat from their surroundings to keep their bodies warm. They can be active at any time.

Warm-blooded animals get their heat energy from the foods they eat. To keep their body temperature high, warm-blooded animals need to eat much more food than cold-blooded animals.

Body coverings of hair, fur, or feathers, or a layer of fat beneath the skin, all act as insulators for warm-blooded animals. Think about the hair on your own head. It helps keep your head warm on cold days.

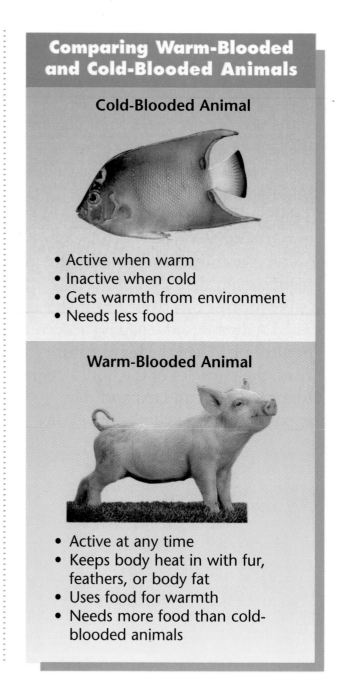

Comparing Warm-Blooded and Cold-Blooded Animals

Cold-Blooded Animal

- Active when warm
- Inactive when cold
- Gets warmth from environment
- Needs less food

Warm-Blooded Animal

- Active at any time
- Keeps body heat in with fur, feathers, or body fat
- Uses food for warmth
- Needs more food than cold-blooded animals

This cold-blooded turtle rests in the sunlight to warm its body.

DID YOU KNOW?

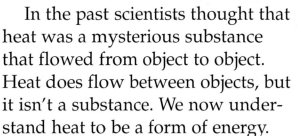

Did you know that the original Celsius scale was different from the scale used today? In 1742 Celsius set the freezing point of water at 100° and the boiling point at 0°. Carolus Linnaeus actually changed the scale by reversing the numbers. However, a textbook claimed that Celsius changed the scale, and his name has been associated with it ever since. What problems might have occurred if the original scale had not been changed?

WHY IT MATTERS

In the past scientists thought that heat was a mysterious substance that flowed from object to object. Heat does flow between objects, but it isn't a substance. We now understand heat to be a form of energy.

Heat is no longer mysterious, but it does affect you in many ways. Understanding heat and how it is transferred has allowed us to create clothing to keep us warm or cool. Buildings are built to prevent as much heat loss as possible. As a result we burn less fuel and create less pollution as we warm our homes.

REVIEW

1. What is heat?
2. How can energy be transferred?
3. What is the difference between how cold-blooded and warm-blooded animals depend on heat?
4. **INFER** Bob at "Bob's Bike Shop" says it isn't wise to fill tires full of air on a cold day. What is Bob worried about?

5. **CRITICAL THINKING** *Analyze* A room is 70°F. In it object A touches object B. Object A has a temperature of 70°F, and it doesn't change. What is the temperature of object B?

WHY IT MATTERS THINK ABOUT IT
What ways can you think of that we use or save heat energy every day?

WHY IT MATTERS WRITE ABOUT IT
Write a short paragraph describing three ways you used heat energy in the last two days.

FIGHT A

Have you ever heard people say, "I'm so sick. I think I have a temperature!"

Of course they do! Everyone has a temperature, sick or well! The average body temperature for humans is 37°C (98.6°F).

How does your body produce this heat? As you digest food your body produces heat. You lose some of this heat in your breath and through your skin. (That's why chocolate candy melts in your hand AND in your mouth!)

When you're sick your body temperature rises. You have a "fever." You don't sweat, so you keep the heat inside. The heat helps kill the germs that are making you sick!

A cool cloth on the forehead transfers some of the heat of a high fever out of the body to help cool it.

Once the germs are gone, your body temperature goes down. You sweat to release the extra heat.

Fevers help our bodies fight disease. A very high fever, however, or one that lasts too long can be harmful. Usually medicine can help to lower that kind of fever.

Science, Technology, and Society

FEVER?

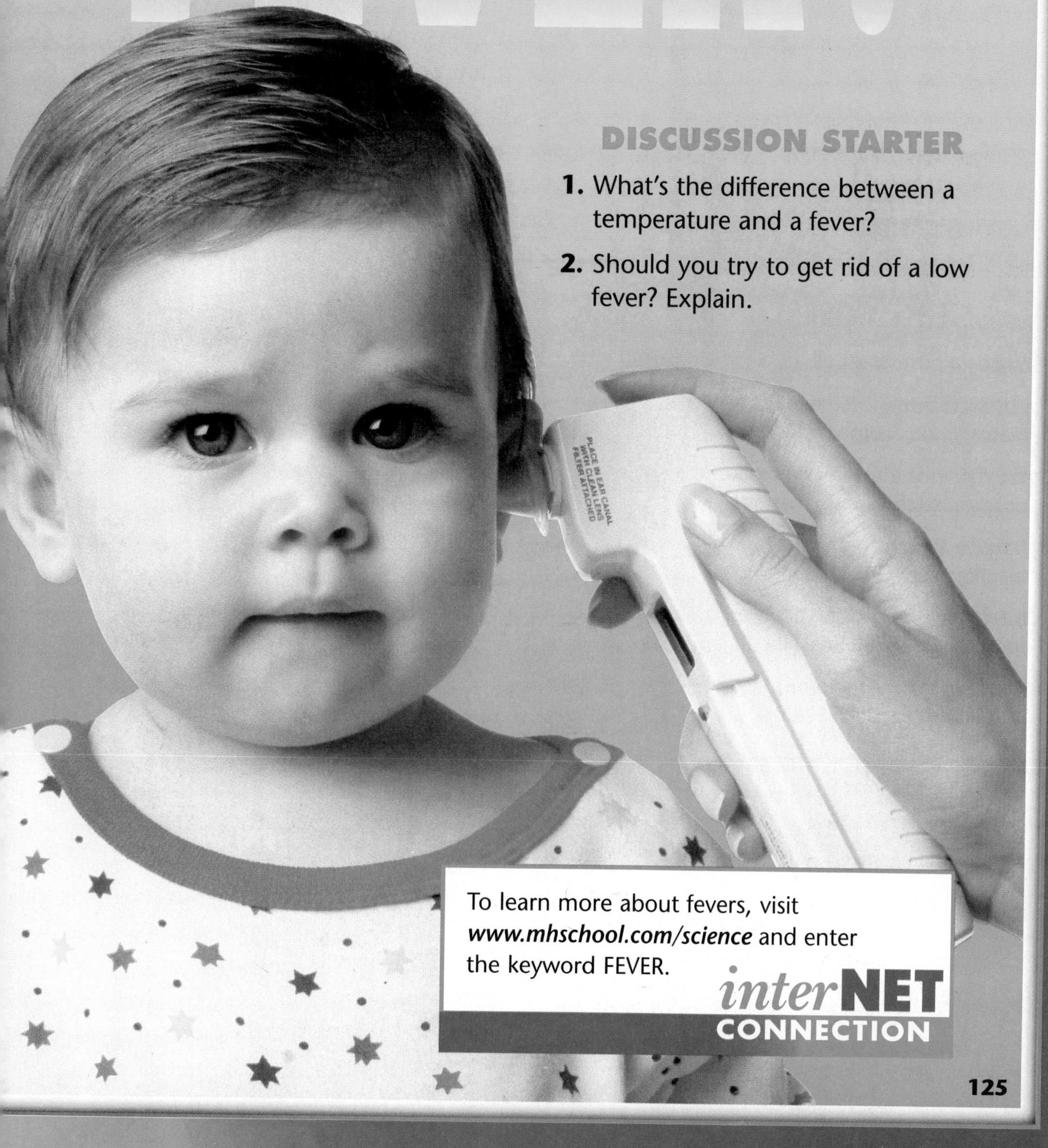
PLACE IN EAR CANAL
WITH CLEAN LENS
FILTER ATTACHED

DISCUSSION STARTER

1. What's the difference between a temperature and a fever?
2. Should you try to get rid of a low fever? Explain.

To learn more about fevers, visit ***www.mhschool.com/science*** and enter the keyword FEVER.

inter **NET**
CONNECTION

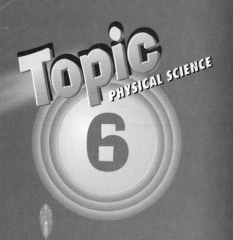

WHY IT MATTERS

Your life would be very different if there were no tools or machines.

SCIENCE WORDS

force a push or a pull

work to apply a force that makes an object move

energy the ability to do work or to cause changes in matter

simple machine a machine with few parts

load the object being lifted or moved by a simple machine

effort force the force put into a simple machine

Energy and Tools

How are the movers going to get this heavy chest of drawers to the third floor? The building has no elevator. Talk about a hard job! What could they do besides just carry it up?

EXPLORE

HYPOTHESIZE **How could the movers get the chest to the third floor? Write a hypothesis in your *Science Journal*.**

Investigate What It Takes to Move Something

Use a pulley to lift a book.

MATERIALS

- pulley
- 2 pieces of cord (thick string)
- book
- spring scale
- *Science Journal*

PROCEDURES

1. Tie the longer piece of cord around the book. Have a partner hold the pulley as shown in figure A. Thread the cord through the pulley's groove.

2. **OBSERVE** Pull down on the cord. What happens? Draw the pulley, cord, and book system in your *Science Journal*. Use arrows to show the direction you pull and the direction the book moves.

3. **OBSERVE** Attach one end of the second cord to something that won't move, as shown in figure B. Attach the book to the hook on the pulley. Pull up on the other end of the cord. What happens to the pulley? What happens to the book? Draw the system in your *Science Journal*. Use arrows to show the direction you pull and the direction the book and pulley move.

CONCLUDE AND APPLY

1. **COMPARE AND CONTRAST** Was it easier to lift the book in step 2 or 3? Why do you think so?

2. **INFER** In which step did you pull one way and the book moved the opposite way?

GOING FURTHER: Apply

3. **EXPERIMENT** Repeat the procedures but attach a spring scale to the end of the cord you pull on. Record the readings on the scale for each trial. Also measure the weight of the book. What do you notice?

A

B

127

What Does It Take to Move Something?

The Explore Activity showed that the book would not move unless you pulled the cord. Pulling is not the only way you can move something. You can also move something by pushing it. The push or pull needed to make something move is called a **force** (fôrs).

When you make something move by using a force, you are doing **work** (wûrk). The word *work* means different things to different people. What does it mean to you? You certainly know what homework is! In science the word *work* means that a force makes an object move. The object may move a little or a lot. However, the object must move a distance to call what happens *work*.

What types of things are work? Pushing a lawn mower is work. Pulling a door open is work. Lifting up a book is work, but holding the book in the air is not work. Why not? No matter how tired you get, the book does not move.

You do a lot of work every day. You do work when you walk, play at sports, and write with a pencil. However, if a friend asks you to help push a heavy box and the box does not move, no work is done. If four more friends pitch in and help move the box, work is done.

Brain Power

Is work being done in both pictures? Explain.

What Else Do You Need to Do Work?

You need something else to do work besides a pushing or pulling force. You need **energy** (en′ər jē). Energy is the ability to do work or to cause changes in matter. No work can be done without energy.

There are different kinds of energy. Sound is one kind. Heat, light, and electricity are other kinds. The energy your body uses to walk, run, and lift things is chemical energy. It comes from the food you eat.

Energy can be transferred from one thing to another. When you kick a ball, you push it hard with your foot. You do work to make the ball move. What happens when your foot stops pushing? The ball keeps rolling. The ball now has moving energy. Where did it get the energy? From you! You transferred energy from your body to the ball when you kicked it.

You even transfer energy to a rubber band when you stretch it. That energy is stored energy. How can you tell? Let one end of the rubber band go. All on its own, it will snap against your other hand.

When you rub a piece of wood with sandpaper, you do work. You are moving the sandpaper. However, the wood does not move. Does the wood gain energy because you do work on it? Yes, it does. It gains heat energy, which you can feel if you touch the rubbed area.

Ignition! The fuel burns and energy is released. Hot gases push on the rocket engine—lift off!

A rocket engine burns rocket fuel. Burning fuels give off hot gases that push on the inside of the engines. The force of this push moves the rocket. When a rocket moves, work is done and energy is transferred.

Clovis point

Ax

Knife

These tools are thousands of years old. The Clovis point was the end of an object that was tossed or thrown. The knife and the ax were used as we use them today.

What Are Machines?

How would you describe a *machine*? It is anything that helps you do work or makes work easier. What machines do you use?

Many machines, such as cars, cranes, and clocks, have lots of parts. Some machines have few parts, like a hammer or a screwdriver. These are **simple machines** (sim'pəl mə shēnz'). There are six different types of simple machines. They are the lever, the pulley, the wheel and axle, the inclined plane, the screw, and the wedge.

Have you ever used any of these simple machines? What were you doing? You might be surprised to learn that you use many simple machines every day!

Some simple machines are often called tools. Think about all the men and women who use tools every day. Builders cannot build without tools. Cooks can't cook, pilots can't fly planes, and gardeners can't dig.

Do you know how the first tools were made by people? They hit one stone with another until pieces with sharp edges broke off. With these sharp-edged pieces, a hunter could easily cut the skin from a dead animal or shape spears.

People invented tools to help them hunt, gather plants, make clothes, build shelters, and protect themselves. Everything had to be invented—axes, hammers, scrapers, saws—even the wheel. No one knows who invented the wheel. Most likely it was invented between 5,000 and 6,000 years ago. Among the first people to use the wheel were the Sumerians. They lived where the country of Iraq is today.

Try to imagine the world without simple machines. How would your life be different?

HISTORY LINK

What Are Some Simple Machines in Nature?

What made ancient people start inventing tools? Maybe they got their ideas by watching animals. Lions, for instance, use their sharp teeth to slice the meat off the bones of animals they kill. Some vultures use stones to help them crack the thick shells of ostrich eggs.

Some types of birds, called finches, use sticks to loosen bark from trees. Under the bark there may be insects the birds eat. Certain ants cut through leaves with their sharp jaws. In the ants' under-ground nest, a fungus that the ants eat grows on the leaves.

A beaver can cut down a tree by gnawing around the trunk with its front teeth. Then it cuts the fallen tree into the pieces it needs to build a dam and the lodge in which it lives. A mole digs underground tunnels by scooping soil with its big front paws.

Many of the tools people invented work just like the body parts of some of these animals. A chisel chips through wood like a beaver's front teeth. A shovel scoops out soil like a mole's paws.

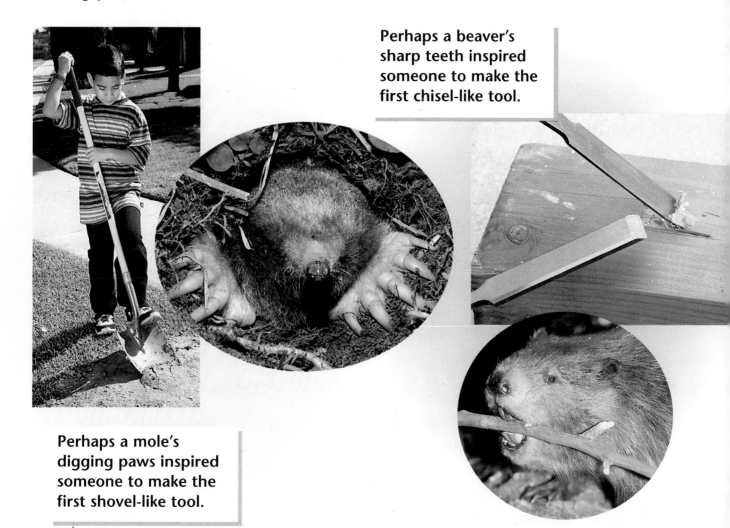

Perhaps a beaver's sharp teeth inspired someone to make the first chisel-like tool.

Perhaps a mole's digging paws inspired someone to make the first shovel-like tool.

How Do Levers Work?

How are a wheelbarrow, a see-saw, and a shovel alike? They are all examples of simple machines called *levers* (lev'ərz).

A lever is a bar that can turn or pivot on a fixed point, called the *fulcrum* (fŭl'krəm). The fulcrum supports the bar. It can be in the middle of the bar, at one end, or in between.

Levers can make it easier for people to lift heavy objects or open things. An object being moved by a simple machine such as a lever is called a **load** (lōd).

How could you move a rock too heavy to lift? You could first put one end of a pole under it. You would then place a small stone under the pole close to the heavy rock. The small stone is the fulcrum. If you pushed down on the long end of the pole, the short end would lift the rock.

A lever doesn't make you stronger. It changes how much force you use to move something, the **effort force** (ef'ərt fôrs). The effort force is the force put into a simple machine. You would need a small effort force to push down on the long end of the pole. The short end of the pole pushes up against the rock with a force greater than the effort force. You would use less energy using a lever than if you simply tried to lift the rock.

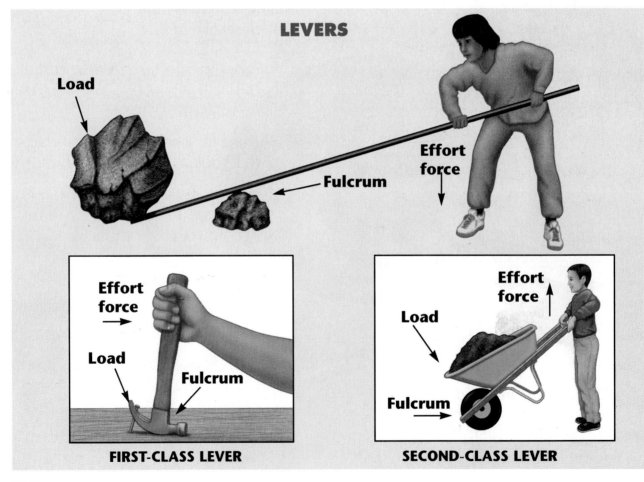

LEVERS

Load

Fulcrum

Effort force

Effort force

Load

Fulcrum

FIRST-CLASS LEVER

Effort force

Load

Fulcrum

SECOND-CLASS LEVER

There is one catch. Which moves more, the short or the long end of the pole? The long end does. You have to push the long end down a greater distance than the rock moves up.

Kinds of Levers

There are three kinds of levers. The difference between kinds is where the fulcrum is.

- A first-class lever changes the direction of the force and changes the effort force.

- A second-class lever only changes the effort force.

- A third-class lever multiplies the distance, but the effort force is greater than the force put out.

READING /\/ DIAGRAMS

1. **DISCUSS** What class of lever is the pole and the small rock in the top picture?
2. **DISCUSS** What class of lever has the load in between the fulcrum and the effort force?
3. **DISCUSS** What class has the effort force between the fulcrum and the load?

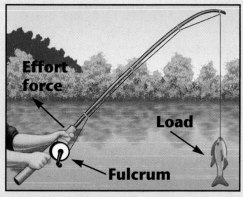

THIRD-CLASS LEVER

QUICK LAB

Make Levers

HYPOTHESIZE What happens to the direction of the force when you use a lever? Write a hypothesis in your *Science Journal*.

MATERIALS
- book
- ruler
- pencil
- *Science Journal*

PROCEDURES

1. **MAKE A MODEL** Place about an inch of the ruler under the edge of the book. Place the pencil under the ruler close to the book.

2. Push down on the other end of the ruler. Record what happens in your *Science Journal*.

3. Place as much of the ruler under the book as fits. Remove the pencil.

4. Lift up on the end of the ruler sticking out from under the book. Record what happens.

CONCLUDE AND APPLY

1. When you pushed down in step 2, which way did the lever push?

2. **DRAW CONCLUSIONS** Can a lever change the direction of the force? Explain.

3. **DRAW CONCLUSIONS** What kind of lever did you make? Explain.

133

How Do Pulleys Work?

In the Explore Activity, the *pulley* (pŭl′ē) made it easier to move an object. A pulley is a simple machine made up of a rope, belt, or chain wrapped around a wheel with a groove in it.

There are two types of pulleys. In a *fixed pulley,* the wheel is attached to something so that it cannot change position. One end of the rope is passed around the wheel. The other end is tied to an object—the load. Pulling the rope lifts the load.

A single fixed pulley makes work easier by changing the direction of the effort force. You pull down, and the load moves up. However, a fixed pulley can't change how much effort force you need to apply to move a load. A force equal to the weight of the load is needed.

A *movable pulley* is not attached to anything. It can be used to increase the force to move the load.

Look at the drawing of a fixed and a movable pulley hooked up together. In this system the rope runs around both pulleys. The load is attached to the movable pulley.

When two or more pulleys are hooked up together, they can change the amount of effort force needed to lift a load. The more pulleys, the less force is needed. However, the rope needs to be pulled a great distance to lift the object a small distance.

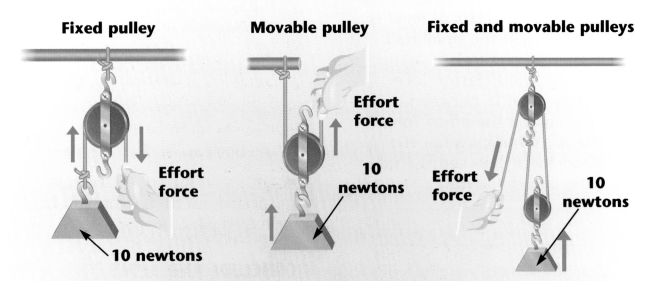

Fixed pulley **Movable pulley** **Fixed and movable pulleys**

Effort force

10 newtons

Effort force

Effort force

10 newtons

Effort force

10 newtons

Force is measured in units called newtons.

READING DIAGRAMS

1. **WRITE** What is the amount of weight being lifted by each pulley?
2. **WRITE** Which pulleys take less effort force to lift the weight? How are these pulleys alike?

134

How Do Wheels and Axles Work?

When you turn a doorknob, you are using a simple machine, a *wheel and axle* (ak'səl). It has two parts. One part is a wheel. The other part is a bar that passes through the center of the wheel.

Why don't you have to use a lot of force to open a door with a doorknob? A small effort force applied to the doorknob, or wheel, turns into a larger force from the axle. The larger force can lift the latch, which is the load. However, the wheel has a larger diameter than the axle, so you have to turn the wheel a long way around for the axle to turn a short distance.

A Ferris wheel is a wheel and axle. However, in a Ferris wheel, the effort force is applied to the axle, not the wheel. The large Ferris wheel moves farther and faster than the axle. To make the wheel move faster and farther takes a lot of effort force from an engine.

A screwdriver is a wheel and axle. The thick handle is the wheel. The shaft is the axle. Try turning a screw into a piece of wood while holding the shaft. Now try it holding the handle. Which way required less effort force?

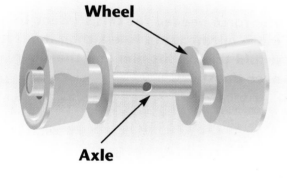

Wheel

Axle

A Ferris wheel is a wheel and axle.

Brain Power

What types of items could you use to make a model of a wheel and axle? Explain how you would assemble the items. How would your model demonstrate how a wheel and axle works?

How Do Inclined Planes Work?

There is a simple machine that has only one part. An *inclined plane* (in klīnd' plān) is a flat, slanted surface.

A ramp is an inclined plane. So is a long board that slants from the back of a truck to the ground. Movers use inclined planes to slide heavy objects in and out of their trucks.

Inclined planes make work easier by reducing the effort force needed to move an object. Imagine if you had to move a very heavy barrel onto a truck 120 centimeters (4 feet) off the ground. You could not lift it, but you could roll it up the inclined plane. It helps you do the work by holding up, or supporting, most of the barrel's weight. Your muscles have to give only a small push to move the barrel. However, you have to push the barrel up the entire length of the board instead of lifting it only 120 centimeters.

Do you think it takes more force to push something up a steep ramp or a less steep ramp? If you are not convinced that inclined planes make work easier, just try using one the next time you have to lift a heavy object!

The force needed for this student to move up the ramp is less than it would take to lift him and the chair over the stairs.

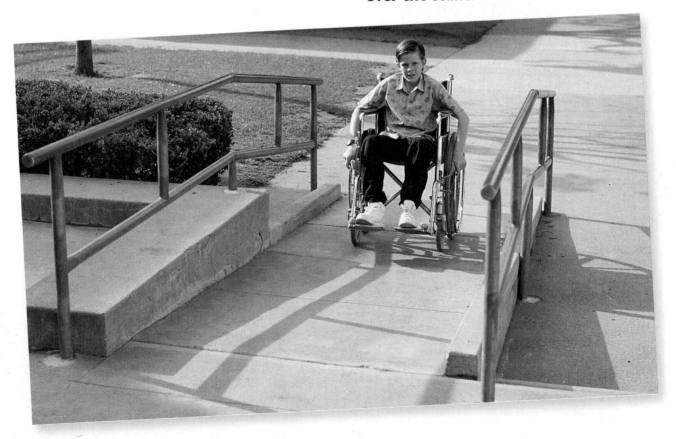

How Do Wedges and Screws Work?

What do you get if you put two inclined planes back to back? You get one machine called a *wedge* (wej). A wedge changes a downward or forward force into a sideways force. Can you think of any wedges?

Many common items are wedges. A needle pushes apart threads of fabric. Wedges in a zipper change your effort force to unhook the teeth or push them together. The blade of an ax is a wedge with a sharp edge. So are razor blades, saw teeth, snippers, knives, and just about all cutting tools.

How does a knife work? As you push and pull the sharp end of a wedge into food, the sides of the wedge push the food apart with a greater force than you use.

Believe it or not, a screw is an inclined plane twisted into a spiral. To see how, cut a piece of paper into a right triangle. Wrap the triangle around a pencil. Watch how the slanted edge of the triangle goes up and around the pencil.

When a screw is turned, it moves forward. It also presses on whatever is around it, such as wood. You have to keep turning a screw for it to move a short distance. You need only a small effort force to turn the screw. The screw increases the force to move deeper into the wood.

TWO KINDS OF INCLINED PLANES

Downward force

A Wedge
Sideways force

A Screw

READING DIAGRAMS

WRITE How are a wedge and a screw alike? How are they different?

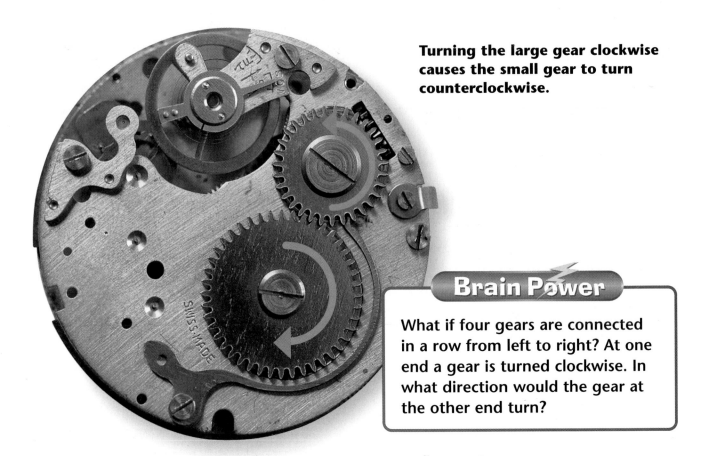

Turning the large gear clockwise causes the small gear to turn counterclockwise.

How Do Gears Work?

Have you ever looked closely at a bicycle? There are wheels with teeth that make the chain and tires turn as the pedals are pushed. These wheels with teeth are *gears* (gîrz).

One gear cannot work on its own. The teeth on one gear have to fit into, or be connected to, the spaces between the teeth on another gear. When a gear is attached to the axle of a wheel-and-axle system, it will turn as the axle turns. When one gear turns, the other gear turns, too.

Look at the picture. One gear is larger than the other. Count the teeth on each. The large wheel has more teeth. When you turn the large wheel once, the small wheel turns more than once in the same amount

of time. It also turns in the opposite direction. There are three advantages to this:

- It is usually easier to turn a larger gear than a smaller gear.
- For every one turn of the larger gear, the smaller gear turns more than once.
- Gears can change the direction and amount of the applied force.

Think about the bicycle again. Bicycle gears are connected by a chain. When you push the pedals, gears make the wheels turn faster than the pedals are turning. When you switch gears, you change to a different-sized gear. That way you can make your bike move faster or slower.

Combining Simple Machines

Not all machines are simple machines. A *compound machine* (kom'pound mə shēn') is a machine that is made up of two or more simple machines. Most machines are compound machines. For example, the entire scissors are a lever. They are also made up of a screw and a wedge. What types of simple machines make up a bicycle?

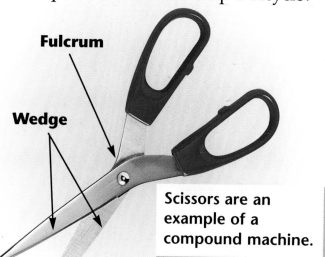

Fulcrum

Wedge

Scissors are an example of a compound machine.

WHY IT MATTERS

Did you know that your lower arm is an example of a third-class lever? When you lift a ball in your hand, your arm muscles supply the effort force. Your hand lifts the ball. Where is the fulcrum? It is in your elbow joint.

How different the world would be without machines. It took people thousands of years to understand how simple machines make work easier. Once they did they also understood more about the human body and the animal world. With time people invent newer and better machines that save time and energy. Who knows what you may invent because of what you know about forces, work, energy, and simple machines!

REVIEW

1. Name one thing you do every day that is work. Name another that is not work. Explain your answers.

2. What is energy?

3. How does a lever make work easier?

4. **COMPARE** What is the difference between a fixed and a movable pulley?

5. **CRITICAL THINKING** *Analyze* How are a screw and a wedge both kinds of inclined planes?

WHY IT MATTERS **THINK ABOUT IT** Is there any tool or machine that you wish existed? Why? How would it work? What would it do?

WHY IT MATTERS **WRITE ABOUT IT** Write an advertisement for an existing or imaginary machine. Explain how it works and how it makes work easier.

There's No Tool Like an Old Tool!

through the water, lifting the oil and leaving the water behind.

It was invented more than 2,000 years ago to make work easier. It never really went "out of style," but today it's got new uses. What is it? Archimedes' screw!

Archimedes' invention was a machine used to irrigate farms. It was simply a large spiral, or screw, in a container. As the screw was turned, water was lifted by the screw blades to the farm.

Today Archimedes' screw is used in factories, but not to move water. Screw conveyors move things like cereal flakes, soap powders, and coffee crystals! It's also used to clean up oil spills. The screw turns

Archimedes must really be proud of his long-standing, ever-turning invention!

DISCUSSION STARTER

1. Can you think of another use for Archimedes' screw? Draw your idea.

2. Do you think the screw would be as effective if the blades were at a steeper angle? Flat? Explain.

To learn more about Archimedes' screw visit *www.mhschool.com/science* and enter the keyword ARCHIMEDES.
*inter*NET CONNECTION

CHAPTER 4 REVIEW

SCIENCE WORDS

chemical
  change p. 104
conduction p. 118
conductor p. 116
convection p. 118
effort force p. 132
energy p. 129
force p. 128
heat p. 116

insulator p. 116
load p. 132
physical
  change p. 107
radiation p. 119
simple
  machine p. 130
work p. 128

USING SCIENCE WORDS

Number a paper from 1 to 10. Fill in 1 to 5 with words from the list above.

1. The ability to do work is ___?___.

2. The movement of heat energy from one material to another is called ___?___.

3. A material that does not conduct heat very well is a(n) ___?___.

4. Heat travels through space by the process of ___?___.

5. An object being lifted or moved by a simple machine is called a(n) ___?___.

6–10. Pick five words from the list above that were not used in 1 to 5, and use each in a sentence.

UNDERSTANDING SCIENCE IDEAS

11. Explain the difference between a physical change and a chemical change.

12. What is the difference between the Fahrenheit and Celsius scales of thermometers?

USING IDEAS AND SKILLS

13. **READING SKILL: CAUSE AND EFFECT** Explain how a pulley helps move an object.

14. **EXPERIMENT** Describe the types of things you would do in an experiment to determine if something has undergone a physical or chemical change.

15. **THINKING LIKE A SCIENTIST** Describe a job that needs to be done, such as moving or building something. What simple machines can help get the job done? How and in what order would they be used?

PROBLEMS and PUZZLES

Penny Pop Put an empty plastic bottle in the freezer for one hour. Wet the top of the bottle. Put a penny on the top. Warm the bottle with your hands. What happens? What effect did the heat from your hands have on the air inside the bottle?

SCIENCE WORDS

buoyancy p. 69
chemical
    change p. 104
density p. 84
effort force p. 132
evaporation p. 93

force p. 128
heat p. 116
matter p. 68
mixture p. 92
physical
    change p. 107

USING SCIENCE WORDS

Number a paper from 1 to 10. Beside each number write the word or words that best complete the sentence.

1. Solids, liquids, and gases are three different forms of ___?___.

2. Boats float on water because of the upward force called ___?___.

3. A push or a pull is a(n) ___?___.

4. The ___?___ of a material is the amount of the material in a given amount of space.

5. If you can separate material with a filter, you know that the material must have been a(n) ___?___.

6. A liquid changes to a gas by ___?___.

7. Breaking a rock is a(n) ___?___.

8. When a nail gets rusty, a(n) ___?___ has occurred.

9. Conduction is one way that ___?___ moves from one place to another.

10. The force put into a simple machine is a(n) ___?___.

UNDERSTANDING SCIENCE IDEAS

Write 11 to 15. For each number write the letter for the best answer. You may wish to use the hints provided.

11. Matter with a definite volume but not a definite shape is a
    a. gas
    b. liquid
    c. mass
    d. solid
    (Hint: Read page 71.)

12. Which of the following is a metric unit of measurement?
    a. cubic centimeter
    b. mass
    c. element
    d. buoyancy force
    (Hint: Read page 80.)

13. Which of the following is an element?
    a. water
    b. heat
    c. volume
    d. gold
    (Hint: Read page 90.)

14. Water turning into ice in a freezer is an example of
    a. radiation
    b. evaporation
    c. physical change
    d. chemical change
    (Hint: Read page 107.)

15. Heat moves through space by
    a. insulation
    b. conduction
    c. convection
    d. radiation
    (Hint: Read page 119.)

USING IDEAS AND SKILLS

16. Imagine that you find a jar in your refrigerator with a strange substance in it. Tell how you might figure out what the substance is.

17.  **INFER** Do you think a broom is a lever? Why or why not? How could you find out?

18. How are compounds and mixtures alike? How are they different? Give some examples.

19. A heavy coat and a fireplace can keep you warm in the winter. What are the different ways they do this?

THINKING LIKE A SCIENTIST

20. **EXPERIMENT** How easy is it for people to taste salt? Think up an experiment to find out how much salt must be in water for the water to taste salty to people.

WRITING IN YOUR JOURNAL

SCIENCE IN YOUR LIFE

What are four mixtures that you use just about every day? Why are they important?

PRODUCT ADS

A new product containing powerful chemicals prevents rust when it is sprayed on metal. Make a list of things people should do to use this product safely. How could the label be used to explain your instructions?

HOW SCIENTISTS WORK

When scientists want to learn about something, they often take measurements. Why is it important for all scientists to use the same system of measurement? What would happen if they did not?

Design your own Experiment

Is newspaper a good insulator? Plan an experiment to find out. Review your experiment with your teacher before you carry it out.

inter**NET** CONNECTION

For help in reviewing this unit, visit *www.mhschool.com/science*

PROBLEMS and PUZZLES

Dipped in Silver

A jeweler is making silver-plated boxes. A 1-ounce silver cube will cover 20 square inches in silver. How many silver cubes will you need to cover this box?

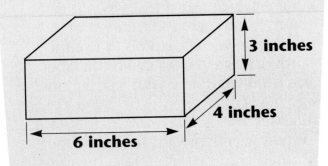

3 inches

4 inches

6 inches

Coin-Sorting Machine

A multilevel machine can separate a mixture of nickels, dimes, and quarters into neat stacks. What size filter would you put at each level? Which coins would be separated out at each level? Which coins would fall through to the next level?

PORTABLE PIZZA

The Pizza That Heats Itself

Portable Pizza to Go!

THE PROBLEM

The Handy-Pie Pizza Company wants to develop a self-heating Portable Pizza. The Portable Pizza will contain top-quality pizza ingredients. It will also cook itself without an oven! How can the Handy-Pie scientists develop this new product?

THE PLAN

Write a hypothesis that outlines how the Portable Pizza can cook itself. How should the package be made? What special chemicals or ingredients should it have? How can you make sure that the Portable Pizza heats itself *only* when you want it to? Include a design for how the Portable Pizza will be packaged.

TEST YOUR HYPOTHESIS

Explain how you would test your hypothesis. What would you expect to happen? How would you change your design if it didn't work?

ANALYZE THE RESULTS

How would you judge whether or not your design worked?

Write a report in your *Science Journal.* Describe your plan in detail. Tell how you would test it.

UNIT 3

LEARNING ABOUT EARTH'S HISTORY

CHAPTER 5

INTERPRETING EVIDENCE IN ROCKS

Most people don't think about rocks very much. However, rocks have many interesting stories to tell. In this chapter you will learn about the types of information you can learn from rocks. You will learn about how different rocks form. You will also learn about the clues they hold about the past.

 As you read this chapter, find the main idea in each reading passage. Look for the sentence that tells you what a passage is about.

WHY IT MATTERS

Rocks are used in many different ways and hold clues to Earth's past.

SCIENCE WORDS

mineral a naturally occurring substance, neither plant nor animal

igneous rock "fire-made" rock formed from melted rock material

sedimentary rock rock formed from bits or layers of rocks cemented together

relative age the age of something compared with the age of another thing

metamorphic rock rock whose form has been changed by heat and/or pressure

rock cycle a process by which rocks are changed from one type to another

What You Can Learn from Rocks

Have you ever given much thought about a rock you kicked as you walked along the street? You might not have stopped to think that the rock had a story to tell.

Take a close look at this rock. Write down some observations that you can make about it. What do you think it is made of? Where do you think it might have been formed?

EXPLORE

HYPOTHESIZE What evidence can you find in a rock that tells about its formation? Write a hypothesis in your *Science Journal.*

Investigate How You Interpret Clues in Rocks

Infer how these rocks were formed by observing their physical properties.

MATERIALS

- 5 different rock samples
- hand lens
- *Science Journal*

PROCEDURES

1. OBSERVE Carefully observe each rock. Describe and record its properties in your *Science Journal*. Look for properties such as color, hardness, texture, and shininess. Is it made of smaller particles that you can see? Does it have any layers?

2. OBSERVE Use a hand lens to observe each rock sample. Record your observations in your *Science Journal*.

3. COMMUNICATE Compare your observations with those of your classmates. Make a class list of all the properties you observed.

CONCLUDE AND APPLY

1. INFER Which rocks may have formed from sand or gravel? What evidence supports your answer?

2. INFER Which rock may have formed on an ocean bottom? What evidence supports your answer?

3. Compare samples B and E. How are they alike? How are they different?

GOING FURTHER: Problem Solving

4. INFER How do you think sample E formed? Why do you think so?

How Do You Interpret Clues in Rocks?

Have you ever noticed how rocks come in different colors, shapes, and sizes? Rocks are solid materials that make up the outer layer of Earth. As in the Explore Activity, *geologists* (jē ol'ə jists) also study the physical properties of rocks to tell how the rocks may have formed.

One way to study a rock is to look for **minerals** (min'ər əlz) in the rock. Rocks are made of minerals. Minerals are naturally occurring substances that are neither plants nor animals. Minerals are the building blocks of rocks.

For example, granite is a rock found in many areas. It is made of several minerals, as shown below. If you find a rock with these minerals in it, you have found granite.

How can you identify minerals? Become a mineral detective. Each mineral has properties you can use as clues. One property of minerals is color. What is the color of each mineral in the granite?

However, color is not always a useful property. A mineral may come in several colors. Mica, for example, can be silvery or black. Quartz can be white, pink, or purple. What's more, both mica and quartz may be colorless.

Mica (mī'kə)

Quartz (kwôrts)

Feldspar

Hornblende (hôrn'blend')

Granite

Granite is a rock made of several minerals. How are the minerals different?

How Can You Tell Minerals Apart?

A mineral detective looks for properties other than just color.

- You can tell some minerals by the way light bounces off them. This property is called luster. For example, some are shiny like a new metal pan or coin. Other minerals are not shiny like metals. They may look dull, glassy, or even "greasy."

- Another clue comes from rubbing a mineral gently but firmly on a "streak plate." You often see a streak that's the same color as the mineral surface. However, pyrite is a yellow mineral. When you rub it on a streak plate, you see a trail of black powder. What a clue!

- Another clue is how hard a mineral is. The harder it is, the less likely it will be scratched. Test a mineral's hardness with three testers—a fingernail, a copper penny, and an iron nail.

A soft mineral, like talc or mica, can be scratched by all three. Calcite is a harder mineral than mica. It cannot be scratched by a fingernail. It can be scratched by the edge of a copper penny. A harder mineral, like fluorite, can be scratched by an iron nail. Many minerals are too hard to be scratched by any of the testers.

Diamond is the hardest mineral. It looks glassy.

Pyrite is brassy yellow but has a greenish black streak.

Galena has a metallic luster. You can scratch it with a copper penny.

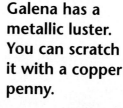

Talc is the softest mineral. It looks greasy.

QUICK LAB

Identifying Minerals

HYPOTHESIZE How can you tell minerals apart? Write a hypothesis in your *Science Journal.*

PROCEDURES

ANALYZE Use the tools and this table to identify each mineral sample. Write the properties and names in your *Science Journal.*

MATERIALS

- 5 mineral samples, labeled 1 to 5
- hardness testers— copper penny, steel nail
- streak plate
- *Science Journal*

CONCLUDE AND APPLY

EVALUATE Which properties helped you most to identify each mineral?

How Else Can You Tell Minerals Apart?

Some minerals split easily along flat surfaces. For example, mica splits easily into thin sheets. *Galena* (gə lē'nə) splits along flat surfaces in three directions. The result is a cube. Many minerals break unevenly, such as quartz and talc.

Some minerals have special properties. For example, magnetite is attracted by a magnet. The table below lists the different properties of some minerals.

MINERAL IDENTIFICATION TABLE

MINERAL	COLOR	LUSTER	STREAK	HARDNESS	OTHER
Galena	silver gray	shiny like a metal	gray	scratched by copper and iron	splits into cube shapes
Pyrite	brassy yellow	shiny like a metal	greenish black	not scratched by testers	looks like gold; breaks unevenly
Quartz	colorless, white, pink, purple	glassy	white	not scratched by testers	breaks unevenly
Mica	colorless, silvery, brown	may look glassy	white	scratched by fingernail	splits into thin sheets
Talc	pale green, white	pearly, dull, greasy	white	scratched by fingernail	flakes or crumbles easily
Feldspar (Orthoclase)	yellow, white, gray, red, brown	glassy, pearly	white	not scratched by testers	splits easily in two directions
Hornblende	green, black	glassy	brown, gray	not scratched by testers	splits easily in two directions

What Is One Main Group of Rocks?

Geologists can tell rocks apart by the minerals that are in the rocks. They also look to see how large the minerals or grains in a rock are. Large grains give rocks a coarse or rough texture. Smaller grains give rocks a fine texture.

Geologists also see how the grains fit together. Are the grains closely locked together, or do they stand out like separate pieces?

By checking these properties, geologists can tell how rocks formed. Geologists classify rocks into three main groups based on how they formed.

Many rocks are classified as **igneous rocks** (ig′nē əs roks). The word *igneous* means "fire-made." An igneous rock is formed from hot, molten rock material that has cooled and hardened.

This molten material may cool and harden below or above Earth's surface. Below the surface this molten material is called magma. Because it is below the surface, magma may cool and harden slowly over time. The slower it cools, the larger the mineral grains can become. The result is a rock with coarse texture. Granite is an example.

Magma tends to rise upward toward Earth's surface. If it reaches the surface before it hardens, it can escape through volcanoes or cracks. Magma that reaches the surface is called lava.

Lava cools quickly as it is exposed to air. As a result the minerals do not have a chance to form large grains. The grains are small, producing rocks with a fine texture. *Basalt* (bə sôlt′) is an example of this type of rock. Some of these rocks may have tiny holes that are the result of escaping steam and gases.

Sometimes lava can cool so quickly that mineral grains do not have time to form. The rocks that result are volcanic glass.

THREE MAIN IGNEOUS ROCKS

Granite is a coarse-grained rock.

Basalt is a fine-grained rock.

Obsidian is an example of volcanic glass.

What Is Another Group of Rocks?

Did you ever see rocks that looked like bits of sand glued together into a clump? These rocks are classified into a group called **sedimentary rocks** (sed'ə men'tə rē roks).

There are several types of sedimentary rocks. One type of sedimentary rock is formed from smaller bits of rock that become pressed or cemented together. They start out as small, broken-down pieces of rock carried away by water, wind, or ice. In time the pieces are dropped off in other places in layers.

Deposited rock particles and other materials that settle in a liquid are called *sediments* (sed'ə məntz). With time the weight of new layers of sediments packs together the layers on the bottom. The sediments change to rock as air and water are squeezed out of the layers.

Sandstone is an example of this type of sedimentary rock. It is made up of grains of sand that have been cemented together. Conglomerate is made up of larger pieces cemented together. Shale is made up of fine mud particles cemented together.

Some sedimentary rocks are made of substances that were once part of living things. Shells and skeletons of dead sea animals build up in layers on the ocean floor. Eventually they become cemented together. They may form a kind of limestone.

In some cases certain minerals become dissolved in the waters of lakes and small seas. When the water evaporates, the minerals are left behind as sediments. Rock salt and some kinds of limestone are formed this way.

FOUR EXAMPLES OF SEDIMENTARY ROCKS

Conglomerate

Rock salt

Shale

Limestone

152

How Do Sediments Form Layers?

Sediments, like bricks in a wall, are laid down in time order. Those at the bottom are laid down first. Those at the top are laid down last. Time order tells us about age. While we cannot always give the age of something in units of time—such as years—we can give its **relative age** (rel'ə tiv āj). Relative age is age expressed by words like *older, oldest, younger,* and *youngest*. It describes the age of something compared with the age of another thing.

For example, in this drawing layer A is the oldest. Layer D is the youngest. Layer B is younger than layer A but older than layers C and D.

Brain Power

How would you describe another layer that might have formed over layer D?

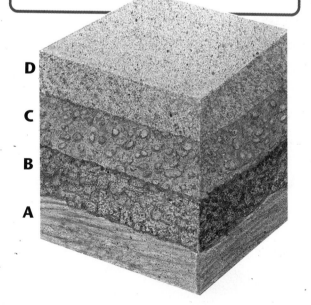

D
C
B
A

Observing the Layering of Sediments

HYPOTHESIZE What will happen if you put some rock particles and sand in water? Which will settle first? Last? Do you think the size of the particles matters? Write a hypothesis in your *Science Journal.*

MATERIALS

- clear quart jar with a lid, half-filled with water
- gravel
- fine-grained sand
- spoon
- *Science Journal*

PROCEDURES

1. MAKE A MODEL Put the gravel and sand in the jar of water. Cover it with the lid. Shake the jar. Set it aside.

2. PREDICT What do you think will happen? Write a prediction in your *Science Journal.*

CONCLUDE AND APPLY

1. COMPARE How did your prediction compare with the results?

2. OBSERVE How many layers formed? Which layer settled first? Last?

3. INFER How does this illustrate the formation of sedimentary rocks?

What Is the Third Group of Rocks?

In a way some rocks result from being cooked. They are classified as **metamorphic rocks** (met'ə môr'fik roks). The word *metamorphic* means "changed in form." A metamorphic rock is a rock that has been changed by heat, by pressure, or by both. Before the change the rock may have been any kind of rock, even another metamorphic rock.

Heat from nearby rising magma can cause a chemical change in the minerals making up a rock. The weight of rocks stacked on top of a rock builds up pressure that can cause the rock to change.

Geologists classify metamorphic rocks into two groups. In one group pressure causes minerals to spread out in bands. The rocks can break apart along these bands. One

Marble is one type of metamorphic rock.

example of this type of rock is *gneiss* (nīs). It can form when granite or shale are heated under pressure.

Rocks classified in the other group of metamorphic rocks do not have bands of minerals. They do not break in layers. Marble is one example of this type of rock. Marble forms when limestone is heated under pressure.

HOW ROCKS CAN BE CHANGED

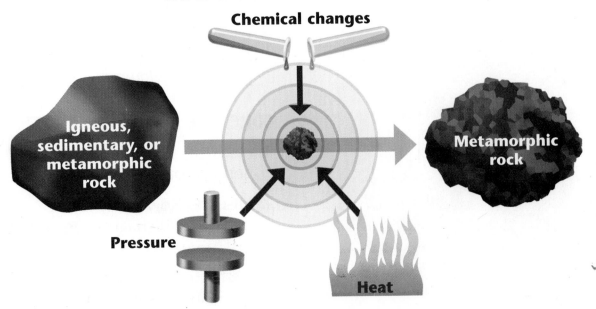

Chemical changes

Igneous, sedimentary, or metamorphic rock

Metamorphic rock

Pressure

Heat

How Do Rocks Change?

Rocks are always changing. All rocks are part of the **rock cycle** (rok sī′kəl). The rock cycle is a never-ending process by which rocks are changed from one type into another. A cycle is something that happens over and over again.

HOW THE ROCK CYCLE WORKS

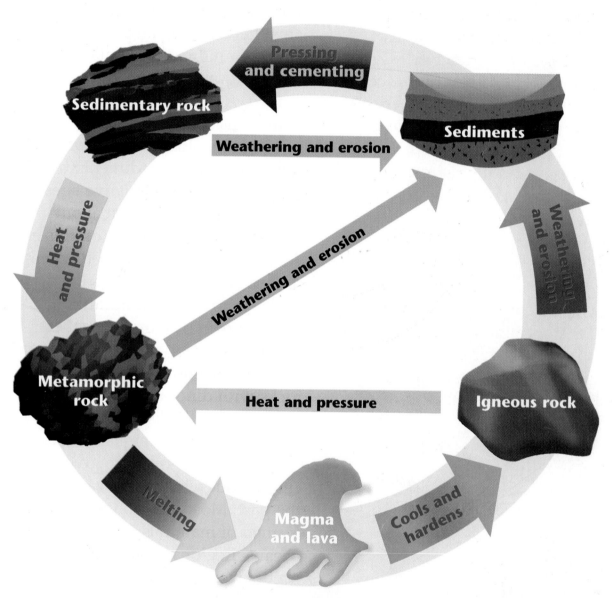

Sedimentary rock

Pressing and cementing

Weathering and erosion

Sediments

Weathering and erosion

Heat and pressure

Weathering and erosion

Metamorphic rock

Heat and pressure

Igneous rock

Melting

Magma and lava

Cools and hardens

READING ∿ DIAGRAMS

1. **WRITE** How can an igneous rock become a sedimentary rock?
2. **DISCUSS** What causes a sedimentary rock to become a metamorphic rock?

What Can You Learn from Rock Layers?

Did humans ever have to fight off dinosaur attacks or saber-toothed tigers? How do we know? Rock layers contain *fossils* (fos′əlz) that can reveal a lot about organisms that lived in the past. Most fossils are found in sedimentary rocks and are found where they were formed. A fossil is any trace, mark, or remains of an organism at least 10,000 years old that has usually been preserved in sedimentary rock. Scientists study the relative ages of rocks and fossils to learn about extinct organisms. Based on this evidence, they have concluded when certain plants and animals lived.

For example, all dinosaurs became extinct before any saber-toothed tigers or humans appeared on Earth. We now know that all rocks with dinosaur remains are older than all rocks with saber-toothed tiger or human remains.

Rocks and fossils also give us clues about what Earth was like in the past. Most limestones are formed of materials deposited in the oceans. Regions where limestone occurs were probably once underwater. Corals live only in warm, shallow parts of the ocean. Places where we find rocks with fossil coral were once tropical areas covered by shallow seas. Fossil ferns in polar regions tell us these areas were once warmer than today.

Fossils provide evidence of plants and animals that lived in the past. They also provide clues about what Earth was like in the past.

Rocks occur everywhere on or near Earth's surface, and we use them in many different ways. Pieces of rock are mixed into cement used to build things. They are also mixed with asphalt used to pave roads. Some rocks, like marble, are even used to make beautiful sculptures.

However, rocks are also important in other ways. By studying the properties and ages of rock layers, scientists have explained what they think Earth was like in the past. The next time you kick a rock, stop and pick it up. Who knows what you might learn from it!

REVIEW

1. Describe some of the properties of minerals to help tell them apart.

2. Compare and contrast how igneous and sedimentary rocks are formed.

3. How can you identify the relative ages of rock layers?

4. **COMMUNICATE** Design another way to communicate the steps of the rock cycle. It can be a chart, a list, a paragraph, or another diagram.

5. **CRITICAL THINKING** *Analyze* A fossil of a polar organism is found in a warm area. What does it tell you about what this area was like in the past?

WHY IT MATTERS THINK ABOUT IT Look around at school or at home. In how many ways are rocks used?

WHY IT MATTERS WRITE ABOUT IT Write a short paragraph describing one way rocks are used at school or at home.

READING SKILL What is the main idea discussed on page 155?

Marvelous MINERALS

Graphite leaves dark marks on paper.

Calcite bends light in two directions, creating a double image.

158

A Closer Look

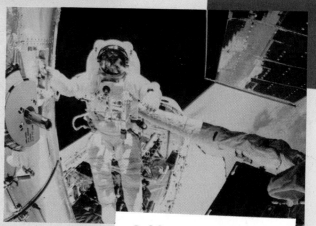

Can you name a mineral you use every day? How about graphite, that stuff we call "lead" in pencils? It's a mineral, and there are lots more.

All rocks are made of minerals. Some rocks are made of several minerals. Other rocks have just one.

One way to identify a mineral is by doing a streak test. Rub the mineral across a white surface. The mineral may leave a streak of color that can help you tell what the mineral is. When you write with a pencil, you're conducting a streak test. Graphite leaves a black streak!

Minerals do all kinds of things. Clear calcite bends light in two directions. If you look at the print in this book through a piece of calcite, you'll see a double image! Gold reflects heat radiation better than any other metal. A thin film of gold on a window can help keep a building cool in summer.

Other minerals do other things. How do you think magnetite got its name? From its magnetic properties! Lodestone, a rock made of magnetite, can pick up iron filings. Diamonds are the hardest mineral on Earth, so they're often used as cutting tools. What's the only thing that can scratch or cut a diamond? Another diamond!

Have you used a mineral yet today?

Gold on an astronaut's helmet reflects radiation from the Sun and protects the astronaut's face.

Discussion
Starter

1 Could you conduct a streak test with a diamond? Explain.

2 Why would lodestone be used in making compasses?

Topic 2
EARTH SCIENCE

WHY IT MATTERS

Fossils give us information about living things in the past.

SCIENCE WORDS

imprint a fossil created by a print or impression

mold a hollow fossil form clearly showing the outside features of the organism

cast a fossil formed or shaped within a mold

amber hardened tree sap, often a source of insect fossils

Clues from Fossils

What do you think happened in each picture? Like a detective you can use clues to help you figure out what took place. The tracks are your clues. Count how many different kinds of tracks you see. Describe what you think happened in each picture.

EXPLORE

HYPOTHESIZE How can you interpret clues left from millions of years ago? What types of things can you look for in fossils to learn the story they tell? Write a hypothesis in your *Science Journal.*

Investigate What You Can Learn from Fossils

Study this drawing of fossilized footprints. How many animals made them? What do you think happened first? Last?

MATERIALS

- footprint puzzle
- *Science Journal*

PROCEDURES

1. **OBSERVE** Carefully study the footprints. Look for clues in the sizes and types of prints. Think about which were made first, next, and last.

2. **COMMUNICATE** Discuss the evidence with your partner. How can you work together to interpret it?

3. **DRAW CONCLUSIONS** Record the "story" you think the prints tell in your *Science Journal*.

CONCLUDE AND APPLY

1. **INFER** How many animals made the tracks? Are all the animals the same kind? How can you tell?

2. **INFER** Were all the animals moving in the same direction? How do you know? Which came first? Next? Last?

3. **COMPARE AND CONTRAST** How does your story compare with those of your classmates? On what points do you agree? Disagree? Be prepared to defend your interpretation with evidence.

GOING FURTHER: Problem Solving

4. **INTERPRET DATA** Create another footprint puzzle. Challenge a classmate to figure out the story the footprints tell.

What Can You Learn from Fossils?

Scientists use clues from fossils to learn about the past, just as was shown in the Explore Activity. By studying fossils they can learn about past events, past environments, and past organisms.

For example, scientists studied the fossil footprints shown in the picture. From them they learned that dinosaurs did not drag their tails. They saw only footprints and no signs of dragged tails.

How Fossils Form

What happens when a plant or animal dies? The soft parts quickly decay or are eaten. Hard parts, such as bones, teeth, and shells, last longer. They are more likely to become fossils.

Most fossils are found in sedimentary rocks. The remains are gently and rapidly buried by sediments. They may become fossils if they remain undisturbed as the sediments become rocks.

Sometimes a shallow print or impression is the only evidence of a plant or animal that once existed. Fossils of this kind—such as animal tracks, body outlines, leaf prints, and grooves made by tiny fish bones—are called **imprints** (im'prints'). An imprint is a mark made by pressing.

From fossil evidence like these dinosaur tracks, scientists determined that dinosaurs did not drag their tails as they walked. How could they tell?

Shells often leave behind fossils known as **molds** (mōldz). A mold is a hollow form with a particular shape. A mold forms when water seeps into the rocks where a shell is buried. The water eventually dissolves the shell. This leaves a hollow space where the shell once was. The hollow space, often clearly showing the outside features of the shell, is a mold.

Another type of fossil is known as a **cast** (kast). A cast is something that is formed or shaped in a mold. A cast forms when minerals slowly accumulate in a mold. Eventually they fill it. The minerals take the shape of the original shell and form a copy. If you have ever made gelatin in a shaped cup, you can understand the difference between molds and casts. The cup is a mold. The hardened gelatin is a cast.

At left is a mold of a fern leaf. At right is a cast of the leaf. What features of the fern can you see?

Making Molds and Casts

HYPOTHESIZE **What is the difference between a cast and a mold? Write a hypothesis in your** *Science Journal.* **Try to make them.**

MATERIALS

- seashells
- modeling clay
- petroleum jelly
- container of plaster of Paris
- *Science Journal*

PROCEDURES

1. MAKE A MODEL Coat a shell with petroleum jelly. Then firmly but gently press the shell into the clay.

2. Carefully remove the shell from the clay. Fill the clay with plaster of Paris.

3. When the plaster has dried, remove it from the clay.

CONCLUDE AND APPLY

1. IDENTIFY Which is the mold? Which is the cast?

2. COMPARE How are they similar and different?

3. OBSERVE What shell characteristics can you see in the mold? In the cast? Record your observations in your *Science Journal.*

163

What Are Some Other Ways Fossils Form?

Imprints, molds, and casts are some types of fossils. Organisms of the past were also preserved in other interesting ways.

Sometimes entire insects became trapped in sticky sap oozing from certain trees. The trapped insects were preserved as the sap hardened into **amber** (am′bər).

Sometimes entire animals were preserved by being frozen. Mammoths are relatives of modern elephants. Fossilized mammoths have been found in ice and frozen ground in the northern parts of Asia and North America. Bones, hair, skin, flesh, and even internal organs have been preserved.

Many fossils have been discovered in tar pits. Many animals—including saber-toothed tigers, camels, lions, and mammoths—became stuck in tar pits and died. Their flesh decayed, while their bones sank. The bones were preserved as the tar around them hardened. Rancho La Brea in California is famous for fossils in its tar pits.

FOUR DIFFERENT TYPES OF FOSSILS

This picture shows a baby woolly mammoth that was once frozen in ice. Studying such specimens allows scientists to test their educated guesses that were made based only on bones.

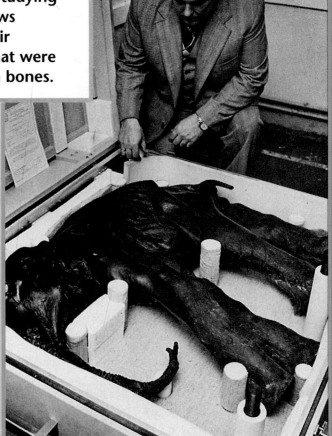

This insect was trapped as sap oozed down a tree. Today it is a perfectly preserved fossil in amber.

Sometimes animal remains are preserved as mummies, slowly dried out in hot, dry regions like deserts. These fossils have changed little if at all since they formed.

Plants and animals that decay slowly may leave behind a thin film of the element carbon. Carbon films of ferns, leaves, and fish often show detailed outlines of the organisms.

Parts of plants and animals, especially wood and bones, may also be preserved by being *petrified* (pet′rə fid′). *Petrified* means "turned to stone."

How do you think bones become petrified? Bones have a hard, compact outer layer. Inside is a spongy layer with connected openings, or pores. When a bone is buried, minerals may slowly seep into the pores and fill them. When this happens the bone is partly petrified. The fossil still has the original bone material. Later the bone itself may be dissolved and replaced by minerals. The bone is then completely petrified.

The woody parts of plants are preserved in the same way as completely petrified bones. Minerals filled the hollow spaces and also replaced all the once-living parts.

This plant left behind a carbon film that shows many details. What observations can you make about the plant?

What observations can you make about this petrified wood?

What Happens Once Fossils Are Found?

Fossils represent only a very small part of all the plants and animals that lived in the past. Most organisms die without leaving a single trace. Even hard parts, such as bones, are usually scattered, broken, and mixed. Complete skeletons are rare, lucky, and exciting finds.

Collecting is the first step. Workers at fossil sites carefully excavate the skeleton, bone by bone, from the rock. Each bone is wrapped in a plaster jacket to prevent damage. Each is carefully labeled and sent to a museum or university.

The next step is removing the last bits of rock from the bones. People use tools much like those used by dentists to file and pick away the rock. They also soak the bones in a type of solution that dissolves the rock. The prepared specimens are then ready for study or display.

What do you think the next step is? The next step is assembling the bones. Sometimes they are put on display in museums. Metal rods and wires are often used to hold up a skeleton so it appears to be standing. Sometimes gaps are left where bones are missing. Sometimes missing bones are replaced by artificial bones. Fossil bones used in exhibits are usually coated with shellac or varnish to help protect them.

Some fossils are stored safely for further study. Casts are used in the exhibits, not the real fossils. Models may be made to show what an extinct animal probably looked like when it was alive.

A lot of work goes into a display of a fossilized dinosaur skeleton.

MATH LINK

Skill: Using Numbers

COMPARING SIZES

Footprint size gives a good idea of overall size and height. Scientists have determined that the length of a footprint is generally equal to one-quarter the length of the hind-leg bone of the animal that made it. The length of the bone gives a good idea of the animal's overall size. In this activity you will use numbers to determine the approximate lengths of dinosaur leg bones.

MATERIALS
• *Science Journal*

PROCEDURES

1. COLLECT DATA This table gives the footprint length of six adult dinosaurs. Copy the table into your *Science Journal.*

2. USE NUMBERS Determine how to calculate the lengths of the hind-leg bones. Complete column C.

3. COMPARE Rank the dinosaurs in order of probable overall size. Write 1 for the largest and 6 for the smallest in column D.

CONCLUDE AND APPLY

1. INTERPRET DATA Which dinosaur probably had the largest hind-leg bone? The smallest?

2. COMPARE Which two dinosaurs were probably close in size? The most different in size?

A	B	C	D
Name of Dinosaur	Length of Footprint	Probable Length of Hind-Leg Bone	Probable Rank in Overall Size
Triceratops	15 inches ($1\frac{1}{4}$ feet)		
Tyrannosaurus	30 inches ($2\frac{1}{2}$ feet)		
Stegosaurus	18 inches ($1\frac{1}{2}$ feet)		
Velociraptor	6 inches ($\frac{1}{2}$ foot)		
Compsognathus	3 inches ($\frac{1}{4}$ foot)		
Ultrasaurus	78 inches ($6\frac{1}{2}$ feet)		

What Other Clues Do Fossils Provide?

Fossils also give information about the age of organisms when they died. Annual-growth rings in petrified wood tell the age of fossil trees. Similar footprints of different sizes tell if organisms were young or old.

Fossils also give many clues about the characteristics of organisms. Footprint size is a clue to an animal's size. Distances between footprints may tell whether an animal was walking or running. Footprints also tell if an animal walked on two or four legs.

What types of clues would tell you what animals ate? Meat eaters usually had strong jaws with many pointed teeth. Plant eaters usually had weaker jaws with flat or peglike teeth. Fossilized stomach contents can tell what an animal ate.

Fossils can also tell about past environments. Fossilized aquatic organisms tell where rivers, lakes, or oceans once existed. Fossils also tell that parts of the world were once colder or hotter than they are today. Fossil ferns tell that an area had a warm or hot, moist climate. Fossil evergreen leaves tell that an area was cool.

How can you tell which dinosaur was most likely a meat eater and which a plant eater?

Brain Power

A fossil of a dinosaur's head is found. It has only a few pointed teeth. What conclusions can you draw from this evidence?

FUNtastic Facts

Fossils show us how animals changed over time. Some animals haven't changed much in millions of years. We call those animals "living fossils." Alligators, lobsters, cockroaches, and horseshoe crabs are living fossils. They look much like their ancestors did 100 million years ago. Can you name another living fossil?

WHY IT MATTERS

Finding, preserving, and studying fossils gives us a lot of interesting information about the past. The fossils provide evidence about the characteristics of extinct organisms. They also tell about the environments in which organisms lived. That is why fossils have been called the "keys to the past."

Finding fossils can be fun!

REVIEW

1. What types of things can be determined from animal tracks and footprints?

2. Describe how imprints, molds, and casts are formed.

3. What are three ways, other than imprints, casts, and molds, that organisms of the past have been preserved?

4. **USE NUMBERS** A fossil of an adult dinosaur foot measures 69 centimeters (27 inches). About how long would its hind-leg bone have been?

5. **CRITICAL THINKING** *Analyze* What if a fossil of a saltwater organism is found in a very dry, hot place? What does it tell you about that area?

WHY IT MATTERS THINK ABOUT IT
Choose a type of organism that lived in the past. What would you like to know about it? How could you find answers to some of your questions?

WHY IT MATTERS WRITE ABOUT IT
Do some research to answer your questions. Write a short report, and share it with your classmates.

WHAT GOOD ARE FOSSILS?

About 200 years ago, people really began to dig Earth's crust. Engineers built long canals and bridges and dug deep mines. They constructed roads and tunnels right through mountains. Scientists discovered that many of the rocks in Earth's crust held the remains of animals no one had ever seen before!

In 1822 an English doctor and his wife found giant teeth in a pile of rocks. He thought the teeth were from an animal that looked like a modern iguana. The creature they found became the first recognized dinosaur, the Iguanodon.

Since then scientists have found fossils of different kinds of giant dinosaurs that lived millions of years ago. Studying the fossils helps us know the history of the continents and understand modern animals.

Fossil hunters have made mistakes, too. They found many sauropod dinosaur fossils without a skull attached. They created two different models. Each had a different type of skull created for it. They called one dinosaur the Apatosaurus and the other the Brontosaurus. Eventually a skeleton with a skull was found. It resembled the Apatosaurus model. They realized the Brontosaurus was really an Apatosaurus all along.

This early Iguanodon model shows how people viewed dinosaurs.

History of Science

Dr. Lisa D. White studies fossilized microorganisms that were alive 70 million years ago. She gets microfossils by working with other scientists who bring up layers of sediment from the ocean floor. A large tube, much like a drinking straw, is forced into the crust under the ocean. The tube is then brought up to the surface with its contents. When the tube is opened, scientists can see layers of sediment in the same order in which they were deposited. By examining the layers and the microfossils, Dr. White has been able to find out about events that took place on Earth millions of years ago.

DISCUSSION STARTER

1. Fossils were known from ancient times. Why did they become more important 200 years ago?
2. Dinosaurs were land animals. If fossils from one species were found in South America and Africa, what would that tell about the continents?

To learn more about fossils, visit *www.mhschool.com/science* and enter the keyword BONES.

*inter*NET
CONNECTION

SCIENCE WORDS

amber p. 164

cast p. 163

igneous rock p. 151

imprint p. 162

metamorphic
~rock p. 154

mineral p. 148

mold p. 163

relative age p. 153

rock cycle p. 155

sedimentary rock
p. 152

USING SCIENCE WORDS

Number a paper from 1 to 10. Fill in 1 to 5 with words from the list above.

1. The process by which rocks are broken down and formed is known as the __?__.

2. One type of __?__ is formed from smaller bits of rock that become cemented together.

3. A fossil that is a hollow form with a particular shape is called a(n) __?__.

4. You can tell a layer's __?__ by comparing it with other rock layers.

5. A type of fossil that is formed or shaped in a mold is a(n) __?__.

6–10. **Pick five words from the list above that were not used in 1 to 5, and use each in a sentence.**

UNDERSTANDING SCIENCE IDEAS

11. Describe different tests you can perform to tell minerals apart.

12. What types of things happen to fossils once they are found?

USING IDEAS AND SKILLS

13. **READING SKILL: FIND THE MAIN IDEA** What is the main idea of the passage on pages 162 and 163? Represent it in a graphic organizer like a table or chart.

14. **USE NUMBERS** Dinosaur A has an adult footprint length of 30 inches. Dinosaur B has an adult footprint length of 18 inches. Dinosaur C has an adult footprint length of 3 feet. Which dinosaur was probably the tallest?

15. **THINKING LIKE A SCIENTIST** Fossils of tropical ferns are found in an area that has a cold winter season. What do these fossils tell you?

PROBLEMS and PUZZLES

Snack Dig Fill one-third of a shoe box with soil. Add a snack food, like crackers. Cover them with more soil. Add other snacks, like raisins. Cover them with more soil. Work with a partner to dig up the evidence with any tools you choose. Why do scientists have to dig carefully? Why do they need to use small as well as large tools?

CHAPTER 6
LEARNING ABOUT EARTH

In this chapter you will learn about ways Earth's surface is shaped. You will also learn about the importance of soil and what Earth is like on the inside.

In this chapter you will have many opportunities to draw conclusions. A conclusion is a decision or judgment based on information. You draw conclusions all the time. What conclusion can you draw about the temperature if you see that it is snowing?

Topic
EARTH SCIENCE
3

WHY IT MATTERS

Glaciers—huge sheets of moving ice—affect Earth in many different ways.

SCIENCE WORDS

glacier a large mass of snow and ice that moves over land

terminus the end, or outer margin, of a glacier

moraine rock debris carried and deposited by a glacier

glacial till an unsorted mixture of rock materials deposited as a glacier melts

erratic an isolated boulder left behind by a glacier

outwash plain gravel, sand, and clay carried from glaciers by melting water and streams

Shaping Earth's Surface

Do you know what caused the luxury ship *Titanic* to sink on April 14, 1912? *Titanic* struck an iceberg, which tore holes in the ship's side. Water flowed in. The ship sank.

Where did the iceberg come from? It came from a **glacier** (glā'shər), a large mass of ice that moves over land. When a glacier meets the sea, icebergs break off. Glaciers also affect the land. How did a glacier affect the land in this picture?

EXPLORE

HYPOTHESIZE **The main component of a glacier is ice. How can a block of ice help shape Earth's surface? Write a hypothesis in your *Science Journal*. How could you test your ideas?**

Design Your Own Experiment

HOW DO GLACIERS SCRATCH AND MOVE ROCKS?

PROCEDURES

1. **PREDICT** Which ice cube do you think is more like a real glacier? Record your prediction and reasons in your *Science Journal.*

2. **USE VARIABLES** Think about how you could use the materials to test your ideas. Which ice cube will scratch a surface? Record your observations for each ice cube.

3. **OBSERVE** Which ice cube will leave "rocks" behind? Place the ice cubes on a folded paper towel. Allow them to melt. Observe and record what is left behind.

MATERIALS

- paper towel
- clean ice cube
- ice cube made with sand
- aluminum foil
- wood scrap
- *Science Journal*

CONCLUDE AND APPLY

1. **COMMUNICATE** How did each model feel as you rubbed it over a surface?

2. **OBSERVE** Which model scratched the foil? The wood? What happened when you pushed down harder?

3. **INFER** What made the scratches?

4. **OBSERVE** What happens to the sand when the ice cube melts?

GOING FURTHER: Problem Solving

5. **COMPARE** How does this model help you explain how a glacier scratches and moves rocks?

How Do Glaciers Scratch and Move Rocks?

A *glacier* is a large mass of snow and ice that moves downward and outward over the land. Glaciers form when more snow falls in winter than melts in summer. With time the snow collects in layers. The weight of the upper layers forms the lower layers into ice.

What do you think causes a glacier to move? The weight of the snow and the force of gravity cause the layers to "creep" or flow downhill. Heat from friction and from Earth below may melt some of the bottom layer of ice. The resulting thin layer of water aids in movement. The Explore Activity shows how the bottom of an ice cube melts if someone presses down on it and pushes it along. When a mass of ice and snow begins to move, a glacier is born.

Glaciers are also made up of *rock debris* (rok də brē′) that includes boulders, rock fragments, gravel, sand, and soil. Glaciers pick up rock debris as they move.

Most debris is found at the bottom and along the sides of a glacier. These are places where glaciers come in contact with solid rock below the soil. This rock is known as bedrock. As the Explore Activity shows, this debris often creates deep scratches in the solid bedrock.

PARTS OF A GLACIER

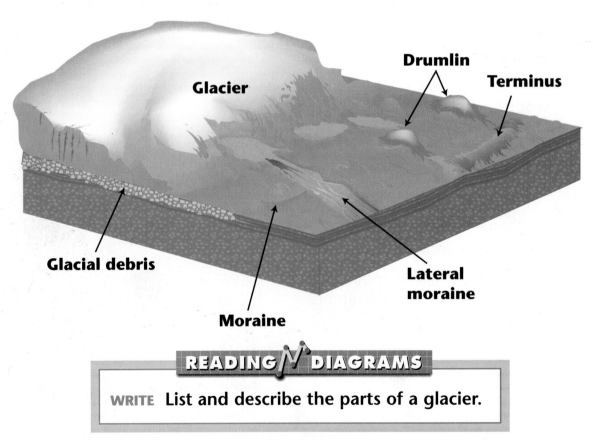

Glacier

Drumlin

Terminus

Glacial debris

Lateral moraine

Moraine

READING DIAGRAMS

WRITE **List and describe the parts of a glacier.**

Rock debris collects at a glacier's **terminus** (tûr'mə nəs). The terminus is the end, or outer margin, of a glacier. The terminus moves forward when a glacier grows and backward when it shrinks.

When a glacier melts, the rock debris is left behind. Rock debris carried and deposited by a glacier is called **moraine** (mə rān'). The sand left behind by the melting ice cube in the Explore Activity represents moraine.

Moraines are made up of **glacial till** (glā'shəl til). Glacial till is an unsorted mixture of rock materials deposited as a glacier melts. Rock materials that make up till vary greatly in size, from large fragments to fine clay. An oval mound of till is called a *drumlin* (drum'lin).

Glaciers leave distinctive features on Earth's surface. They act like giant bulldozers, pushing and piling up anything in their paths. As glaciers move they loosen and scrape away broken rocks, sometimes even plucking out giant blocks of bedrock. Loosened material from valley walls also falls into glaciers. This leaves steep cliffs and circular basins.

Rock fragments in the ice act like sandpaper. They grind away the bedrock. They may carve deep, parallel scratches, similar to the marks made in the foil and wood in the Explore Activity. They can smooth and polish the rock below.

The general effect of erosion by *continental glaciers* is to flatten and round the land. However, some types of glaciers carve out valleys, making them deeper and U-shaped.

This is an example of a U-shaped valley.

177

Skill: Defining Terms Based on Observations

FLOW OF A GLACIER

You know what *flow* means. You can see water flow in a stream or down a drain. What do we mean when we say that a glacier flows? In this activity you will make and observe a model to see how glacial ice flows. Then you will be able to describe glacial ice flow based on your experiences and observations.

MATERIALS

- prepared corn-starch mixture
- mixture of sand, gravel, and soil
- waxed paper
- metal spoon
- ruler
- *Science Journal*

PROCEDURES

1. **MAKE A MODEL** Place a spoonful of the cornstarch mixture on a piece of waxed paper. This represents a glacier. Record what happens in your *Science Journal.*

2. **OBSERVE** Place another spoonful on top of the first. This represents new snow. Record what happens.

3. Sprinkle some of the sand mixture in a 3-cm band around the edges and on top. Mark the edges of the sand on the waxed paper.

4. **OBSERVE** One at a time, add four more spoonfuls of the cornstarch mixture. After adding each, mark how far the glacier moves and the sand's position.

5. **OBSERVE** Flip the glacier over onto another piece of waxed paper. Measure and draw the bottom.

CONCLUDE AND APPLY

1. **EXPLAIN** Did the sand mixture sprinkled on top of your model in step 3 eventually reach the bottom?

2. **INTERPRET DATA** What do you think happens when a real glacier moves over rocks and boulders?

3. Define *glacial ice flow*.

Did Glaciers Exist in the Past?

Scientists have learned about glaciers of the past by studying present-day glaciers and their features. You have read about some of these features, such as scratched bedrock, and U-shaped valleys. Other glacial features include **erratics** (i rat′iks). Erratics are isolated boulders left behind by a glacier. **Outwash plains** (out′wôsh plānz) are gravel, sand, and clay carried from glaciers by melting water and streams. They are deposited over large areas.

Glacial features are found today in places at great distances from those where glaciers now exist. They are evidence that in the past glaciers covered much larger parts of the world than they do today. Periods of very cold temperatures and many glaciers are called ice ages. During the ice ages, vast ice sheets as thick as several miles covered as much as one-third of Earth's surface. Temperatures were very low. Snowfall was heavy. Only places far from the glaciers were even slightly warm. As more and more water became ice, the oceans were greatly reduced in size.

Periods of warmer weather existed between ice ages. They are known as interglacial periods. Some scientists think that we are now in an interglacial period. They also believe that far in the future, Earth will undergo another ice age.

Brain Power

What do you think might happen to your hometown if an ice age came? Why?

GLACIATION DURING THE ICE AGE

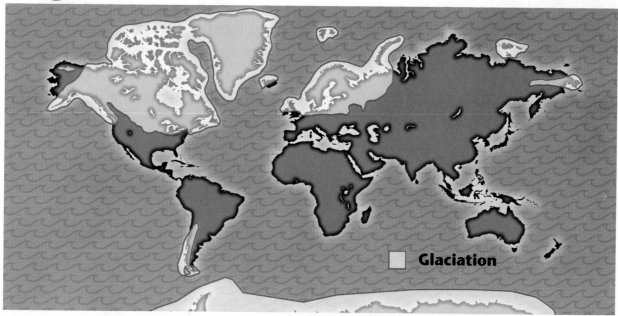

Glaciation

What Other Forces Shape Earth?

Glaciers are not the only things that slowly change and affect Earth's surface. Other agents of erosion include wind, waves, running water, and gravity.

As wind blows across Earth's surface, it picks up small particles of dust, soil, and sand. With time, exposed rocks and soil are worn down by them as if rubbed by sandpaper. When the wind finally slows down or stops, the particles drop to the ground, often far from where they were picked up.

Gravity and running water caused these rocks to move down the hillside.

Have you ever stood in ocean waves? After a few minutes you begin to feel like you are sinking in the sand. That is because the water is pulling sand from under your feet each time a wave pulls away.

Pounding waves break up rocks, coral, and shells into smaller pieces. As the pieces rub against each other, they grind down into particles. Waves also carry these materials away from the shore and can drop them in other places. With time, waves can change a coastline.

Which agent of erosion do you think causes the greatest changes? Running water. Examples include streams, rivers, and flowing rainwater that pick up and carry particles of rock and soil. As these particles move, they may eventually cut a valley in the bedrock.

Running water drops particles in places far from where they were picked up. When they settle at a river's mouth, they form a delta.

How do you think gravity can shape Earth's surface? Gravity causes any loose materials such as rocks, boulders, soil, water, and glaciers to move from a higher place to a lower place. Gravity can also cause landslides and mudflows.

Landslides occur when rocks and other materials are shaken loose by an earthquake or heavy rain. Mudflows typically occur after a heavy rain, when the soil can no longer absorb water.

Studying glaciers and the evidence they leave behind can be exciting and interesting. However, there are more important reasons to study glaciers. Understanding glaciers helps us learn how they can change the landscape. Studying glaciers can also help us understand how Earth's climate was different in the past and how it might change in the future.

This scientist is studying a glacier. What types of things do you think scientists might look at?

REVIEW

1. Explain what glaciers are and how they form and move.

2. Name and describe a glacier feature made up of glacial till.

3. Describe two features that result from glacial erosion.

4. DEFINE Why do you think isolated boulders left behind by a glacier are called erratics?

5. CRITICAL THINKING *Apply* A giant boulder, different from the bedrock in the area, sits in New York's Central Park. How do you think it might have gotten there?

WHY IT MATTERS THINK ABOUT IT
Some scientists believe that the world is gradually becoming colder and that another ice age will occur in the future. What do you think?

WHY IT MATTERS WRITE ABOUT IT
Write a short story about what the world might have been like during the ice ages.

The Work of

Wind and

Is erosion always a bad thing? Millions of people who've marveled at the view at Arizona's Grand Canyon don't think so! Over thousands of years, the Colorado River carved out this beautiful 1,753-meter (5,750-foot) deep canyon. What a great use of water erosion!

Rivers are created by rainfall. As rain flows downhill, it cuts into the soil. In time it produces a deep canal or canyon. The water wears away river banks and soil and rocks are slowly deposited on the sides. This creates a flat plain where the river begins to curve. Much of the soil and rocks a river carries is dropped off

on the inside of the curves, where the flow is the slowest.

Wind can wear away the surface of soft rocks, especially in dry areas like deserts. Strong winds pick up bits of sand and gravel that beat against the hillsides. This erosion can create unusual shapes in the rocks. Some look like faces!

Wind can also cause dust storms in drought areas. Without enough rain the topsoil dries up and becomes loose. If strong winds blow across the land, they pick up the soil and carry it miles away. This is wind erosion.

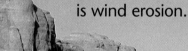

Water

DISCUSSION STARTER

1. Is a pothole in the street an example of erosion? Why?

2. How did the Colorado River carve the Grand Canyon?

To learn more about erosion, visit *www.mhschool.com/science* and enter the keyword WEATHERING.

*inter*NET
CONNECTION

WHY IT MATTERS

It is important to protect soil and use it wisely.

SCIENCE WORDS

humus leftover decomposed plant and animal matter

horizon a layer of soil differing from the layers above and below it

topsoil the top layer of soil, rich in humus and minerals

subsoil a hard layer of clay and minerals that lies beneath topsoil

soil profile a vertical section of soil from the surface down to bedrock

pore space the space between soil particles

permeability the rate at which water can pass through a material

The Story of Soil

What do you think would happen if there was no soil? Think about the many ways we use soil to help you answer the question.

One of the most important things on Earth is soil. Water flows through it. We walk and build on it. Most importantly plants grow in it. If there was no soil, few things would be able to live on Earth.

EXPLORE

HYPOTHESIZE The picture shows three different types of soil. What kinds of materials do you think make up different soils? How can you separate soil into its different parts? Write a hypothesis in your *Science Journal.*

Investigate What Soil Is Made Of

Test different soils to find out what they might be made of.

MATERIALS

- 3 types of soil
- hand lens
- eye dropper
- water
- newspaper
- paper towel
- 3 sharp pencils
- *Science Journal*

PROCEDURES

1. Spread the newspaper on a desk or table. Place one soil sample on each paper towel. Put the paper towels on the newspaper.

2. OBSERVE Use a pencil to push around the soil a little bit. Observe each sample with the hand lens. Record as many observations as you can of each soil sample in your *Science Journal*.

3. CLASSIFY Use the pencil tip to classify the particles of each sample into two piles—pieces of rock and pieces of plant or animal material.

4. OBSERVE Put four drops of water on each sample. After a few minutes, check which sample leaves the biggest wet spot on the newspaper.

CONCLUDE AND APPLY

1. INFER What kinds of materials make up each soil sample?

2. COMPARE How do the particles you sorted in each soil sample compare by size? By color?

3. OBSERVE Describe the properties you observed of each sample.

4. COMPARE Which sample absorbed the most water? How can you tell?

GOING FURTHER: Apply

5. INFER What do you think soil is made of? How do you think it is made?

What Is Soil Made Of?

Soil begins to form when bedrock is broken apart into small rock pieces and minerals. This break-down is caused by rain, ice, wind, freezing and thawing, or chemical changes.

What other things break apart rocks? Plants and animals that live in these small rock pieces help break them apart further. As plant roots grow downward, they pry apart rocks. Burrowing animals, such as earthworms and ants, create tunnels in between rock pieces. Some of these tunnels fill with air and water. Water expands as it freezes, further breaking apart the rocks.

Bacteria and fungi also help create soil. They decompose dead plants and animals for energy. The leftover decomposed plant and animal matter is called **humus** (hū′məs). Humus becomes mixed with the rock pieces. Finally, a material that can be called *soil* is produced. Soil is a mixture of tiny rock particles, minerals, humus, water, and air. How does this definition compare with the one developed in the Explore Activity?

HOW SOIL FORMS

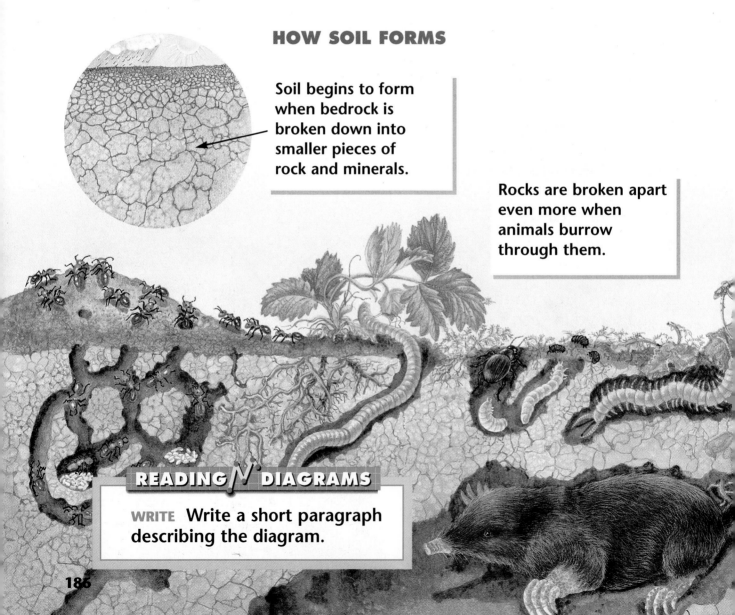

Soil begins to form when bedrock is broken down into smaller pieces of rock and minerals.

Rocks are broken apart even more when animals burrow through them.

READING N DIAGRAMS

WRITE Write a short paragraph describing the diagram.

What Are Soil Layers?

The process of soil formation is a very long one. It may take hundreds to thousands of years for one inch of soil to form.

As soil forms, different layers result. A layer of soil differing from the layers above and below it is called a **horizon** (hə rī′zən).

Soils typically have three horizons. They are named from the top downward by the capital letters *A*, *B*, and *C*. Each horizon has certain characteristics.

The A horizon is made up of **topsoil** (top′soil′). Topsoil is the top layer of soil. It is rich in humus and minerals. Topsoil is usually dark in color. It is the part of soil in which most plants grow and in which many organisms live.

The B horizon lies below the A horizon. This horizon is known as **subsoil** (sub′soil′). Subsoil is normally a fairly hard layer. It is made up of clay particles and minerals that have filtered down from the A horizon. It is usually light in color. Sturdy plant roots may grow down into the B horizon.

The C horizon is made up of coarse material broken down from the underlying bedrock. It is typically beyond the reach of plant roots.

The soil horizons make up a **soil profile** (soil prō′fĭl). A soil profile is a vertical section of soil from the surface down to bedrock.

A horizon: topsoil

B horizon: subsoil

C horizon: broken-down bedrock

Bedrock

How Are Soils Alike and Different?

In what ways were the soils on page 184 and in the Explore Activity alike and different? There are dozens of different kinds of soils, each with its own set of properties. The properties include texture, composition and thickness, mineral content, and the place it formed.

Texture refers to the size of the particles making up the soil. Sandy soil, for example, has a coarse texture. Soil with a lot of silt, or fine minerals, has a medium texture. Soil with a lot of clay has a fine texture. Most soils are mixtures of particles of several different sizes.

The composition and thickness of soils depend on several factors. They include the kind of bedrock from which the soils are formed, organisms, climate, steepness of the land, and time.

The kinds of minerals and rock fragments that make up different soils vary with the bedrock. The amount of humus depends on the kinds and numbers of organisms in the region. High temperatures and heavy rainfall cause rock to break down into soil quickly.

Soil that forms on steep slopes is usually quite thin because it is eroded quickly. Where soil is eroded, new soil begins to form as bedrock is exposed at the surface.

Time is another important factor that determines soil thickness. In general undisturbed soil becomes thicker with the passing of time.

Soil with a lot of clay has a fine texture.

Silty soil has a medium texture.

Sandy soil has a coarse texture.

Soils also differ based on the minerals they contain. The minerals in soil depend on the minerals found in the bedrock from which it was formed. Soil formed from limestone has minerals different from soil formed from granite.

Soil in one area may have more or fewer minerals than soil in another area. The amount of minerals in soil depends on how much water passes through the soil. Water can dissolve and wash away minerals. Plants also use up minerals as nutrients to make their own food. Areas with many plants may have few minerals in the soil.

Soils also differ based on where they were formed. That is because soil may be eroded from where it was formed by water, wind, or ice. This can provide a geological history of a region.

When this eroded soil is deposited in other places, it is called transported soil. Minerals in transported soil may be quite different from those found in the bedrock below. This is a good clue that the soil has not always been there. For example, large parts of the central United States are covered by soil that has been eroded by glaciers or wind.

Water passes through some soils more quickly than through others. The rate at which water travels through soils is another way in which soils differ.

Farmers often add fertilizers to soil. This replaces minerals that were washed away or used up by crops.

There are more microorganisms in one spoonful of soil than there are people on Earth. Among these organisms is a bacteria that the antibiotic *streptomycin* (strep'tə mī'sin) is extracted from. An antibiotic is a medicine used to help treat and cure certain types of infections.

Why do you think it is important not to pollute soil and to treat it with respect?

Rate of Water Flow

HYPOTHESIZE What variables might affect the rate of water flow through soil? Write a hypothesis in your *Science Journal*.

MATERIALS

- 2 prepared containers
- sandy soil
- clay-rich soil
- water
- 2 measuring cups
- stopwatch or clock with second hand
- *Science Journal*

PROCEDURES

1. Put one soil sample in each container. Hold the container of sandy soil over a measuring cup. Slowly pour 1 c of water over the soil, and start timing.

2. **MEASURE** When water drops begin to "hang," record the total time. Determine the amount of water left in the soil. Record your findings in your *Science Journal*.

3. **REPEAT** Repeat with the other soil.

CONCLUDE AND APPLY

1. **COMPARE** Through which soil did the water pass more quickly?

2. **COMPARE** Through which soil did more water pass?

3. **INTERPRET DATA** Can you relate your findings to soil texture?

How Does Particle Size Affect Water Flow?

On page 188 you learned that sandy soil has a coarser texture than clay-rich soil. Does it surprise you that water flowed through sandy soil more quickly than through clay-rich soil?

Remember that soil is made up not only of rock particles, minerals, and humus but also of water and air. Even in tightly packed soil there are spaces between the solid materials. The spaces between soil particles are called **pore spaces** (pôr spās'əz). Water and air fill these spaces.

As water travels through a soil's pore spaces, the soil acts like a filter. It filters certain pollutants out of the water as it passes through.

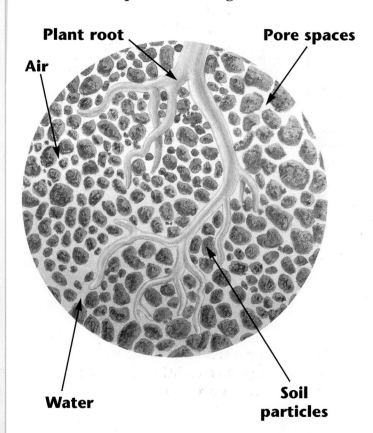

Plant root

Pore spaces

Air

Water

Soil particles

Materials with pore spaces are said to be *porous* (pôr′əs). Coarse-grained soils, like sandy soils, have numerous pore spaces. That is because the larger particles are not packed together as tightly as smaller particles. This creates larger pore spaces where water can be stored.

The size of pore spaces and the way in which they are connected affect **permeability** (pûr′mē ə bil′i tē). Permeability is the rate at which water can pass through a porous material. Soils through which water passes quickly have a high permeability. Sandy soils have a high permeability. The smaller particles are packed tightly together, holding little water.

Importance of Soil Permeability

Soil permeability is important to plants that live on land. Therefore, the type of soil in which plants grow is important. Coarse soil is very porous. It absorbs water quickly. Water moves downward quickly. It often travels to depths beyond the reach of plant roots. It dissolves minerals in the topsoil and carries them along with it.

How do you think fine soil affects a plant? Fine soil is not very porous. Water soaks into it slowly. It may remain in the pore spaces for a long time. The soil layers in which plant roots grow may become soaked. The plants drown from too much water.

The small particles of a fine soil are packed together tightly. This type of soil has small pore spaces.

The large particles of a coarse soil are not packed together tightly. This type of soil has large pore spaces.

Why Is Soil Important?

Without soil few things would live on Earth. Soil supports the growth of plants on land. Plants use water, energy from the Sun, and nutrients in soil to make their own food. Plants, in turn, provide food for other organisms. Some animals eat plants directly. Others eat animals that eat plants.

Farmers who grow food crops must take good care of soil. Soil supplies the crops with water and nutrients, such as nitrogen, potassium, and phosphorus. It also supports the crops' roots.

Land is often cleared of its natural vegetation to make it available for farming. Soon dramatic changes may take place in the soil. For example, when tropical forests are cut down, the soil is broken up and exposed. It becomes more permeable, and minerals are dissolved and carried downward. In a short time, the soil is unable to support plants.

Soil is also important in other ways. It filters pollutants out of water. We build houses, cities, and roads on it. We plant grass, flowers, and trees in it.

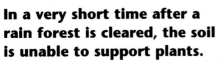

In a very short time after a rain forest is cleared, the soil is unable to support plants.

Brain Power

Soil is a very important natural resource. What are some things we can do to use it wisely and preserve it?

Soil is one of our most important resources. It supplies us with food and filters our water. Soils are also living systems, providing homes for many organisms. It is hard to imagine that more microorganisms grow in a spoonful of soil than there are people on Earth.

Soils are sensitive to changes in water, temperature, and human activity. That is why many people work to protect them. Soil scientists learn about soils and work to help conserve them. Some work with farmers to help them manage the soils in their fields.

We can all be "soil scientists" in a way. Treat the soil around you well, and it will treat you well in return.

Do you think you might like to be a soil scientist some day? Why or why not?

REVIEW

1. Briefly explain how soil is formed.

2. Name and describe at least three properties of soil.

3. How is soil permeability related to how porous a soil is?

4. COMPARE What is the difference between a soil horizon and a soil profile?

5. CRITICAL THINKING *Evaluate* Do you agree that without soil there would be no land plants, and without land plants there would be no soil? Explain your answer.

WHY IT MATTERS THINK ABOUT IT
What do you think happens to soil when it becomes polluted?

WHY IT MATTERS WRITE ABOUT IT
Why is it important to protect our soil from pollution and overuse? What can you do to help?

The Ever-Changing Planet

Did you think Earth has always looked as it does today? No way! Earth is constantly changing.

Deep inside Earth is a huge pool of magma—melted rock and gas. When there's too much pressure underground, the magma spills or explodes out of a volcano as lava. It flows downhill, destroying everything. However, when it cools and hardens, the lava creates new islands, or enlarges old land!

If heavy rainfall weakens soil and rocks on a hillside, they may suddenly break loose and slide down the slope. A landslide can knock over trees, cover houses, and deposit land in a new area!

An avalanche of snow quickly tumbles down a mountain, picking up rocks as it goes. They scrape the mountain's surface, changing it forever. Soil and rocks carried with the snow build up the land below after the snow melts.

Rainfall or the sudden melting of snow and ice can cause rivers to overflow. Floods wash away fertile topsoil and may even change the course of a river!

Earthquakes quickly create new landforms and destroy others. Earthquakes under the ocean can cause tidal waves, or tsunamis, with waves as high as 30 meters (100 feet). When they reach land, they rearrange the landscape.

Even tornadoes, hurricanes, and lightning can quickly change Earth's surface. Wind storms rip up trees and blow away soil. Lightning can cause forest fires that destroy land.

DISCUSSION STARTER

1. How do these quick changes help to build Earth's surface?

2. Could humans create these kinds of quick changes? How?

To learn more about how Earth changes, visit *www.mhschool.com/science* and enter the keyword LAVA.

*inter***NET**
CONNECTION

Topic
EARTH SCIENCE
5

WHY IT MATTERS

Studying earthquakes helps us learn about Earth's structure.

SCIENCE WORDS

earthquake a movement or vibration in Earth

fault a break in Earth's outer layer caused by the movement of rocks

seismic wave a vibration caused by rocks moving and breaking along faults

crust the solid rock that makes up Earth's outermost layer

outer core a liquid layer of Earth lying below the mantle

mantle the layer of rock lying below the crust

inner core a sphere of solid material at Earth's center

Inside Earth

Have you ever received a wrapped package? Half the fun is guessing what's inside! "Is it the book I wanted to borrow from Cousin Ted?" Clues on the outside may tell you something about what is inside. What clues might tell you about what could be inside this package?

Earth is something like a wrapped package. However, we cannot open this package to find out what is inside. How do you think scientists learn what Earth is like inside?

EXPLORE

HYPOTHESIZE How can you learn about something that you can't see directly? Write a hypothesis in your *Science Journal.*

Design Your Own Experiment

WHAT'S INSIDE?

PROCEDURES

1. What kinds of observations can you make about the objects in the containers? Make a plan with your group. Outline different things you can test. Record your plan in your *Science Journal.*

2. OBSERVE Make your observations. Be sure not to damage the containers. Each group member should have a turn with each container. Record all the observations in your *Science Journal.*

3. INTERPRET DATA Look at all your data. Come to a conclusion about what you think might be in each container.

MATERIALS

- 3 sealed opaque containers
- *Science Journal*

CONCLUDE AND APPLY

1. INFER What do you think is in each container? Include a diagram or model that supports your observations.

2. COMMUNICATE Present your observations for each test. Explain how they support your conclusions.

GOING FURTHER: Apply

3. INFER In what ways might these types of observation skills help you in everyday life?

What's Inside?

How far down into Earth do you think you would get if you dug the deepest hole possible? Would the bottom of your hole be near Earth's center? Not even close!

The deepest wells and mines extend only a relatively short distance into the bedrock that makes up Earth's outer layer. Even deeply eroded canyons barely scratch Earth's surface. The Grand Canyon is almost 2 kilometers (about 1 mile) deep. However, this distance is nothing compared with the total distance from Earth's surface to its center. That is a distance of almost 6,400 kilometers (4,000 miles)!

As shown in the Explore Activity, one of the ways to learn about the contents of containers is to shake them. In a similar way, scientists learn about Earth by studying **earthquakes** (ûrth′kwāks). Earthquakes are movements or vibrations in Earth. They are caused by the release of stored energy in Earth's outer layer. This release of energy causes sudden shifts of rock as well as other kinds of disturbances.

Shaking containers allows you to hear and feel what is inside. Scientists "feel" and "listen to" Earth by using instruments called *seismographs* (sīz′mə grafs′). A seismograph detects, measures, and records the energy of earthquake vibrations.

Brain Power

What would you do to try to find out what is inside something that is too large for you to lift or shake?

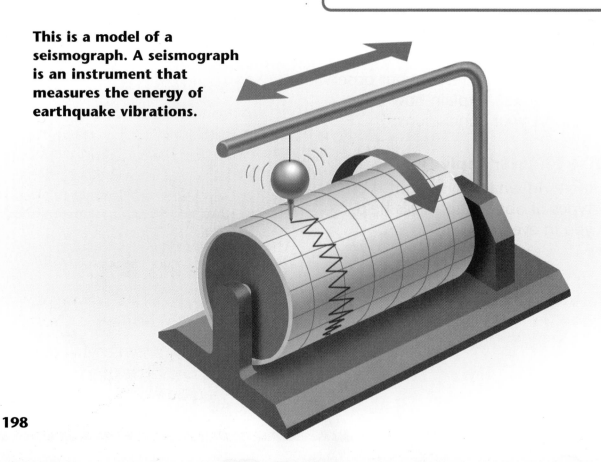

This is a model of a seismograph. A seismograph is an instrument that measures the energy of earthquake vibrations.

Imagine the world as an apple. The Grand Canyon and the deepest wells and mine shafts would not even extend through the apple's skin. They provide only information about Earth's very thin, rocky outer layer.

Scientists have spent many years trying to answer the question of what lies below Earth's thin surface. They can't cut Earth open to see, weigh, or observe what is there. They must depend on information obtained in several different ways, such as from earthquakes. Then they combine and interpret it to come up with an answer.

In this model of Earth, even the deepest wells and mine shafts would not extend through the apple's skin.

QUICK LAB

PHYSICAL
LINK
SCIENCE

Earthquake Vibrations

HYPOTHESIZE **How do you think the energy of earthquakes travels through Earth? Write a hypothesis in your** *Science Journal.* **In this activity you will make a model to observe how energy waves travel during an earthquake.**

MATERIALS

- marble
- pan of water
- newspaper
- flashlight
- *Science Journal*

PROCEDURES

1. Spread out some newspaper to absorb splashed water. Place the pan of water on the newspaper.

2. OBSERVE Take turns dropping the marble into the water from a height of about 15 cm (6 in.). Shine the flashlight on the water to help you see what happens more clearly. Record your observations of the wave patterns in your *Science Journal.*

CONCLUDE AND APPLY

1. COMMUNICATE What type of wave pattern did the marble create?

2. INFER How do you think this pattern might relate to the way earthquake vibrations travel?

199

What Causes Earthquakes?

Pressure within Earth can cause rocks in its outer layer to break. If the rocks found along a break move, the break is called a **fault** (fôlt). The place where the movement begins is called the *focus*. The focus may lie as far as 700 kilometers (450 miles) below Earth's surface. When an earthquake begins, pressure from within Earth causes rocks along faults to move and break. As they move, energy is released as vibrations. These vibrations are called **seismic waves** (sīz′mik wāvz), or earthquake waves.

In what direction do you think seismic waves travel? Seismic waves travel out from the focus in all directions. They travel in much the same way as the water waves in the Quick Lab. As seismic waves move through Earth and along its surface, they are felt as shakings and vibrations.

EARTHQUAKE FEATURES

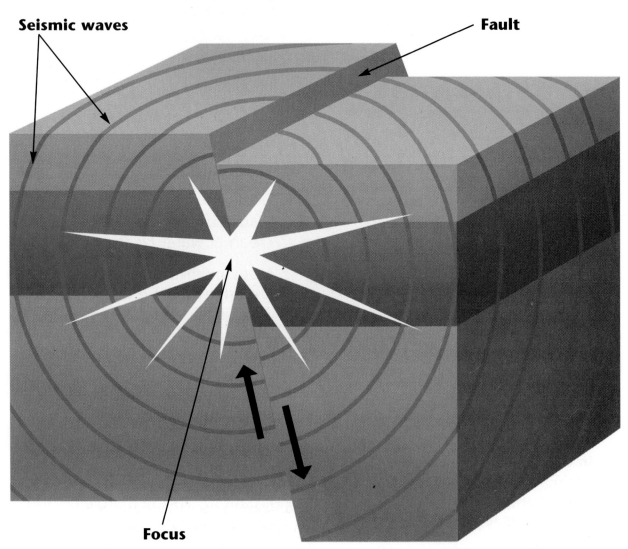

Seismic waves

Fault

Focus

200

What Information Do We Get from Earthquakes?

The farther waves travel away from the focus, the weaker they become. Seismographs in different places record the strength of the waves. They can detect even very weak waves at great distances from the focus. The printed record made by a seismograph is called a *seismogram* (sīz′mə gram′).

By comparing seismograms scientists can track waves and determine their speed and direction of travel. They can also learn about Earth's interior. That is because there are several different kinds of seismic waves, and they travel at different speeds.

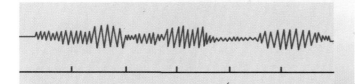

This seismogram was recorded during a weak earthquake.

This seismogram was recorded during a strong earthquake. How are the two seismograms similar? Different?

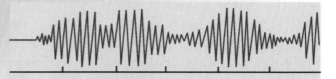

TYPES OF WAVES

- **PRIMARY WAVES.** Also called P waves, these are the fastest seismic waves. They are the first to arrive at a distant point. P waves can travel through solids, liquids, and gases.

- **SECONDARY WAVES.** Also called S waves, they travel slower than P waves. They arrive later at a distant point. S waves travel only through solids.

- **SURFACE WAVES.** Also called L waves (long waves), these are the slowest waves of all. They are felt at the surface as they slowly move the ground up and down, and from side to side. These waves cause the damage that often comes with an earthquake.

What have scientists learned by studying earthquake waves? They have learned that the waves travel at different speeds through solids, liquids, and gases. They use this information to infer what Earth is like on the inside.

What Is Earth's Structure?

By observing the characteristics of different waves, scientists have determined that different layers of Earth are solid or liquid.

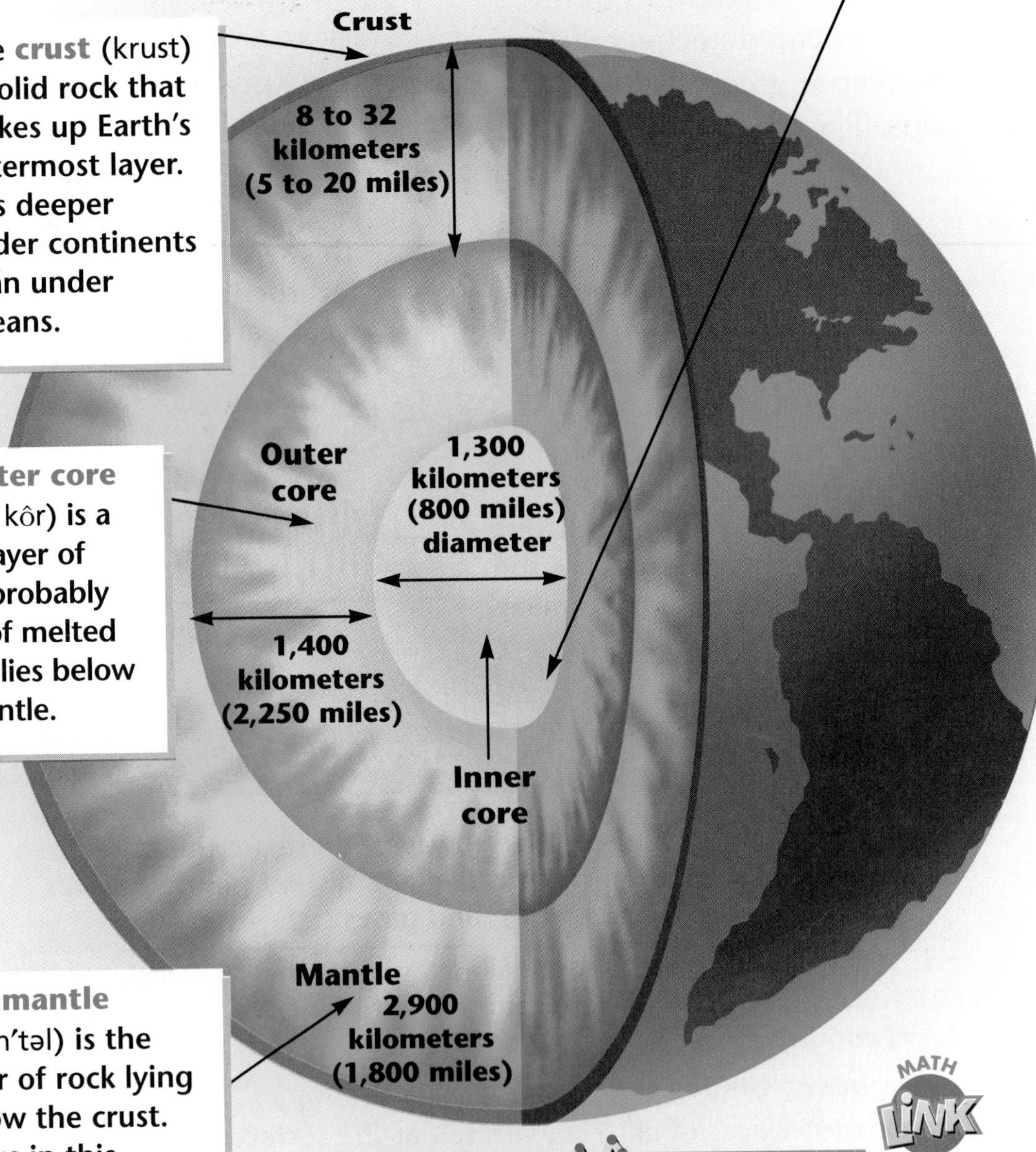

4 The **inner core** (in′ər kôr) is a sphere of solid material at Earth's center.

1 The **crust** (krust) is solid rock that makes up Earth's outermost layer. It is deeper under continents than under oceans.

Crust

8 to 32 kilometers (5 to 20 miles)

2 The **outer core** (ou′tər kôr) is a liquid layer of Earth, probably made of melted iron. It lies below the mantle.

Outer core

1,300 kilometers (800 miles) diameter

1,400 kilometers (2,250 miles)

Inner core

3 The **mantle** (man′təl) is the layer of rock lying below the crust. Rocks in this region can move or slowly flow because of great pressure and high temperatures.

Mantle
2,900 kilometers (1,800 miles)

MATH LINK

READING DIAGRAMS

1. **WRITE** Make a list of Earth's layers. Start with the outermost layer.
2. **DISCUSS** What is the total thickness of Earth's core?

Scientists use instruments to try to learn as much as possible about when an earthquake might occur. A gravity meter tells scientists about the rise and fall of the land surface. A strain meter measures how much rocks expand and contract. A tilt meter measures changes in the tilt of the surface of Earth. A creep meter measures how much the land moves along a fault. This information may help scientists warn people of a possible earthquake.

This scientist studies earthquakes. Would you like to study earthquakes? Why or why not?

REVIEW

1. How have scientists learned about Earth's interior?

2. What causes earthquakes? What have scientists learned from studying earthquakes?

3. List the following seismic waves in order of increasing speed— S waves, L waves, and P waves. Through what kinds of materials can P waves and S waves pass?

4. **COMMUNICATE** Name Earth's layers in order from the surface to the center. Describe each.

5. **CRITICAL THINKING** *Evaluate* What is Earth's approximate total diameter?

WHY IT MATTERS THINK ABOUT IT Do you think it is important to study earthquakes? Why or why not?

WHY IT MATTERS WRITE ABOUT IT Design a way to warn people in your area of a potential earthquake.

READING SKILL What conclusions can you draw about the strength of an earthquake by looking at a seismogram?

A Closer Look

What's Inside the Moon?

Is the Moon made of green cheese? No, scientists think it's pretty similar to Earth inside. On the Moon's surface are igneous rocks, formed from cooled lava. Astronauts set up seismometers to record data about moonquakes. Using that data, scientists made a model of the Moon's insides!

The Moon has a crust, a mantle, and a core. The crust is about 61 kilometers (38 miles) thick.

The Moon's mantle is a layer of dense rock up to 1,000 kilometers (620 miles) thick. Deep moonquakes occur there.

The core is less than 500 kilometers (311 miles) from the outside edge to the center. Little else is known about it.

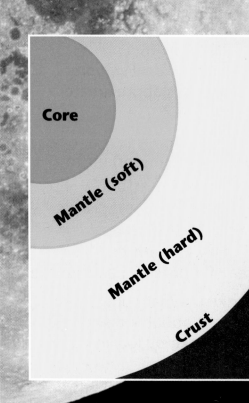

Core

Mantle (soft)

Mantle (hard)

Crust

To learn more about the Moon, visit
www.mhschool.com/science
and enter the keyword LUNAR.

*inter*NET
CONNECTION

SCIENCE WORDS

crust p. 202

earthquake p. 198

erratic p. 179

fault p. 200

glacial till p. 177

horizon p. 187

humus p. 186

inner core p. 202

mantle p. 202

moraine p. 177

outer core p. 202

outwash
  plain p. 179

permeability p. 191

pore space p. 190

seismic wave p. 200

soil profile p. 187

subsoil p. 187

terminus p. 177

topsoil p. 187

USING SCIENCE WORDS

Number a paper from 1 to 10. Fill in 1 to 5 with words from the list above.

1. The A horizon is made of ___?___.

2. Movements or vibrations in Earth caused by the release of stored energy in Earth's outer layer are called ___?___.

3. The gravel, sand, and clay that are carried from glaciers by melting water and streams and deposited over large areas form a(n) ___?___.

4. The end, or outer margin, of a glacier is known as the ___?___.

5. The layer below Earth's crust is known as the ___?___.

6–10. **Pick five words from the list above that were not used in 1 to 5, and use each in a sentence.**

UNDERSTANDING SCIENCE IDEAS

11. How does studying earthquakes help scientists learn about Earth's structure?

12. How does pore size affect the rate of water flow through soil?

USING IDEAS AND SKILLS

13. **READING SKILL: DRAW CONCLUSIONS** What information can lead you to draw the conclusion that glaciers are powerful agents of erosion?

14. **DEFINE** How did studying the cornstarch mixture in Topic 3 help you describe how a glacier moves?

15. **THINKING LIKE A SCIENTIST** A soil scientist finds that a sample of soil contains minerals different from the bedrock below it. What conclusions can she make about the soil?

PROBLEMS and PUZZLES

Soil from Garbage A compost pile turns some garbage into rich soil. How could you start your own compost pile? What garbage could you use? How would you maintain the pile? Describe how composting helps people and the land around them.

SCIENCE WORDS

amber p. 164   imprint p. 162

crust p. 202   inner core p. 202

earthquake p. 198   mantle p. 202

erratic p. 179   sedimentary

glacial till p. 177   rock p. 152

horizon p. 187   subsoil p. 187

humus p. 186   topsoil p. 187

igneous rock p. 151

USING SCIENCE WORDS

Number a paper from 1 to 10. Beside each number write the word or words that best complete the sentence.

1. Granite is "fire-made" or __?__ .

2. Sandstone layers are a kind of __?__ .

3. Insect fossils have been found in hardened tree sap called __?__ .

4. Fossil animal footprints are a type of __?__ fossil.

5. Mixed rock and soil rubble left behind by melted glaciers is called __?__ .

6. A boulder left behind by a melted glacier is called a(n) __?__ .

7. The layer of soil at Earth's surface is called __?__ .

8. Decaying material mixed into the soil to help plants grow is called __?__ .

9. A violent jolting movement in Earth's crust is a(n) __?__ .

10. The solid sphere that makes up Earth's center is the __?__ .

UNDERSTANDING SCIENCE IDEAS

Write 11 to 15. For each number write the letter for the best answer. You may wish to use the hints provided.

11. All rocks are made of
    a. humus
    b. magma
    c. minerals
    d. sand
    (Hint: Read page 148.)

12. Fossils of wood formed when minerals fill in spaces and replace cells are called
    a. casts
    b. imprints
    c. petrified
    d. preserved
    (Hint: Read page 165.)

13. Rock debris collects at a glacier's
    a. glacial till
    b. moraine
    c. terminus
    d. drumlin
    (Hint: Read page 177.)

14. One property usually *not* used to describe soil is
    a. texture
    b. mineral content
    c. the place it formed
    d. smell
    (Hint: Read page 188.)

15. Where are soil layers found?
    a. in Earth's crust
    b. in Earth's mantle
    c. in Earth's outer core
    d. in Earth's inner core
    (Hint: Read page 202.)

USING IDEAS AND SKILLS

16. Tell how the metamorphic rock marble is formed.

17.  **USE NUMBERS** You find an imprinted dinosaur footprint while you are on a field trip in Montana. Tell how to estimate the length of the dinosaur's hind-leg bone.

18. Draw a simple "cut in half" diagram of Earth, showing its center. Label the major features.

19. **DEFINE** Based on the activity on page 178, explain what glacial flow is.

THINKING LIKE A SCIENTIST

20. When Suzie waters her lawn, the water forms puddles and doesn't soak in. Tell what you think the soil in Suzie's yard is like. Why do you think so?

WRITING IN YOUR JOURNAL

SCIENCE IN YOUR LIFE
List different ways rock is used in your neighborhood. Use your list to describe how rocks are important to you and your neighbors.

PRODUCT ADS
In the spring, garden nurseries advertise products such as large bags of decaying bark and peat moss. Who would buy these products, and how would they use them? How could you test the claims of the advertisements?

HOW SCIENTISTS WORK
Scientists know it is important to gather evidence. What kinds of scientific evidence have been discussed in this unit?

Design your own Experiment

Think about the soil where you live. Make a hypothesis about the properties of the soil. Design an experiment to test your hypothesis. Think safety first. Review your experiment with your teacher before you do it.

interNET CONNECTION

For help in reviewing this unit, visit
www.mhschool.com/science

PROBLEMS and PUZZLES

Frozen Footprints

This is a drawing of fossil footprints from a three-toed, two-legged dinosaur. Make a drawing of what you would expect to see if

- the dinosaur walked slowly
- the dinosaur ran
- the dinosaur stood still
- the dinosaur jumped
- the dinosaur stood in thick mud
- a larger, heavier dinosaur of the same type made footprints nearby
- a smaller, lighter dinosaur of the same type made footprints nearby

Showbiz Science

Enormous Pictures movie company has just hired you as their chief Science Advisor! Your job is to judge each of the following movie ideas. Write a short paragraph describing why each idea is valid or not.

- **The Big Shaker** Plot: A giant earthquake strikes Los Angeles, California, causing massive destruction.
- **Electric Dinosaurs** Plot: Fossil evidence shows that dinosaurs invented such things as toasters, motorcycles, and television sets.
- **Scrodzilla** Plot: A volcano erupts in Boston, freeing a group of pre-historic scrod fish that are the size of garbage trucks from deep underground.

Soil Test

How do soils drain differently? To find out cut the top off three small milk cartons. Poke a hole in the bottom of each carton. Fill each carton with soil from a different area.

Pour water into each carton. Time how long it takes for the water to drain through the hole in the bottom. Which soil held water best? What type of soil do you think it was? Why?

CHAPTER 7
DESCRIBING ANIMALS

In this chapter you will learn about the characteristics of animals. You will also learn about the two large groups into which all animals are classified. When you are done studying this chapter, you will be able to classify all the pets you know!

In this chapter you will have many opportunities to represent information in an outline. An outline describes a subject, its main ideas, and its supporting details.

WHY IT MATTERS

Sometimes it is not easy to tell whether or not an organism is an animal.

SCIENCE WORDS

food chain shows the steps in which organisms get the food they need to survive

food web shows how food chains in an ecosystem are related

vertebrate an animal with a backbone

invertebrate an animal without a backbone

symmetry the way an animal's body parts match up around a point or central line

sponge the simplest kind of invertebrate

Animal Characteristics

How would you describe an animal? Think about any animals you know. Don't forget that you are an animal, too. What types of characteristics, or traits, do animals have in common?

EXPLORE

HYPOTHESIZE Animals come in many sizes and shapes, yet they all have certain characteristics. For example, what are the main characteristics of a fish and snail? Write a hypothesis in your *Science Journal*. How could you test your ideas?

Investigate the Characteristics of Animals

Observe the characteristics of a snail and a fish to compare how they are similar and different.

MATERIALS

- clear container with aquarium water
- water snail
- goldfish or guppy
- fish food
- ruler
- *Science Journal*

PROCEDURES

1. Obtain a beaker with a fish and a snail in it.

2. OBSERVE Record the shape and approximate size of both animals in your *Science Journal*. Describe how each animal moves and any other observations that you make.

3. OBSERVE Add a few flakes of fish food to the beaker. What do the animals do? Record your observations.

4. DRAW CONCLUSIONS What does the fish eat? The snail?

CONCLUDE AND APPLY

1. IDENTIFY What body parts does each animal have? How do they use these parts?

2. COMPARE Compare how the fish and the snail move. Is movement an advantage for the animals? Explain.

3. INFER Do you think the fish and the snail are made of one cell or many cells? Why?

4. IDENTIFY What characteristics do the fish and the snail have? Make a list. Compare your list with other groups' lists. Make a class list.

GOING FURTHER: Apply

5. COMPARE How are you similar to the fish and the snail? How are you different?

What Are the Characteristics of Animals?

The Explore Activity showed some of the characteristics that all animals have in common.

1. Animals are made of many cells.

• Each cell has a nucleus and a cell membrane.

• Animal cells do not have a cell wall or chlorophyll, like plants.

• Different cells have different jobs. Bone cells support and protect. Nerve cells carry messages.

2. Animals reproduce.

• Some animals have thousands of offspring, or young, in their lifetimes. Others have only a few.

• Many animals care for and protect their offspring.

3. Animals move in some way.

• Most animals move during some time of their life.

• Animals move by walking, running, flying, gliding, crawling, and swimming.

• Animals move to find food, escape danger, find mates, and find a new home.

4. Animals grow and change.

• Some animals change form as they grow.

• Some animals just grow larger.

5. Animals eat food.

• Animals cannot make their own food, like plants.

• They get food by eating plants or other animals.

• Animals digest food for energy.

• Animals use oxygen to turn their food into energy.

Some animals change form as they grow older. This moth began its life as a caterpillar.

How Do Organisms Get Energy?

All living things need energy to stay alive. Animals get energy from food. A **food chain** (füd chān) tells you the steps of how energy flows among a group of organisms. An ecosystem can have many different food chains. Combined they form a **food web** (füd web). A food web shows how food chains in an ecosystem are related.

A FOOD CHAIN

1 Energy comes from the Sun.

5 After organisms die, decomposers like fungi and bacteria break down their remains into chemicals.

2 Producers use it to make food.

6 Now all the energy in the food chain has been converted to heat. The chemicals are absorbed into the soil. They are used by producers as nutrients to make more food, along with energy from the Sun. The cycle starts again.

3 Consumers that eat the plants are primary consumers. They use some of the energy to maintain life functions. The rest is lost as heat.

4 Secondary consumers get energy by eating other consumers.

READING DIAGRAMS

REPRESENT **Draw and label another food chain.**

How Are Animals Different?

All animals have the same things in common. They all have five basic characteristics—they are made of cells, they reproduce, they move in some way, they grow and change, and they eat food.

However, animals are also different in many ways. One major difference is having or not having a backbone. An animal with a backbone is called a **vertebrate** (vûr′tə brāt′). An animal without a backbone is called an **invertebrate** (in vûr′tə brit). You will learn more about vertebrates and invertebrates later in this chapter.

Brain Power

Which animal in the Explore Activity was a vertebrate? Which one was an invertebrate?

How Body Plans Differ

Another difference among animals is the way their body parts match up around a point or central line. This is known as **symmetry** (sim′ə trē). Body parts with symmetry match up as mirror images when they are folded over.

Some animals have no symmetry. One example is a **sponge** (spunj), the simplest kind of invertebrate. No matter how you fold a sponge, its body parts do not match up.

A sponge has no symmetry.

An animal with *radial* (rā′dē əl) symmetry has body parts that extend outward from a central point. You could fold a sea star through its center five ways and it would match up.

An animal with a sphere-shaped body, like a sea urchin, has *spherical* (sfer′i kəl) symmetry. You could fold a sea urchin any way through its center and it would match up.

An animal with *bilateral* (bī lat′ər əl) symmetry has only two sides, which are mirror images. You could fold a butterfly only one way through its center to have it match up. Organisms with bilateral symmetry have a definite front end, back end, upper side, and lower side. Invertebrates most commonly have radial and bilateral symmetry.

TYPES OF SYMMETRY

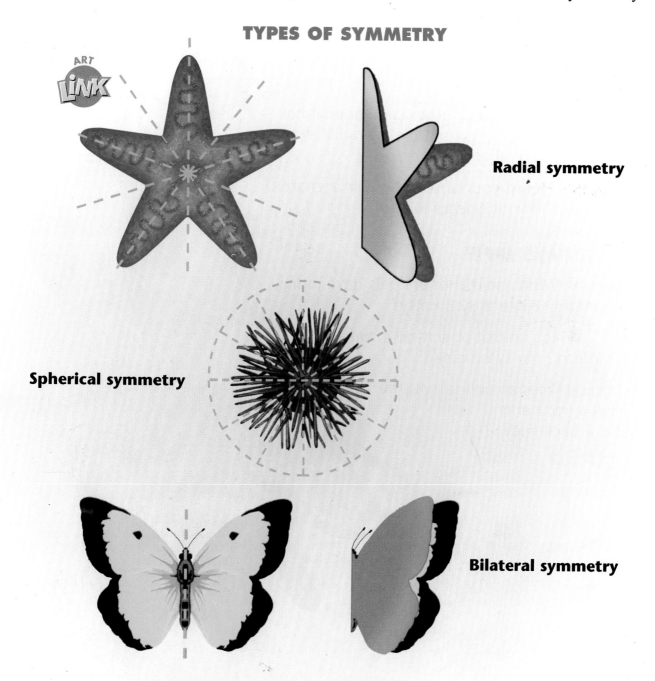

Radial symmetry

Spherical symmetry

Bilateral symmetry

215

Skill: Observing

ANIMAL SYMMETRY

A scientist's most important job is to *observe*, or look closely at, things. When you observe carefully, you often see things that you didn't know were there. You can practice your observation skills by looking for symmetry in different animals.

PROCEDURES

1. IDENTIFY Determine whether each animal has no symmetry, spherical symmetry, radial symmetry, or bilateral symmetry.

2. CLASSIFY Record your observations in a chart you create in your *Science Journal*.

CONCLUDE AND APPLY

1. IDENTIFY Which animal or animals have radial symmetry? Bilateral symmetry?

2. INFER Which animal or animals have spherical symmetry? No symmetry?

3. EXPLAIN Does an animal with radial symmetry have a front end and a back end? Explain.

FUNtastic Facts

It looks like a cross between a horse and a salad, but it's a fish. This foot-long animal—the leafy sea dragon—lives off the coast of Australia. Its wavy spines and leaflike appearance help conceal it on the seabed where it feeds. How might the fish's appearance help it survive?

Before you can learn about the different animals with which you share the world, you need to know how to identify an animal. Sometimes you can be confused or even fooled. Look at the organism in the picture. Do you think it is a plant or an animal? What characteristics would you look for to identify it as an animal?

Is this a plant or an animal? How could you find out?

REVIEW

1. What characteristics do all animals have?

2. What is the difference between a vertebrate and an invertebrate?

3. How is radial symmetry different from bilateral symmetry?

4. 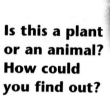 OBSERVE What kind of symmetry does your own body have? Draw a diagram that shows how you could fold your body so each half matched up.

5. CRITICAL THINKING *Analyze* What do you think would happen if one organism was removed from a food chain?

WHY IT MATTERS THINK ABOUT IT
How do you know that you are an animal?

WHY IT MATTERS WRITE ABOUT IT
What if you discovered a new organism? How would you test to see if it was an animal? Describe some observations and tests you would do.

Once in the Wild

Drawing of aurochs on cave wall

History of Science

Mouflon

Did you know that the kinds of animals people have as pets were once wild? So were the kinds of animals now raised on farms.

Thousands of years ago, people began domesticating wild animals, or adapting them to live with and around humans. Over time, the animals began to look and act different from their wild ancestors.

Wolves

The ancestor of the dog is the wolf. Wolves probably hung around ancient people to get leftover scraps of meat. Wolves lived and hunted in packs. Training them to live and hunt with humans was a natural development.

Ancient people hunted the cow's ancestor, the dangerous aurochs. They drew it on cave walls. Over time, people began keeping and raising cattle. They bred some cows to give milk and others to produce meat.

The mouflon is the sheep's ancestor. It still lives in parts of Europe and Asia. Before there were farms, humans gathered wool from wild sheep. Then people learned to raise sheep for wool. Trained dogs may have helped people round up the sheep.

Discussion
Starter

1 Why did people domesticate some animals?

2 How did domesticating wolves help people? How did it help wolves?

*inter*NET CONNECTION To learn more about domesticated animals, visit **www.mhschool.com/science** and enter the keyword **DOMESTIC.**

WHY IT MATTERS

Many interesting animals do not have a backbone.

SCIENCE WORDS

cnidarian an invertebrate with poison stingers on tentacles

mollusk a soft-bodied invertebrate

echinoderm a spiny-skinned invertebrate

endoskeleton an internal supporting structure

arthropod an invertebrate with jointed legs and a body that is divided into sections

exoskeleton a hard covering that protects an invertebrate's body

Animals Without Backbones

Have you ever seen an organism like this? What do you think it is?

In 1909 Charles Walcott, an American scientist, found an interesting rock. It contained more than 100 fossils of animals that lived about 530 million years ago! Some animals were very strange. One, like the fossil and model below, show five eyes. Another was so strange that scientists couldn't tell if it was right-side up or upside down!

EXPLORE

HYPOTHESIZE Many of Walcott's fossils were invertebrates. What characteristics do you think invertebrates have? Write a hypothesis in your *Science Journal*. How could you test your ideas?

Investigate the Characteristics of Invertebrates

Observe some invertebrates to find out what common characteristics they have.

MATERIALS

- living planarian
- living earthworm
- hand lens
- petri dish
- water
- damp paper towel
- toothpick
- *Science Journal*

PROCEDURES

1. **OBSERVE** Place the worm on the damp paper towel. Get a petri dish with a planarian (plə när′ē ən) in it from your teacher. Observe each organism with a hand lens. Record your observations in your *Science Journal*.

2. **OBSERVE** Gently touch the worm with your finger and the planarian with the toothpick. What do they do? Record your observations in your *Science Journal*.

3. **OBSERVE** What characteristics of the praying mantis and magnified hydra do you observe? Record your observations.

CONCLUDE AND APPLY

1. **DRAW CONCLUSIONS** What characteristics do you think invertebrates have? Make a list.

2. **COMPARE AND CONTRAST** Compare your list with those of other classmates. Based on your observations, make a class list of invertebrate characteristics.

3. **COMPARE AND CONTRAST** How are Walcott's ancient invertebrates like invertebrates that live today? Do they have similar characteristics? How are they different?

GOING FURTHER: Apply

4. **IDENTIFY** Think of other organisms that you would classify as invertebrates based on your observations. Make a list. Check your list as you continue this topic.

What Are the Characteristics of Invertebrates?

As the Explore Activity showed, invertebrates come in a variety of shapes and sizes. The one thing that they have in common is the one thing that they lack—a backbone.

Classifying Invertebrates

How many different types of animals do you think there are in the world? Would you believe more than one million? Keeping track of them must be a BIG JOB! The first step is to classify them into groups. Animals can be classified into two large groups—vertebrates and invertebrates.

Nearly 95 out of every 100 animals are invertebrates. Invertebrates are divided into smaller groups based on their characteristics. Each group is called a *phylum* (fī′ləm). You will learn about eight invertebrate phyla in this lesson. *Phyla* is the plural of *phylum*.

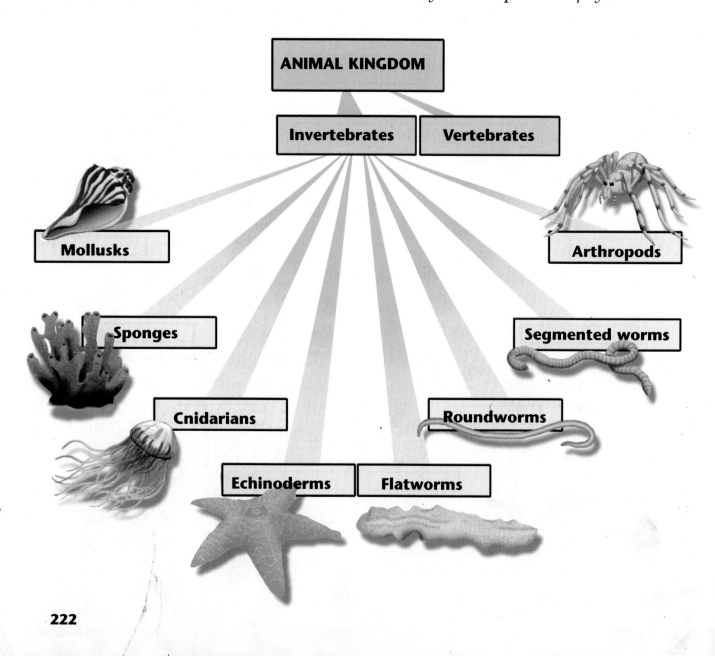

ANIMAL KINGDOM

Invertebrates   Vertebrates

Mollusks

Arthropods

Sponges

Segmented worms

Cnidarians

Roundworms

Echinoderms   Flatworms

Slime on the clown fish's body protects it from the sea anemone's stingers.

Some natural sponges are collected, dried, and sold for household use.

How Simple Is Simple?

Sponges

Sponges are the simplest invertebrates. You've already seen some sponges on page 214. A sponge's body is shaped like a sack, with an opening at the top. A sponge's body has no symmetry, is hollow, and does not have bones. A sponge's body is made of two cell layers with a jelly-like substance between the layers.

Water and food flow into the sponge through holes in its body. Water and wastes move out through the opening at the top.

A young sponge moves about until it finds a place to settle. An adult doesn't move from place to place. It filters the water passing through its body, eating bacteria, single-celled algae, and protists. A sponge can also grow back a missing part.

Cnidarians

Imagine an animal that shoots poison darts at its enemies! Cnidarians (nī dâr′ē ənz) are invertebrates that use poison stingers on tentacles to capture prey and for protection. Cnidarians, like sponges, have bodies that are two cell layers thick. However, they are more complex than sponges. Cnidarians have simple tissues and a mouth. They also have radial symmetry.

There are three major cnidarian groups, or classes. The hydra in the Explore Activity is one example. A hydra has a tube-shaped body and lives anchored to a surface. A jelly-fish has a body shaped like an umbrella and floats freely in the water. Sea anemones and corals make up the third group. Groups of coral form coral reefs.

How Are Worms Classified?

Flatworms

Worms are classified into several phyla. You will learn about three phyla.

The planaria in the Explore Activity is a type of flatworm. Flatworms are more complex than cnidarians or sponges, but they are the simplest worms. They have flat, ribbonlike bodies with a head and a tail. Their bodies have bilateral symmetry and are three cell layers thick.

One group of flatworms includes the planaria. They live in fresh water and eat food with a mouth. Undigested food and wastes pass out through the mouth, too. Another group includes parasites. They have no mouth or digestive system, and live and feed inside the bodies of other animals. They absorb digested food in the host's intestines.

An adult roundworm *Ascaris* can grow to 40 centimeters (16 inches) long. It can also lay up to 200,000 eggs a day!

Roundworms

Roundworms have a slender, rounded body with pointed ends. The *Ascaris* (as′kə rəs), hookworm, and vinegar eel are typical roundworms. Some roundworms, like the *Ascaris* and hookworm, are parasites. They cause illness in people and other animals. About 2,500 species of roundworms are parasites of plants and animals. Others, like the vinegar eel, do not depend on one particular organism for food or a place to live. They can live on land and in water.

Roundworms are more complex than flatworms. They have a one-way digestive system. In a one-way system, food comes into the body through one opening. Waste leaves through another opening at the opposite end of the animal's body.

A tapeworm is a parasite that can live in many host animals, including people!

Segmented Worms

Have you ever seen or touched an earthworm? Earthworms, sand-worms, and leeches are in the phylum of segmented worms.

Segmented worms have bodies that are divided into sections called segments. They have more complex bodies than other worms. Their blood travels through blood vessels. They have a three-layer body and bilateral symmetry. They have a digestive system with two openings. Food enters through the mouth. Wastes leave through an opening at the other end of the body.

The best-known segmented worm is the earthworm. An earthworm has a head end and a tail end. Every segment of its body, except for the first and last, has four pairs of tiny bristles. These bristles help the earthworm move through the soil.

An earthworm also has complex organ systems that keep it alive. One system breaks down food into nutrients the earthworm can use. Blood is pumped through blood vessels by five pairs of simple hearts. Nerves give the worm information about its surroundings.

THE EARTHWORM

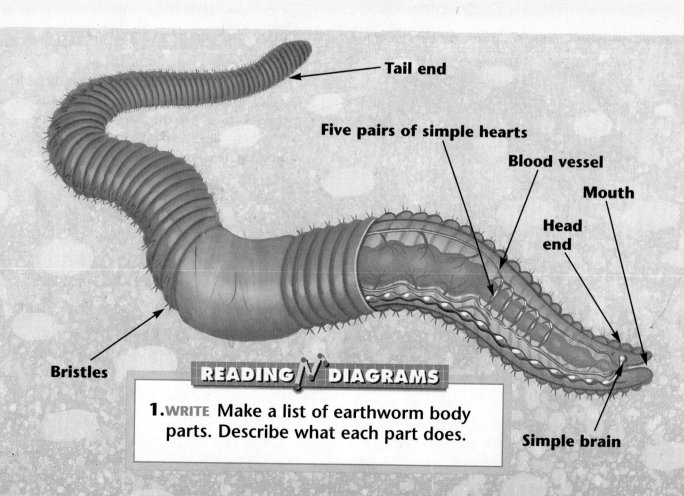

Tail end

Five pairs of simple hearts

Blood vessel

Mouth

Head end

Bristles

Simple brain

READING DIAGRAMS

1. WRITE Make a list of earthworm body parts. Describe what each part does.

What Are Some More-Complex Invertebrates?

Mollusks

Do you have a seashell collection? Most seashells come from **mollusks** (mol'əsks). Mollusks are soft-bodied invertebrates. Some, like snails and slugs, live on land. Others, like clams, oysters, and squids, live in water. Most mollusks have bilateral symmetry and many organ systems. Mollusks are among the largest, swiftest, and most intelligent sea animals.

Most mollusk classes have either one shell, two shells, or an inner shell. Snail-like mollusks have one shell. Clamlike mollusks have two shells. The group that includes the octopus and the squid has an inner shell.

Echinoderms

Have you ever seen a sea star? It is an **echinoderm** (i kī'nə dûrm'). Echinoderms are spiny-skinned animals. You can identify most echinoderms by their star design and spiny skin. Echinoderms include sea stars, sand dollars, sea cucumbers, and sea urchins.

Echinoderms have an internal supporting structure called an **endoskeleton** (en'dō skel'i tən). Usually the endoskeleton has many protective spines. A sea star has hard, rounded spines. A sea urchin has long, sharp spines. A sea cucumber does not have spines at all.

Many echinoderms move and grab things with tiny tube feet. Each tube foot is powered by suction.

This squid is a mollusk that lives in water. There are more than 70,000 different types of mollusks.

The sea star uses its arms and tube feet to pry open the oyster. Then it turns its own stomach inside out. It sticks its stomach out to digest the oyster.

What Is the Largest Phylum of Invertebrates?

The largest invertebrate phylum is **arthropods** (är′thrə podz′). It is also the largest of all animal phyla. Arthropods live almost everywhere on Earth. Scientists think there are more than a million arthropod species!

Arthropods have jointed legs and a body that is divided into sections. Some arthropods breathe with gills. Others have an open-tube breathing system.

Arthropods have a hard skeleton on the outside of their bodies called an **exoskeleton** (ek′sō skel′i tən). It protects them and keeps them from drying out. Exoskeletons are made of a light but tough material called *chitin* (kī′tin). An exoskeleton does not grow, but is shed by a process called molting (mōl′ting).

There are more arthropods than all other types of animals combined! You will learn about four main arthropod classes— arachnids (ə rak′nidz), centipedes and milli- pedes, crustaceans (krus tā′shənz), and insects.

Brain Power

Design your own invertebrate. Give your animal at least one characteristic from each phylum. Draw it, and list its characteristics.

Arachnids

Includes: Spiders, mites, scorpions, ticks, daddy-longlegs
Head: No antennae
Legs and Body: Four pairs of legs, two-section body, up to eight eyes
Home: A wide variety of habitats
Food: Most arachnids are hunters, mainly eating insects.
Special Features: Many arachnids are poisonous, including spiders and scorpions. Some arachnids, such as spiders, can spin webs to trap their food.
Fact: Not all spiders are dangerous. Many are helpful to people. They eat insects and other pests.

Scorpions feed on spiders and insects. Their sting can be dangerous to people.

227

Crustaceans

Includes: Crabs, lobsters, shrimp, barnacles, crayfish, sow bugs

Head: Jawlike structures for crushing food and chewing; two pairs of antennae for sensing

Legs and Body: Ten or fewer legs, including claws. The body has sections.

Home: Some have ocean and freshwater homes. A few live on land.

Food: Dead animal remains, seaweed, other leftovers

Special Features: Crabs and lobsters can have huge claws. One claw is often much bigger than the other. They use their claws to fight and to scare off predators.

Fact: Millions of shrimp, crabs, and lobsters are eaten every year. Billions of tiny copepods (kō′pə podz) live in the sea. They are the main food for whales and other animals.

Centipedes and Millipedes

Includes: Centipedes, millipedes

Legs and Body: Centipedes: usually less than 100 legs. Millipedes: more than a hundred legs. Both have long, thin, segmented bodies.

Home: Under rocks, in rotting wood and dark, damp places

Food: Centipedes eat worms, slugs, and insects. Millipedes are plant eaters.

How to Tell Them Apart: Centipedes have one pair of legs per segment and can move quickly. Millipedes have two pairs of legs per segment and move slowly.

Facts: Although *centi-* means "100" in Latin, most centipedes have only 30 legs. Some centipedes have poison claws. A millipede's legs move in a wavelike motion.

Lobsters can live 50 years and grow to lengths of 60 centimeters (2 feet) or more.

Scolopendra (skä′lə pen′drə) centipedes can grow to a length of 30 centimeters (1 foot)!

Insects

Includes: Beetles, flies, bees, ants, mosquitoes, butterflies, dragonflies, fleas, termites, many others

Head: One pair of antennae

Legs and Body: Three pairs of legs; one or two pairs of wings; three body sections: head, thorax, abdomen

Home: All land habitats, air and freshwater habitats

Food: Other animals and plants

Special Features: A special tube system for breathing; compound eyes made of hundreds of lenses.

Facts: There are more different kinds of insects than there are all other kinds of animals. The first insects appeared about 350 million years ago. Flight speed can reach 58 kilometers (36 miles) per hour. At that speed how far could an insect fly in three hours?

MATH LINK

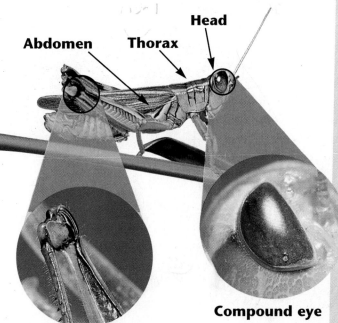

Abdomen   Thorax   Head

Compound eye

Jointed leg

QUICK LAB

Classifying Invertebrates

HYPOTHESIZE What characteristics would you use to classify these invertebrates? Write a hypothesis in your *Science Journal*.

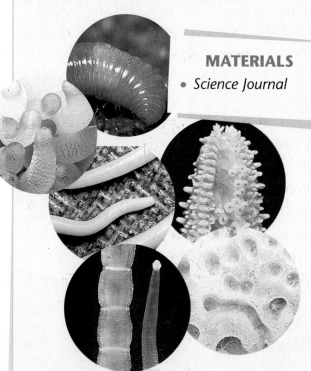

MATERIALS
- *Science Journal*

PROCEDURES

1. **IDENTIFY** Use the clues in each picture to identify which type of invertebrate is shown.

2. **COMMUNICATE** Make a table in your *Science Journal* to show how you classified each picture. List key characteristics for each phylum.

CONCLUDE AND APPLY

EXPLAIN How do you know the phylum that each animal belongs to?

What Invertebrates Live in Coral Reefs?

Imagine an animal that forms its own island! Corals do. Coral is made by colonies of polyps. Each polyp looks like a tiny sea anemone. For protection polyps build cup-shaped skeletons around their bodies. When polyps die the skeletons remain. After many years they pile up. A coral reef or island forms.

Coral reefs contain invertebrates of almost every size and shape. A typical reef will have anemones, prawns, worms, lobsters, sea stars, jellyfish, and giant clams. Reefs also have more that 2,000 different kinds of fish—many with brilliant colors and unusual shapes. Coral reefs are among the richest communities on Earth.

Coral reefs are delicate. Coral needs warm, clean water to grow. Unfortunately many coral reefs are threatened by pollution, souvenir hunters, ships, and boats. People take chunks of a coral reef as souvenirs. Ships crash into reefs. Small boats damage reefs with heavy anchors. It may take hundreds of years for the damaged reef to grow back.

What can we do to help protect coral reefs? We can stop pollution, boat carefully, not buy coral souvenirs, and learn more about reefs.

The Great Barrier Reef, located near Australia, is about 2,000 kilometers (1,240 miles) long.

Did you know that most animals on Earth are invertebrates? Between 90 and 95 of every 100 animal species are invertebrates! Invertebrates are important because they are a food source for other animals. People also depend on them for many things. In some parts of the world, mollusks like squids, clams, and oysters are important foods. Earthworms help enrich soil. This helps healthy plants grow. Coral reefs protect islands and provide homes to animals. Water-absorbing sponges have many household uses.

Arthropods also help people. Most people are not allergic to the chitin in an arthropod's exoskeleton. That is why chitin is often used to make contact lenses, artificial skin, and thread for stitches!

Chitin from arthropod exoskeletons has many interesting uses.

REVIEW

1. What is an invertebrate? How can you identify invertebrates?

2. How are segmented worms different from other types of worms?

3. How are echinoderms similar to and different from arthropods?

4. **COMMUNICATE** What kinds of things threaten coral reefs? How can reefs be saved?

5. **CRITICAL THINKING** *Analyze* Which invertebrate phyla have the simplest body systems? Which have the most complex systems?

WHY IT MATTERS THINK ABOUT IT
What do you think might happen if all the earthworms in an area suddenly died?

WHY IT MATTERS WRITE ABOUT IT
What if all invertebrates suddenly disappeared? How do you think this would affect life on Earth?

CONTROL
WITHOUT CHEMICALS

What's another name for an insect or a bug? A pest! Farmers know what pests can do to their crops. Some pests stop plant growth. Others cause spots, cracks, lumps, or other marks on fruits and vegetables. How can anyone get rid of these pests? One way is to spray crops with chemical pesticides.

Unfortunately, pesticides themselves are a problem. They can kill fish, bees and other helpful insects, and can make humans sick, too. That's why it's important to carefully wash any pesticides off fruits and vegetables before you eat them.

Can you safely control pests? Sure, paper or plastic around fruit trees will stop some insects. Electric light traps can destroy other pests. Scientists use radiation on male insects. When the males mate, any eggs the females lay won't hatch! That cuts down on the pest population.

Science, Technology and Society

Insects can also be used to kill other insects. Some wasps eat the larva of problem insects. Some bacteria and other organisms also feed on problem insects.

Scientists continue to look for ways to eliminate pests and help useful insects survive. It's important to control insects, but scientists know it's more important to keep a balance in nature.

Better insect control could help to cut down America's use of pesticides. Then we could grow pest-free food and also keep harmful chemicals out of our food, our water, and our air.

DISCUSSION STARTER

1. How can insects be controlled without using pesticides?

2. Pesticides can be dangerous. Why do people still use them?

To learn more about harmful pesticides, visit *www.mhschool.com/science* and enter the keyword PESTS.

*inter*NET
CONNECTION

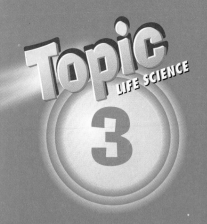
SCIENCE WORDS

cold-blooded describes an animal with a body temperature that changes with its surroundings

warm-blooded describes an animal with a constant body temperature

amphibian a cold-blooded vertebrate that spends part of its life in water and part of its life on land

reptile a cold-blooded vertebrate that lives on land and has waterproof skin with scales or plates

mammal a warm-blooded vertebrate with hair or fur that feeds milk to its young

Animals with Backbones

Did you know that you are classified into the same large group as fish, toads, snakes, birds, and rabbits? What could you all possibly have in common?

All these animals have a backbone. They are classified into a large group known as vertebrates. However, these animals are also very different from one another. These differences are used to make smaller groups.

EXPLORE

HYPOTHESIZE What characteristics are used to classify vertebrates? Write a hypothesis in your *Science Journal*. How could you test your ideas?

Investigate What Vertebrates Are Like

Observe some vertebrates. What characteristics set each of these animals apart from the others?

PROCEDURES

OBSERVE As you observe each animal, look for answers to these questions. Record your observations in your *Science Journal*.

a. Where does it live—in water, on land, or both?

b. What color is it?

c. What kind of outer covering does it have?

d. What body parts does it have?

e. Do you see eyes, ears, nostrils, or other sense organs?

f. How does it move?

MATERIALS

- goldfish
- frog
- chameleon, turtle, or lizard
- parakeet
- hamster, gerbil, or guinea pig
- hand lens
- *Science Journal*

CONCLUDE AND APPLY

1. COMMUNICATE What major characteristics did you observe in each animal?

2. COMPARE What are the main differences between a fish and a frog?

3. COMPARE What are the major differences between a bird and a hamster?

GOING FURTHER: Problem Solving

4. IDENTIFY Which animal are you most like in this activity? Why do you think so?

235

What Are Vertebrates Like?

The Explore Activity showed several vertebrates. Although they have very different characteristics, they all have a backbone that is part of the endoskeleton made of bones.

An endoskeleton has two important jobs. First, it supports the body. It also protects the soft inner organs.

Classifying Vertebrates

The animal kingdom is divided into the invertebrate phylum and the chordate phylum. Vertebrates are part of the chordate phylum. Most chordates are vertebrates.

Vertebrates are divided into seven classes based on characteristics such as body structure.

Vertebrates are also classified by how they control body temperature.

Fish, amphibians, and reptiles are **cold-blooded** (kōld'blud'id). A cold-blooded animal gets heat from outside its body. Its body temperature changes with the temperature of its surroundings.

Birds and mammals are **warm-blooded** (wôrm'blud'id). Their body temperature doesn't change much. They use the energy from food to keep a constant body temperature.

Brain Power

How is an endoskeleton different from an exoskeleton?

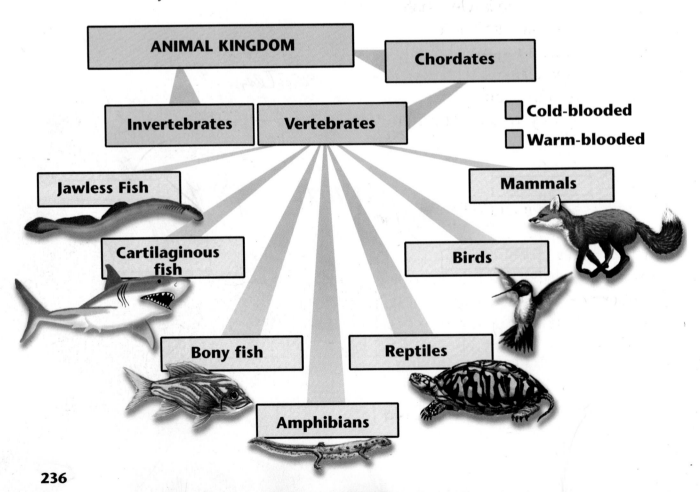

ANIMAL KINGDOM

Chordates

Invertebrates

Vertebrates

☐ Cold-blooded
☐ Warm-blooded

Jawless Fish

Mammals

Cartilaginous fish

Birds

Bony fish

Reptiles

Amphibians

What Are the Characteristics of Fish?

There are three classes of fish—jawless fish, *cartilaginous* (kär'tə laj'ə nəs) *fish*, and bony fish. All fish have several characteristics.

- Fish are cold-blooded vertebrates that live in fresh or salt water.
- Fish have streamlined bodies and gills for breathing.
- Gills take oxygen out of water the way your lungs take oxygen out of the air. They also get rid of carbon dioxide.

Jawless Fish

What is the first thing you notice about these fish? They do not look anything like other fish! These eel-like animals are jawless fish.

Jawless fish are soft, slimy, and vicious. Instead of jaws they have powerful suckerlike mouths. A jawless fish uses its mouth to attach itself to its prey. It uses a horn tooth to cut a hole in its prey. Then it slowly sucks out the fluids and insides of the prey.

Jawless fish include lampreys and hagfish. These fish have no scales and unusual fins. Their bodies have a rubbery cartilage skeleton. Cartilage is a tough, flexible tissue. Your outer ears are made of cartilage.

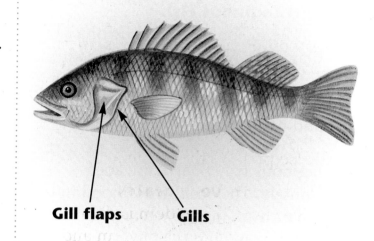

GENERAL FISH CHARACTERISTICS

Gill flaps **Gills**

Most lampreys, like these, live in fresh water.

What Are the Other Classes of Fish?

Cartilaginous Fish

The major characteristic of a cartilaginous fish is a skeleton made entirely of cartilage. Cartilaginous fish also have movable jaws, fins, and tough, sandpaper-like skin.

Rays, skates and sharks are cartilaginous fish. Sharks are keen hunters. They can smell blood in the water from many meters away. With their razor-sharp teeth, sharks can tear apart their prey in seconds. Most sharks, however, do not attack people. They feed on small fish and invertebrates.

Bony Fish

Have you ever gone fishing? If you ever caught a fish, it most likely was a fish from this class. Bony fish are the largest vertebrate class. They have jaws and skeletons made of bone. More than 21,000 different kinds of bony fish swim both in the ocean and in fresh water.

What makes bony fish so successful? Tough, overlapping scales protect their skin. Gill flaps protect their gills. Fins help the fish steer in the water.

Bony fish have different body plans. Predator fish have sleek bodies and powerful muscles. Reef fish have box-shaped bodies that fit in small spaces. Bottom dwellers are flat. Eels have snakelike shapes to fit into tight spaces.

Rays are bottom dwellers that eat invertebrates. This manta ray can grow to a length of more than 6 meters (20 feet).

The cichlid (sik'lid) fish keeps its eggs in its mouth until the fish hatch. What type of advantage does this give the young fish?

What Are Amphibians?

Have you ever seen a frog, toad, or salamander? If you have, how would you describe it? Frogs, toads, and salamanders are **amphibians** (am fib′ē ənz). An amphibian is a cold-blooded vertebrate that spends part of its life in water and part of its life on land.

Amphibians start out their lives in the water. A tadpole is a young frog. It has gills and fins. It cannot live on land because it has no lungs or legs. Over time the tadpole turns into a frog. It loses its gills and breathes through lungs and its skin. It also loses its fins and grows legs.

Although adult frogs live most of their lives on land, they are never far from water. An amphibian's skin will dry out without water. That is why amphibians live in wet or damp places.

Do you know how to tell a frog from a toad? This table will help you.

This is a young tadpole.

Frog or Toad?		
	Frog	**Toad**
Body	sleek	plump
Movement	jump	hop
Skin	moist and smooth	dry and bumpy

With time a tadpole changes and grows into a frog.

READING ⋀ TABLES

WRITE Write a short paragraph comparing and contrasting the characteristics of a frog and a toad.

What Are the Characteristics of Reptiles?

Do you think that a snake has slimy skin? Some people think that **reptiles** (rep′ təlz) like snakes are slimy. In fact reptile skin is dry. Reptiles have skin with scales or larger plates. Strong, waterproof skin helped reptiles become the first vertebrate group to live on land.

Reptiles are cold-blooded animals with a backbone and an endoskeleton. How could they survive on land when other vertebrates could not? Reptiles have lungs. Their skin keeps water from escaping out of their bodies. Their eggs are tougher than amphibian eggs. All of these traits helped reptiles become successful on land.

Reptiles can be classified into four smaller groups, called orders. There are four main reptile orders—tuataras (tü′ə tär′əz), turtles, lizards and snakes, and alligators and crocodiles.

Tuataras are the smallest order. There are only two members, both of which are endangered. Tuataras live on islands off New Zealand.

Turtles and tortoises are among the longest-living animals. Some tortoises live more than 100 years. Sea turtles can swim at speeds of 9 kilometers (6 miles) per hour.

Lizards and snakes outnumber the other groups. Most lizards have limbs, although a few types do not. Lizards are insect eaters. Snakes are meat eaters. Some snakes kill their prey by squeezing them, others use poison. More than 500 species of snakes are poisonous.

Dinosaurs were reptiles that walked on Earth for 150 million years. They disappeared about 66 million years ago. Today crocodiles and alligators are their closest living relatives. A large adult crocodile can weigh as much as 900 kilograms (1 ton) and eat prey as large as deer. Without a backbone, these large animals would not be able to support their weight on land.

Tuataras are not very different from their prehistoric ancestors.

What Are the Characteristics of Birds?

Birds are vertebrates with several distinct characteristics.

- Birds have feathers. Feathers are light but very warm. Some birds have feathers with dull colors. This allows them to blend into their surroundings and hide from enemies. Others have bright colors to attract mates.

- Birds have beaks without teeth. Some birds, like finches, have a beak designed for eating seeds. A meat-eating bird like a hawk has a sharp, curved beak for tearing flesh. A flamingo has a beak designed for catching fish.

- Birds have two legs with clawed feet. Birds have scales on their feet, like reptiles. A bird's feet are well designed for its needs. Hawks have sharp claws for catching and tearing prey. A penguin has flat feet for walking. Birds like swifts have tiny feet. They spend most of their time flying, not perching.

- Birds are warm-blooded like you.

- Birds lay eggs with strong shells. Most birds sit on their eggs to keep them warm until they hatch.

- All birds have wings. However, not all birds can fly. Penguins and ostriches cannot fly, but this is not a problem. Ostriches can run at speeds up to 72 kilometers (45 miles) per hour! Penguins are excellent swimmers.

The wings of a frigate bird measure more than 200 centimeters (80 inches) across, yet its entire skeleton weighs only a little more than 100 grams (4 ounces)! Frigate birds can fly at speeds of more than 150 kilometers (95 miles) per hour.

- Most birds can fly. A bird's body is designed for flight. Bird bones are hollow and thin. Bird lungs and flight muscles are powerful. Bird feathers are strong and light. They fit together to form an air-tight wing surface. Together these features help birds fly.

There are four main bird groups. One group includes perching birds, like the robin. The second group includes water birds, like the duck. The third group includes predator, or hunting, birds, like the hawk. The fourth group includes flight-less birds, like the penguin.

What Are the Characteristics of Mammals?

How would you describe the characteristics of a human? Make a list. The characteristics you named describe a **mammal** (mam' əl). You and about 4,000 different vertebrates are classified as mammals.

What is a mammal? A mammal is a warm-blooded vertebrate with three major characteristics. How do the characteristics you named compare with this list?

1. Most mammals have body hair or fur.
2. Females feed milk to their young.
3. All but a few mammals are born live rather than hatching from an egg.

On land the fastest animal is a mammal, the cheetah. The tallest land animal is a mammal, the giraffe. The largest and heaviest creature in the animal kingdom is also a mammal, the blue whale.

Types of Mammals

There are three basic types of mammals. Mammals that lay eggs make up one group. Members of this group include the platypus and spiny anteater. After the young hatch, they drink milk made by the female's body.

The second group includes animals with pouches. Members of this group include koalas, kangaroos,

Mammals like this platypus and her young live in distant parts of Tasmania, Australia, and New Guinea.

and opossums. The female has a pouch that holds the immature offspring until it is fully developed.

The third group includes animals like cats, horses, whales, bats, mice, apes, and you. All of these animals have offspring that develop inside the female's body. Most mammals are born at a well-developed stage. Larger mammals generally develop inside the female's body longer than smaller mammals. For example, rabbits have offspring after 30 days. A rhinoceros takes over a year to develop before it is born.

Where Do Mammals Live?

Mammals live in almost every kind of habitat and move in almost every kind of way. The horse lives on land and walks on legs. The walrus lives in salt water and swims. Bats live in caves and fly through the air. Gophers are mammals that live underground. Otters are mammals that live in fresh water and swim.

An interesting mammal from the past lived on what is now Seymour Island, near the Antarctic Peninsula. This mammal was a giant relative of the armadillo. It had an armored tail and was about the size and shape of a small car! The plates that covered its body were different sizes. Some were as small as a saucer, others were as big as a dinner plate. Scientists think that this animal lived near streams and ate plants. Mammals really are an interesting class of vertebrates!

This ancient mammal was nearly as big as a small car!

QUICK LAB

Classifying Vertebrates

HYPOTHESIZE What characteristics would you use to classify these vertebrates? Write a hypothesis in your *Science Journal.*

MATERIALS
• *Science Journal*

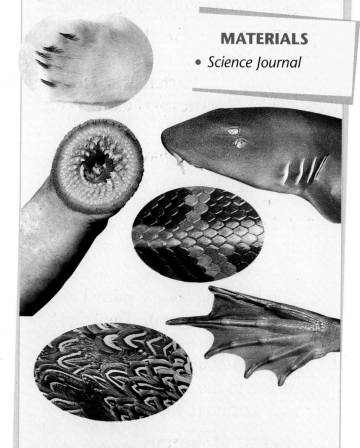

PROCEDURES

1. **CLASSIFY** Use the clues in each picture to help you classify each animal.

2. **COMMUNICATE** Make a table in your *Science Journal* to show how you classified each picture.

CONCLUDE AND APPLY

EXPLAIN How do you know which class each animal belongs to?

How Can Animals Help People?

People are warm-blooded mammals who sometimes get ill or become sad. When people have troubles, animals can often help.

Duffy is a dog who is part of a program called Pet Partners. Every week Duffy and other Pet Partners go to hospitals and other places. Their job is to help people who are very sick, sad, or lonely feel better.

How did Duffy get to become a Pet Partner? It wasn't easy. First, Duffy needed to pass many different tests. Testers put food in front of Duffy. They bounced balls in front of him. They even brought in other dogs to distract him. In each case Duffy had to stay still until his trainer told him it was okay to move.

After Duffy passed all his tests, he needed to be trained. During his training Duffy learned how to help people. He learned to be patient with strangers. He learned how to be gentle with young children and very old people. After four months of training, Duffy was ready to be a Pet Partner.

Pet Partners work in hospitals and nursing homes. Do Pet Partners really help people? Take a look at the smile you see on this page!

Duffy wears a special uniform. He has a blue harness and a special badge that says, "I am a visiting dog."

The blue whale can weigh up to 150 metric tons (165 tons). How many pounds is that?

WHY IT MATTERS

How does a backbone make a difference? Think about the invertebrates and vertebrates you have studied. Invertebrates are generally small. Many vertebrates are very large, like the rhinoceros, the great white shark, and the polar bear. This is no coincidence. Backbones and endoskeletons give animals support. This support allows vertebrates to grow to very large sizes. That is why the largest animals on Earth are vertebrates.

REVIEW

1. How are vertebrates different from invertebrates?

2. What is the difference between the three types of fish?

3. How can a Pet Partner help people?

4. **EXPLAIN** Why is a platypus classified as a mammal even though it lays eggs?

5. **CRITICAL THINKING** *Analyze* A newt looks like a lizard, but it is an amphibian. What traits must a newt have?

WHY IT MATTERS THINK ABOUT IT Droopy Dogs are made only out of clay. They have a problem—they droop. Big Droopy Dogs can't hold up their own weight. How could you fix them?

WHY IT MATTERS WRITE ABOUT IT Write a short paragraph about how you would fix Droopy Dogs. Try it. Does it work?

READING SKILL Make an outline showing how animals are classified as invertebrates or vertebrates. Include an example of each and its characteristics.

HELPING ENDANGERED ANIMALS

What's that gliding through the water? It's a manatee. This mammal spends its days slowly munching grasses in the water. That's why manatees are also called "sea cows!"

Unfortunately, people hunted the manatee. Its tough hide was used for making shoes and canoes. Oil from its body was burned in lamps. Its bones had many uses, and the animal could be eaten.

In Florida, where most manatees live, it's illegal to hunt them. Still, manatees are endangered. Trash poisons their water. Fishing nets trap them. Boat propellers scar or kill them.

Many manatees are identified by their scars. Some are equipped with radio transmitters so researchers can track them. When researchers find sick or injured manatees, they nurse them back to health.

Making a Difference

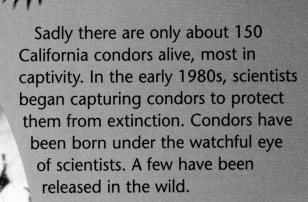

The California condor is the largest flying land bird in North America. It has a wingspan of about 2.5–3.1 meters (8–10 feet). Once thousands of these graceful giants soared over the wilds of southern California. Now much of that territory has been developed. Hunting and poisoning by pesticides also pushed the condor close to extinction.

Sadly there are only about 150 California condors alive, most in captivity. In the early 1980s, scientists began capturing condors to protect them from extinction. Condors have been born under the watchful eye of scientists. A few have been released in the wild.

DISCUSSION STARTER

1. What is killing manatees today?

2. Why would it be important to track manatees and condors?

To learn more about manatees and condors, visit *www.mhschool.com/science* and enter the keyword INDANGER.

*inter*NET
CONNECTION

SCIENCE WORDS

arthropod p. 227   food web p. 213

cnidarian p. 223   invertebrate p. 214

cold-   mollusk p. 226

   blooded p. 236   symmetry p. 214

echinoderm p. 226   vertebrate p. 214

endo-   warm-

   skeleton p. 226   blooded p. 236

exoskeleton p. 227

USING SCIENCE WORDS

Number a paper from 1 to 10. Fill in 1 to 5 with words from the list above.

1. An animal that has a constant body temperature is called ___?___.

2. One example of a soft-bodied invertebrate is a(n) ___?___.

3. An animal with a backbone is called a(n) ___?___.

4. An inner supporting structure is called a(n) ___?___.

5. The hard covering that protects an invertebrate's body is a(n) ___?___.

6–10. **Pick five words from the list above that were not used in 1 to 5, and use each in a sentence.**

UNDERSTANDING SCIENCE IDEAS

11. What is the difference between a mammal and a reptile?

12. What are the major characteristics of birds?

USING IDEAS AND SKILLS

13. **OBSERVE** Make a chart that shows the symmetry of ten different animals.

14. **READING SKILL: OUTLINING** Scientists group living things according to similar characteristics. Explain how this helps them study all the animals in the world. Make an outline of the groups and characteristics scientists use.

15. **THINKING LIKE A SCIENTIST** All very large invertebrates, like the giant squid, live underwater. Can you explain why they don't live on land?

PROBLEMS and PUZZLES

Thumbprint Symmetry Use an inkpad and white paper to make a thumbprint. Does it have symmetry? Use the reflection of a mirror to find out. Stand a mirror with a straight edge in the middle of the print. Try this method to see if other natural objects have symmetry.

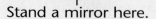

Stand a mirror here.

CHAPTER 8
SEE HOW THEY WORK

How do you think this animal gets food? What parts of its body does the animal use to get food? Besides getting food, what else does this animal do to survive? How do the organs in its body work together keeping this animal alive? In this chapter, you'll find out how organs work together.

In this chapter you will locate details that support a main idea. As an example you may use details to describe how a fish can get oxygen underwater.

WHY IT MATTERS

Organ systems work together to keep animals alive.

SCIENCE WORDS

circulatory system the organ system that moves blood through the body

respiratory system the organ system that brings oxygen to body cells and removes waste gas

excretory system the organ system that removes liquid wastes

digestive system the organ system that breaks down food for fuel

skeletal system the organ system made up of bones

muscular system the organ system made up of muscles that move bones

nervous system the organ system that controls all other body systems

Organ Systems

How are a fish and a frog similar and different? Think about their bodies and where they live. The frog is a more complex animal than a fish. A frog breathes with lungs instead of gills. A frog has limbs instead of fins. A frog can live both on land and in water. Do you think a frog also has more complex organs and organ systems than a fish?

EXPLORE

HYPOTHESIZE **Which do you think is more complex—a frog's heart or a fish's heart? Write a hypothesis in your** *Science Journal.* **How could you test your ideas?**

EXPLORE ACTIVITY

Investigate How Blood Travels

Compare models of fish and amphibian hearts.

PROCEDURES

1. Label each small cup "atrium." Label each large cup "ventricle."

2. MAKE A MODEL: FISH HEART Tape the paper circle with one flap over the top of one ventricle. Center the top of an atrium over the flap in the circle. Tape it to the paper.

3. Label one straw "From gills and body." Place it in the hole in the bottom of the atrium. Label another straw "To gills and body." Place it in the hole in the bottom of the ventricle. Draw the model in your *Science Journal*.

4. MAKE A MODEL: AMPHIBIAN HEART Tape the paper circle with two flaps over the top of a ventricle. Center the top of an atrium over each flap. Tape the cups to the paper.

5. Label one straw "From the body." Place it in the hole in the bottom of the right cup. Label another straw "From lungs." Place it in the hole in the bottom of the left cup. Label the third straw "To lungs and body." Place it in the hole in the paper between the two small cups. Draw the model.

CONCLUDE AND APPLY

COMPARE AND CONTRAST How are the fish heart and the amphibian heart alike? Different?

This is a model of a fish heart.

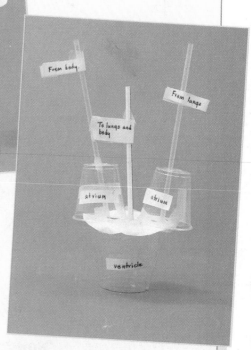

This is a model of an amphibian heart.

How Does Blood Travel?

Do you know what blood is? Blood is a liquid tissue made up mostly of red blood cells, white blood cells, and a liquid called *plasma* (plaz′mə). Blood carries food, oxygen, and water to the body's cells and removes wastes from cells.

The heart is part of an organ system called the **circulatory system** (sûr′kyə lə tôr′ē sis′təm). The circulatory system's job is to move blood through the body.

Sponges and cnidarians don't need a circulatory system because materials can move freely in and out of each thin body layer. Insects and other invertebrates have open circulatory systems. The heart simply bathes the tissues in blood, which slowly drains back to the heart.

All vertebrates have a closed circulatory system, where blood travels through tubes called blood vessels. Some of the more complex invertebrates, like the earthworm, also have a closed system.

As the Explore Activity showed, complex animals have complex hearts. A fish has a simple heart with two parts, or chambers. It allows blood carrying wastes and oxygen to mix. An amphibian has a heart with three chambers. The most complex animals, mammals, have hearts with four chambers. They do not allow blood carrying waste gas to mix with blood carrying oxygen.

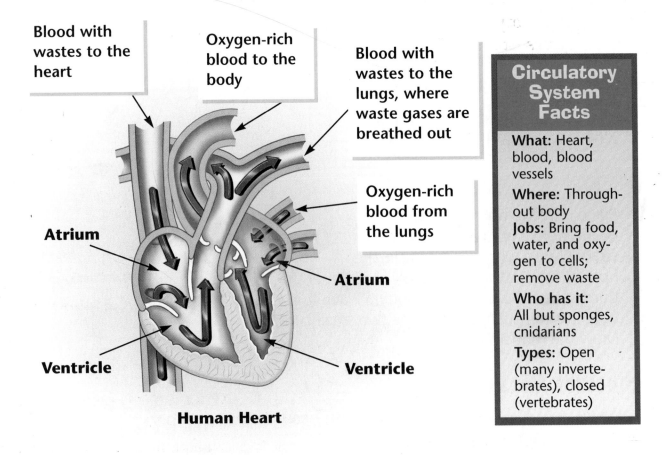

Blood with wastes to the heart

Oxygen-rich blood to the body

Blood with wastes to the lungs, where waste gases are breathed out

Oxygen-rich blood from the lungs

Atrium

Atrium

Ventricle

Ventricle

Human Heart

Circulatory System Facts

What: Heart, blood, blood vessels

Where: Through-out body

Jobs: Bring food, water, and oxygen to cells; remove waste

Who has it: All but sponges, cnidarians

Types: Open (many invertebrates), closed (vertebrates)

How Do Animals Get Oxygen?

Cells need the oxygen carried by blood to get energy from food. The **respiratory system** (res'pər ə tôr'ē sis'təm) brings oxygen to body cells and removes the waste gas carbon dioxide. Respiratory systems become more complex in more complex animals.

Most invertebrates don't have a specialized respiratory system at all. Their bodies usually are small, and gases can easily move in and out of tissues, even through their skin. An insect's exoskeleton has holes connected to tubes that bring oxygen to different tissues.

Larger, more complex animals and animals with waterproof skin need a respiratory system. Each has a respiratory system well designed for its body and where it lives. Fish and young amphibians, such as tadpoles, have gills that take oxygen out of the water and get rid of carbon dioxide. Adult amphibians breathe through both their skin and lungs.

How You Breathe

What do you think causes you to breathe in and out between 12 and 16 times per minute? The plastic bottle on the right is a good model.

Mammals have a muscle called the *diaphragm* (dī'ə fram') below the lungs. When relaxed the diaphragm pushes up. Air leaves the lungs. When the diaphragm flattens and pulls down, the lungs fill with air.

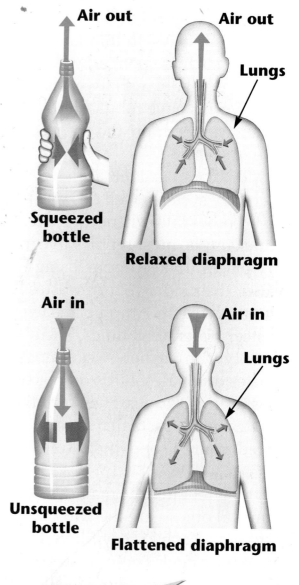

Air out — Air out — Lungs

Squeezed bottle

Relaxed diaphragm

Air in — Air in — Lungs

Unsqueezed bottle

Flattened diaphragm

Brain Power

Why does air leave the lungs when the diaphragm relaxes?

How Do Liquid Wastes Leave the Body?

Animals create many types of wastes. The waste gas carbon dioxide is removed from the body by the lungs. Liquid wastes, created when cells break down chemicals, are removed by the **excretory system** (ek′skri tôr′ē sis′təm).

Animals get rid of liquid wastes in different ways. In thin-layered animals such as sponges, wastes simply wash away. Flatworms and earthworms have tubules into which wastes drain and are passed from the body.

More complex animals have excretory systems well designed for their bodies and where they live. For example, most reptiles live in dry places. To keep from losing water, their kidneys turn wastes into a dry paste. Amphibians live in or near water at all times. Their *urine* (yùr′in) is more wet than the wastes of reptiles. Birds do not store wastes in a bladder. They turn their wastes into a paste that is eliminated from the body with solid wastes.

In vertebrates the main waste-removal organs are the two *kidneys* (kid′nēz). Each kidney filters wastes from the blood. These wastes are concentrated into a liquid called urine. Urine is stored in the *bladder* (blad′ər) until it is removed from the body.

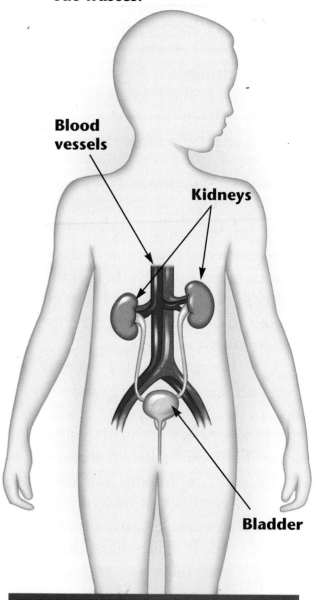

Blood from the body enters the kidneys. The kidneys filter out wastes.

Blood vessels

Kidneys

Bladder

Excretory System Facts

What: Kidneys, special cells, tubules

Where: Different body locations

Jobs: Remove liquid wastes from the body

Who has it: Vertebrates, some invertebrates

Works with: The circulatory system to filter blood

How Is Food Broken Down?

Before body cells can use food for energy, it must be broken down. That is the job of the **digestive system** (di jes'tiv sis'təm).

In simple animals like sponges and cnidarians, cells along the body walls break down food into small particles. These cells transfer the particles to cells in the body.

Other simple invertebrates, like some flatworms, have a digestive system with one opening. Food enters through the mouth. Wastes and undigested food leave through the same opening.

A segmented worm has a digestive system with two openings. Food enters through the mouth. Wastes exit through the other end of the body.

Birds do not chew food. A muscular organ called a *gizzard* (giz'ərd) stores pebbles that grind food before it enters the rest of the system.

What happens to your food?

HUMAN DIGESTIVE SYSTEM

1 Food is broken down by teeth and saliva.

2 It passes to the stomach through the *esophagus.*

3 Acids break down the food. Stomach muscles mix it.

4 Food passes into the *small intestine.* Chemicals from the liver and other glands mix with the food. When it is digested, nutrients are absorbed into the blood through the small intestine's walls.

5 Solid wastes are passed to the *large intestine.*

Mouth

Esophagus

Liver

Stomach

Large intestine

Small intestine

Digestive System Facts

What: Teeth, saliva, esophagus, stomach, intestines, liver, glands

Where: Hollow tube through body

Job: Break down food

How: Chewing, grinding, squeezing, chemicals

Types: One or two openings

Who has it: Vertebrates, most invertebrates

Works with: Circulatory system

How Do Animals Move?

A vertebrate's bones form its **skeletal system** (skel′i təl sis′təm). Bones are living tissues. Minerals make bones hard. The skeletal system supports the body and protects body organs. It works with the **muscular system** (mus′kyə lər sis′təm) to allow a vertebrate to move. The muscular system is made of the body's muscles. Muscles are tough tissues that can move.

How do invertebrates move? Almost all invertebrates that can move have some kind of muscle tissue. An earthworm shortens and stretches its body to move.

In vertebrates muscles produce movement by shortening and pulling on bones. Vertebrates use bones and muscles together to move in different ways. Powerful muscles allow a fish to wriggle back and forth as it swims. A snake uses its muscles to slither along. Its bones are designed to wriggle as its muscles shorten and relax.

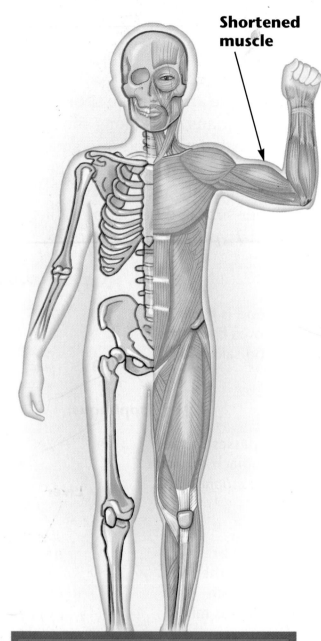

Shortened muscle

Birds have powerful muscles in their chests. Some use them to fly at incredible speeds. A racing pigeon can fly at speeds of 177 kilometers (110 miles) per hour. How far can it fly in five hours? In ten hours?

Muscular and Skeletal Systems Facts

What: Bones, muscles, cartilage

Where: Entire body

Jobs: Support, protection, movement

Types: Exoskeleton and endoskeleton

Who has it: Vertebrates and some invertebrates

Works with: Nervous system

How Do Animals Control Organ Systems?

How do animals sense changes in their world and control their organ systems? The **nervous system** (nûr′vəs sis′təm) is the body's master control system. A nervous system is made of nerve cells and nerves. More complex animals have a brain and some or all of the senses—seeing, tasting, hearing, touching, and smelling.

Simple animals have simple nervous systems. More complicated animals have more complicated nervous systems. Vertebrates have the most complex nervous systems.

The structure of an animal's nervous system relates to its lifestyle. Compare the parts of the brain related to the senses of sight and smell in these three organisms.

COMPARING ANIMAL BRAINS

Shark Brain

Vision

Smell

The shark has a keen sense of smell and poor eyesight. Brain parts related to smell are large in the shark brain.

Frog Brain

Vision

Smell

The frog relies on eyesight to catch prey. The visual part of the brain in the frog is larger than the part used for smell.

Human Brain

Vision

Thinking

Smell

Smell is not as important to humans as eyesight. Brain parts related to vision are much larger in the human brain than those for smell. The largest region of all is used for thinking and memory.

Nervous System Facts

What: Nerve cells, spinal cord, brain
Where: Body network
Jobs: Control the senses; control muscles, breathing, heart rate, and many other body functions
Who has it: Vertebrates and almost all invertebrates

READING CHARTS

REPRESENT **Draw or make your own models to help you compare these brains.**

QUICK LAB

Fooling Your Senses

HYPOTHESIZE Can your eyes be fooled? Write a hypothesis in your *Science Journal.*

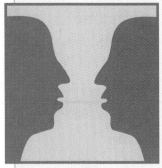

A

MATERIALS
• *Science Journal*

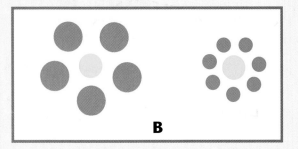

B

PROCEDURES

1. **OBSERVE** Look at drawing A. What do you see?

2. **OBSERVE** Observe the center circles in drawing B. Compare their sizes by just observing.

3. **MEASURE** Measure each yellow circle in drawing B. Which yellow circle is bigger?

CONCLUDE AND APPLY

DRAW CONCLUSIONS Can your eyes fool you? Explain.

Do Some Animals Have Special Sense Organs?

Do you think an animal can "see" with its ears? A bat can. Many animals, like bats, have specialized sense organs that collect information about their surroundings. For example, a bat makes a series of clicking sounds, then listens for echoes. A click makes certain echo patterns when it bounces off different objects. A bat can detect these changes with its ears. Using echoes it can find prey in the dark.

Can an animal "taste" the air? A snake's forked tongue collects tiny odor particles. These particles tell where prey or enemies are.

An insect eye has many lenses. This allows an insect to see light and movement in several directions, but not a clear image. To an insect the world probably looks like a newspaper photo viewed through a hand lens. Try it.

The lenses in an insect eye focus an image on many spots.

What do you think the line of small holes along this fish's body does? Cells along the line have tiny hairs. When the hairs move, the fish knows the water is disturbed. This helps the fish sense tiny waves in the water to detect prey or enemies.

lateral line

WHY IT MATTERS

Everything you do depends on organ systems. Think what happens when you kick a ball. Your nervous system sees the ball and sends a message to kick. Your circulatory system brings food and oxygen from your digestive and respiratory systems to your foot. Then your skeletal and muscular systems kick the ball! Understanding the parts that make up your organ systems and how they work lets you take good care of them.

REVIEW

1. Name and describe the function of seven body systems. Which system controls all of the other systems?

2. What is the difference between an open and a closed circulatory system?

3. How does a bat use its ears to "see"? How is this different from the way you use your ears?

4. **COMPARE** Which body systems get rid of wastes? How are they different?

5. **CRITICAL THINKING** *Analyze* How are body systems different from one animal group to another? Which animals have simple body systems? More complicated body systems?

WHY IT MATTERS THINK ABOUT IT
Suppose you could shrink to microscopic size and take a tour of one of your body systems. Which system would you choose? Why?

WHY IT MATTERS WRITE ABOUT IT
Describe what your tour would be like. Draw pictures to add to your description.

HELP WANTED:

Animal Doctor

Love working with animals? A veterinarian may be the career for you. First, you must complete two to four years of college. Then you apply to a veterinary college.

The United States has nearly 30 veterinary schools and colleges. Most veterinary schools offer a four-year program. In order to be a licensed vet, students must pass a state test and one or more national tests.

Most vets work with sick or injured pets. Some vets treat only zoo animals. Others help only farm animals. They might work on a cattle ranch or a large chicken farm.

Would it surprise you to know that some animals treat themselves? Dr. Eloy Rodriguez is a famous biochemist who works and travels all over the world. His specialty is studying the

It appeared that these chimps were eating healing substances. They were practicing "self-medication." Dr. Rodriguez tries to create these natural healing substances in the laboratory. His goal is to make these remedies available for human diseases.

DISCUSSION STARTER

1. Why do so many people want to be vets? Would you like to work with animals?

2. How do you think the chimps knew which plants to eat?

natural chemicals that plants and animals produce. He tries to discover how the chemicals work.

During a trip to the rain forests of Africa, Dr. Rodriguez noticed that sick chimpanzees ate plants that didn't taste good. He analyzed these plants and found that they contained substances that were poisonous to fungi and certain viruses.

To learn more about veterinarians, visit *www.mhschool.com/science* and enter the keyword VETS.

*inter*NET
CONNECTION

Development and Reproduction

What observations can you make of this dog and her puppies?

You may notice that some puppies are colors different from their mother. They are also all smaller than their mother. Even though the puppies are different from their mother in some ways, they all look like a small copy of an adult dog. Do all animals look like small copies of their parents?

WHY IT MATTERS

Animals develop and reproduce in many interesting ways.

SCIENCE WORDS

metamorphosis is a process of changes during certain animals' development

life cycle the stages of an animal's growth and change

life span how long an animal can be expected to live

asexual reproduction produces offspring with only one parent

sexual reproduction produces offspring with two parents

heredity the passing of traits from parent to offspring

EXPLORE

HYPOTHESIZE **Do you know of young animals that look very different from their parents? How do you think they change as they grow older? Write a hypothesis in your *Science Journal*. How could you test your ideas?**

262

Design Your Own Experiment

HOW DO MEALWORMS CHANGE AS THEY GROW?

PROCEDURES

1. OBSERVE As a group choose a Mealworm Observation Station that your teacher has set up. Each station has three jars labeled A–C.

2. OBSERVE Break into smaller groups. Each group should observe the animals in one jar. Record your observations in your *Science Journal*. Share your observations with the other members of your larger group.

3. ASK QUESTIONS Record any questions you have about mealworms and how they change and grow. How could you find the answers?

4. EXPERIMENT Design simple experiments to find out as much as you can about the mealworms. Do they prefer light or dark places? Damp or dry places? Make a group table to display your findings.

5. OBSERVE Make observations of the animals every few days. Record your observations. Draw the different stages of development that you observe.

MATERIALS

- jars containing food and mealworms in different stages of development
- 3 hand lenses
- 3 rulers
- *Science Journal*

CONCLUDE AND APPLY

1. COMMUNICATE Describe all the stages of mealworm development.

2. DRAW CONCLUSIONS Use your drawings to arrange the stages in the order in which you think mealworm development occurs.

GOING FURTHER: Apply

3. COMPARE How does the way a mealworm grows and changes differ from other animals like cats and dogs?

How Do Mealworms Change as They Grow?

Most young animals look like smaller copies of their parents. Puppies look like small dogs. Chicks look like small birds. They grow larger as they grow older. As the Explore Activity showed, other young animals don't look like their parents at all.

Certain animals, like mealworms, go through changes during their development. This process is called **metamorphosis** (met′ə môr′fə sis), meaning "a change in body form." There are two types of metamorphosis—complete and incomplete. Insects such as mealworms and butterflies go through complete metamorphosis.

COMPLETE METAMORPHOSIS

① Egg Stage
An adult mealworm is known as a grain beetle. After mating a female grain beetle lays eggs.

② Larva Stage
A wormlike *larva* (lär′və) hatches from each egg. A larva is a young organism with a form different from its parents. After hatching a larva begins to eat.

③ Pupa Stage
When the larva reaches a certain stage, it becomes a *pupa* (pū′pə). A pupa is a stage where many changes take place. Adult tissues and organs form.

④ Adult Stage
When the adult is fully formed, it comes into the world. An adult grain beetle is completely unlike its larva. It has a smooth body, wings, and six legs.

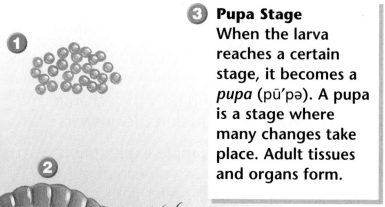
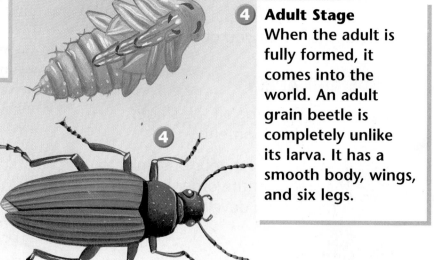

Why Metamorphosis?

Metamorphosis allows animals to specialize. Larvae and nymphs specialize in eating and growing. Adult animals specialize in breeding. They come to a new environment where their eggs have a better chance of surviving.

Insects such as grasshoppers, termites, and damselflies go through incomplete metamorphosis. Incomplete metamorphosis has three stages.

METAMORPHOSIS	
Complete stages	**Incomplete stages**
1. Egg	1. Egg
2. Larva	2. Nymph
3. Pupa	3. Adult
4. Adult	
Time: several weeks	**Time:** up to 2 years
Who does it: wasps, ants, bees, flies, beetles, fleas, butterflies, moths	**Who does it:** bugs, mayflies, dragonflies, grasshoppers, cockroaches, termites

INCOMPLETE METAMORPHOSIS

3 Adult Stage
The damselfly nymph molts several times until it becomes an adult.

2 Nymph Stage
The young damselfly, called a *nymph* (nimf), hatches from an egg. A nymph is a young insect that looks like an adult. The damselfly nymph lives in water and has gills. The nymph keeps growing and changing. After many weeks the damselfly nymph comes out of the water. It has lungs for breathing. Soon the nymph sheds its skin, or molts. Small wings appear.

1 Egg Stage
A female damselfly lays her eggs on a reed underwater. After some time the eggs hatch.

READING *N* DIAGRAMS

WRITE Study both diagrams. Write a paragraph comparing how complete and incomplete metamorphosis are different.

265

What Are the Stages of an Animal's Life?

The Explore Activity shows how a mealworm changes as it grows into an adult. These stages of growth and change make up an organism's **life cycle** (līf sī′kəl).

Each different organism has its own particular life cycle. However, all organisms follow the same general pattern of birth, growth, reproduction, and death.

Humans have their own life cycle. Stages in the human life cycle are shown below. Each person's life cycle is different. You may go through different stages at very different ages. Even so, all people have a life cycle that follows the same general pattern. At what stage of the human life cycle are you?

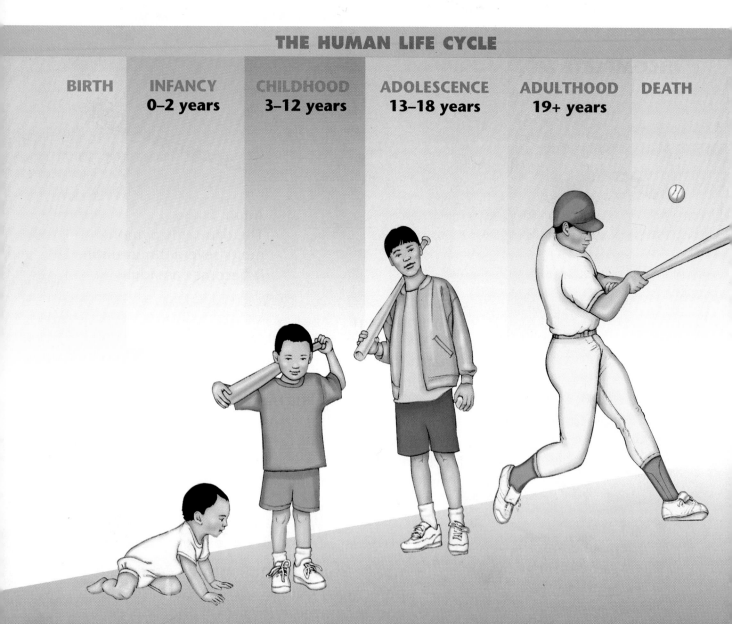

THE HUMAN LIFE CYCLE

BIRTH | INFANCY **0–2 years** | CHILDHOOD **3–12 years** | ADOLESCENCE **13–18 years** | ADULTHOOD **19+ years** | DEATH

How Long Do Animals Live?

The **life span** (līf span) of an animal tells you how long it can be expected to live. The average life span of a human is about 75 to 80 years. Compare this with life spans of other organisms in the bar graph. Do you see any trends? Do certain animals live longer than others?

Scientists aren't sure what decides an animal's life span. They think cell division may control how long an animal lives.

Throughout an animal's life, its cells divide many times. Scientists think that after many divisions, cells get damaged. Older animals have more damaged cells than younger animals. Therefore, older animals are more likely to develop diseases that weaken them.

What might happen if scientists could slow down cell division? It is possible that animals—including people—could have longer life spans!

MATH LINK

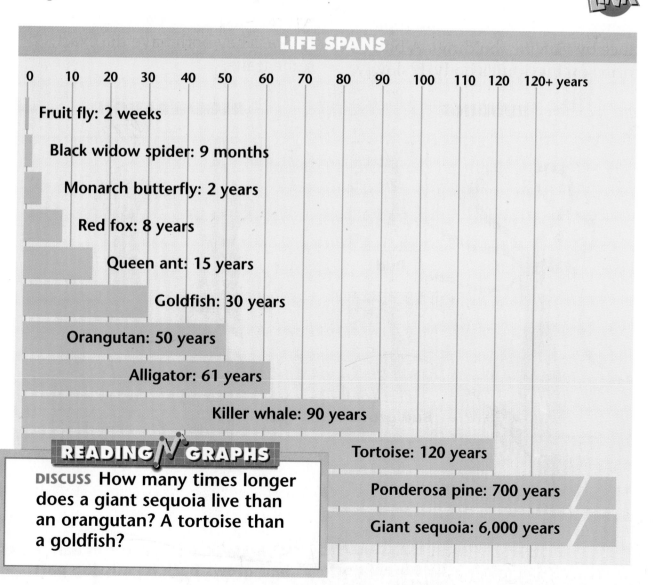

LIFE SPANS

| 0 | 10 | 20 | 30 | 40 | 50 | 60 | 70 | 80 | 90 | 100 | 110 | 120 | 120+ years |

- Fruit fly: 2 weeks
- Black widow spider: 9 months
- Monarch butterfly: 2 years
- Red fox: 8 years
- Queen ant: 15 years
- Goldfish: 30 years
- Orangutan: 50 years
- Alligator: 61 years
- Killer whale: 90 years
- Tortoise: 120 years
- Ponderosa pine: 700 years
- Giant sequoia: 6,000 years

READING GRAPHS

DISCUSS How many times longer does a giant sequoia live than an orangutan? A tortoise than a goldfish?

How Do Animals Reproduce?

The life cycle of every animal includes reproduction, the making of new animals. There are two types of reproduction. **Asexual reproduction** (ā sek'shü əl rē'prə duk'shən) produces offspring from only one parent. **Sexual reproduction** (sek'shü əl rē'prə duk'shən) requires two parents.

Asexual Reproduction

Simple invertebrates, like sponges and cnidarians, can reproduce by *budding* (bu'ding). A bud forms on the adult's body. It slowly develops into a new animal. After some time the bud breaks off. Each animal then continues its own life cycle.

Regeneration (ri jen'ə rā'shən) is another form of asexual reproduction. A whole animal develops from just a part of the original animal. Sponges and planaria reproduce through regeneration.

Asexual reproduction produces *clones* (klōnz). A clone is an exact copy of its parent. Its traits, or characteristics, are identical to the traits of its parent. For example, a budded hydra is a copy of the original hydra. They both have the exact same traits.

BUDDING

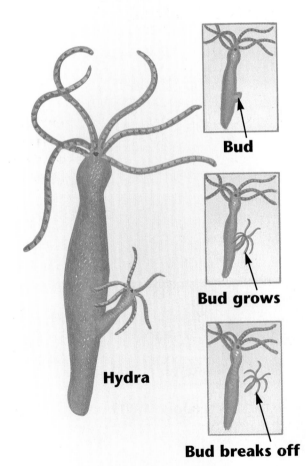

Bud

Bud grows

Hydra

Bud breaks off

REGENERATION

A single planaria is cut in half. Each half grows back its missing part.

Sexual Reproduction

In animals sexual reproduction is more common than asexual reproduction. Sexual reproduction requires two parents. Their offspring are not clones. They are similar to their parents but not identical. These offspring are new individuals. They have traits from both parents.

Sexual reproduction is more complicated than asexual reproduction. Animals produce special sex cells. The female sex cell is called an *egg*. The male sex cell is called a *sperm* (spûrm).

Do you think an egg can become a new organism by itself? It cannot. Neither can a sperm. To reproduce, an egg and a sperm must join. This joining is called *fertilization* (fûr′tə lə zā′shən). It produces a developing animal called an *embryo* (em′brē ō′). An embryo can go on to become a new organism, with traits from both parents.

Some animals lay eggs. Egg-laying animals include most invertebrates, reptiles, amphibians, birds, fish, and a very few mammals. In most cases the embryo grows inside a protective shell. The embryo uses stored food in the egg to develop. After maturing the offspring hatches into a newborn animal.

In most mammals the embryo grows inside the female's body. The female's body provides the nutrients the offspring needs to develop. All but a few mammals give birth to live young. One mammal that lays eggs is the platypus.

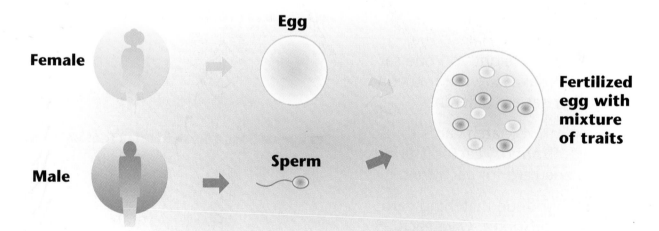

Female → **Egg**

Male → **Sperm** → **Fertilized egg with mixture of traits**

COMPARING ASEXUAL AND SEXUAL REPRODUCTION

	Asexual	Sexual
Parents	1	2
Male and female	no	yes
Clones	yes	no
Offspring traits	same as parent	mixed
Egg and sperm	no	yes

QUICK LAB

Heredity Cards

HYPOTHESIZE How many possible offspring can come from six different traits? Write a hypothesis in your *Science Journal.*

Brown Eyes   Short

Green Eyes   Tall

MATERIALS

- pink construction paper
- blue construction paper
- scissors
- marker
- *Science Journal*

PROCEDURES

1. Cut three cards from each paper. Pink cards represent the female, blue cards the male.

2. Write a trait for "Hair," "Eye color," and "Height" on one set of cards. Make sure the traits on the other set are different.

3. **COLLECT DATA** Match cards to make "offspring." Each offspring needs one card for each trait.

4. **REPEAT** Continue matching cards to create offspring. Give each a number. Record the traits in a table in your *Science Journal.*

CONCLUDE AND APPLY

1. **OBSERVE** How many different offspring did you get?

2. **PREDICT** How many offspring would you get with eight cards?

How Are Traits Passed to Offspring?

The passing of traits from parent to offspring is called **heredity** (hə red′i tē). Offspring inherit traits from both parents.

Each parent has different traits. For example, the mother may have light eyes, while the father's eyes are dark.

When an egg and a sperm join, the traits they carry are mixed like a deck of cards. The offspring ends up with a mixture of traits. Some traits come from the father. Other traits come from the mother.

Female Parent's Traits

■ Eyes ■ Ears ■ Nose ■ Hair ■ Teeth ■ Height ■

+

Male Parent's Traits

■ Eyes ■ Ears ■ Nose ■ Hair ■ Teeth ■ Height ■

Offspring's Traits

■ Eyes ■ Ears ■ Nose ■ Hair ■ Teeth ■ Height ■

How Can Mammals Be Clones?

In 1997 Scottish scientist Dr. Ian Wilmut got a sheep to produce a clone. The clone, named Dolly, is an exact copy of her mother. Sheep are mammals that reproduce sexually. Never before had a mammal reproduced asexually, and it created a huge sensation around the world. Why do you think his discovery created such a sensation?

How could Dr. Wilmut clone a sheep? He recognized that every cell in the body has special hereditary material. This material contains information for making a sheep.

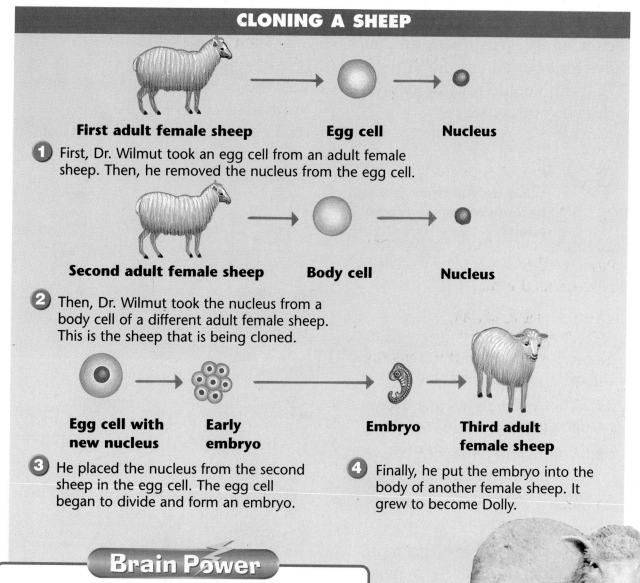

CLONING A SHEEP

First adult female sheep   **Egg cell**   **Nucleus**

1 First, Dr. Wilmut took an egg cell from an adult female sheep. Then, he removed the nucleus from the egg cell.

Second adult female sheep   **Body cell**   **Nucleus**

2 Then, Dr. Wilmut took the nucleus from a body cell of a different adult female sheep. This is the sheep that is being cloned.

Egg cell with new nucleus   **Early embryo**   **Embryo**   **Third adult female sheep**

3 He placed the nucleus from the second sheep in the egg cell. The egg cell began to divide and form an embryo.

4 Finally, he put the embryo into the body of another female sheep. It grew to become Dolly.

Brain Power

Identical twins are natural clones. Identical twins form when a fertilized egg splits in half. Each half goes on to be a complete person. How are identical twins different from Dolly and her mother?

Dolly is the first mammal in the world who never had a father.

271

Where are you in your life cycle right now? You are probably in the childhood stage. In a few years, you'll reach adolescence, then adulthood. What challenges lie ahead for you? What dangers and opportunities? Knowing about life cycles can help you identify some of the problems that lie ahead and plan for a better future. What plans do you have for your adolescent years? What can you do now to help you achieve your goals?

HEALTH LINK

What do you think you will become when you are an adult?

ASTRONAUT?
TEACHER?
MOTHER?

REVIEW

1. What is the difference between a life cycle and a life span?

2. What is the difference between complete and incomplete metamorphosis?

3. What is heredity?

4. COMPARE How is sexual reproduction different from asexual reproduction? Give some examples of asexual reproduction.

5. CRITICAL THINKING *Evaluate* Do you think that mammals should be cloned? Why or why not?

WHY IT MATTERS THINK ABOUT IT What would you like to accomplish in your adult years? Why?

WHY IT MATTERS WRITE ABOUT IT Write a plan for how you would like to achieve your goals for your adult years.

READING SKILL Describe the details of how a mammal can be cloned.

The Science of BREEDING

What could you do if you wanted your cows to give really rich milk? Farmers learned long ago that they could choose and mate, or breed, animals with desirable traits. So they bred cattle that produced very rich milk or sheep with longer hair.

How was this done? Let's imagine you have some corn that has many ears on a stalk. You also have corn with very few ears, but those ears are really juicy and full! You want corn with many juicy ears. Here's what you do.

Take pollen from the corn that's juicy and full. Sprinkle it on the flowers of the many-eared plant. Wait until the next harvest, and wow! What a feast!

Of course, this is a simplified version of breeding. It's really a science, and one that's used by farmers everywhere!

DISCUSSION STARTER

1. What animals or foods do you think were bred for specific traits?

2. Why would farmers want to breed animals or plants?

To learn more about breeding, visit **www.mhschool.com/science** and enter the keyword BREEDING.

*inter*NET CONNECTION

Topic 6
LIFE SCIENCE

WHY IT MATTERS

A variety of characteristics helps animals survive.

SCIENCE WORDS

camouflage blending with surroundings

adaptation a trait that helps an organism survive

mimicry when one organism imitates the traits of another

inherited behavior a behavior that is inborn, not learned

instinct a pattern of behavior

learned behavior behavior that is not inborn

Animal Survival

Have you ever played hide-and-seek? Where did you hide? How did you cover yourself up? An animal in this pictures is also hiding. Can you find it? Here is a hint: It is hiding in plain sight.

EXPLORE

HYPOTHESIZE What role does body color play in the types of places an animal can stay without being noticed? Write a hypothesis in your *Science Journal.* How could you test your ideas?

Investigate How Body Color Can Help an Animal Survive

Test your ideas by pretending to be a bird searching for worms. Which color worms are easiest to see?

MATERIALS

- colored toothpicks
- plastic bag or shoe box
- label or piece of masking tape
- marking pen
- *Science Journal*

PROCEDURES

1. Label your bag or box with your name. This is your "nest." Use it to hold all the toothpick "worms" that you collect.

2. **OBSERVE** Follow the rules given by your teacher to capture the worms. Record the rules in your *Science Journal*. Also record any observations that you make while collecting the worms.

3. **COMMUNICATE** When you are done, record your results in a bar graph like the one shown.

CONCLUDE AND APPLY

1. **EXPLAIN** Which color worms were easiest to see? Why?

2. **EXPLAIN** Which color worms were hardest to see? Why?

3. **DRAW CONCLUSIONS** If you were to become a toothpick worm, what color would you want to be? Why?

GOING FURTHER: Problem Solving

4. **PREDICT** Colors help certain animals blend in with their surroundings. Why do you think some animals have bright colors? How could you find out?

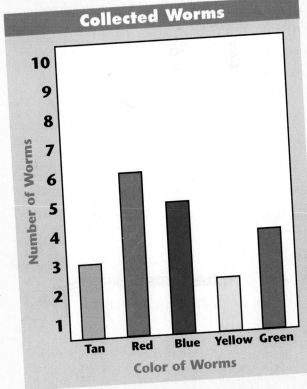

Collected Worms

Number of Worms — Color of Worms: Tan, Red, Blue, Yellow, Green

Light and dark peppered moths

What do you see in this picture?

How Can Body Color Help an Animal Survive?

The Explore Activity shows how an animal's color can help it blend into its surroundings. Blending because of color is called **camouflage** (kam′ə fläzh′).

The peppered moth is a good example of how camouflage helps an animal survive. In the early 1800s, there were two types of peppered moths in England, dark and light. Dark moths were rare. Light moths were common. As a result of increased industry, England's air became polluted in the late 1800s. Suddenly dark moths outnumbered light moths.

Why do you think that happened? Dark moths stood out on light-colored trees. Birds could spot them easily and ate them. However, pollution slowly darkened the trees. The light moths stood out and were eaten.

Why do you think some animals have bright colors? Some display bright colors to attract a mate. Others use bright colors to warn predators not to eat them.

What do you see in the picture above? That isn't a leaf—it's an insect! The insect's body resembles its environment very closely. This is *protective resemblance* (prə tək′tiv ri zem′bləns). The fact that an animal resembles something else protects it.

Camouflage and protective resemblance are examples of **adaptations** (ad′əp tā′shənz). Adaptations are traits that help organisms survive.

What Are Some Other Adaptations?

Body adaptations are called physical adaptations. Physical adaptations help animals survive in their environments. Can you think of physical adaptations other than those listed here? What adaptations do you have?

- **Gills and Fins** They allow fish to breathe and swim underwater.

- **Fur** Thick white fur helps a polar bear blend in with its snowy surroundings. It also keeps the bear warm.

- **Legs** The long legs of the horse help it run at great speed.

- **Neck** A giraffe's long legs and neck allow it to reach leaves high up in trees, where other animals can't reach.

- **Shell** A hard outer shell protects a turtle's soft body parts.

- **Trunk** A trunk helps an elephant grasp things, and feed itself.

- **Eyes and Ears** The keen eyes of an owl help it spot prey from great distances. Sensitive ears allow it to detect prey in the dark.

Do you think that an animal chooses its adaptations? It does not. Adaptations happen naturally. The peppered moths didn't choose to be dark or light. The birds simply ate the light-colored moths because they were easier to see on the dark trees.

For any adaptation survival is the key. An adaptation that helps an animal survive is likely to become more common. Adaptations that do not increase survival are unlikely to become common.

This giraffe can reach leaves high up in trees.

Is That What You Think It Is?

Monarch butterflies have an important adaptation that helps them survive—they don't taste good. Predators spit out monarch butterflies if they eat them. Monarch butterfly bodies contain a poison that they get from feeding on the milkweed plant.

Most predators stay away from monarch butterflies. They recognize the bold, bright coloring. Predators also stay away from the viceroy butterfly. The viceroy is not poisonous, nor does it taste bad. However, it looks very similar to the monarch. Most predators won't take a chance eating it.

The viceroy butterfly is protected by **mimicry** (mim′i krē). Mimicry occurs when one organism imitates another. What advantage does mimicry give animals?

How did the viceroy come to resemble the bad-tasting monarch? At one time there probably was a variety of viceroy butterflies. The ones that looked like monarchs survived. The ones that looked less like monarchs got eaten. As time passed, the viceroys that looked more and more like monarchs survived.

Monarch butterfly

Viceroy butterfly

SKILL BUILDER

Skill: Forming a Hypothesis

HOW DO ADAPTATIONS HELP AN ANIMAL SURVIVE?

Every science experiment begins with a hypothesis. A hypothesis is a statement you can test. "Dogs like big bones best" is a hypothesis. You could test this hypothesis by giving dogs different-sized bones.

In this activity you will design two different kinds of animals—a super predator and an animal that is skilled at avoiding predators. Then form a hypothesis about how the adaptations would help each animal in different situations.

MATERIALS

- modeling clay
- construction paper
- drawing materials
- *Science Journal*

PROCEDURES

1. PLAN What traits should your predator have? Record them in your *Science Journal*. Describe how these traits would help the animal.

2. REPEAT Do the same for your avoider animal.

3. COMMUNICATE Make a table like the one shown for each animal. Fill in each category that applies. Add any extra categories that you need.

4. MAKE A MODEL Make models or colored drawings of your animals. Label all the features of your animals. Tell how they function.

5. HYPOTHESIZE How would these features help the animal survive?

CONCLUDE AND APPLY

1. COMMUNICATE What are the animals' most important features? How would they use these features?

2. EXPLAIN Review your hypothesis. How could you test it?

3. PREDICT Predict what would happen if you could test your hypothesis.

Animal Name _____
Predator ☐   Avoider ☐
Food _____
Enemies _____
Environment _____

Trait	How It Helps
Length	
Weight	
Shape	
Coloring	
Pattern	
Skin	
Arms	
Legs	
Tails	
Fins	
Eyesight	
Hearing	
Smell	
Strength	
Quickness	
Intelligence	

How Do Actions Help Animals Survive?

You learned how physical adaptations help animals survive. Another kind of adaptation involves behaviors, or actions.

One type of behavior is not learned. It is an **inherited behavior** (in her'it əd bi hāv'yər). The simplest inherited behavior is a *reflex* (rē'fleks'). A reflex is automatic, like scratching an itch.

A spider knows how to spin a web because of instinct.

Complicated inherited behavior is called **instinct** (in'stingkt'). Instincts are patterns of behavior, like spinning a web and building a nest. The behavior is complicated, but automatic. The spider and bird do not think about what to do, they just know.

The dormouse is a true hibernator. It loses up to half its body weight while hibernating.

When salmon swim thousands of miles to mate and lay eggs, they are *migrating* (mī'grāt ing). Migration is an instinct. Animals migrate for three main reasons. First, they avoid cold weather. Second, they find new food supplies. Third, they find a safe place to breed and raise their young.

How do migrating animals find their way? Many birds navigate by the Sun and the stars. Other migrators may use magnetic "compasses" inside their bodies.

Surviving a cold winter is hard. Some animals struggle to find food. Others *hibernate* (hī'bər nāt'), or sleep through the winter. True hibernation is a deep sleep. All body processes slow down. Body temperature can drop to just above freezing. Mice and bats are true hibernators.

Bears and chipmunks go into a less deep sleep. Their body temperatures drop, but their heartbeats remain high. They can wake up in an emergency.

Can Animals Learn Behaviors?

Some animal behaviors are inherited. Others aren't. Behavior that is not inborn is called **learned behavior** (lûrnd bi hāv'yər). Animals learn through experience and change their behavior. Learning starts with a need, such as escaping predators, protection, and food. All animals do not learn in the same way.

- **Learning to Ignore** Moving shadows pass over a frog. At first the frog jumps. Later it doesn't. It learned that the shadow is not a threat.

- **Copying** Newborn ducks follow their mother wherever she goes. They copy her to learn to find food.

- **Learning from Experience** At first it takes a rat a long time to get through a maze. It is unsure of where to go. Finally, it reaches the food at the end of the maze. After many trips the rat learns to find its way. The rat learns from experience.

- **Using Two Unrelated Things** A trainer shouts, "Up!" If the dolphin jumps, the trainer gives it a fish. At first the dolphin gets a fish every time it jumps. After a while the dolphin doesn't need the fish. It jumps simply because the trainer shouts, "Up!"

Almost all learning involves some form of trial and error. For example, the rat in the maze uses trial and error to find its way. It makes mistakes but learns from them. After a while it can find its way through the maze.

Trial and Error

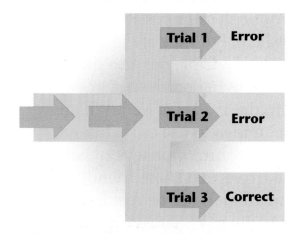

Making mistakes helps you find the correct path.

Dolphin learning also brings together two unrelated things—food and the word *up*. The idea of food causes the dolphin to jump. This is known as cause and effect. The cause is the fish. The effect is the jump. Can you think of any other similar cause-and-effect situations?

Brain Power

Your cat comes running when he hears someone use the electric can opener. Is this an instinct or a learned behavior? Why?

Can Animals Be Trained to Help People?

Can you imagine what it would be like to lose the use of your arms and legs? Quadriplegics (kwod'rə plē'jiks) are people who are paralyzed from the neck down. For them simple everyday tasks can be difficult or impossible. Attendants can help, but they are expensive. Many quadriplegics also like the idea of living on their own.

In the 1970s Dr. M. J. Willard got an idea to use capuchin (kap'yə chin) monkeys to help quadriplegics. These friendly, intelligent animals are perfect for the job. By 1979 Dr. Willard's first monkey was ready to work. It was part of a program called Helping Hands.

Helping Hands trains monkeys, then places them with quadriplegics. First, a baby monkey is placed in a human foster home. The foster family carefully teaches the monkey to perform tasks.

After about five years, the monkey is ready to help quadriplegics. Monkeys are matched with their owners very carefully. For example, an owner who works on a computer is matched with a monkey trained to perform computer tasks.

What do Helping Hands monkeys do? They open books and fetch snacks. They change radio and TV stations. They turn on computers. They perform dozens of other tasks quickly and easily. Monkeys also become companions to their owners and make them more independent. What impact do you think Dr. Willard's program has on the lives of many quadriplegics?

The Helping Hands program needs all the help it can get. It takes a long time and a lot of money— about $25,000—to train a monkey successfully. How can you help? Visit the McGraw-Hill Web site for more information on how to contact Helping Hands.

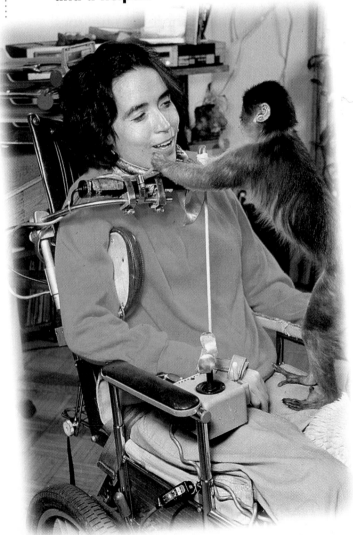

This monkey helps its owner live a better life. It is a companion and a helper.

Understanding adaptations helps us learn about ways we can help animals survive. For example, we know that certain animals hibernate. This can make us more aware of not disturbing their resting sites while exploring during the winter. Knowing how animals learn helps us, too. We can train them to help people in need.

It also makes us more aware of our own adaptations—our eyes, nose, ears, and tongue to name a few. Your greatest adaptation of all is your brain. It can produce more learned behavior than any other organism. In fact you are using it right now—to learn!

This dog is a Canine Companion. Similar to a Helping Hands monkey, it is trained to help its owner do many things.

REVIEW

1. How is protective resemblance different from mimicry? How do both help animals survive?

2. Compare and contrast reflexes and instincts.

3. Use "trial and error" and "stimulus and response" to describe how a dog might learn to open the cabinet where his food is kept.

4. **HYPOTHESIZE** How might having a bright color instead of camouflage help a bird survive?

5. CRITICAL THINKING *Evaluate* A sheepdog is an expert at herding sheep. Do you think this is learned or inherited behavior? Why?

WHY IT MATTERS THINK ABOUT IT
Choose an adaptation you would like to have. What would it be? Why would you choose that adaptation?

WHY IT MATTERS WRITE ABOUT IT
Write a paragraph describing the adaptation you would like to have. How would it help you in your life?

Dancing Bees

If the bee moves up the comb, the food's toward the Sun. If the bee moves down, it's away from the Sun. Moving to the right means it's to the right of the Sun. The closer the food, the faster the bee moves.

The other bees smell the nectar on the dancing bee. They copy its movements, then leave the hive. They fly in wider and wider circles until they find the nectar.

Honeybees dance to tell each other where to find nectar, the sweet juice of a flower. After a bee finds a flower, it fills its honey sac with nectar and returns to the hive.

If the flower is very close by, the bee does a circle dance on the hive's honeycomb. It circles in one direction, then the other. If the nectar's farther away, the bee does a "waggle" dance, moving in a figure-eight across the honeycomb.

DISCUSSION STARTER

1. Why is the bees' dance so important?

2. What would happen if each bee just ate the nectar it found?

To learn more about bees, visit **www.mhschool.com/science** and enter the keyword BEES.

inter**NET** CONNECTION

SCIENCE WORDS

adaptation p. 276

camouflage p. 276

circulatory
  system p. 252

digestive
  system p. 255

excretory
  system p. 254

heredity p. 270

inherited
  behavior p. 280

instinct p. 280

life cycle p. 266

life span p. 267

metamorphosis
  p. 264

mimicry p. 278

muscular
  system p. 256

nervous
  system p. 257

USING SCIENCE WORDS

Number a paper from 1 to 10. Fill in 1 to 5 with words from the list above.

1. The organ system that removes liquid wastes is called the __?__.

2. The stages of an animal's growth and change are part of its __?__.

3. Organisms use __?__ to blend with their surroundings.

4. A pattern of behavior is called a(n) __?__.

5. All other body systems are controlled by the __?__.

6–10. **Pick five words from the list above that were not used in 1 to 5, and use each in a sentence.**

UNDERSTANDING SCIENCE IDEAS

11. Describe the processes that must take place for you to catch a ball. Include all the body systems that are involved.

12. Why does sexual reproduction produce more variation in offspring than asexual reproduction?

USING IDEAS AND SKILLS

13. **READING SKILL: LOCATING DETAILS** Describe some details about organisms to support the idea that learned behavior is not inborn.

14. **HYPOTHESIZE** What causes animals to hibernate? Cold weather? Short days? Low food supply? State a hypothesis that explains why animals hibernate. Then describe an experiment that would test your hypothesis.

15. **THINKING LIKE A SCIENTIST** What advantage would sexual reproduction have in a changing environment? How might it help an animal species survive?

PROBLEMS and PUZZLES

Hot Rhythm By counting the number of times a cricket chirps in one minute, dividing the number of chirps by 7, and adding 4, you can find the air temperature in degrees Celsius. If a cricket chirps 196 times in one minute, what is the air temperature? Will a cricket chirp more or less times if it is colder? If it is warmer?

MATH LINK

SCIENCE WORDS

arthropod p. 227
camouflage p. 276
circulatory
    system p. 252
cold-blooded p. 236
digestive system
    p. 255
echinoderm p. 226
heredity p. 270

learned behavior
    p. 281
life cycle p. 266
mimicry p. 278
mollusk p. 226
sexual
    reproduction
    p. 268
symmetry p. 214
vertebrate p. 214

USING SCIENCE WORDS

Number a paper from 1 to 10. Beside each number write the word or words that best complete the sentence.

1. Fishes and reptiles have backbones and are known as __?__.

2. Invertebrates with jointed legs and bodies divided into parts are __?__.

3. Soft-bodied invertebrates that have shells are __?__.

4. An animal that cannot control its body temperature is __?__.

5. The system that moves blood though the body is the __?__.

6. The system that breaks down food for energy is the __?__.

7. The passing of a trait from parents to offspring is __?__.

8. An animal with a male and a female parent is the result of __?__.

9. Bike riding is not done by instinct but is a(n) __?__.

10. An animal that blends in with its surroundings uses __?__ for survival.

UNDERSTANDING SCIENCE IDEAS

Write 11 to 15. For each number write the letter for the best answer. You may wish to use the hints provided.

11. Which is not a characteristic of all animals?
    a. They grow and change.
    b. They have backbones.
    c. They need food.
    d. They are made of cells.
    (Hint: Read page 212.)

12. The largest phylum (group) of invertebrates are the
    a. flatworms
    b. sponges
    c. arthropods
    d. cnidarians
    (Hint: Read page 227.)

13. Only warm-blooded animals have
    a. hearts and lungs
    b. backbones
    c. legs and feet
    d. fur or feathers
    (Hint: Read pages 241–242.)

14. The system that carries oxygen to body cells is the
    a. circulatory system
    b. respiratory system
    c. excretory system
    d. digestive system
    (Hint: Read page 253.)

15. Which animals go through metamorphosis?
   a. mealworms
   b. chickens
   c. snakes
   d. all mammals
   (Hint: Read page 264.)

USING IDEAS AND SKILLS

16. OBSERVE Give examples of how symmetry is used to help classify animals.

17. What are the major characteristics of flatworms?

18. What are the major characteristics of fish?

THINKING LIKE A SCIENTIST

19. HYPOTHESIZE Imagine finding two animals. The animals look different, but they might be similar in some ways. How could you find out if they were in the same phylum? Write a hypothesis to help you decide.

20. Explain what the nervous system does.

WRITING IN YOUR JOURNAL

SCIENCE IN YOUR LIFE
What if people were cold-blooded instead of warm-blooded? How might your life be different?

PRODUCT ADS
Identify the kinds of products or services for animals you might see advertised. What different phyla of animals might they be for?

HOW SCIENTISTS WORK
Give an example from the unit that shows how scientists use classification. Show how and why the classification works.

Design your own Experiment

Do ants change as they grow? Design an experiment to find out. Check with your teacher before doing the experiment.

interNET CONNECTION

For help in reviewing this unit, visit *www.mhschool.com/science*

PROBLEMS and PUZZLES

Identify and Classify

Make a poster that displays information about an animal you find interesting. Explain how you know it is an animal. Classify it as a vertebrate or invertebrate. Does it go through metamorphosis? List any other interesting characteristics. Illustrate your poster.

Market Mimicry

Look for examples of mimicry in store products. Choose a food, clothing, music, or sporting goods store, or some other store. Keep a record of products that seem to mimic one another. Which product is the original? Which do you think is better? Is mimicry a good strategy for store products? Explain.

A Faulty Heart

THE PROBLEM

The Heart-Throb 2000 artificial heart isn't working properly. Blood carrying waste gas is mixed with blood carrying oxygen.

THE PLAN

Study the diagram carefully. Think of a hypothesis that would fix the faulty heart. Your hypothesis should prevent mixed blood from being pumped out of chambers 2 and 4.

TEST

Think of a way that you could test your hypothesis. Show how you could build a model of a four-chambered heart similar to the models in the Topic 4 Explore Activity. Describe how you would test your model.

ANALYZE THE RESULTS

Predict how your model would work. Write a letter to the Heart-Throb company describing how they can fix their faulty hearts. Describe how your heart design might improve the health of their customers.

From body cells

From lungs

1

3

2

4

To lungs

To body

288

UNIT 5

ELECTRICITY AND MAGNETISM

CHAPTER 9
PATHS FOR ELECTRICITY

Electricity. Everyone knows what it does. Flip a switch—a light comes on. Flip another—a computer turns on. Electricity runs the appliances in your home. It runs the traffic lights that let you cross a street safely. It even runs some new cars! Yet few people can tell you what electricity is or how it gets from one place to another. In this chapter you will learn about what electricity is and the paths it travels to get to you.

 In this chapter you will have many opportunities to read diagrams for information.

WHY IT MATTERS

A balloon can stick to a wall for the same reason that lightning hits the ground.

SCIENCE WORDS

static electricity a buildup of electrical charge

discharge when a buildup of electrical charge empties into something

conductor a material through which electricity flows easily

insulator a material through which electricity does not flow

It's Shocking!

Have you ever been "zapped"? You pull off a sock that got stuck to a sweater in your gym bag and—zap!—you hear a loud crackling sound. You rub a balloon on a sweater and—zap!—the balloon sticks to the wall. What do you think is going on? The answer may shock you.

EXPLORE

HYPOTHESIZE What do you think will happen when two rubbed balloons are brought next to each other? Will they pull together or push apart? Write a hypothesis in your *Science Journal.*

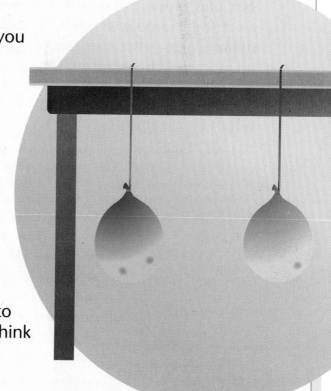
Investigate What Happens to Rubbed Balloons

Test what happens when two rubbed balloons are brought next to each other.

MATERIALS

- two 9-in.-round balloons, inflated
- 2 pieces of string, 50 cm each
- tape
- wool cloth scrap or old wool sock
- *Science Journal*

PROCEDURES

1. **OBSERVE** What happens to the balloons when you hang them as shown in the picture? Write about it in your *Science Journal.*

2. **PREDICT** What will happen if you rub one balloon with a piece of wool? Both balloons? Test your predictions.

3. **PREDICT** What will happen if you hold the wool cloth between the balloons? Test your prediction.

4. **PREDICT** What will happen if you put your hand between the two balloons? Test your prediction.

CONCLUDE AND APPLY

1. **COMMUNICATE** What happened when you rubbed one balloon with the wool cloth? Both balloons?

2. **COMMUNICATE** What happened when you put the wool cloth between the balloons?

3. **COMMUNICATE** What happened when you placed your hand between the balloons?

GOING FURTHER: Apply

4. **EXPERIMENT** Untie one balloon. Rub it with the wool. Try to stick the balloon to the wall. What happens? Why do you think this happened?

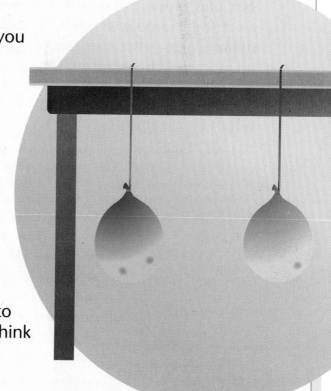

What Is Electricity?

You are probably familiar with electricity. It makes your toaster hot and your refrigerator cold. It runs through wires that you plug into the wall. However, electricity also affects things without wires—things like balloons and like socks in your gym bag. What exactly is electricity?

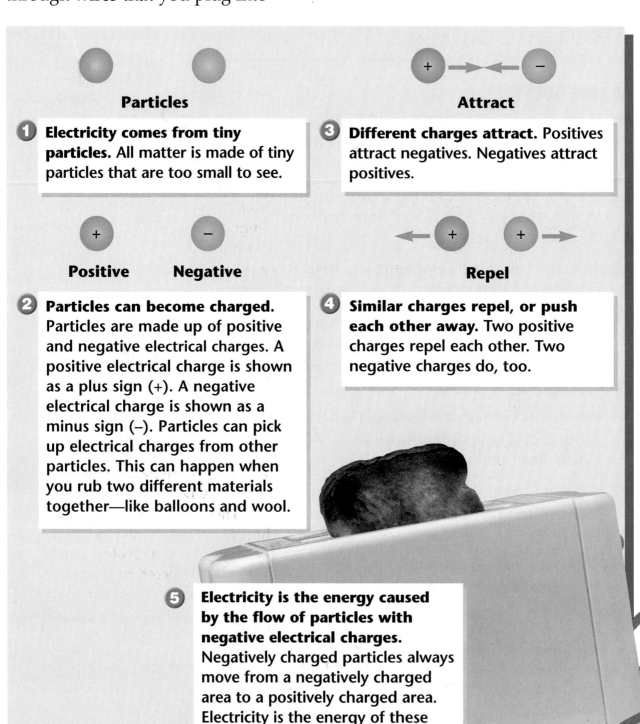

Particles

1 **Electricity comes from tiny particles.** All matter is made of tiny particles that are too small to see.

Positive **Negative**

2 **Particles can become charged.** Particles are made up of positive and negative electrical charges. A positive electrical charge is shown as a plus sign (+). A negative electrical charge is shown as a minus sign (–). Particles can pick up electrical charges from other particles. This can happen when you rub two different materials together—like balloons and wool.

Attract

3 **Different charges attract.** Positives attract negatives. Negatives attract positives.

Repel

4 **Similar charges repel, or push each other away.** Two positive charges repel each other. Two negative charges do, too.

5 **Electricity is the energy caused by the flow of particles with negative electrical charges.** Negatively charged particles always move from a negatively charged area to a positively charged area. Electricity is the energy of these moving negative particles.

What Happens to Rubbed Balloons?

What do you think electrical charges and electricity have to do with what happened to the balloons in the Explore Activity? This diagram will help you understand why the balloons behaved as they did.

ATTRACT AND REPEL

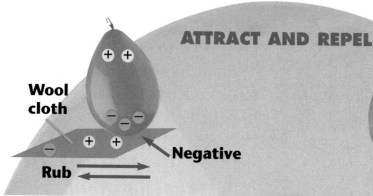

Wool cloth

Negative

Rub

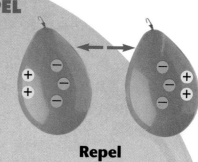

Repel

❶ Rubbing the balloon knocks negative charges off the cloth. These negative charges collect on the balloon and make it negative.

❸ The balloon repels other negative things, such as another rubbed balloon.

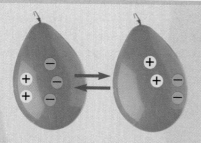

Attract

Attract

❷ Now the balloon is attracted to more positively charged things, such as an unrubbed balloon.

❹ The balloon's negative charges repel negative charges on the wall. This leaves a row of positive charges on the outside edge of the wall. The negatively charged balloon is attracted to the wall's positive charges and sticks to it.

READING Ⓝ DIAGRAMS

1. **DISCUSS** How does rubbing a balloon with a wool cloth affect the charge of the balloon?
2. **REPRESENT** Why does a rubbed balloon stick to a wall? Draw your own model.

QUICK LAB

Testing How Long Charges Last

HYPOTHESIZE Dylan plans to rub balloons and stick them to the wall for his 2-hour party. Will they stay up? Write a hypothesis in your *Science Journal*.

MATERIALS

- 3-in. balloon, inflated
- clock or watch
- *Science Journal*

PROCEDURES

1. Rub the balloon on your shirt or hair. Stick it to the wall.

2. Time how long it takes the balloon to fall. Record the time in your *Science Journal*.

CONCLUDE AND APPLY

1. **OBSERVE** How long did the balloon stay on the wall?

2. **INTERPRET DATA** Does the electrical charge last long enough to hold the balloons up for Dylan's entire party? Explain.

3. **INFER** Why do you think the balloons fell?

Why Do Balloons Fall from the Wall?

To answer this question, you need to know about the type of electricity that causes the balloons to stick. It is called **static electricity** (stat'ik i lek tris'i tē).

Static electricity is a buildup of electric charge. When the buildup of negative charge on a balloon becomes strong enough, it will attract the positively charged particles in a wall. Soon charges on the balloon "leak" away. That is why Dylan's party balloons eventually will fall.

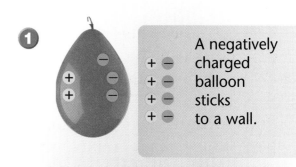

A negatively charged balloon sticks to a wall.

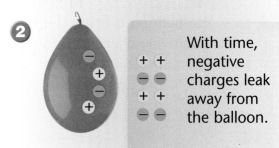

With time, negative charges leak away from the balloon.

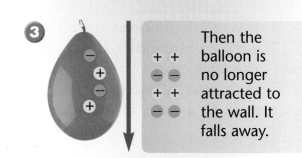

Then the balloon is no longer attracted to the wall. It falls away.

What Other Things Happen to Charges?

The Quick Lab activity showed evidence that charges move between objects. Electrical charges can also travel through certain materials. When you walk on a rug, static electricity builds up on your shoes. The charge keeps building until you touch something. Then—zap! It suddenly empties, or **discharges** (dis chärj′əz), into the object. You might feel this discharge as a small shock. The shocks you often feel when you touch objects like doorknobs, water fountains, and even other people are all small discharges.

Static electricity doesn't discharge into all types of materials. "Why not?" you might wonder. The answer is that electricity flows where it can. It flows easily through materials called **conductors** (kən duk′tərz). An **insulator** (in′sə lā′tər) is a material through which electricity does not flow.

What types of materials do you think are good conductors? Metal is a very good conductor. That is why you might feel a shock when you touch a metal doorknob. The static electricity on your shoes travels through your body to your hand. When your hand gets near the metal knob—zap! The charges jump the gap, and you feel a shock.

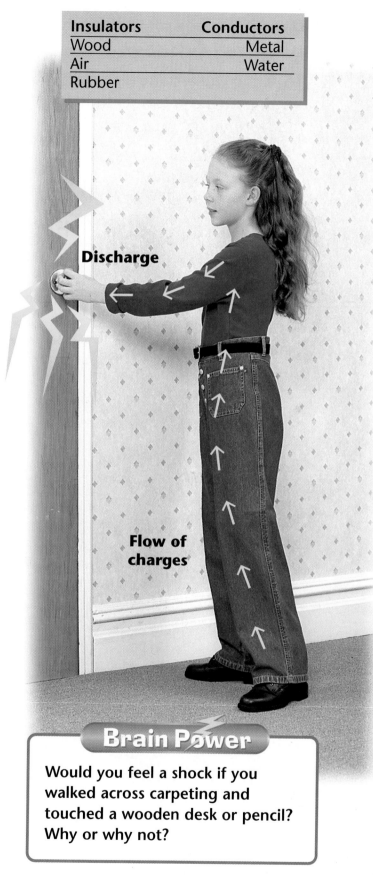

Insulators	Conductors
Wood	Metal
Air	Water
Rubber	

Discharge

Flow of charges

Brain Power

Would you feel a shock if you walked across carpeting and touched a wooden desk or pencil? Why or why not?

How Does Lightning Form?

How big can a static electricity buildup get? It can form a lightning bolt! *Lightning* (lit′ning) is a discharge of static electricity from a huge cloud called a thundercloud. It is no different from the zap you get from touching a doorknob—just bigger. A single lightning bolt has enough power to light 100 million light bulbs!

LIGHTNING

1 Inside a thundercloud water and ice particles rub together. This separates positive and negative charges.

2 Light, positive ice particles gather at the top of the cloud.

Thundercloud

3 Heavy, negative water particles settle at the bottom of the cloud. The charge keeps building up.

5 Soon the buildup is too great. Charges jump the gap between the cloud and the ground as a discharge. Zap! Lightning strikes.

4 Compared to the cloud bottom, the ground below is positively charged.

READING N' DIAGRAMS

1. **DISCUSS** What causes positive and negative charges to separate within a thundercloud?

2. **REPRESENT** Where do negative charges build up in a cloud? Draw a picture.

Where Does Lightning Go?

Sometimes lightning bolts occur inside the thundercloud and never leave it. Sometimes lightning bolts occur between two clouds. Other times lightning strikes the ground or objects on the ground.

Lightning gives off energy in several forms. One form is light energy. Another form is heat energy. You can see evidence of heat energy in burn marks on a struck tree. A third form is sound energy. You hear this as thunder. Some electrical energy can also travel through a struck object. This energy moves into the ground, or is grounded.

Why does lightning strike some places and not others? Lightning targets the clearest, shortest path to the ground. That may be through a tall tree or building. Lightning also targets the best conductor.

That is why people often use lightning rods. A lightning rod safely discharges lightning into the ground. A lightning rod is made of metal. It is usually placed at the very top of a building. A wire connects the lightning rod to the ground. When lightning strikes the rod, the electrical energy flows through the wire and into the ground.

Lightning often strikes tall objects such as buildings and trees.

Lightning rod

Underground discharge

How Do You Keep Safe from Lightning?

Lightning is a very dangerous discharge of static electricity. You should always take lightning very seriously. Getting struck by lightning can cause severe injuries and even death. Understanding how lightning behaves can help keep you safe. Following these simple rules can keep you safe, too.

LIGHTNING DOS AND DON'TS

HEALTH LINK

If you hear thunder, or see or suspect lightning:

1. Stay away from high places, like the top of a hill.

2. Stay away from trees and other tall objects.

3. Crouch down if you feel your hair stand on end.

4. Get out of the water.

5. Don't use the telephone.

6. If you are in a car, stay inside. Close the windows and doors.

7. Don't touch electrical devices or anything made of metal.

READING ∕ DIAGRAMS

1. **WRITE** Make a list of lightning "dos and don'ts" for your home.
2. **DISCUSS** Why do you think you should not touch anything during a lightning storm?

About 2,600 years ago, the ancient Greeks noticed the effects of static electricity when they rubbed fur on amber, which is hardened tree sap. They named the force they felt after *elektron*, their word for amber. Today our understanding of static electricity has come a long way.

Knowing what static electricity is and how it is formed explains what causes shocks to be felt and balloons to stick to walls. Understanding shocks and lightning allows you to keep safe.

Lightning is a dangerous form of static electricity.

REVIEW

1. Why does a rubbed balloon stick to the wall?

2. You rub two balloons on the same cloth. Explain what happens when you bring them close together. Draw a diagram.

3. How is lightning formed? What are some things you can do to keep safe from lightning?

4. **DRAW CONCLUSIONS** Balloon A was rubbed with a wool cloth. Balloon B was rubbed with plastic wrap. The balloons attracted each other. Did the plastic wrap make balloon B positive or negative? How did it do that?

5. **CRITICAL THINKING** *Analyze* Would a wooden lightning rod work? Why or why not?

WHY IT MATTERS THINK ABOUT IT Why do you think the ancient Greeks might have first started thinking about static electricity?

WHY IT MATTERS WRITE ABOUT IT The ancient Greeks made static electricity by rubbing fur on amber. Explain how this created static electricity.

World of SCIENCE

A SHOCKING Story

Franklin built little devices to use in his experiments.

B enjamin Franklin was a leader of the young United States. He was also a scientist.

In 1746 Franklin began to experiment with electricity. He believed electricity was a fluid. He thought that objects with lots of it had a positive charge. He thought that electricity jumped from them to objects with less of it—those with a negative charge.

Franklin found that electricity jumped quickly to a sharp, pointed object. It jumped more slowly to an object that wasn't pointed. He also noted that electricity was like lightning. Both were the same color, made the same noise, and could destroy things!

Franklin suggested some experiments to find out if lightning was electricity. However, he didn't do them right away. He was waiting for the construction of a church steeple with a sharp point. Franklin hoped the steeple would attract lightning from the clouds.

In 1752 Franklin decided not to wait any longer. He tied a key to a kite string and flew the kite in a storm. Suddenly threads on the string stuck straight out. A spark jumped from the key to Franklin's knuckle! Luckily Franklin let go of the string before he was killed.

Thanks to Franklin we now know that lightning is static electricity. We also have the lightning rod!

Franklin's most famous experiment was a shocker!

Discussion
Starter

1 Why did threads on the kite string stick out?

2 Why was the kite experiment so dangerous?

*inter*NET CONNECTION To learn more about Benjamin Franklin, visit www.mhschool.com/science and enter the keyword FRANKLIN.

Topic 2
PHYSICAL SCIENCE

WHY IT MATTERS

We use and depend on many electrical pathways in our daily activities.

SCIENCE WORDS

circuit a complete path that electricity can move through

current electricity a moving electrical charge

closed circuit a complete circuit

open circuit an incomplete circuit

resistor a material through which electricity has difficulty flowing

short circuit when too much current flows through a conductor

switch a device that can open or close a circuit

Electrical Pathways

Have you ever had one of those camping trips where everything went wrong? Unfortunately Corky is having one of those trips. Now something is wrong with her flashlight. She made a list of what could be wrong.

Could the problem be something else? What else might it be?

EXPLORE

HYPOTHESIZE What parts are needed to make a light bulb light? How should they be arranged? Write a hypothesis in your *Science Journal.* What kind of experiment can you design to test your ideas?

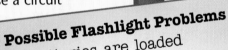

Possible Flashlight Problems

1. The batteries are loaded incorrectly.
2. The batteries are dead.
3. The bulb is no good.
4. The flashlight was damaged when it fell in muddy water.

Investigate What Makes a Bulb Light

Test what makes a bulb light by arranging the materials in different ways.

PROCEDURES

1. EXPERIMENT Work with your group to try to light the bulb using the materials. Draw each setup in your *Science Journal*. Record your results.

2. PREDICT Study the drawings on this page. Predict in which setups the bulb will light and in which it will not light. Record your predictions.

3. EXPERIMENT Work with another group of students to test each setup. Can you see a pattern?

CONCLUDE AND APPLY

1. OBSERVE How many ways could you arrange the materials to make the bulb light in step 1?

2. COMPARE How were the ways to light the bulb using only one wire similar?

3. COMPARE How were the ways that did *not* light the bulb using only one wire similar?

4. COMPARE In which drawings did the bulb light? How are the setups similar?

GOING FURTHER: Problem Solving

5. PREDICT Draw another setup. Challenge a classmate to determine if the bulb will light.

MATERIALS
- flashlight bulb
- 20 cm of wire with stripped ends
- D-cell
- D-cell holder
- *Science Journal*

What Makes a Bulb Light?

The Explore Activity showed a pattern in the setups that made the bulb light. All the setups that worked had one thing in common. They formed a complete path. The path went from one end of the D-cell. Then, it went through the bulb. Next, it went back to the other end of the D-cell. A complete path that electricity can move through is called a **circuit** (sûr′kit). A circuit is a system made up of many parts that work together to allow electricity to flow.

Here are four circuits that will make a bulb light using the materials from the Explore Activity. Trace the path in each.

Electricity Flow in a Circuit

The electricity that flows through a circuit is a little different from static electricity. Remember, static electricity is a buildup of electrical charge. The electricity that flows through a circuit is called **current electricity** (kûr′ənt i lek tris′i tē). Current electricity is moving electrical charge.

Can you think of something else that flows? What about a liquid, like water? Water flows in streams, rivers, pipes, and hoses. Current electricity itself is not *like* water. However, in many ways it *behaves like* flowing water. Both flow only if they have a clear path. For example, if the path of flowing water is clear, it flows freely. If the path isn't clear, it stops flowing.

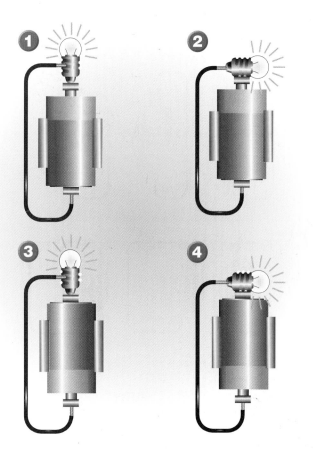

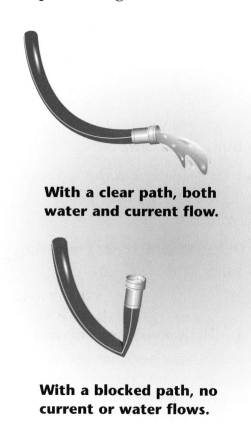

With a clear path, both water and current flow.

With a blocked path, no current or water flows.

When Will Current Flow in a Circuit?

With electric circuits a complete path is called a **closed circuit** (klōzd sûr′kit). In a closed circuit, there are no gaps or places where current cannot flow.

An incomplete path is called an **open circuit** (ō′pən sûr′kit). No current flows in an open circuit. The path is not complete. There are gaps, or places where current cannot flow. As in any system, when a part is missing, the system does not work properly.

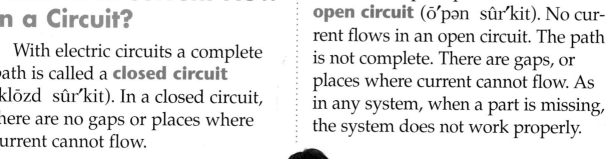

CLOSED CIRCUIT

Current flows.

No gaps

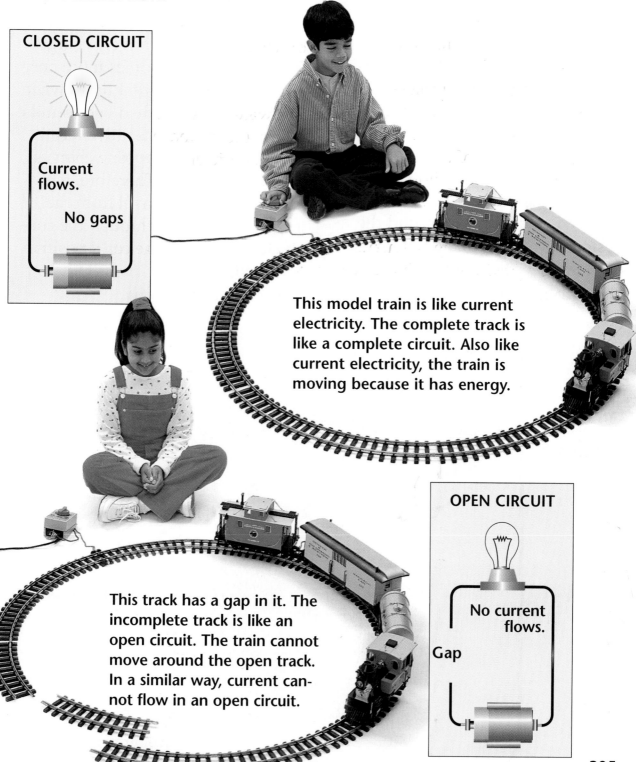

This model train is like current electricity. The complete track is like a complete circuit. Also like current electricity, the train is moving because it has energy.

This track has a gap in it. The incomplete track is like an open circuit. The train cannot move around the open track. In a similar way, current cannot flow in an open circuit.

OPEN CIRCUIT

No current flows.

Gap

305

Where Does Current Come From?

One way to make current is by using a cell. A cell changes chemical energy into electrical energy. A battery is made up of several connected cells. One type of cell is a wet cell. You will learn about wet cells in Topic 5. Another type of cell is a dry cell.

What parts of a dry cell can you identify in this diagram? This diagram shows what is inside one type of dry cell. Down the center is a rod made of the element carbon. Surrounding the carbon rod is a moist chemical paste. Around the paste is a container made of the element zinc. *Never* open a cell. The paste inside can harm your skin.

On the outside of the dry cell are two places where wires can be attached. These are called *terminals* (tûr′mə nəlz). The positive terminal is attached to the carbon rod. The negative terminal is attached to the zinc container.

A chemical change takes place within the cell. This makes the zinc container more negatively charged. The carbon rod becomes more positively charged. Current flows when a conductor is attached between the cell's positive and negative terminals. Remember, opposite charges attract each other. Therefore, the negative charges travel from the negative terminal, through the conductor, and on to the cell's positive terminal.

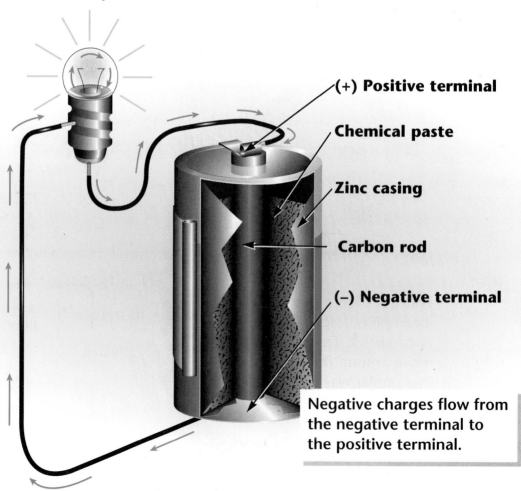

(+) Positive terminal

Chemical paste

Zinc casing

Carbon rod

(–) Negative terminal

Negative charges flow from the negative terminal to the positive terminal.

How Does a Light Bulb Work?

The circuit on page 306 includes a light bulb. Current from the dry cell lights the bulb. How do you think this happens? To understand how a light bulb works, you must first learn about its parts.

1 A light bulb is a ball of glass. Inside the bulb most of the air has been removed.

2 The bulb has a metal base that can be screwed into a socket. The metal socket is a good conductor. You remember from Topic 1 that electricity flows easily through a conductor. Electricity does not flow through an insulator.

4 Between the two wires is a thin, coiled wire. It is called a filament (fil′ə mənt). The filament, however, is a poor conductor. It is a **resistor** (ri zis′tər). Current does not flow easily through a resistor. This resistance causes the filament to get so hot that it glows. That is how the bulb creates light and heat. The air in the bulb has been removed to keep the filament from burning up.

3 Two wires extend into the bulb from the base. These wires are also good conductors.

READING DIAGRAMS

1. **WRITE** What are the parts of a light bulb? Make a list.
2. **DISCUSS** What parts of a light bulb are good conductors?
3. **DISCUSS** Why does the bulb give off light and heat?

QUICK LAB

Conductor Test-Off

HYPOTHESIZE The base and wires of a light bulb are good conductors. The filament is a poor conductor. What other materials are good conductors or insulators? Write a hypothesis in your *Science Journal.*

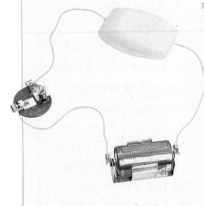

MATERIALS

- flashlight bulb
- bulb socket
- D-cell
- cell holder
- 3 wires with stripped ends, 20 cm each
- assorted test objects
- *Science Journal*

PROCEDURES

1. **EXPERIMENT** Make a circuit as shown, using one of the test objects. Record your observations in your *Science Journal.*

2. **REPEAT** Test the other objects. Record your observations.

CONCLUDE AND APPLY

1. **OBSERVE** Which objects were good conductors? Which were not? How could you tell?

2. **INFER** Examine a length of wire. Which part of the wire is a conductor? Which part is an insulator? Why do you think the wire is made this way?

What Can Go Wrong in a Circuit?

Current always follows the path with the least resistance. If at all possible, it would flow through a conductor rather than a resistor.

How does the current flow in the diagram below? In this diagram the connecting wire is a better conductor than the filament. It has less resistance than the filament. Therefore, current avoids the bulb. It takes the path with less resistance to the cell.

That causes too much current to flow through the conductors. This is called a **short circuit** (shôrt sûr′kit).

In your home a short circuit can also occur if frayed or broken wires touch. This heats up the wires and can cause a fire.

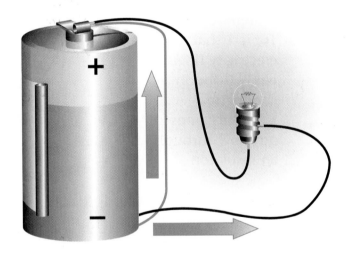

This is one example of a short circuit

How Can You Control Current in a Circuit?

This circuit is set up to make an electric door buzzer. In this system some of the electricity is transformed into sound energy. When the circuit is closed, the buzzer makes a sound.

What do you think might be wrong with the circuit in figure A? The buzzer never stops buzzing because the circuit stays closed. Figures B and C show a different setup that uses a **switch** (swich). A switch is a device that can open or close a circuit. It is used to control current in a circuit.

What do you see in figure B? Figure B shows the switch in the open position. No current flows. The buzzer doesn't buzz.

What do you see in figure C? Figure C shows what happens when you push the switch button. The circuit closes. Current flows. The buzzer buzzes. When you stop pushing the button, the switch opens again. Current stops flowing. The buzzer stops buzzing.

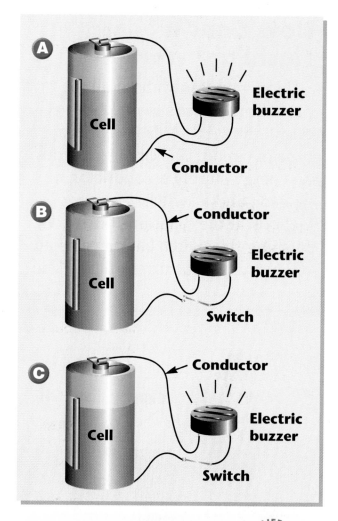

A Cell — Electric buzzer — Conductor

B Conductor — Cell — Electric buzzer — Switch

C Conductor — Cell — Electric buzzer — Switch

Brain Power

Somebody rang your doorbell. Now it won't stop ringing! What could be wrong?

FUNtastic Facts

Electric eels can produce enough current to stun or even kill a human. An electric eel's body has layers of tissue, one under the other, like the plates in a car battery. Chemicals in the eel's body flow through these tissues and produce electricity. How does this feature help the eel survive?

How Does a Flashlight Work?

Now you know about all the parts Corky needs to make her flashlight work. A flashlight is a type of circuit. The circuit includes an energy supply, a conductor, a resistor, and a switch.

Look at the diagrams below. Pushing the switch back creates an open circuit. No current flows. The flashlight is off. Pushing the switch forward creates a closed circuit. Current flows from the cells to the bulb. The filament in the bulb gets very hot and glows.

Current completes the circuit by traveling through the wire to the other end of the cells. Pushing the switch back to the open position will open the circuit and turn off the flashlight.

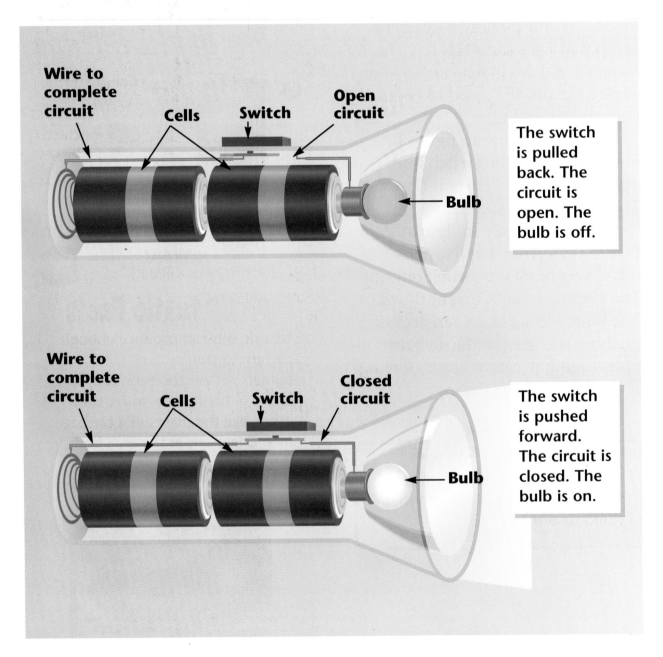

Wire to complete circuit

Cells

Switch

Open circuit

Bulb

The switch is pulled back. The circuit is open. The bulb is off.

Wire to complete circuit

Cells

Switch

Closed circuit

Bulb

The switch is pushed forward. The circuit is closed. The bulb is on.

Electricity has become an important part of our lives. As a matter of fact, almost every part of our lives depends on electricity. We use it to create light. We use it to communicate. Electricity powers machines large and small. We use it to keep our food cold and our homes warm.

Knowing how electricity travels allows us to investigate the parts of a circuit to see what is wrong when electricity doesn't flow. This is important when there is a power loss or something like a flashlight doesn't work. Electricity—imagine trying to live without it!

How many ways did you use electricity today? Keep a log.

REVIEW

1. How does a dry cell work to provide electricity?

2. What is a short circuit?

3. What does each part of a flashlight circuit do? What causes the bulb to light?

4. **INFER** Why does a radio go off when you unplug it? Explain in terms of closed and open circuits.

5. **CRITICAL THINKING** *Analyze* How could dirt inside a flashlight prevent it from working? Think of two ways.

WHY IT MATTERS THINK ABOUT IT How would our lives be different if we did not know how to create and control electricity?

WHY IT MATTERS WRITE ABOUT IT Write about a morning that you get up and there is no electricity. What can't you do without it? What can you do instead?

READING SKILL Use the information you find in the diagram on page 310 to describe the closed circuit that makes the bulb light.

MAKING LIGHT OF ELECTRICITY

What did people do at night before there were electric lights? Most people stopped working shortly after sunset. At night they lighted their homes with fires, candles, or gas lamps. It was too hard to sew or read by such dim light, so people went to bed!

Then came the invention of electric lights. People could do things at night that they once could do only by day. They stayed up later to visit friends, read, and sew. They slept longer in the morning because they could work later in the evening!

Some of the first electric lights were arc lights. They're created when a strong electric current jumps through the air and hits a target made of carbon. The carbon glows with a bright, white light.

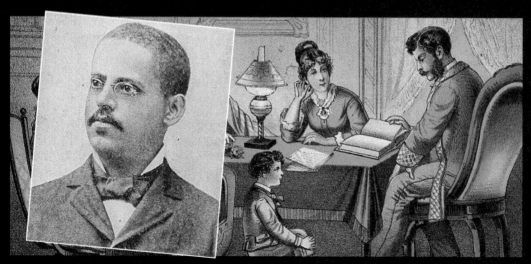

Lewis H. Latimer

312

Science, Technology, and Society

Thomas Edison's first light bulb

Inventors found that a thin wire of carbon glows when a current passes through it. Lewis H. Latimer developed the process to manufacture carbon filaments.

The first successful carbon-wire lamps were built by Thomas Edison and Joseph Swan in 1879. This event is called "the invention of the electric light." About 20 years later, a metal called tungsten (tung°stæn) was found to be the best filament. We still use tungsten-wire light bulbs today.

DISCUSSION STARTER

1. How did the way people live change as a result of the invention of electric lights?

2. How are neon lights different from other electric lights?

You see "neon" lights that spell out the names of theaters, restaurants, and stores. These lights contain gases, including neon, that glow when a current flows through them.

To learn more about electricity, visit **www.mhschool.com/science** and enter the keyword FILAMENT.

*inter*NET CONNECTION

Modern light bulb

313

WHY IT MATTERS

Different circuit types let you control how electricity works.

SCIENCE WORDS

series circuit a circuit in which the current must flow through one bulb in order to flow through the other

parallel circuit a circuit in which each bulb is connected to the cell separately

fuse a device that keeps too much electric current from flowing through wires

circuit breaker a switch that protects circuits from dangerously high currents

Different Circuits

What if you could use only one electrical device at a time? What if you had to turn off all the lights to iron clothes, dry your hair, or use a computer?

Luckily you can usually turn on more than one electrical device at the same time. Do you think each has its own circuit? Might they be part of the same circuit?

EXPLORE

HYPOTHESIZE How can you light two bulbs with one cell? Can you have one bulb on and one bulb off? Write a hypothesis in your *Science Journal.* What kind of experiment can you design to test your ideas?

Investigate How to Light Two Bulbs with One Cell

Build two different circuits. Observe how electric energy interacts with the parts of a circuit to light bulbs.

MATERIALS

- D-cell
- cell holder
- 2 flashlight bulbs
- 2 bulb holders
- 4 pieces of wire with ends stripped, 20 cm each
- *Science Journal*

PROCEDURES

1. **EXPERIMENT** Build a circuit that will light two bulbs. Use one D-cell and the fewest number of wires. Draw it in your *Science Journal*. Label it Circuit 1.

2. **PREDICT** When both bulbs are lit, predict what will happen if you remove one bulb. Test your prediction. Record your results.

3. **EXPERIMENT** Construct another circuit that will light two bulbs. One bulb should remain lit if you remove the other. Draw it in your *Science Journal*. Label it Circuit 2.

4. **COMPARE** Record in which circuit the bulbs were brighter.

CONCLUDE AND APPLY

1. **INFER** Why do you think the bulbs were brighter in one circuit than the other?

2. **COMPARE AND CONTRAST** How can removing and replacing a bulb be like opening and closing a switch?

3. **DRAW CONCLUSIONS** When you removed a bulb, why did the other bulb go out in one circuit but not in the other?

GOING FURTHER: Apply

4. **INFER** What kind of circuit do you think works best in your home? Why?

315

How Can You Light Two Bulbs with One Cell?

The Explore Activity showed that each one of two different types of circuits behaved in a certain way. Now take a closer look at two different circuits to understand why.

The first type is like circuit 1 in the Explore Activity. It shows two light bulbs connected in a **series** circuit (sîr′ēz sûr′kit). A series circuit puts both bulbs in the same circuit. The arrows show how the current flows through the parts of the circuit.

Can you think of some other things that follow one after another and are called "a series"?

When both bulbs are in place in a series circuit, it is a closed circuit. When one bulb is removed, an open

SERIES CIRCUIT

D-cell

– + Wire

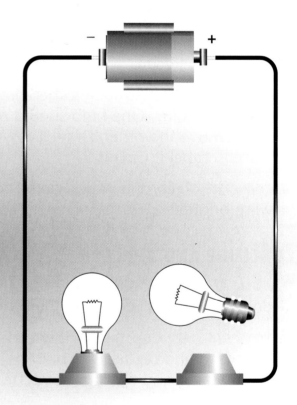

– +

	Series	Parallel
Connection	Both bulbs are on the same circuit.	Each bulb is on a separate circuit.
Removing one bulb	Both bulbs go off.	Only the removed bulb goes off.
Brightness	Dim	Bright

circuit is created. In an open circuit, current can't complete its path. The remaining bulb does not light without current flowing through its filament. A series circuit is a type of system that does not work when a part is removed.

This second type is like circuit 2 in the Explore Activity. It shows two light bulbs connected in a **parallel circuit** (par′ə lel′ sûr′kit). A parallel circuit connects each bulb to the cell separately.

When one bulb is removed from a parallel circuit, the other bulb is still a part of a complete circuit. That is why it remains lit. A parallel circuit is a type of system that still works when a part is removed because there is still a complete circuit.

The table on page 316 compares series and parallel circuits that contain two bulbs.

PARALLEL CIRCUIT

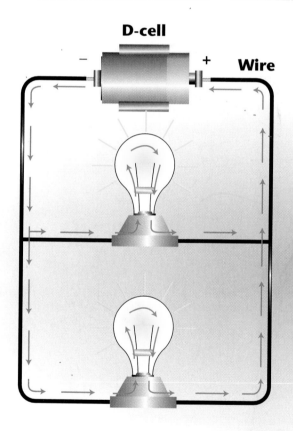

D-cell

Wire

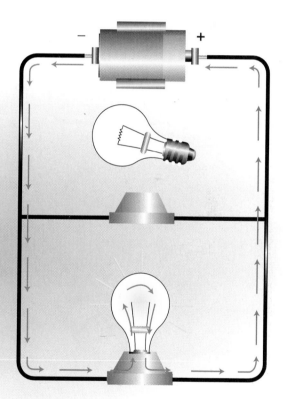

READING DIAGRAMS

1. **DISCUSS** How are the series and parallel circuits on these two pages different?
2. **REPRESENT** How are the circuits similar? Make a chart.

Why Are Bulbs Brighter in a Parallel Circuit than in a Series Circuit?

Why do you think the light bulbs were brighter in the parallel circuit than in the series circuit in the Explore Activity? Comparing electric current with cars traveling along a road will help you find out.

This diagram compares a road with a series circuit. Each construction area narrowing the road acts like a resistor in a circuit. Cars traveling along this road would be slowed down as they passed each "resistor," or construction site.

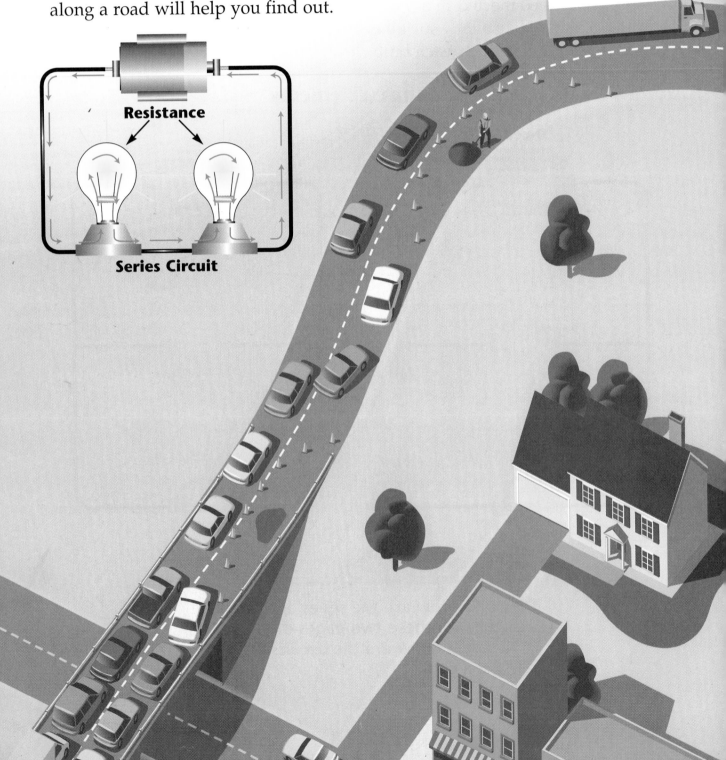

Resistance

Series Circuit

In a series circuit with two bulbs, current has only one path to follow. This path has one resistor after another in it. However, there are two paths along which current can flow in a parallel circuit. This diagram compares a parallel circuit with a split road. Each section of road has only one "resistor." More cars can travel along this road, just as more current can flow through a parallel circuit.

As you can see, more cars are traveling along this road than along the road with two narrow areas in a row. More paths are provided for cars to travel. Each path has only one narrow area, or "resistor."

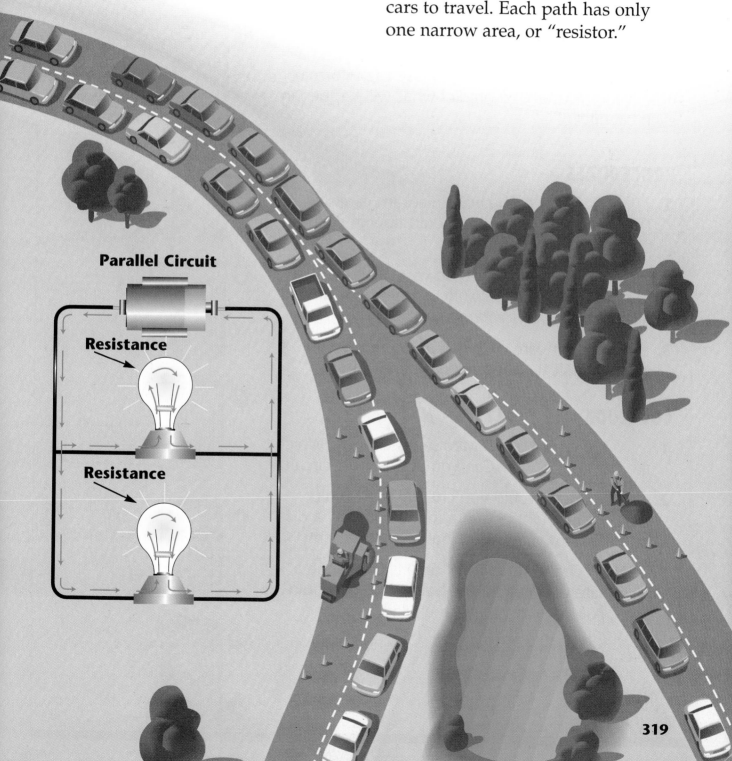

Parallel Circuit

Resistance

Resistance

Skill: Predicting

PREDICT IF IT WILL LIGHT

Making predictions is like telling the future. You can't be sure of the future. However, you can sometimes use what you know to make a good prediction.

How do you make good predictions? Look closely at each circuit. How is it similar to circuits you have seen before? How is it different? Use the information in the diagrams to predict what will happen in each circuit.

PROCEDURES

1. OBSERVE Study each circuit diagram carefully. Think about how current would flow in each circuit.

2. PREDICT In which circuits do you think the bulb or bulbs would light up? Record your predictions in your *Science Journal*.

3. PREDICT Compare circuits 4 and 5. Predict in which circuit the bulbs would be brightest.

CONCLUDE AND APPLY

1. IDENTIFY Which circuits are series circuits? Which are parallel circuits? Can you find a short circuit?

2. EXPLAIN How would you change the circuits that will not light? Make a model or draw a diagram to show how you would change them.

3. PREDICT Draw yet another circuit. Challenge a classmate to predict if the bulb or bulbs would light. Ask your classmate to explain his or her thoughts about the prediction.

MATERIALS

- *Science Journal*

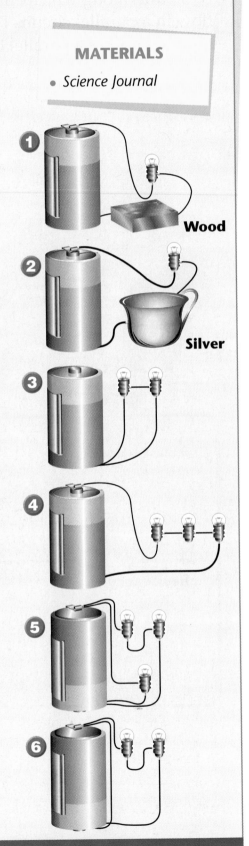

1 — Wood

2 — Silver

3

4

5

6

What Types of Circuits Are Found in Homes and Other Places?

Now that you know more about circuits, do you think those in homes and other places are series or parallel circuits? Why?

Electrical devices in homes and other places are connected in parallel circuits. If they were series circuits all the lights would go out if one bulb burnt out. Do you remember that the bulbs in the series circuit were dim? If many lights in your home were part of a series circuit, they would probably be so dim you couldn't see by them!

Circuits in homes and other places are controlled by switches. For example, flipping a light switch to the up position closes a circuit. The light goes on. Flipping the light switch on the wall down opens the circuit. The light goes off.

CLOSED CIRCUIT

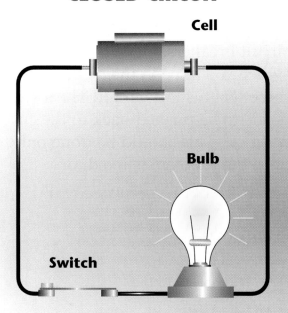

Cell

Bulb

Switch

OPEN CIRCUIT

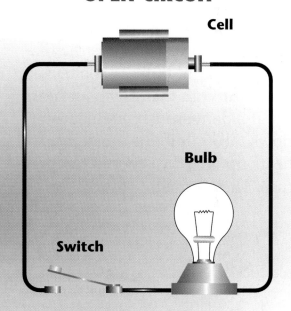

Cell

Bulb

Switch

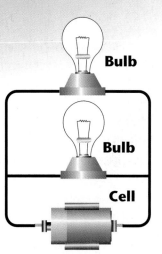

Bulb

Bulb

Cell

Brain Power

How can switches and one power source control more than one light in a parallel circuit? Where would you put switches to control each light in this circuit?

How Can Circuits in Homes Be Protected?

In the Skill Builder activity, circuit 6 would create a short circuit. That would happen because there is no resistance, such as a light bulb, in one of the paths. A short circuit is dangerous. Too much current flows in a short circuit. This can cause wires to heat up. Hot wires can start a fire. Too much current can also damage electrical devices.

One device that keeps too much electrical current from flowing through wires is called a **fuse** (fūz). A fuse has a thin strip of metal in it. The strip is a resistor, like the filament in a light bulb. When current flows through the resistor, it heats up. If a dangerously high current flows through it, the metal strip heats up only to a certain temperature. Then it melts. This creates an open circuit. The current stops flowing. Once a fuse melts, it cannot be reused. It must be replaced with a new fuse.

Most new homes do not have fuses. They are built with **circuit breakers** (sûr′kit brā′kərz). A circuit breaker is a switch that protects circuits. When a dangerously high current flows through the switch, the metal becomes heated. The overheated metal in the switch expands. This pushes the switch open. A spring holds the switch open creating an open circuit.

If some electrical devices stop working, an adult should check the circuit breakers. One or more of the switches will be in the *off* position if there was a short circuit. The switch needs to be pushed back to the *on* position. This should be done only once the problem is fixed, or another short circuit will occur.

A thin metal strip conducts current through a fuse. When too much current flows, the metal strip melts. This creates an open circuit. Current cannot flow through the fuse.

How a Fuse Works

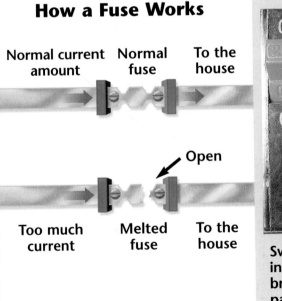

Normal current amount — Normal fuse — To the house

Too much current — Melted fuse — To the house — Open

Switches in a circuit breaker panel

Understanding parallel and series circuits gives you a good idea of how the circuits in your home and school work. When you know how electricity travels through different types of circuits, you can control where it goes and what it does. You are also aware of safety issues. Imagine a world without different kinds of circuits. You couldn't control the individual lights or appliances in your home. Your life would be very different!

What would happen if the circuits in this room were series circuits?

REVIEW

1. What are two ways that a circuit can be connected using two light bulbs and one cell?

2. Describe the differences between a series and a parallel circuit in terms of how the parts are arranged.

3. Why do homes and other places have parallel circuits?

4. **PREDICT** Suppose you added an extra light bulb in a series circuit that already had two bulbs in it. Would the bulbs shine brighter or dimmer? Why?

5. **CRITICAL THINKING** *Apply* Should a fuse be in a series or a parallel circuit with the main power coming into a house? Explain.

WHY IT MATTERS THINK ABOUT IT How would your life be different if only one type of circuit existed?

WHY IT MATTERS WRITE ABOUT IT Write about a day when all the circuits in your home or school suddenly changed to series circuits.

Critical Circuits

Any electrical tool must have a complete circuit or current can't flow to make the tool work! Most circuits, like those in flashlights and video games, can fit into the palm of your hand.

Other circuits are gigantic! Electric power plants are linked in a giant circuit called a grid. Power demands from one plant can interrupt the whole circuit. On November 9, 1965, one switch failed near Toronto, Canada. The power overload spread throughout eastern North America, causing a blackout over the entire region for hours!

Other circuits are tiny. The heart of a computer is a small silicon chip. It's about the size of

Greatly enlarged picture of a chip

a fingernail but may contain hundreds of thousands of tiny regions. Together they do the computer's "thinking." Each region must be connected to the others by a tiny circuit that's on the chip.

There can be hundreds of circuits on a single computer chip. That's why the computer-chip circuits are so tiny. If they were made of regular electrical parts with wires and switches, they'd cover a gym floor!

It's important to fit as many circuits as possible on a computer chip. Why? The farther apart they are, the farther the electrical signal has to travel and the slower the computer! The more circuits, the faster and more powerful the computer.

Creating the tiny circuits on computer chips is a difficult process. Workers wear protective suits to

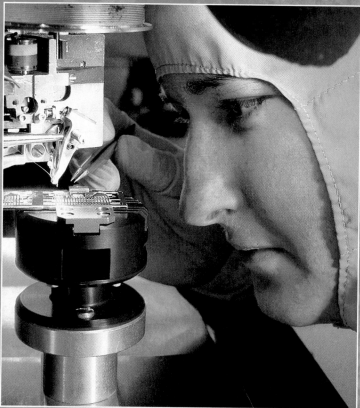

prevent dust and dirt from getting into the circuits.

DISCUSSION STARTER

1. What's the advantage of making smaller and smaller circuits for computer chips?

2. How small or large do you think circuits can get? Why?

To learn more about circuits, visit *www.mhschool.com/science* and enter the keyword MAZE.

*inter*NET
CONNECTION

SCIENCE WORDS

circuit p. 304

circuit
  breaker p. 322

closed
  circuit p. 305

conductor p. 295

current
  electricity p. 304

discharge p. 295

fuse p. 322

insulator p. 295

open circuit p. 305

parallel
  circuit p. 317

resistor p. 307

series circuit p. 316

short circuit p. 308

static
  electricity p. 294

switch p. 309

USING SCIENCE WORDS

Number a paper from 1 to 10. Fill in 1 to 5 with words from the list above.

1. A buildup of electric charge that causes lightning is called __?__ .

2. A light bulb is a type of __?__ .

3. Current must flow through one device to get to another in a(n) __?__ .

4. A circuit that has a gap is a(n) __?__ .

5. A thin piece of metal in a(n) __?__ melts when current is dangerously high.

6–10. Pick five words from the list above that were not used in 1 to 5, and use each in a sentence.

UNDERSTANDING SCIENCE IDEAS

11. How does a dry cell work to produce current?

12. What is the difference between a series and a parallel circuit?

USING IDEAS AND SKILLS

13. **READING SKILL: READING A DIAGRAM FOR INFORMATION** Look at the diagram on page 296. Describe the difference in charge between the ground and the bottom of the cloud.

14. **PREDICT** A company makes a lightning rod out of plastic. It is lighter, stronger, and cheaper to make than a metal lightning rod. Predict if this rod will work. Why or why not?

15. **THINKING LIKE A SCIENTIST** A fixture has six light bulbs in a row. How can you find out if the bulbs are wired in a series or a parallel circuit?

PROBLEMS and PUZZLES

Circuit Map How would you light a house? Draw a floor plan of a room or floor. Show where you would put lights. Map the circuits. Where will the electricity come from?

CHAPTER 10
MAKING AND USING ELECTRICITY

Have you ever thought about where electricity comes from? In Chapter 9 you learned how a dry cell creates current. However, this current is not enough to power homes, businesses, and large machines. Most people know that power comes from a power station. Yet few think about how it is produced. In this chapter you will learn about ways people make and use electricity.

In this chapter you will have several opportunities to read for cause and effect. Knowing why something happens helps you to understand how events are connected.

WHY IT MATTERS

Television and stereo speakers couldn't work without magnets.

SCIENCE WORDS

pole one of two ends of a magnet; where a magnet's pull is strongest

magnetic field a region of magnetic force around a magnet

electromagnet a temporary magnet created when current flows through wire wrapped in coils around an iron bar

Electricity and Magnets

Did you know that a compass needle always points north? That is how a compass helps you find your way in unfamiliar places.

When Jenna's toy crane lifted a bar magnet, the magnet always pointed in the same direction. When the crane lifted a nonmagnet, it pointed in any direction. Jenna wondered if a hanging magnet is like a compass. Do you think so?

EXPLORE

HYPOTHESIZE How does a bar magnet compare with a compass? Write a hypothesis in your *Science Journal.* How could you find out?

EXPLORE ACTIVITY

Investigate How a Bar Magnet Is Like a Compass

Play around with magnets to test how they compare with a compass.

PROCEDURES

1. OBSERVE How do the bar magnets interact when you place them next to each other in different positions?

2. PREDICT Which way will the bar magnet point if you hang it as shown? Record your prediction in your *Science Journal*.

3. OBSERVE Test your prediction. Record the results.

4. COMPARE Place the compass on a flat surface away from the magnets. Compare the directions in which the compass and magnet point.

5. OBSERVE Hold the compass near the hanging magnet. What happens?

CONCLUDE AND APPLY

1. COMMUNICATE How do the two magnets interact with each other?

2. COMPARE How did your hanging magnet compare with other students' magnets?

3. COMMUNICATE What happened when you brought the compass near the hanging magnet?

4. INFER Of what must a compass be made?

GOING FURTHER: Problem Solving

5. INFER What do you think was pulling the magnet and compass?

MATERIALS

- 2 bar magnets
- 1 m of string
- compass
- ruler
- tape
- heavy book
- *Science Journal*

How Are a Compass and a Magnet Alike?

The Explore Activity showed that Jenna was correct. The hanging magnet pointed north, just as the compass did. Magnets also interacted when they were placed next to each other. Study these pages to learn more about the properties of magnets and compasses.

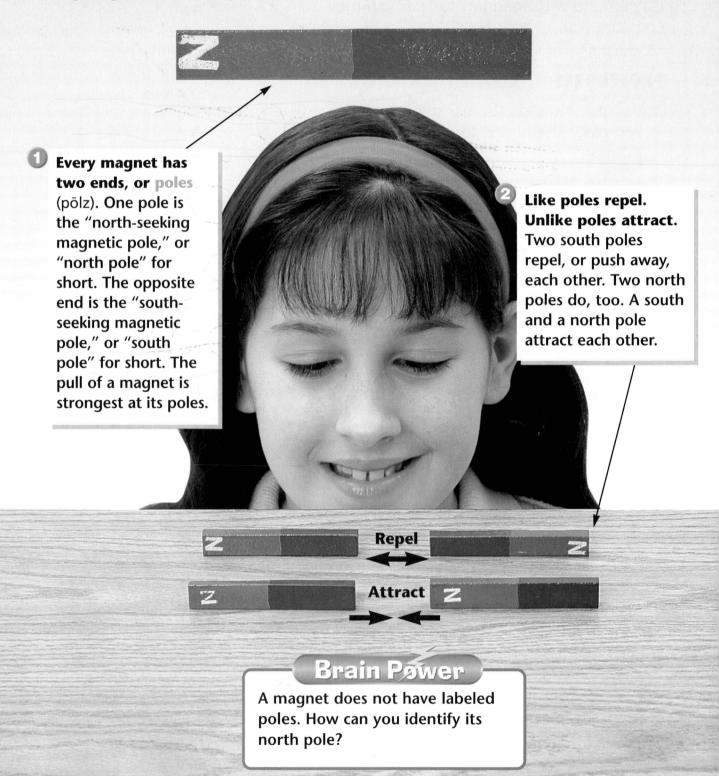

1 Every magnet has two ends, or poles (pōlz). One pole is the "north-seeking magnetic pole," or "north pole" for short. The opposite end is the "south-seeking magnetic pole," or "south pole" for short. The pull of a magnet is strongest at its poles.

2 Like poles repel. Unlike poles attract. Two south poles repel, or push away, each other. Two north poles do, too. A south and a north pole attract each other.

Repel

Attract

Brain Power
A magnet does not have labeled poles. How can you identify its north pole?

Did you know that there is even a plant that can determine which way is north? A plant known as the compass plant grows in the United States Midwest. It is also known as the pilotweed in some places.

A compass plant can grow taller than a tall adult. Its lower leaves line up in a north-south direction, which allows it to avoid the hot noon sunlight. How could the compass plant help you find your way?

3 **When free to move, magnets will line up in a north-south direction.** Jenna's hanging magnet is like a compass. It points north. You can make a compass by hanging a magnet like Jenna's.

North

4 **A compass is a magnet.** The needle of a compass is a small magnet. It is attached to the base by a small pin. The pin does not move but allows the needle to turn toward Earth's North Pole.

QUICK LAB

How Magnets Interact

HYPOTHESIZE It seems that there is an invisible force at work between magnets. What do you think causes magnets to interact the way they do? Write a hypothesis in your *Science Journal.*

MATERIALS
- safety goggles
- 2 bar magnets
- piece of white paper
- iron filings in a sealed plastic bag
- tape
- *Science Journal*

PROCEDURES

 Safety: Wear safety goggles.

1. **OBSERVE** Tape a bar magnet flat on your desk. Place the paper over it. Put the bag of iron filings over the paper. Sketch the pattern of the filings in your *Science Journal.*

2. **OBSERVE** Repeat step 1 using two bar magnets with their poles 2 cm apart. Try different north/south combinations. Sketch each setup and the patterns you see.

CONCLUDE AND APPLY

1. **OBSERVE** Describe the pattern of the filings when like and unlike poles were next to each other.

2. **COMPARE** How was the pattern of a single bar magnet different from the pattern of two magnets?

Why Do a Hanging Magnet and Compass Turn?

What attracted Jenna's hanging magnet and made it line up in a north-south direction? The answer may surprise you. Earth itself is a magnet.

Imagine a huge bar magnet running along Earth's center. This magnet would create a region of magnetic force called a **magnetic field** (mag net'ik fēld). Jenna's magnet lined up with Earth's magnetic field in a north-south direction. In other words the north-seeking magnetic pole faced Earth's north magnetic pole. The south-seeking magnetic pole faced Earth's south magnetic pole. You can't see a magnetic field. However, the iron filings in the Quick Lab let you "see" the magnetic field of bar magnets.

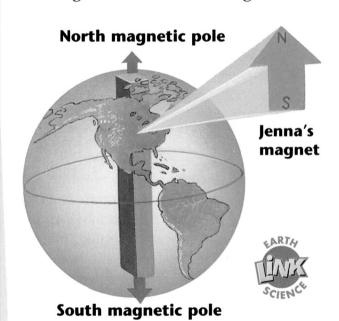

North magnetic pole

Jenna's magnet

South magnetic pole

Jenna's magnet lined up with Earth's magnetic field.

Where Do Magnets Come From?

A magnet is a material or device that attracts items containing the elements iron, nickel, or cobalt (kō′bôlt).

About 2,000 years ago, people from an area called Magnesia (mag nē′shə) found rocks that would attract small pieces of iron. The rocks are called magnetite (mag′ni tīt′). They contain magnetized iron.

What gives a magnet its properties? A piece of magnetized iron, like all matter, is made up of particles. Each particle of iron has its own magnetic field. When the particles are all lined up in the same direction, their magnetic fields act together. This makes the piece of iron have a strong magnetic field.

Magnets can also be created using electric current. Current running in a wire creates a weak magnetic field. When current flows a magnetic field forms around the wire. When the current is turned off, the magnetic field goes away.

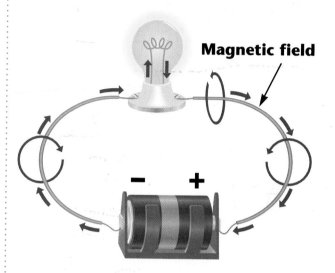

Magnetic field

You can make a stronger magnetic field by winding the wire in loops around an iron bar. When current flows this creates a temporary magnet called an **electromagnet** (i lek′trō mag′nit).

Magnetized iron

Nonmagnetized iron

Electromagnet

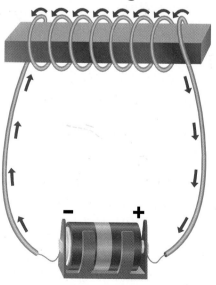

QUICK LAB

Stronger Electromagnets

HYPOTHESIZE What will make an electromagnet stronger? Write a hypothesis in your *Science Journal.*

MATERIALS

- nail
- 2 D-cells and holders
- wire with stripped ends
- 10 paper clips
- *Science Journal*

PROCEDURES

1. Wind the wire 20 times around the nail near its head. Attach each end of the wire to the D-cell to complete the circuit.

2. **OBSERVE** Record in your *Science Journal* how many paper clips your electromagnet can hold.

3. **EXPERIMENT** Repeat using two D-cells in series. Record how many paper clips the nail held.

4. **EXPERIMENT** Wind the wire 20 more times. Repeat steps 2 and 3.

CONCLUDE AND APPLY

INTERPRET DATA How did increasing current affect the strength of the electromagnet? Increasing the number of coils?

How Are Electromagnets Used?

This junkyard crane uses a powerful electromagnet. It attracts all items made of iron, steel, nickel, and cobalt.

Electromagnets also have many other uses. Doctors use electromagnets to take iron splinters out of a patient's skin. Recyclers use them to separate scrap metals. Electromagnets are also used in machines such as tape players, bells, motors, buzzers, loudspeakers, and televisions.

A junkyard crane uses an electromagnet to move large pieces of metal.

How Does a Doorbell Work?

An electric doorbell is made up of an electromagnet and a power source. Figure A shows the doorbell circuit before you push the button. The gap leaves the circuit open. No current flows.

Figure B shows that when you push the button, the gap closes. Current flows. This pulls the electromagnet and makes the hammer hit the bell.

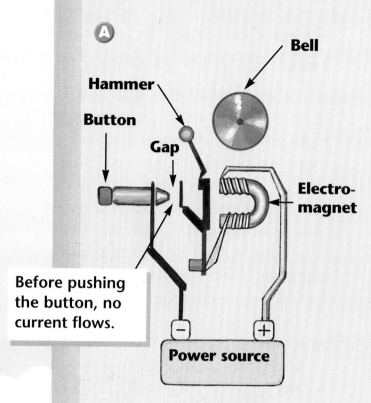

A

Bell

Hammer

Button

Gap

Electro-magnet

Before pushing the button, no current flows.

Power source

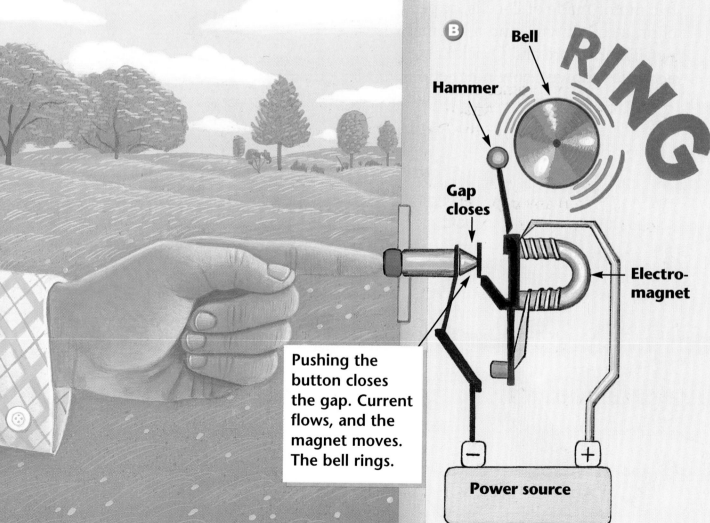

B

RING

Bell

Hammer

Gap closes

Electro-magnet

Pushing the button closes the gap. Current flows, and the magnet moves. The bell rings.

Power source

335

How Can You Put Electricity to Work?

Electric motors are clean and quiet power sources. They transform electrical energy into movement, or mechanical energy. This energy can power video recorders, some appliances, and other devices.

One of the first electric motors was built in 1829 by an American scientist, Joseph Henry. In his electric motor, electromagnets made a beam that was balanced on a pivot move up and down.

How does an electric motor work? Here you see a simple electric motor made of D-cells, paper clips, a coil of wire, and a bar magnet. The Explore and Quick Lab activities showed how magnetic fields can interact with each other.

You also learned that current passing through a conductor creates a magnetic field.

When the switch of an electric motor is closed, current passes through the coiled wire. This creates an electromagnet. When the bar magnet is brought near it, their magnetic fields interact. As the two magnets attract and repel each other, they make the coil spin.

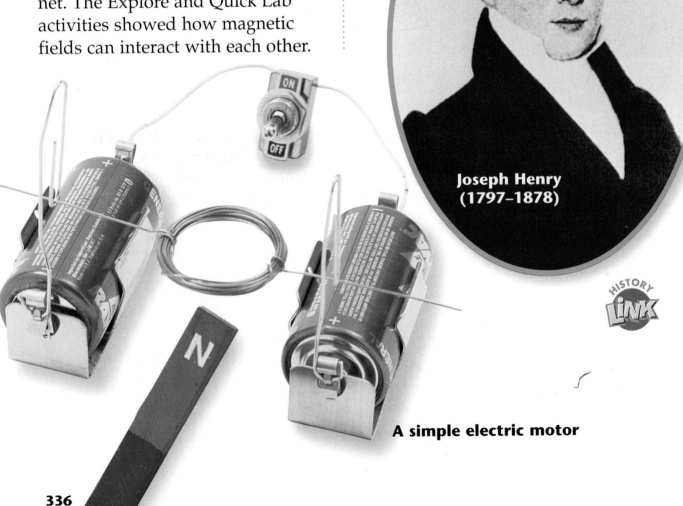

Joseph Henry (1797–1878)

HISTORY LINK

A simple electric motor

WHY IT MATTERS

The use of magnets has come a long way. By A.D. 1000 Chinese travelers used magnetic stones to find their way. In 1820 Danish scientist Hans Oersted discovered that magnetism and electricity were linked. By the 1880s electric motors were powering many different kinds of machines.

Today electromagnets play important roles in our everyday lives. They are used to separate recycled materials, to sound car horns, and to record data on computer disks. Cassette players, stereo speakers, and televisions contain electromagnets. Electromagnets are useful because we can change parts of the system to turn them on and off, and make them as strong as needed.

REVIEW

1. How are a magnet and a compass similar?

2. What happens when like poles of magnets are brought together? When opposite poles are brought together?

3. What is an electric motor? What does it do?

4. **COMPARE** How is a magnetic stone different from an electromagnet?

5. **CRITICAL THINKING** *Analyze* Would a compass be useful on a spaceship in outer space? Why or why not?

WHY IT MATTERS THINK ABOUT IT
Why isn't it a good idea to store computer disks near a television, VCR, or stereo speaker? Think about what a warning on a package of disks should say.

WHY IT MATTERS WRITE ABOUT IT
Based on everything you've learned and observed, in your own words, write a definition of an electromagnet.

READING SKILL Write a short paragraph that explains what causes a doorbell to ring.

Flips, Slides,

Let's create geometric patterns by moving figures around. Try these three ways.

Flip It!

Flip a figure over a line, and the second figure looks like a mirror image of the first! Hold out your hands in front of you, palms up. Spread out your fingers. The shape of your right hand is like a mirror image of your left. Check it out. Flip your left hand over onto your right, palms facing each other. Then open your hands!

Slide It!

Slide a figure across a line. The second figure looks the same, but it's in a different place!

Turn It!

Turn a figure around a point on a line. Imagine holding one end of the figure and moving the other end in a circle!

338

Math Link

and Turns

One of those patterns is made inside an electric motor! There's a metal coil sitting between the poles of a magnet. Electric current flows through the coil and magnetizes it. Because it's between the magnet's poles, the coil spins as its magnetic field interacts with the magnet's magnetic field. That movement keeps the motor running. The spin follows one of the geometric patterns. Which one do you think it is?

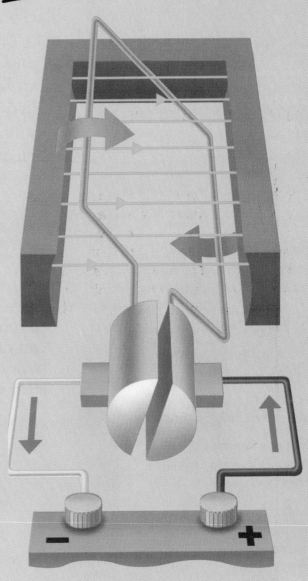

DISCUSSION STARTER

1. Why does the coil in an electric motor spin?

2. Which of the geometric patterns do you think a coil in an electric motor represents? Why?

To learn more about geometric patterns, visit *www.mhschool.com/science* and enter the keyword FLIPS.

*inter*NET
CONNECTION

Topic 5

WHY IT MATTERS

Electricity may have to travel a long way from where it is made to where it is used.

SCIENCE WORDS

direct current current that flows in one direction through a circuit

alternating current current that flows in a circuit first in one direction, then in the opposite direction

generator a device that creates alternating current

volt a unit for measuring the force that makes negative charges flow

transformer a device in which alternating current in one coil produces current in a second coil

Making Electricity

Have you ever been in a blackout? A blackout occurs when the electrical system in an area stops working. What happened during the blackout? How long did it last?

In 1965 a blackout affected the eastern United States. Cities from Boston to New York had no power! You may not think much about the electricity in your home or where it comes from—until it's gone!

EXPLORE

HYPOTHESIZE **You know that electric current can produce a magnetic field. Do you think that a magnetic field can produce electric current? Write a hypothesis in your *Science Journal*. How can you test your ideas?**

Investigate Another Way to Make Electric Current

Test another way to make electric current using wires and a magnet.

MATERIALS

- "current detector"
- paper-towel tube wrapped with enameled wire
- bar magnet
- D-cell
- D-cell holder
- tape
- *Science Journal*

PROCEDURES

1. Turn your "current detector" until the needle points north. Line up the wire loops with the needle. Tape the detector to your desk.

2. OBSERVE Connect one end of the wire to the D-cell in its holder. Briefly touch the other end of the wire to the other end of the cell. Record your observations in your *Science Journal*.

3. Obtain a cardboard tube wrapped in wire from your teacher. Connect the current detector to the ends of the wires to make a circuit.

4. OBSERVE Insert the bar magnet into the tube. Observe what happens to the detector.

5. PREDICT What will happen if you take out the magnet? Try it. Record your observations.

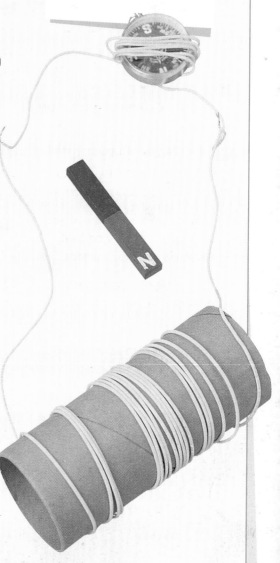

CONCLUDE AND APPLY

1. OBSERVE What happened to the current detector when current passed through the wire?

2. INTERPRET DATA What did the loops of wire around the compass form when current passed through them?

3. INFER How does the moving compass needle show that current passed through the wire?

GOING FURTHER: Problem Solving

4. INFER What made a current in the wire?

What Is Another Way to Make Electric Current?

In Topic 4 you learned that electric current creates a magnetic field. The Explore Activity showed that the reverse is also true. A magnet can create electric current.

Here are three ways to make electric current.

1 Move a magnet inside a closed loop or coil.

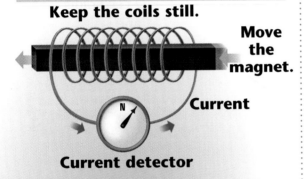

Keep the coils still.

Move the magnet.

Current

Current detector

2 Keep the magnet steady, and move the coil.

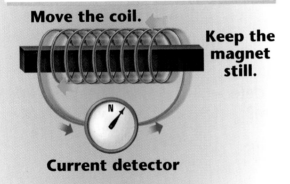

Move the coil.

Keep the magnet still.

Current detector

3 Change chemical energy to electric energy using a cell.

Current flow →

Different Types of Current

There are two types of current. The type of current that you have studied was created by dry cells. It is called **direct current** (di rekt′ kûr′ənt). Direct current is like a one-way street. It flows in one direction through the circuit. Cells and batteries make direct current.

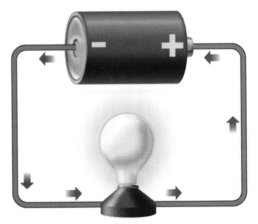

Negative charges flow from the negative terminal along the wire, through the light bulb, and on to the positive terminal. It flows in only one direction.

In the Explore Activity, the compass needle moved in one direction when the magnet was placed into the tube. When the magnet was pulled out, the needle moved the other way. This is like the current that flows in your home.

The two-way current in your home is called **alternating current** (ôl′tər nāt′ing kûr′ənt), or AC for short. The current first flows in one direction. Then it flows in the opposite direction. This happens many times every second. It is so quick that lights don't flicker.

What Makes the Electricity You Use?

Where do you think alternating current comes from? A device that creates alternating current is called a **generator** (jen′ə rā′tər). How does a generator work? These diagrams will show you.

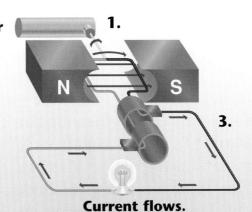

Outside power

1.

Current flows.

① A generator works by spinning a coil between the poles of a powerful magnet.

③ Current flows as the red side of the coil passes up through the magnetic field.

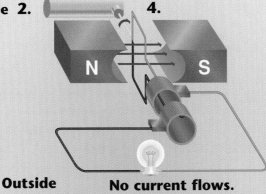

Outside power 2.

4.

No current flows.

② An outside force spins the coil. The force may come from a gasoline engine, from steam heated by a coal or nuclear power plant, or from running water.

④ In this position no part of the coil passes through the magnetic field. No current flows.

Outside power

5.

Current flows in opposite direction.

⑤ Now the red side of the coil passes down through the field instead of up. Current flows in the opposite direction. The cycle continues as the coil spins. The current changes direction many times every second.

READING /\/ DIAGRAMS

1. REPRESENT Make a list showing some things that power a generator.

2. DISCUSS How is a generator different from what was built in the Explore Activity?

Are There Other Types of Cells?

A cell uses the energy stored in chemicals to make electric current. In Topic 2 you learned about dry cells. A dry cell has a chemical acid paste around a carbon rod. Another type of cell is a *wet cell*.

In the simplest case, a wet cell contains two different metal bars placed in a liquid. The liquid contains certain chemicals and is an acid. A car battery is made up of many connected wet cells.

The negative and positive terminals of a cell are called *electrodes* (i lek'trōdz). The positive electrode in some wet cells is made of copper. The acid strips away negative charges from the copper. This leaves the copper bar positive.

The negative electrode is made of the metal zinc. The negative charges that leave the copper move to the zinc bar. This makes it have a negative charge.

When you attach a wire between the electrodes, current from a wet cell flows one way only. It is direct current.

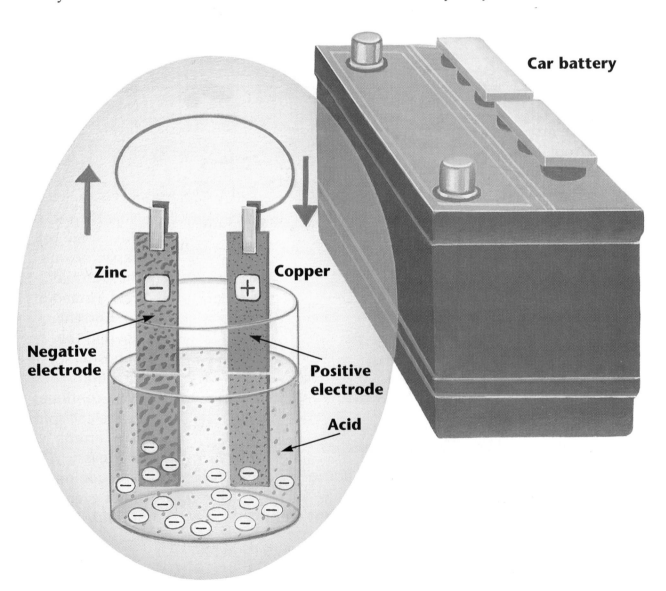

Car battery

Zinc

Copper

Negative electrode

Positive electrode

Acid

Can the Power of a Cell Be Measured?

Have you ever used batteries? If so, what did you use them for? Did you notice that they come in many different sizes? Each battery is labeled to show how many **volts** (vōlts) it has. A volt is the unit used to measure the force that makes negative charges flow. This force is called *voltage* (vōl′tij). A battery is a series of cells that are connected to produce extra voltage.

How much is a volt? A flashlight battery puts out 1.5 volts. Can it give you a shock? Not likely. A car battery puts out 12 volts. It can give you a shock. Your wall socket typically puts out 110 volts. This is enough to kill a person. Never touch any part of a circuit that is plugged into the wall. It is dangerous!

How many volts does this battery put out?

Build a Wet Cell

HYPOTHESIZE How do you think you can make a wet cell? Write a hypothesis in your *Science Journal.*

MATERIALS
- safety goggles
- $\frac{1}{2}$ c of distilled vinegar
- plastic cup
- current detector from the Explore Activity
- copper strip
- zinc strip
- tape
- *Science Journal*

PROCEDURES

Safety: Wear safety goggles.

1. Put on your goggles. Pour the vinegar into the cup.

2. **OBSERVE** Tape one metal strip to each end of the current detector. Place the metal strips in the vinegar. Record your observations of the detector in your *Science Journal.*

CONCLUDE AND APPLY

1. **OBSERVE** Did your wet cell produce current? How do you know?

2. **COMMUNICATE** What function did the vinegar have in your experiment?

What Happens to Current Before It Reaches Your Home?

Power stations near your home have powerful electric generators. Huge magnets inside these generators spin inside huge coils. This produces current. The energy to spin the huge magnets comes from water, wind, or some kind of fuel.

A typical power plant puts out 25,000 volts or more of electrical force. This is far too much to use in your house. The voltage is lowered by use of a **transformer** (trans fôr′mər). A transformer is made up of two wire coils. Alternating current travels through the first coil. This produces a current in the second coil.

In transformer A the right side has twice as many coils as the left. This means that current going from left to right doubles in voltage.

In transformer B the left side has twice as many coils. The voltage of current going from left to right is cut in half.

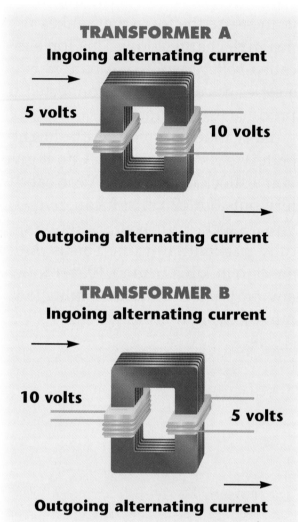

TRANSFORMER A
Ingoing alternating current

5 volts   10 volts

Outgoing alternating current

TRANSFORMER B
Ingoing alternating current

10 volts   5 volts

Outgoing alternating current

Voltage generated by this power plant is reduced by transformers.

Brain Power

How many loops would you put in each side of a transformer to change voltage in a battery from 60 volts to 180 volts? Draw a picture of the transformer.

MATH LINK

Skill: Using Numbers

TRANSFORMERS AND NUMBERS

Numbers help you understand how things work in the real world. In this activity you will be looking for a pattern in the volts going into and out of five different transformers.

MATERIALS
- calculator (optional)
- *Science Journal*

PROCEDURES

1. The left side of transformer A has 10 times as many loops as the right side. Ten times as many volts go into the transformer as go out. The 110 volts going in are reduced 10 times to 11 volts.

2. The right side of transformer B has 10 times as many loops as the left side. Ten times fewer volts go into the transformer as go out. The 15 volts going in are increased 10 times to 150 volts.

3. INTERPRET DATA Do you notice a pattern? Write the number of volts for diagrams C–E in your *Science Journal*.

CONCLUDE AND APPLY

1. INTERPRET DATA What is the pattern that you noticed in the transformers?

2. COMPARE In which transformers is the voltage increased? Decreased? Make a table of your results.

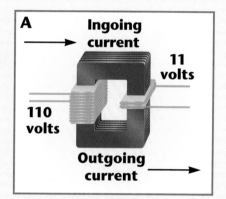

A Ingoing current
11 volts
110 volts
Outgoing current

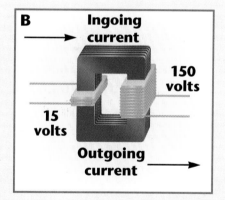

B Ingoing current
150 volts
15 volts
Outgoing current

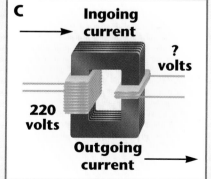

C Ingoing current
? volts
220 volts
Outgoing current

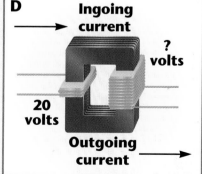

D Ingoing current
? volts
20 volts
Outgoing current

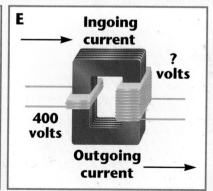

E Ingoing current
? volts
400 volts
Outgoing current

How Does Current Get to Your Home?

Do you think there are large magnets inside your home producing alternating current? Probably not! How do you think current gets to your home? This diagram shows how current gets from a power plant to your home.

1 A power plant gets energy from wind, water, fossil fuel, or nuclear power.

3 Current with high voltage is dangerous. It travels on wires often placed high above the ground.

2 A transformer increases the voltage. High-voltage current is best for traveling long distances. It loses less energy along the way.

4 Another transformer decreases the voltage.

5 An even smaller transformer decreases the voltage.

6 The current enters your home.

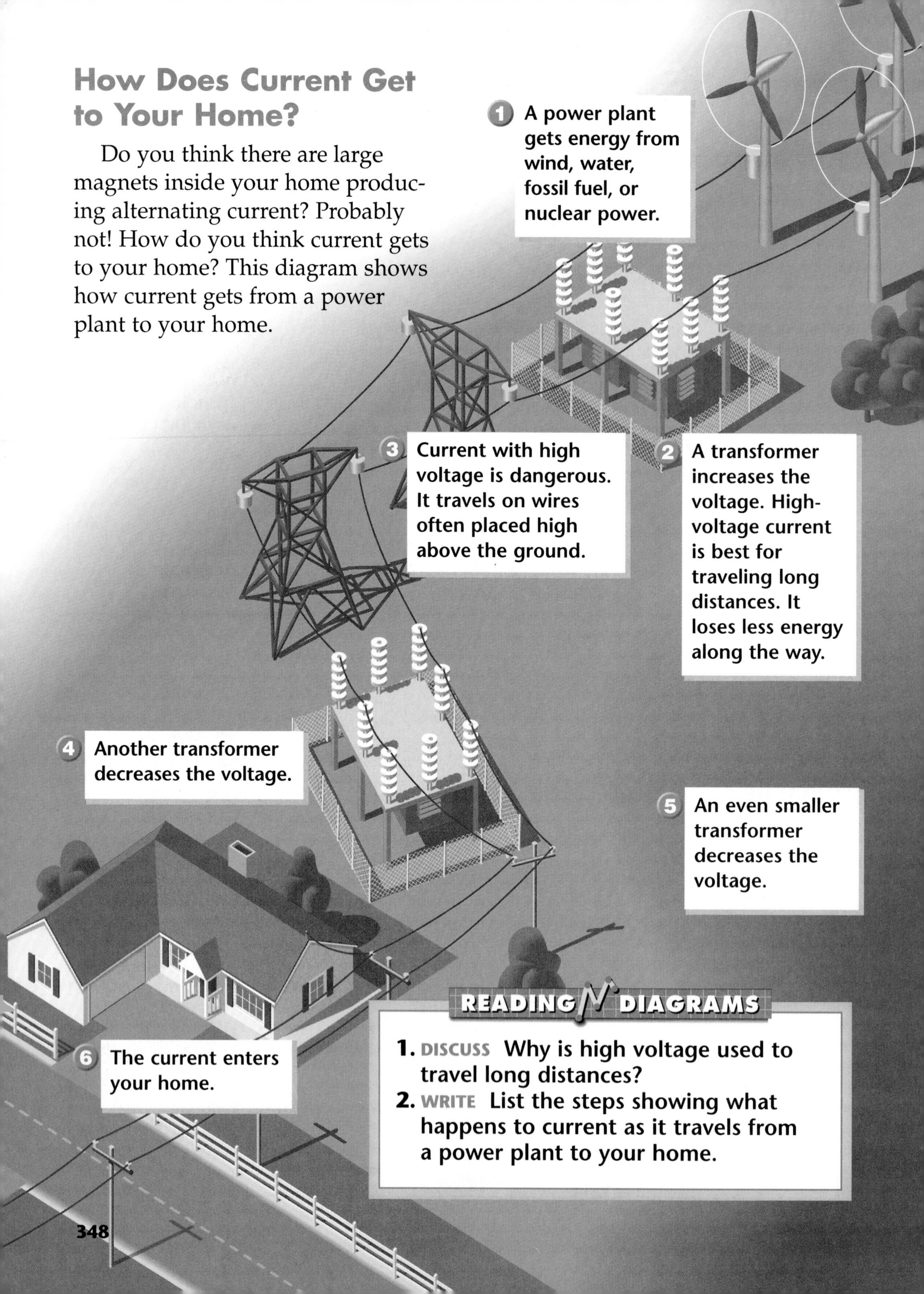

READING ⋀ DIAGRAMS

1. **DISCUSS** Why is high voltage used to travel long distances?
2. **WRITE** List the steps showing what happens to current as it travels from a power plant to your home.

Knowing how to make and use electricity safely is important. We depend on electricity every day to help us perform a variety of tasks. Giant generators produce current that travels all across the continent. Transformers allow us to change voltage to meet our needs. It also makes electricity safer to use.

The electricity we use every day is provided by a generator that works on the ideas and discoveries of scientists like Michael Faraday, Joseph Henry, and many others. Each deserves a big "Thank you!"

HISTORY LINK

Michael Faraday demonstrated the ideas used to make electric motors.

REVIEW

1. What are some ways, other than a dry cell, to make electricity?

2. Use a model to explain how a generator produces alternating current.

3. How are a wet cell and a dry cell similar? Different?

4. **USE NUMBERS** Alternating current going into a transformer has 200 volts. The current coming out has 20 volts. How many loops of wire might each coil have?

5. **CRITICAL THINKING** *Analyze* What do you think might happen if a transformer along the way from a power station was not working properly?

WHY IT MATTERS THINK ABOUT IT
Design a circuit to light a room or to light a matching-game board. Share your design with a classmate.

WHY IT MATTERS WRITE ABOUT IT
Three hundred years ago, no one dreamed of electric lights. Early experiments with electricity were often very dangerous. What uses do you think electricity might have 300 years from now? Do you think it will be even safer to use?

Current Jobs

Do you like to take things apart? Can you put them back together again? Maybe you'd be interested in becoming an electrician!

"What do electricians do?" you might ask. Some put wiring and other electrical parts in new buildings. Others repair electrical parts in older buildings. Some just fix problems.

Electricians must know about all kinds of electrical parts. They must be able to find and fix electrical problems. They also must know how to handle and care for tools.

Electricians must make safe connections and not overload electrical systems. Electricians must check their work for safety, too. Loose or broken wires can cause fires or shock people.

To become an electrician, most people help other electricians for a few years. They also take at least 144 hours of classes each year. In most cities electricians must be licensed. People must pass a test to get the license.

Appliance repairers fix washers, TVs, toasters, and other electrical machines.

They spend at least six months learning on the job. Some take one- or two-year training programs. They also have to pass a test, if they plan to fix refrigerators or air conditioners. Those contain harmful chemicals. Repairers must know how to keep the chemicals out of the air.

Many new machines have electronic parts. They need fewer repairs. That means fewer jobs for repairers. Those who know how to fix electronic parts get the most jobs.

DISCUSSION STARTER

1. Why do electricians need to work carefully?

2. Which is more likely to need an appliance repairer, a new home or an older home? Why?

Would you like to be an electrician or an appliance repairer? Why or why not?

To learn more about electricians, visit *www.mhschool.com/science* and enter the keyword WIRING.

*inter***NET**
CONNECTION

Transforming Electricity

Can you help this group of friends? They have turned on several lights to help them see how all the model pieces fit together. Soon they begin to feel warm. "Boy, it's hot in here!" Maria says. "It certainly is," replies Marco. Why do you think it is so hot? "I bet it's all these lights we have on," Bruce says. What do you think?

WHY IT MATTERS

Electrical energy changes into many other forms of energy.

SCIENCE WORDS

energy transformation a change of energy from one form to another

radiate to travel in all directions

EXPLORE

HYPOTHESIZE Can the light energy of even small flashlight bulbs be changed into heat? Write a hypothesis in your *Science Journal.* Test your ideas.

Design Your Own Experiment

CAN LIGHT ENERGY CHANGE?

PROCEDURES

1. Set up a circuit like this one. You can set up a different circuit if you like.

2. **USE VARIABLES** How would you test to see if painting a bulb affects how warm it gets? Do you think changing the outside of a plain bulb in another way might make it get warmer? Test your ideas. Record your results in your *Science Journal*.

3. **USE VARIABLES** Can you think of any other variable that might affect how warm a bulb gets? Test your ideas. Record your results.

CONCLUDE AND APPLY

1. **COMPARE** Did you feel some heat energy in any of the bulbs? What variables were you testing? What materials were you using?

2. **INFER** What if some light bulbs felt warmer? How can you explain what might have caused that to happen?

3. **INTERPRET DATA** Do you think light energy can be transformed into heat energy? Why or why not?

GOING FURTHER: Problem Solving

4. **EXPERIMENT** What other variables might affect changing light energy into heat energy? How could you test your idea in an experiment?

MATERIALS

- flashlight bulb
- flashlight bulb painted black
- 2 bulb holders
- 5 pieces of hookup wire, 20 cm each
- 2 D-cells
- 2 D-cell holders
- small pieces of foil and cloth
- *Science Journal*

Can Electrical Energy Be Changed?

In the Explore Activity, the painted light bulb felt warmer than the unpainted bulb. What do you think was going on? The answer is an example of an **energy transformation** (en′ər jē trans′fər mā′shən). An energy transformation is a change of energy from one form to another. How does this happen?

Light energy normally **radiates** (rā′dē āts′), or travels in all directions through space. The black paint blocked the light and absorbed its energy. The bulb got hotter and hotter as it absorbed more and more light energy.

Light energy that can't escape from the bulb as light is radiated by the black surface as heat.

In this topic you will learn about five different ways we use changed energy every day.

How Can Electrical Energy Be Changed?

Into heat energy

Into sound energy

Into mechanical energy, the energy of moving things

Into chemical energy

Into light energy

How Can Electrical Energy Be Changed into Heat Energy?

How many appliances in your home create heat? Make a list. Does your list include items like an iron, an electric stove, a toaster, and a hair dryer? All of these things need electricity to work.

How do you think the electrical energy is changed into heat energy? In Topic 2 you learned that a resistor is a material that does not conduct electricity well. In other words a resistor is a poor conductor. One of the most common places to find a resistor is in a typical light bulb. Some, not all, of the electrical energy going into the bulb produces light energy. What do you think happens to the rest?

Have you ever accidentally touched a lit light bulb? It probably felt warm, or even hot. That is because some electrical energy was changed into heat energy.

Many of the devices on your list contain wires that are good resistors. These wires are looped into coils. This allows a long wire to fit into a small space. The more coils an appliance has, the hotter it can get.

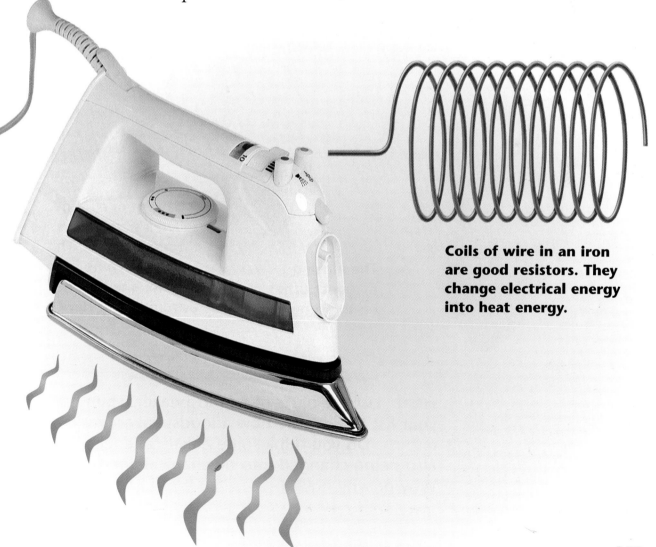

Coils of wire in an iron are good resistors. They change electrical energy into heat energy.

How Can Electrical Energy Be Changed into Sound Energy?

How do you think loudspeakers work? Loudspeakers change electrical energy into sound energy.

Loudspeakers are used in radios, telephones, CD players, and other devices that produce sound. Sound is created by vibration. The job of the speaker is to get a thin cone to vibrate. The cone's vibrations produce sounds.

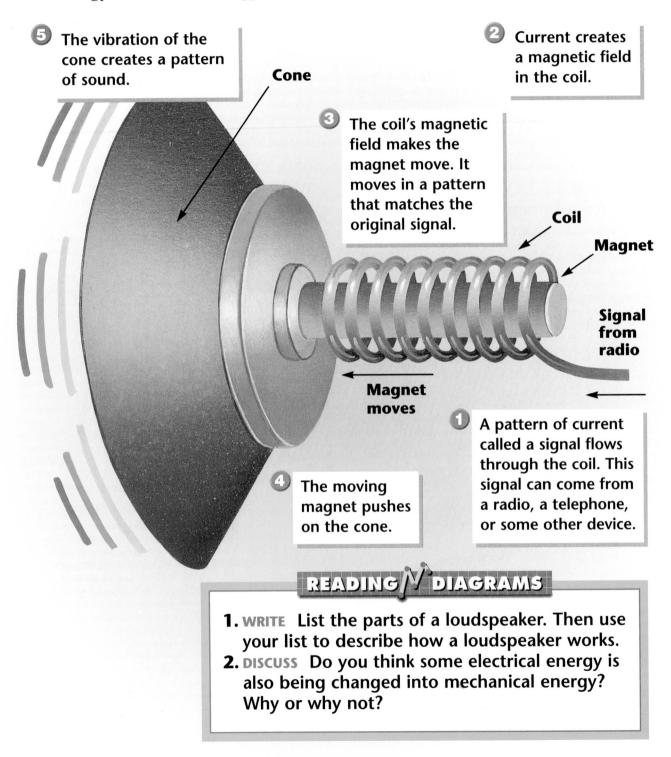

5 The vibration of the cone creates a pattern of sound.

2 Current creates a magnetic field in the coil.

Cone

3 The coil's magnetic field makes the magnet move. It moves in a pattern that matches the original signal.

Coil

Magnet

Signal from radio

Magnet moves

4 The moving magnet pushes on the cone.

1 A pattern of current called a signal flows through the coil. This signal can come from a radio, a telephone, or some other device.

READING DIAGRAMS

1. WRITE List the parts of a loudspeaker. Then use your list to describe how a loudspeaker works.
2. DISCUSS Do you think some electrical energy is also being changed into mechanical energy? Why or why not?

How Can Electrical Energy Be Changed into Chemical Energy?

Have you ever left a video game or flashlight on too long? What happened? After some time the batteries probably "died." The chemicals in the cells were used up. The chemical reaction stopped. The cells could no longer produce an electric current.

When this happens the batteries must be thrown out. However, don't just throw them in the kitchen trash. Remember, cells contain chemicals that can harm someone if the cell is broken open. Place the batteries in a sealed plastic bag. Give them to an adult. He or she should place them with other dangerous materials. Most communities have a recycling center for hazardous household wastes.

Have you ever seen a battery like this one? It is called a *rechargeable* (rē chär'jə bəl) *battery.* A battery made of rechargeable cells works like a normal battery, except that the chemical reactions in it can be reversed.

The batteries are placed into a device called a recharger. The recharger needs to be plugged into an electrical outlet. The recharger produces a current in the opposite direction. This causes the chemical reaction to be reversed. After a time the cells are recharged. Rechargeable batteries can be used again and again.

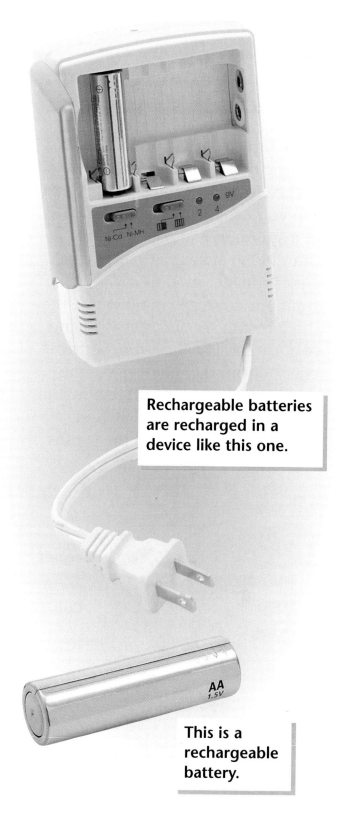

Rechargeable batteries are recharged in a device like this one.

This is a rechargeable battery.

Brain Power

How can using rechargeable batteries be good for the environment?

How Can Electrical Energy Be Changed into Mechanical Energy?

In Topic 4 you learned that an electric motor changes electrical energy into mechanical energy. How can you use the mechanical energy of a spinning motor to do something? One answer is gears (gîrz). Gears transfer motion and force from one source to another.

Here you see a simple drawing of a toy car. How can the electrical energy from the motor make the car's wheels spin? First, review the motor. A battery sends current through a coil. The coil then spins between the two poles of a magnet. The coil is connected to a gear. As the coil spins, the gear spins clockwise.

As this gear turns, it transfers its motion to another gear. The other gear is perpendicular to the first. It is also attached to the car's axle. As this gear turns, it turns the axle. The car moves forward.

Gears can be used to do other things than move the car forward. If the direction of the first gear is reversed, the car can go in reverse. The car can also be made to go faster. It could pull a load. These things can be done using different gear combinations or different-sized gears.

A SIMPLE MOTOR

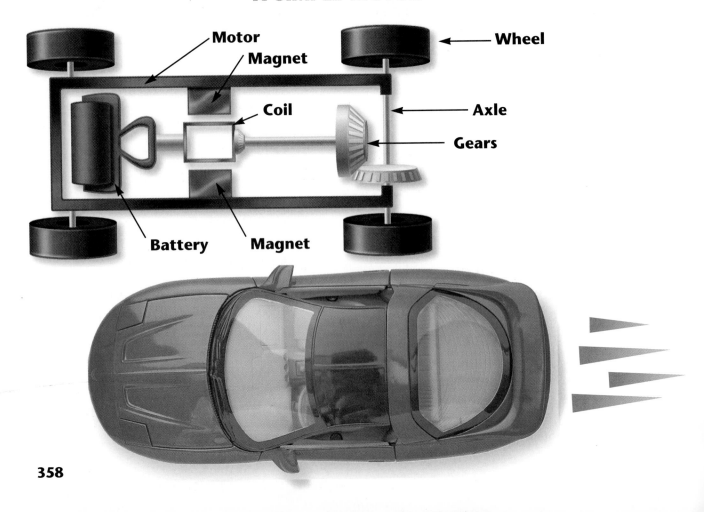

Motor

Magnet

Coil

Battery

Magnet

Wheel

Axle

Gears

How Can Electrical Energy Be Changed into Light Energy?

A television changes a pattern of electrical energy into a pattern of light energy and some sound energy.

How does a television work to make images? A signal, or pattern of current, comes from a cable or antenna. The signal is fed into the television's electron gun. The signal is translated into a beam of negatively charged particles. The electron gun shoots the beam at a screen.

The beam travels back and forth across the screen. It makes hundreds of lines. The screen is bright where many particles hit it. It is dim where few particles hit it. The gun makes an entirely new pattern of lines 60 times each second.

DIAGRAM OF TELEVISION

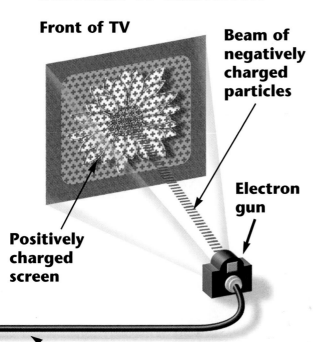

Front of TV

Beam of negatively charged particles

Electron gun

Positively charged screen

Signal from cable or antenna

Identifying Energy Transformations

HYPOTHESIZE What types of clues can you use to identify types of energy transformations in your classroom? Write a hypothesis in your *Science Journal.*

MATERIALS
- *Science Journal*

PROCEDURES

1. **OBSERVE** Look around the classroom. Which items use electrical energy? Make a list in your *Science Journal.*

2. **INFER** Which items change electrical energy into another form of energy? What type of energy? Record your observations in your *Science Journal.*

3. **CLASSIFY** Classify the items into groups based on how they change electrical energy.

CONCLUDE AND APPLY

1. **IDENTIFY** Into what types of energy did the items change electrical energy?

2. **EXPLAIN** What clues did you use to help you identify how the electrical energy was changed?

In this topic you learned about five different ways we use changed energy every day. Study these pictures carefully. What types of energy transformations are taking place in each one?

ELECTRICAL ENERGY

Electrical energy makes this coil on an electric stove glow red-hot.

Sound ENERGY

Heat ENERGY

Into what types of energy does a television transform electrical energy? What lets you see the lion on the screen? What lets you hear it roar?

These bulbs are called infrared (in′frə red′) light bulbs. Infrared bulbs are often used to keep prepared foods warm in restaurants. Why do you think they are called infrared? Into what other type of energy is the electrical energy being transformed?

Light ENERGY

The chemical reactions within a rechargeable battery can be reversed. The recharger produces a current in the opposite direction. This causes the chemical reaction to be reversed. The batteries are recharged and can be used again.

Chemical ENERGY

Into what types of energy does this power tool transform electrical energy? Why is such a tool useful?

This toy gets its power from batteries. Into what types of energy do you think the electrical energy is transformed? Why do you think so?

Mechanical ENERGY

READING ∧ DIAGRAMS

1. **WRITE** Into what other types of energy can electrical energy be transformed? Make a list.
2. **DISCUSS** Did you use electrical energy that was transformed into another type of energy today? What was it?

How Can You Use Electricity Safely?

Plug in a toaster. Turn on the radio. Turn on the light. You use electric energy every day. Do you ever think much about it? Probably not.

Electric devices can be dangerous if they are not used properly. Knowing a few safety rules is important. They can help you make sure electricity doesn't pose a danger to you.

HEALTH
LINK

SAFETY RULE		REASON
• Never touch a wall socket with anything but a plug.		Current could flow from the socket to the item to you.
• Never touch the metal part of a plug when you plug it in.		Your finger could create a short-circuit path for the current.
• Never use a cord that is torn or has a hole in it.		You can create a short circuit.
• Don't pull the cord to remove a plug.		You can damage the plug or create a hole in the cord.
• Don't overload a plug or extension cord with too many devices.		Overloaded plugs draw too much current. They can get hot and cause a fire.
• Stay away from high-voltage cables and train rails.		You could accidentally touch them and be electrocuted.
• Never use electric devices when you are wet. Also do not use them if you are standing in or near water.	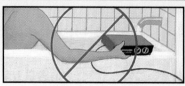	Water is a conductor. Therefore, you are a better conductor when wet. You can get a shock or be electrocuted.

Much of the energy we use is transformed, or changed, from one form into another.

We can cook food and heat our homes because electrical energy can be changed to heat energy. We can turn on a lamp because it can be changed to light energy. We can listen to tapes or CDs because it can be changed in part to sound energy. We can make a milk shake in the blender because it can be changed to mechanical energy. Knowing how to change energy from one form into another is a useful thing!

REVIEW

1. How was light energy transformed into heat energy in the Explore Activity?

2. Give an example of how electrical energy can be transformed into sound energy.

3. Give an example of how electrical energy can be transformed into light energy.

4. **COMMUNICATE** A friend is about to plug a fourth appliance into an extension cord. What would you tell her?

5. **CRITICAL THINKING** *Apply* A battery-operated toy has flashing lights and a siren, and it jumps up and down. Describe all the energy transformations that occur.

WHY IT MATTERS THINK ABOUT IT
How many different ways have you used transformed electrical energy in the past two days?

WHY IT MATTERS WRITE ABOUT IT
List some things you did today that used electrical energy. Write about how the electrical energy was transformed into another form of energy.

a POWER-ful SUN!

A lot of our energy comes from fuels like oil, coal, and gas. One day we'll run out of them, but what can we do? Use energy from the Sun!

When the Sun heats air, it rises and cooler air rushes in to take its place. The Sun's energy is now wind energy! It can turn windmills that, in turn, can produce electrical energy!

The Sun also warms water. It rises and evaporates. Then it falls as rain or snow. Now the Sun's energy fills rivers. We can use this water to run generators that produce electricity!

Solar panels on houses collect the Sun's energy. It can warm a house and heat its water supply.

Special cells collect the Sun's energy and change it into electrical energy.

The more we use the Sun, the less we'll need other fuels, and the cleaner our air will be!

DISCUSSION STARTER

1. Could we have wind energy without solar energy? Why or why not?

2. Why is it important to use as much solar energy as possible?

To learn more about solar energy, visit *www.mhschool.com/science* and enter the keyword DAYSTAR.

*inter*NET
CONNECTION

SCIENCE WORDS

alternating
  current p. 342
direct
  current p. 342
electromagnet
  p. 333
energy transfor-
  mation p. 354

generator p. 343
magnetic
  field p. 332
pole p. 330
radiate p. 354
transformer p. 346
volt p. 345

USING SCIENCE WORDS

Number a paper from 1 to 10. Fill in
1 to 5 with words from the list above.

1. Winding a wire in loops around an
   iron bar creates a(n) __?__.

2. A device that creates alternating
   current is a(n) __?__.

3. Light energy is able to __?__ from
   a lit bulb.

4. Current that travels in only one
   direction is __?__.

5. Electrical energy being transformed into sound energy is an
   example of a(n) __?__.

6–10. **Pick five words from the list
   above that were not used in 1
   to 5, and use each in a
   sentence.**

UNDERSTANDING SCIENCE IDEAS

11. What are some uses for electro-
    magnets?

12. What is a volt?

USING IDEAS AND SKILLS

13. **READING SKILL: CAUSE AND EFFECT**
    What happens when opposite
    poles of magnets are brought
    together? When the same poles
    are brought together? What
    causes this to happen?

14. **USE NUMBERS** Five 4-volt cells
    are connected. What do they
    make?

15. **THINKING LIKE A SCIENTIST** Think
    of a new use for an electric motor.
    How could you harness its energy
    to make a part of your life easier?

PROBLEMS and PUZZLES

Magnetic Strength How far
away can a magnet be from an
object it is trying to attract? Does
it matter if there is paper, plastic,
or wood between the object and
the magnet? Design an experiment to test your ideas.

SCIENCE WORDS

conductor p. 295

discharge p. 295

electromagnet
   p. 333

energy transfor-
   mation p. 354

fuse p. 322

generator p. 343

insulator p. 295

open circuit p. 305

pole p. 330

radiate p. 354

resistor p. 307

series
   circuit p. 316

short circuit p. 308

static
   electricity p. 294

switch p. 309

transformer p. 346

volt p. 345

USING SCIENCE WORDS

Number a paper from 1 to 10. Beside each number write the word or words that best complete the sentence.

1. The unit measuring the force that makes negative charges flow is a(n) __?__.

2. A buildup of an electrical charge on an object, such as a balloon, is called __?__.

3. A material through which electricity flows easily is a(n) __?__.

4. You can use a(n) __?__ to open or close a circuit.

5. If electricity travels first through one light bulb and then through a second light bulb, the bulbs are part of a(n) __?__.

6. A material that restricts the flow of electricity is a(n) __?__.

7. A magnet has both a north and a south __?__.

8. A magnet made by an electric current flowing through a wire coiled around an iron rod is a(n) __?__.

9. A device that keeps too much electric current from flowing through wires is a(n) __?__.

10. Changing electric energy to heat energy is an example of a(n) __?__.

UNDERSTANDING SCIENCE IDEAS

Write 11 to 15. For each number write the letter for the best answer. You may wish to use the hints provided.

11. If two balloons are attracted to each other, they may
    a. both have positive charges
    b. both have negative charges
    c. have different charges
    d. have no charge
    (Hint: Read pages 292–293.)

12. Current electricity
    a. is positive
    b. flows through a circuit
    c. attracts balloons
    d. repels balloons
    (Hint: Read page 304.)

13. Light bulbs that are separately connected to the same cell are
    a. all on or all off
    b. on a series circuit
    c. on a parallel circuit
    d. on the same circuit
    (Hint: Read page 317.)

14. A compass points north because
    a. it is a magnet
    b. it is a closed circuit
    c. it has a generator
    d. it is made of metal
    (Hint: Read pages 331–332.)

15. Electrical energy can be changed
- **a.** into only light energy
- **b.** into only heat energy
- **c.** into only two forms of energy
- **d.** into five forms of energy

(Hint: Read page 354.)

USING IDEAS AND SKILLS

16. Explain why lightning rods should be made of metal.

17. Draw a closed circuit that includes a cell, a light bulb, and a switch.

18.  **PREDICT** You are using the computer. Your sister is listening to the radio. Your mother is using the blender. Your father turns on the vacuum cleaner. Suddenly all the lights go out. The appliances don't work. What do you think happened?

19. Explain how Earth's magnetic field affects magnets. Why is this important?

THINKING LIKE A SCIENTIST

20. **USE NUMBERS** What if a transformer changes an electrical force from 100 volts to 50 volts? How would the same transformer change an electrical force of 20 volts? Explain.

WRITING IN YOUR JOURNAL

SCIENCE IN YOUR LIFE
Describe the two types of cells used to make electric current. What are some of the things you do that use electricity made by cells?

PRODUCT ADS
You may have seen advertisements for batteries (dry cells) that claim that this brand or that brand is the best. Explain what you think would make one kind of battery better than another kind. How could you find out which brand of battery is better?

HOW SCIENTISTS WORK
In this unit you learned that Joseph Henry made the first electric motor more than 100 years ago. In what ways do you think scientists today could try to transform electrical energy into mechanical energy?

Design your own Experiment

You have a circuit with a switch and three light bulbs. Can you have two lights always lit and one light always off? Design an experiment to find out. Review your experiment with your teacher before testing your ideas.

interNET CONNECTION

For help in reviewing this unit, visit *www.mhschool.com/science*

PROBLEMS and PUZZLES

Body Power

Design a device that would use your own body power to light a light bulb. You can use any materials that appeared in this unit, or any others you wish. Build or draw a model.

ON AND OFF

Rewire this circuit so you can flip a switch to do one or two of these things:

1. Turn on both lights.

2. Turn off both lights.

3. Turn on A but not B.

4. Turn on B but not A.

Build or draw a model of your circuit. If possible, test your design.

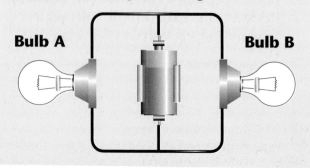

Bulb A   Bulb B

The EAT Mystery

THE PROBLEM

The EAT restaurant sign is made of 57 light bulbs. The sign works when all 57 bulbs are on. If one bulb burns out, the whole sign goes dark. When this happens, the manager needs to test each bulb—one at a time. Finding the burnt-out bulb takes a long time!

Your job is to change the system so one burnt-out bulb doesn't make the whole sign go dark. You should also make it easier for the manager to find the burnt-out bulb.

THE PLAN

Write a hypothesis that will help you solve the problem. Draw a diagram or make a model of the system.

TEST

Test your hypothesis. Explain how you would test your hypothesis. What would you expect to happen? How would you change your plan if it didn't work?

EVALUATE AND PUBLISH

How would you judge whether or not your plan worked?

Write a report in your *Science Journal*. Describe your plan in detail. Tell how you would test it.

EARTH'S WATER

CHAPTER 11

PLACES TO FIND WATER

"Rain, rain, go away. Please come back some other day!" Rain falls from the sky, but how does the water get up there? What happens to the water after it falls on the ground?

In this chapter you will have many opportunities to compare and contrast. When you compare things, you tell how they are alike. When you contrast things, you tell how they are different.

WHY IT MATTERS

Water can be in different forms in different places.

SCIENCE WORDS

atmosphere gases that surround Earth

water vapor water in a gas state

ice cap a thick sheet of ice covering a large area of land

soil water water that soaks into the soil

groundwater water stored in the cracks of underground rocks

Water, Water Everywhere

Thirsty? How do you get water? Unlike the stegosaur, you probably don't have to travel far to a watering hole. The stegosaur became extinct millions of years ago. What about the water it drank? Is it still around today? Where might it be? Could some of that same water be in your next glass of water?

EXPLORE

HYPOTHESIZE What do you think happened to the pond that the stegosaur drank from? Write a hypothesis in your *Science Journal*.

Investigate Where Water Can Be Found

Make a water path to find out about the state of water in different places.

PROCEDURES

1. Form six teams; one team at each location. Record your location in your *Science Journal.* What is the state of the water there? Remember, the states of matter are liquid, solid, and gas.

2. Next, each team will go to the next closest location. Record the location and state of the water. Repeat until every team has visited all six locations.

3. **COMPARE** How did the state of water differ from location to location?

4. **INTERPRET DATA** Use your color markers to draw your team's water path.

MATERIALS

- 6 different-colored markers
- white drawing paper
- *Science Journal*

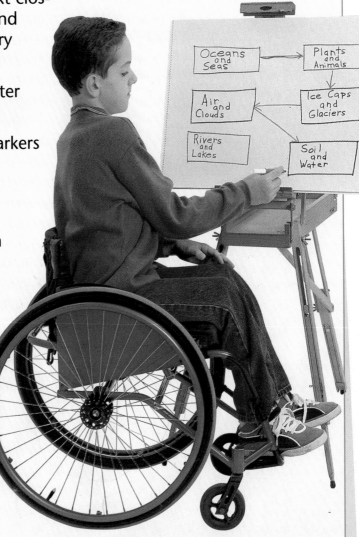

CONCLUDE AND APPLY

1. **PREDICT** Where might water stay in one place for a short time? A long time? Why?

2. **DRAW CONCLUSIONS** Do you think water that was around at the time of the dinosaurs can still be around today? Why or why not?

GOING FURTHER: Apply

3. **INFER** What might have caused the change in the state of water from place to place?

Where Can Water Be Found?

Do some places have more water than others? Where would you find large amounts of water? Very little water? The Explore Activity showed that water is found in different states in different places.

Look at a globe. It shows that we live in a watery world. Oceans and seas are very large bodies of salt water. They cover about $\frac{70}{100}$ of Earth's surface. Oceans and seas are very deep and hold about $\frac{97}{100}$ of all of Earth's water.

Water is also found in the atmosphere (at′məs fîr′). Gases that surround Earth make up its atmosphere. One of these gases is the oxygen you breathe.

In the atmosphere water is in a gas state and is called water vapor (wô′tər vā′pər). The atmosphere always has some water vapor. How much water vapor there is in the atmosphere depends on the location. There is more water vapor in the atmosphere over or near large bodies of water. There is less water vapor in the atmosphere over a desert.

This photograph of Earth was taken from space. Can you point out the oceans and seas?

What Other Places Have Water?

Lakes, rivers, and streams make up a very small part of all of Earth's water. A lake is a large body of water surrounded by land. A river is flowing water that empties into an ocean, a lake, or another river. A stream is flowing water that is smaller than a river. The water in rivers and streams is fresh water, not salty like the ocean. Most lakes are fresh water. However, there are some saltwater lakes, such as the Great Salt Lake in Utah.

About $\frac{2}{100}$ of Earth's water is found in glaciers and polar **ice caps** (īs kaps). Some glaciers form high in the mountains and flow slowly down steep valleys.

Ice caps are types of glaciers. They are very wide, thick sheets of ice that cover large areas of land. Greenland and Antarctica are covered by ice caps.

Some glaciers flow across land until they reach the sea. There large chunks often break off and float out to sea as icebergs.

Some lakes are small. Others are so large that huge ships transport people across them.

Icebergs often break off and float away from glaciers that reach the sea.

WATER GOES UNDERGROUND

Rain

Soil

Soil water

Rock that water can pass between

Groundwater

Rock that water cannot pass between

READING DIAGRAMS

1. DISCUSS Which underground area do plants and trees get water from?
2. WRITE Where does groundwater collect?

Where Can Water Be Found Underground?

How does water get underground? Oceans and lakes are water you can actually see on Earth's surface. There is also water in the soil and in the rocks below the ground. Some water soaks into the soil to become **soil water** (soil wô′tər). Some soil water is used by plants. The rest moves through the soil into the underground rocks.

Many rocks have tiny spaces and cracks in them. Water passes down through these cracks until it reaches a layer of solid rock that it cannot pass through. Then the water begins to fill the spaces and cracks in the rocks above. Water stored in these cracks and spaces of underground rock is called **groundwater** (ground′wô′tər).

The amount of water found in soil water and groundwater is very small. Even so, there is almost 20 times more groundwater than all of the water in rivers and lakes.

How Much Water Is in Plants and Animals?

A small amount of Earth's water can also be found in all living things, large and small. You learned that the jellylike substance inside all cells is made up mostly of water. Water makes up at least half the weight of most plants and animals.

How much water do you drink in a day? All living things need water. Plants soak up water through their roots. People and other animals drink water. They also get water from the foods they eat.

NATIONAL GEOGRAPHIC

FUNtastic Facts

Do fish drink? Ocean fish do! This harlequin fish and other saltwater fish lose water from their bodies into the salty sea around them. But they replace what they lose. They gulp sea water, and their bodies filter out the salt. Freshwater fish don't live in salty water. Do they drink?

This gray timberwolf, like all animals, needs fresh water to survive.

How Much Water?

What's a good way to show all the information you learned about water? How could you show the different places where water can be found? What about the amount of water that can be found in each place?

A chart is one way to present information. It is especially useful in showing information that you want to compare. The chart below gives information about the different amounts of water found in different places on Earth.

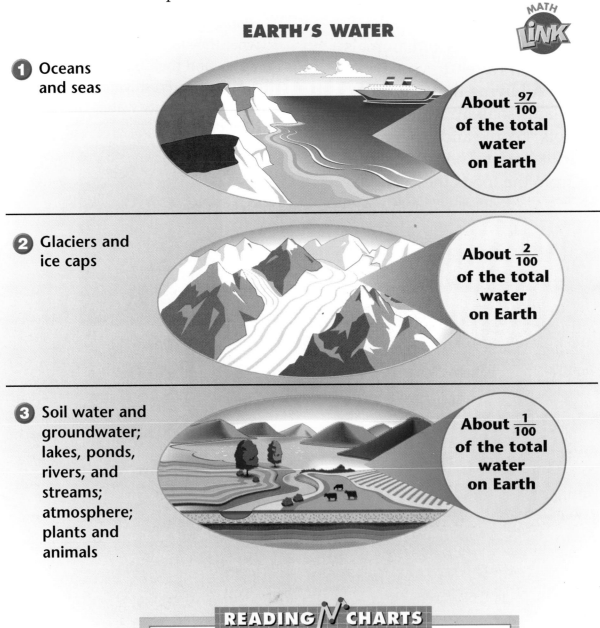

EARTH'S WATER

MATH LINK

1 **Oceans and seas** — About $\frac{97}{100}$ of the total water on Earth

2 **Glaciers and ice caps** — About $\frac{2}{100}$ of the total water on Earth

3 **Soil water and groundwater; lakes, ponds, rivers, and streams; atmosphere; plants and animals** — About $\frac{1}{100}$ of the total water on Earth

READING CHARTS

DISCUSS How much more water is there in oceans and seas compared with glaciers and ice caps?

Skill: Communicating

COMPARING AMOUNTS OF WATER

Graphs are another good way to communicate information. Graphs can help you compare information quickly and easily. A pictograph is one kind of graph. It uses a picture symbol to stand for a certain amount of something.

Make a pictograph to compare the amounts of water in different places. Use the information in the chart on page 376.

MATERIALS

- *Science Journal*

PROCEDURES

1. Suppose that all the water on Earth could be contained in 100 buckets.

2. **USE NUMBERS** In your *Science Journal,* complete the pictograph. Show how much water is found in different places on Earth. Choose a symbol to stand for $\frac{1}{100}$ of all of Earth's water.

3. Give your pictograph a title at the top.

4. Be sure to show what the picture symbol stands for.

CONCLUDE AND APPLY

1. **INTERPRET DATA** How many symbols did you draw to show the amount of water in glaciers and ice caps?

2. **COMPARE** How much more water is found in oceans and seas than in glaciers and ice caps?

3. **COMMUNICATE** How are pictographs similar to charts? How are they different?

Water in an Apple

HYPOTHESIZE Write in your *Science Journal* the amount of water you think is in an apple.

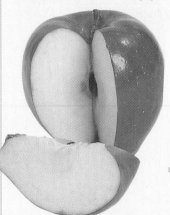

MATERIALS

- apple slices
- tray
- pan balance
- *Science Journal*

PROCEDURES

1. MEASURE Measure the mass of the apple slices, and record the mass in your *Science Journal*.

2. Lay the apple slices on the tray, and place them in a warm place.

3. MEASURE When the slices are completely dried, measure their mass. Record the mass of the dry slices.

CONCLUDE AND APPLY

1. MEASURE What was the mass of the apple before and after drying?

2. USE NUMBERS How much of the apple's mass was water?

What Is That Liquid?

Have you ever bitten into a juicy apple or other kind of fruit? Was it so juicy that liquid came running down from your mouth? What do you think the liquid was made of? It was water. There is water in the cells of an apple.

In the Quick Lab, you will try to find out how much of an apple's mass is water.

Brain Power

You leave a glass of water by a sunny window for a few days. What do you think will happen to the water?

What is in that juicy apple?

Without water there would be no life on Earth. Water is one of our most valuable resources. You use water for drinking and bathing. All the food you eat needs water to grow. If you like to swim or play water sports, you may enjoy spending time near oceans, lakes, and rivers. These places are also homes for different animals and plants.

Many people enjoy spending a hot summer day at the beach.

REVIEW

1. Name the six kinds of places on Earth where water is found.

2. Name the different states of the water in each place.

3. How can you find out how much of a pear is water?

4. **COMMUNICATE** How does a pictograph help you present information?

5. **CRITICAL THINKING** *Analyze* What might happen if there was less water in the oceans and seas?

WHY IT MATTERS THINK ABOUT IT
What if you could no longer get water from faucets? How would your life be different?

WHY IT MATTERS WRITE ABOUT IT
Describe some of your favorite uses of water. What state is the water in when you use it?

W⊕rld of SCIENCE

WATER from Space?

Did the water on Earth come from comets?

Comets are sometimes called "snowballs in space."

Science, Technology, and Society

In 1981 scientist Dr. Louis Frank was studying satellite images of the sky. He noticed dark specks on the images. Other scientists suggested the specks were caused by dust on the satellite's camera lens. However, Dr. Frank thought the specks were small, icy comets entering Earth's atmosphere.

Later evidence supported Dr. Frank's hypothesis. Cameras on NASA's Polar spacecraft took images that seem to show objects streaking across the sky. Instruments on the spacecraft indicate the objects are mostly water. Millions of icy comets may be bombarding Earth!

Dr. Frank thinks these icy comets may be the source of Earth's water. They may have been showering Earth with water for 4.5 billion years.

He estimates that 5 to 20 comets reach Earth's atmosphere every minute. Some of the comets are as big as a house. However, they melt into water vapor 960 to 1,250 kilometers (600 to 800 miles) above Earth.

Some scientists still doubt the comets exist. They point out that the comets would also shower the Moon with water. Well, in 1996 NASA found ice near the Moon's south pole. Did it come from comets?

The *Polar* spacecraft photographed this white streak. Dr. Frank thinks the streak is a comet entering Earth's atmosphere.

Discussion Starter

1 If comets do bring water to Earth, do we still have to conserve water? Why or why not?

2 Illustrate the water cycle with this new theory in mind.

*inter*NET CONNECTION To learn more about space, visit www.mhschool.com/science and enter the keyword **MOONICE.**

381

WHY IT MATTERS

The water cycle affects you every day.

SCIENCE WORDS

evaporation when liquid changes to a gas

condensation when a gas changes to a liquid

cloud tiny drops of condensed water in the atmosphere

precipitation water in the atmosphere that falls to Earth as rain, snow, hail, or sleet

freeze when moving particles in a liquid slow down, lose heat, and change to a solid

melt when a solid absorbs heat energy and changes to a liquid

water cycle the movement of Earth's water through evaporation, condensation, and precipitation

Follow the Water

What happens to a puddle of water after you finish playing in it? You'll probably take some of the puddle's water home with you in your wet shoes and socks. Can you jump into that same puddle tomorrow? Next week? Where does the water go?

EXPLORE

HYPOTHESIZE Where does puddle water go? How long does it take a small puddle to disappear? A big puddle? What causes the water to disappear? Write a hypothesis in your *Science Journal*.

Investigate What Makes Water Disappear

Experiment to find out how long it takes puddles of water to disappear.

MATERIALS

- measuring cup
- water
- 2 index cards
- 2 lunch trays with sides
- *Science Journal*

PROCEDURES

1. **MEASURE** Pour a half cup of water into each tray.

2. Place one tray in a sunny area. Place the other in a dark area.

3. Use an index card for each tray. Label one card Sunny and the other card Dark. On each index card, write your name and the date. Then write the time when you placed your trays in each area.

4. **OBSERVE** Check your trays every hour until the water is gone. Note on the index cards how long it took for each "puddle" to disappear. Record the results in your *Science Journal*.

CONCLUDE AND APPLY

1. **COMPARE** Which puddle disappeared first? Which took the longest to disappear?

2. **DRAW CONCLUSIONS** What do you think made one puddle disappear faster? The other disappear slower?

GOING FURTHER: Problem Solving

3. **EXPERIMENT** Repeat the activity, placing your trays in different places. How were the results similar or different?

Sunny

Dark

What Makes Water Disappear?

Where does the water on the ground go? How does water get from one place to another? In the Explore Activity, water disappeared faster in some places than in others.

You have learned that particles of matter have energy and are always moving. Now you'll find out how heat energy plays a role in how water changes its state. You'll learn how water moves from different Earth surfaces into the atmosphere.

Water in the deepest parts of land and bodies of water is quite cold. Water is warmer on the surface because it is heated by the Sun. Heat energy from the Sun causes the particles of water at the surface to move rapidly. As they absorb heat energy, these moving water particles go through the process of **evaporation** (i vap′ə rā′shən). This means that the water particles change from a liquid to a gas. The gas, known as water vapor, is invisible and rises into the atmosphere.

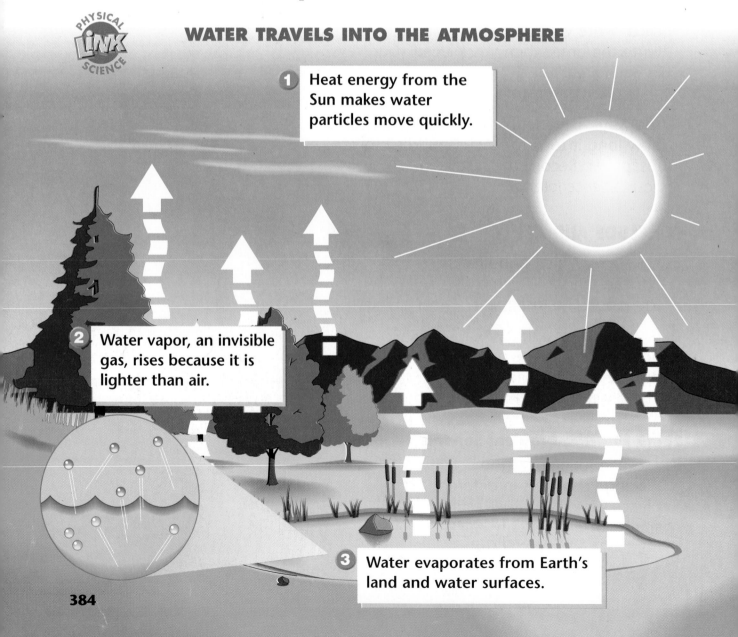

WATER TRAVELS INTO THE ATMOSPHERE

1 Heat energy from the Sun makes water particles move quickly.

2 Water vapor, an invisible gas, rises because it is lighter than air.

3 Water evaporates from Earth's land and water surfaces.

What Happens to Water in the Air?

High in the atmosphere, particles of water move slowly because it is very cold. These water particles lose heat energy, slow down, and *condense* (kən dens'), or change from a gas to a liquid. This process is known as **condensation** (kon'den sā'shən).

Tiny droplets of condensed water in the atmosphere form **clouds** (kloudz). When droplets of water in clouds come together, they get bigger and heavier. Gravity, the force that pulls things toward the center of Earth, causes the heavy droplets to fall.

Brain Power

What happens to water when you heat it on a stove? Where does the water go?

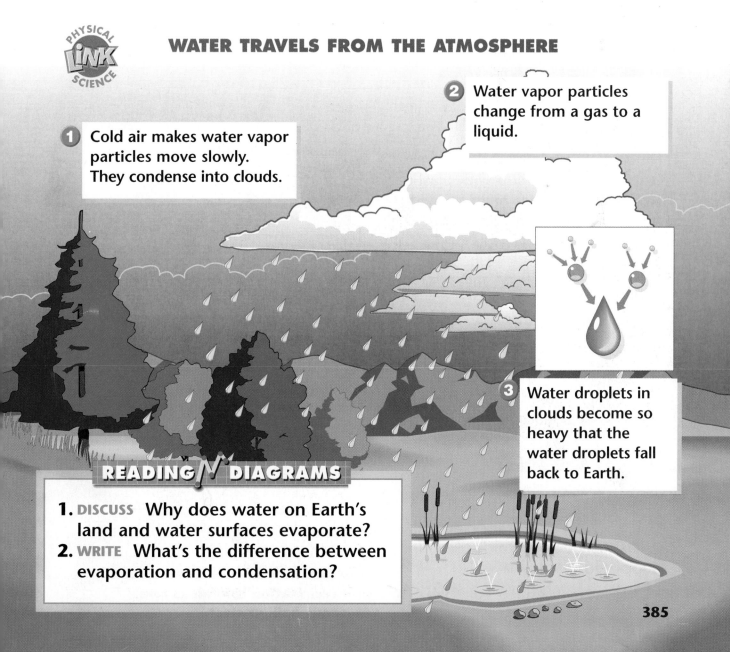

PHYSICAL LINK SCIENCE

WATER TRAVELS FROM THE ATMOSPHERE

1 Cold air makes water vapor particles move slowly. They condense into clouds.

2 Water vapor particles change from a gas to a liquid.

3 Water droplets in clouds become so heavy that the water droplets fall back to Earth.

READING DIAGRAMS

1. DISCUSS Why does water on Earth's land and water surfaces evaporate?
2. WRITE What's the difference between evaporation and condensation?

QUICK LAB

Disappearing Water

HYPOTHESIZE What happens when a glass of water is left uncovered? Write a hypothesis in your *Science Journal.*

MATERIALS

- water
- 2 plastic cups
- piece of clear plastic wrap
- rubber band
- marker
- *Science Journal*

PROCEDURES

1. Fill both plastic cups half full with water. Cover one cup with plastic wrap. Use a rubber band to hold down the plastic. Mark the level of the water in each cup.

2. Place both cups in a warm, sunny spot.

3. **PREDICT** What do you think will happen to the water in each cup?

4. **OBSERVE** Check the water in the cups every hour. Record what you see in your *Science Journal.*

CONCLUDE AND APPLY

1. **EXPLAIN** Where did the water in each cup go?

2. **INFER** Why do you think this happened?

What Falls from Clouds?

Water in the atmosphere falls to Earth as **precipitation** (pri sip'i tā'shən)—rain, snow, hail, or sleet. The form in which precipitation falls depends on the temperature. Most precipitation falls into the oceans. The precipitation that falls over land may also fall directly into lakes and rivers. When rainfall is very heavy, water will flow over land into rivers. Some water also soaks into the ground as soil water or groundwater.

Rain

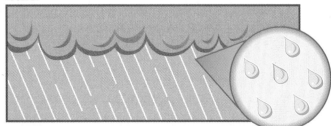

Snow

Hail

Sleet

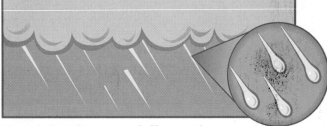

Precipitation can fall as rain, snow, hail, or sleet.

How Does Temperature Affect Precipitation?

Will the water in the atmosphere fall as rain, snow, hail, or sleet? Are there any clues that you see or feel before it rains or snows?

This depends on the temperature outdoors. It also depends on the amount of heat energy in the particles of water. Cold temperatures cause water to release heat energy, or lose heat. When this happens the moving particles in water slow down and may **freeze** (frēz). This means that the water particles change from a liquid to a solid. Ice and snow are solid water.

Warm temperatures allow water particles to absorb heat energy. This causes ice and snow to **melt** (melt), or change from a solid to a liquid.

Use the terms *freeze, melt, evaporation, water vapor,* and *heat energy* to describe what is going on in these pictures.

How Does Water Travel?

By now you know a lot about water. You know that water can be found in many different places and in three different states. Water doesn't stay put! It moves continuously from place to place. This never-ending movement of Earth's water through evaporation, condensation, and precipitation is called the **water cycle** (wô'tər sī'kəl).

THE WATER CYCLE

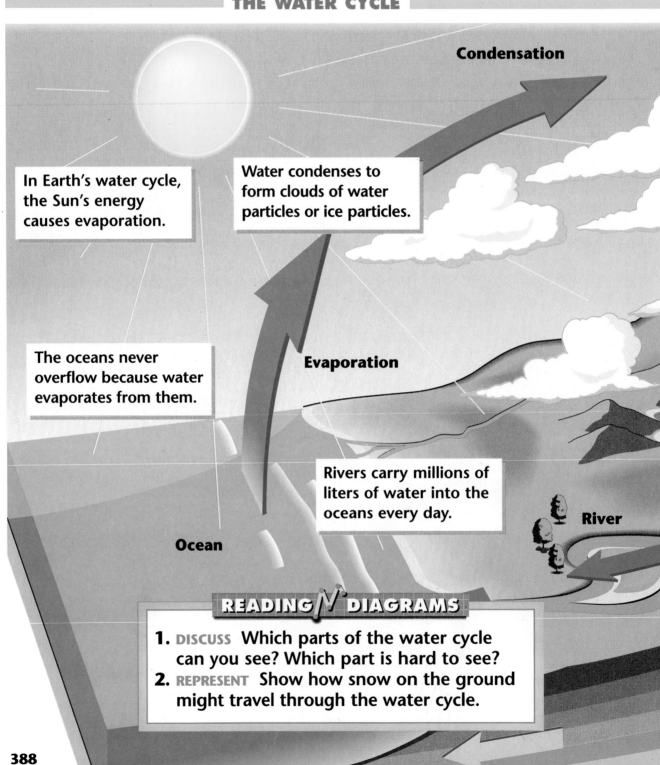

Condensation

In Earth's water cycle, the Sun's energy causes evaporation.

Water condenses to form clouds of water particles or ice particles.

The oceans never overflow because water evaporates from them.

Evaporation

Rivers carry millions of liters of water into the oceans every day.

River

Ocean

READING DIAGRAMS

1. **DISCUSS** Which parts of the water cycle can you see? Which part is hard to see?
2. **REPRESENT** Show how snow on the ground might travel through the water cycle.

This diagram of the water cycle shows how water is used over and over again. However, it is never used up. Believe it or not, all the water that was present when Earth began is still around today!

The Sun is the source of energy for the water cycle. As water moves through the water cycle, it changes form when it absorbs or releases heat energy. The smaller diagram describes this transfer of heat.

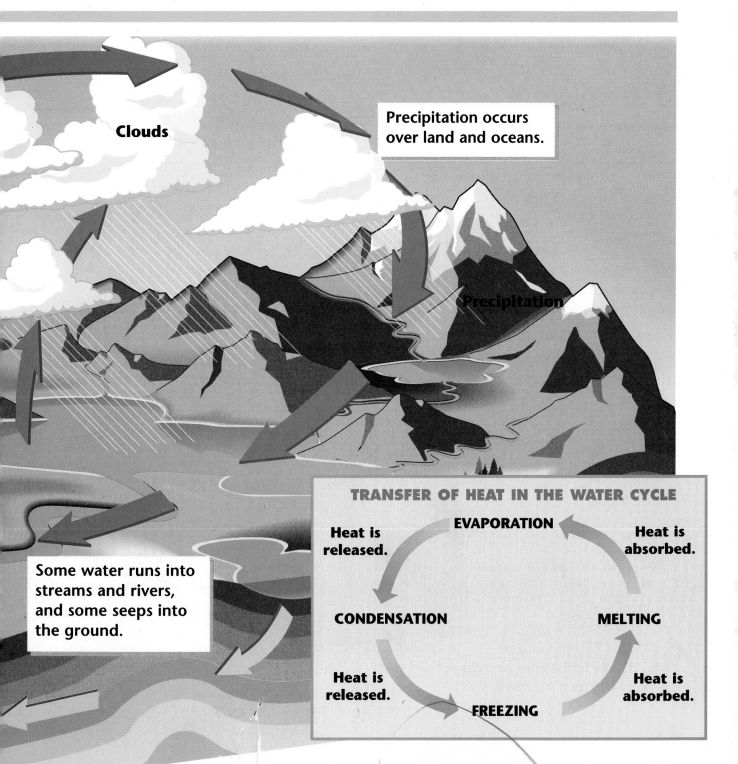

Clouds

Precipitation occurs over land and oceans.

Precipitation

Some water runs into streams and rivers, and some seeps into the ground.

TRANSFER OF HEAT IN THE WATER CYCLE

EVAPORATION

Heat is released.

Heat is absorbed.

CONDENSATION

MELTING

Heat is released.

Heat is absorbed.

FREEZING

What Kinds of Precipitation Do You Get?

How does water in the atmosphere fall where you live? Rain, snow, sleet, and hail are different forms of precipitation. You know that rain falls as a liquid. Snow, sleet, and hail are solids.

Snow is made up of small *crystals*, clear and shiny particles of frozen water. Water vapor in the atmosphere freezes at 0°C (32°F) and below. As gravity pulls the ice crystals toward Earth, they gather together and form snowflakes.

Hail forms when frozen drops of rain fall and are blown back up in the air by the wind. The size of a piece of hail increases each time it goes up and down through the layers of air, collecting more water.

Falling pieces of ice that are 5 millimeters ($\frac{1}{5}$ inch) or larger are called hailstones. There have been hailstones as large as 13 centimeters (5 inches) across and weighing more than 450 grams (1 pound)!

When rain falls through layers of cold air, the raindrops freeze to form sleet. The pieces of ice that are called sleet are usually smaller than 5 millimeters ($\frac{1}{5}$ inch) across.

These hailstones are almost as big as a baseball!

How water moves in the water cycle affects everyone on Earth. You use water every day to drink and cleanse yourself. By looking at clouds, you can tell if you need to bring an umbrella. Maybe it will snow, and you can test your new sled. Knowing what the precipitation in an area might be is also helpful to farmers when planting crops. The water cycle is nature's way of recycling its resources.

How can you tell when it will snow?

REVIEW

1. What causes a puddle of water to seem to disappear?

2. Does water lose or absorb heat energy when it condenses? When it freezes? When it evaporates? When it melts?

3. Give two examples of how water moves from one place to another in the water cycle. Explain how the water changes state in each example.

4. COMMUNICATE What is the difference between snow and hail?

5. CRITICAL THINKING *Apply* What do you think might happen if the only precipitation that fell was snow?

WHY IT MATTERS THINK ABOUT IT
Water is all around us. Do you live near large bodies of water? How do you think a body of water affects the water cycle?

WHY IT MATTERS WRITE ABOUT IT
Where might you see evaporation and condensation occurring in your environment?

READING SKILL How are evaporation and condensation different? What happens to heat energy in each process?

LET IT RAIN!

Do you like rain? In some cultures people do dances or hire rainmakers to bring rain. The dancers and rainmakers get their best results during the normal rainy season. Since long droughts end in time, no one has ever proved he or she shortened a drought!

In 1946 researcher Vincent Schaefer was studying the cause of icing on airplane wings. He sprinkled frozen carbon dioxide, or "dry ice," into a box containing a synthetic cloud. A tiny snowstorm began in the box!

Schaefer rented a plane and went up to sprinkle dry ice in a real cloud. The result: an instant snowstorm!

People thought maybe this new method could be used to end summer droughts. Experiments proved that indeed dry ice could produce rain as well as snow!

Here's how it works: The cold dry ice causes some of a cloud's water vapor to freeze. More water vapor freezes around the first ice to make a snowflake. When the flakes are heavy enough, they fall. In warm weather they melt and become rain.

Native Americans in the Southwest have complex rituals based on the need to have rain for their crops.

Another rain-making researcher, Bernard Vonnegut, noted that the chemical silver iodide has particles shaped much like water ice. He proved that particles of silver iodide, that are light enough to float like dust in air, could also start rain!

Now if there's a drought, tiny amounts of silver iodide are floated up into the sky or dropped from planes. Soon clouds of cool water vapor turn to rain.

DISCUSSION STARTER

1. How does the dry-ice method work?

2. How could the same techniques be used to reduce rainfall when there's too much in a given area?

Dry ice is "dry" because it turns into the gas carbon dioxide instead of melting into a liquid.

To learn more about making it rain, visit *www.mhschool.com/science* and enter the keyword POUR!

*inter*NET
CONNECTION

Topic 3
EARTH SCIENCE

WHY IT MATTERS

The ocean moves in ways that affect the weather, the climate, the land, and you!

SCIENCE WORDS

current an ocean movement; a large stream of water that flows in the ocean

deep ocean current water that flows more than 197 meters (650 feet) deep

surface current the movement of the ocean caused by steady winds blowing over the ocean

tide the rise and fall of ocean water levels

wave an up-and-down movement of water

Motions in the Oceans

Have you ever put a message into a bottle? Did you hope that one day someone on the other side of the ocean might find it?

Long ago people stranded on islands sent messages in bottles to call for help. What are the chances of a bottle traveling across the ocean?

EXPLORE

HYPOTHESIZE How could a message in a bottle travel across the ocean? Write a hypothesis in your *Science Journal*. How could you test your ideas?

Investigate What Makes the Ocean Move

Make a model to find out how water temperature affects the way ocean water moves.

MATERIALS

- clear-plastic shoe box
- medium-temperature tap water
- 500 mL of hot tap water
- small plastic sandwich bag
- twist tie
- food coloring
- dropper
- small rocks
- 2 or 3 ice cubes
- *Science Journal*

PROCEDURES

SAFETY Use caution when handling the hot water, or ask your teacher for help.

1. Fill the box three-fourths full of medium-temperature tap water.

2. Put the rocks in the bag. Fill the bag half full of hot water. Close it with the twist tie.

3. Place the bag in one corner of the box.

4. Float the ice cube in the opposite corner from the bag. If the ice cube melts, put another one in its place.

5. Put food coloring in the dropper. Then place four drops of the coloring in the water next to the ice cube.

6. **OBSERVE** Look at the food coloring for several minutes through the sides of the box. Record what you see in your *Science Journal*.

CONCLUDE AND APPLY

1. **OBSERVE** Where did the water sink? Where did it rise?

2. **EXPLAIN** Why do you think you added food coloring to the water?

GOING FURTHER: Problem Solving

3. **EXPERIMENT** Repeat the activity without using hot water. Compare your results. What are some strengths and weaknesses of this model

What Makes the Ocean Move?

The Explore Activity showed how cold water causes warmer water to move. One way ocean water moves is in currents (kûr'ənts). Currents are large streams of water that flow in the ocean. One kind of ocean current is known as a deep ocean current (dēp ō'shən kûr'ənt). These currents flow more than 197 meters (650 feet) deep, where the water is very cold. Cold water is more dense, or heavier, than an equal amount of warm water. This diagram shows how density causes deep ocean currents.

HOW DEEP OCEAN CURRENTS FORM

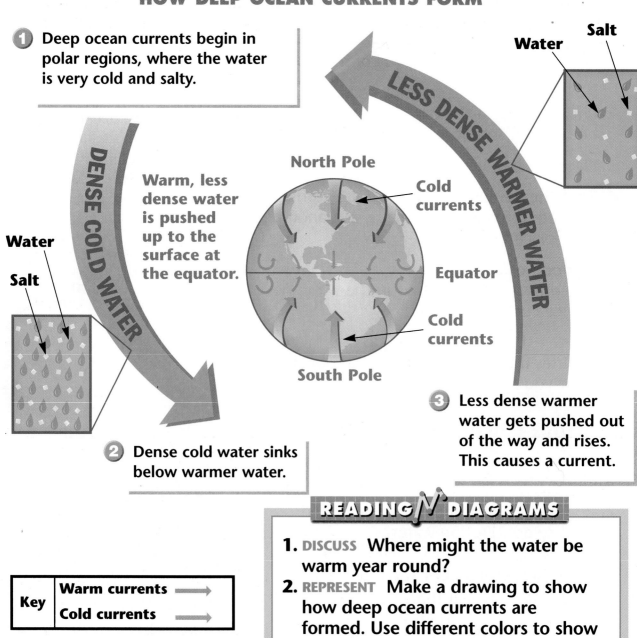

1. Deep ocean currents begin in polar regions, where the water is very cold and salty.

Warm, less dense water is pushed up to the surface at the equator.

DENSE COLD WATER

LESS DENSE WARMER WATER

Water

Salt

Water

Salt

North Pole

Cold currents

Equator

Cold currents

South Pole

2. Dense cold water sinks below warmer water.

3. Less dense warmer water gets pushed out of the way and rises. This causes a current.

Key	Warm currents	⟶
	Cold currents	⟶

READING DIAGRAMS

1. **DISCUSS** Where might the water be warm year round?
2. **REPRESENT** Make a drawing to show how deep ocean currents are formed. Use different colors to show cold water and warm water.

Which Currents Are Caused by the Wind?

Walk along the ocean, and you will see currents moving water at the ocean's surface. When steady winds blow over the ocean, they move the water in currents called surface currents (sûr'fis kûr'ənts).

Some surface currents move warm water from the equator. Other surface currents move cold water from areas near the poles.

The diagram shows you that surface currents move in circular patterns. In the Northern Hemisphere, they move clockwise. In the Southern Hemisphere, they move counterclockwise. This difference in direction is caused by Earth's rotation. It causes winds in the hemispheres to blow in different directions. Large landmasses also cause surface currents to change direction. Surface currents that hit against a continent turn and move along the coast.

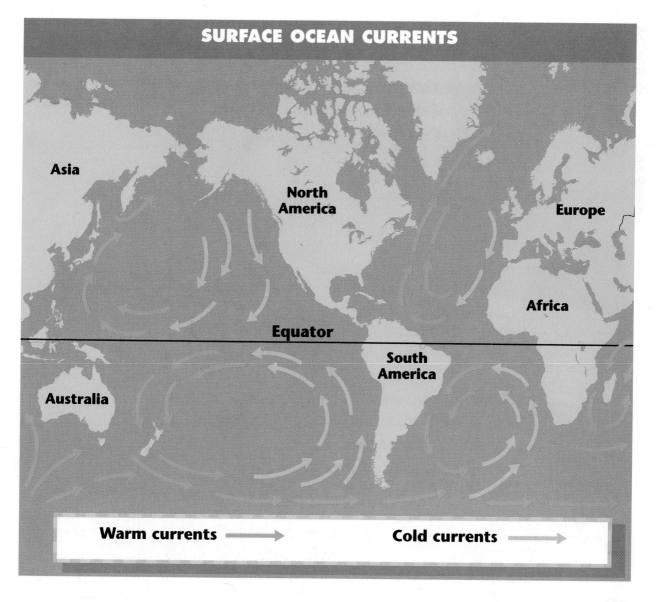

SURFACE OCEAN CURRENTS

Asia

North America

Europe

Africa

Equator

South America

Australia

Warm currents ⟶   Cold currents ⟶

What Ocean Motion Is Caused by Gravity?

The rise and fall of ocean water levels is called a **tide** (tīd). Ocean tides are caused by the pull of gravity between Earth and the Moon and the Sun. The pull is greater by the Moon because it's closer to Earth. Remember what you learned about gravity? The closer objects are together, the stronger the pull of gravity is between them.

The pull of gravity on the side of Earth facing the Moon causes oceans to bulge outward. The bulge moves water higher on the shore, causing a high tide. On the opposite side of Earth, the Moon's pull on solid ground causes oceans to bulge outward, too.

As Earth rotates, the bulge travels around it. Where the water doesn't bulge, there is a low tide. In a low tide, the ocean water doesn't come up as far onto the shore.

The Moon's orbit around Earth also causes daily tide changes. In most places there are two high tides and two low tides each day. During a full Moon and a new Moon, the pull of gravity is stronger. The tides are higher and lower than usual.

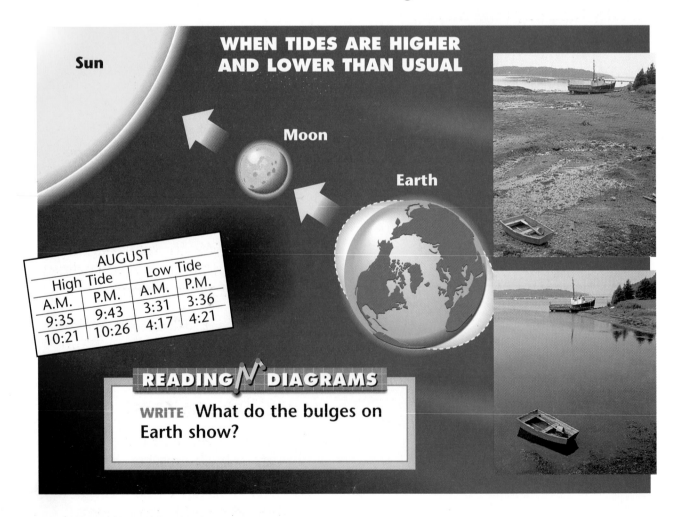

WHEN TIDES ARE HIGHER AND LOWER THAN USUAL

Sun

Moon

Earth

AUGUST			
High Tide		Low Tide	
A.M.	P.M.	A.M.	P.M.
9:35	9:43	3:31	3:36
10:21	10:26	4:17	4:21

READING DIAGRAMS

WRITE What do the bulges on Earth show?

What Is the Up-and-Down Motion?

Along with currents and tides, ocean waters also move in waves. A **wave** (wāv) is an up-and-down movement of water.

The wind causes the ocean's surface water to move up and down in a circular path. The wave moves in the direction of the wind.

As a wave slows down, its lower part reaches toward the ocean bottom. The top of the wave keeps moving and makes the wave steeper. This causes the wave to fall over, or "break" onto the shore. Gravity then pulls the water back into the ocean.

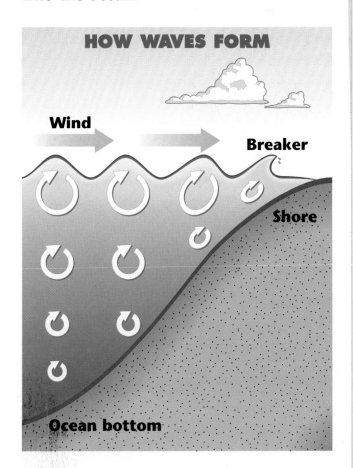

HOW WAVES FORM

Wind

Breaker

Shore

Ocean bottom

QUICK LAB

Make Waves!

HYPOTHESIZE How does the wind affect waves? Write a hypothesis in your *Science Journal.*

MATERIALS

- clear-plastic shoe box
- water
- 2 straws
- cork
- *Science Journal*

PROCEDURES

1. Fill the plastic shoe box halfway with water.

2. Place the cork at one end of the box. Take turns quickly puffing on the water at the other end of the box. Be sure you each use a fresh straw.

3. **OBSERVE** Watch the action of the waves, and record your findings in your *Science Journal.*

4. **EXPERIMENT** Puff on the water surface harder and at different distances.

CONCLUDE AND APPLY

1. **OBSERVE** Describe how the cork moved in the water.

2. **COMMUNICATE** Draw a diagram to show the cork's movements.

How Do Oceans Affect Climate?

How does the size and movements of oceans affect the land nearby? How about the weather and climate?

Surface ocean currents affect the climate of land areas along their path. Some currents carry cold water into areas that would otherwise be warm. Other currents carry warm water into regions that would otherwise be cold. The Gulf Stream helps keep the eastern coast of the United States warmer.

Oceans absorb and release heat more slowly than land areas. In summer air over the ocean is cooler than air over land. Winds blow the cooler ocean air onto the land. Coastal cities have cooler summers than places farther inland.

In winter the opposite occurs. Temperatures along the coasts are warmer than inland areas. As a result winters are warmer along many coastal areas.

Brain Power

What would happen if there were no summer breezes coming from the ocean?

SUMMER SEA BREEZES

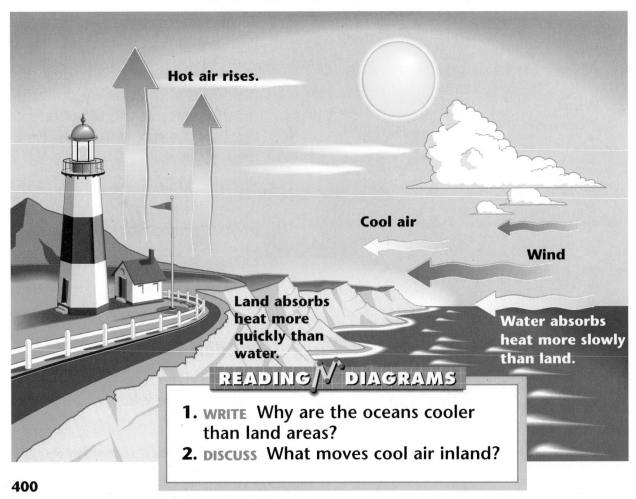

Hot air rises.

Cool air

Wind

Land absorbs heat more quickly than water.

Water absorbs heat more slowly than land.

READING DIAGRAMS

1. **WRITE** Why are the oceans cooler than land areas?
2. **DISCUSS** What moves cool air inland?

How Do Oceans Change Coastlines?

Powerful ocean waves are always changing coastlines. Waves move against the shore and wear away the land. This is called *erosion.* Soil, sand, gravel, and large rocks are carried out to sea. As a result the coastline moves inland.

Waves carry soil, sand, gravel, and rocks from the shore and deposit them in other places. This is called *deposition.* When this happens the coastline is built up and moves out toward the ocean.

Hurricanes

Violent storms with strong winds and heavy rains are called hurricanes. They always begin over the oceans in tropical regions near the equator. Earth's rotation can help start the storm's whirling winds.

Sometimes wind speeds can be more than 240 kilometers (150 miles) per hour. Hurricanes can travel great distances in a short time. They can cause great damage, destroying trees and houses. Giant waves can cause flooding.

What has happened to this coastline?

401

You may not live near an ocean, but oceans are a very important part of your life. Ocean currents help warm or cool land temperatures. If you want to keep track of the weather, it helps to know how these currents move. If you live near an ocean, it helps to know when tides will change. This is especially true if you like to go sailing, swimming, or surfing!

What will happen to the sand castle by the next day?

REVIEW

1. How does water temperature affect the ocean's movement?

2. Explain the difference between surface ocean currents and deep ocean currents.

3. Describe the relationship between gravity and the tides.

4. **COMMUNICATE** Explain how the oceans affect coastlines.

5. **CRITICAL THINKING** *Evaluate* What if the pull of gravity between Earth and the Moon was much less? How would this affect the oceans?

WHY IT MATTERS THINK ABOUT IT
What if the ocean didn't have currents, waves, and tides? How would it affect you?

WHY IT MATTERS WRITE ABOUT IT
Describe some things that you might see happening while spending a day at the beach. Explain what causes each event.

Science, Technology, and Society

TIDAL POWER

In some places people get energy from the Moon. How? By using the ebbing and flowing tides!

People have used rivers and streams to run waterwheels for years. The water is held behind a wall, or dam. It flows over the dam and turns a wheel that powers machinery.

In some coastal areas, the ocean tides rise several meters twice a day. People make the ocean water flow behind a dam as the tide rises. After the tide goes out, the trapped water is used to turn a wheel. Tidal energy can power machinery and make electricity.

Tidal power isn't as easy to get as river-water power. Places with high tides are usually deep bays, where it's hard to build dams. Waves, currents, and storms can damage the dams. Today only a few places get power from the tides.

Tidal power may become more popular. Some people point out that tidal power plants don't pollute oceans as much as other energy sources. As new energy ideas, techniques, and materials are developed, it may also become easier to build dams in ocean bays.

DISCUSSION STARTER

1. Explain why tidal power can be considered energy from the Moon.

2. On a map of the United States, find five places where tidal power plants could be built.

To learn more about tidal power, visit **www.mhschool.com/science** and enter the keyword TIDES.

*inter***NET**
CONNECTION

SCIENCE WORDS

atmosphere p. 372   melt p. 387

cloud p. 385   precipitation p. 386

condensation p. 385   soil water p. 374

current p. 396   tide p. 398

evaporation p. 384   water cycle p. 388

freeze p. 387   water vapor p. 372

ice cap p. 373

USING SCIENCE WORDS

Number a paper from 1 to 10. Fill in 1 to 5 with words from the list above.

1. The process when water particles change from a liquid to a gas is called ___?___ .

2. The movement of Earth's water through evaporation, condensation, and precipitation is the ___?___ .

3. When a gas changes its form to a liquid, it has gone through the process of ___?___ .

4. Water in the atmosphere is in a gas state and is called ___?___ .

5. Rain, snow, hail, and sleet fall to Earth and are known as ___?___ .

6–10. **Pick five words from the list above that were not used in 1 to 5, and use each in a sentence.**

UNDERSTANDING SCIENCE IDEAS

11. What happens to water in the soil?

12. How do clouds form?

USING IDEAS AND SKILLS

13. **READING SKILL: COMPARE AND CONTRAST** How are sleet and snow alike and different?

14. **COMMUNICATE** Make a table to show the different states of water. Then show places where each state of water can be found.

15. **THINKING LIKE A SCIENTIST** The coastline in your area is changing. How can you tell if it is from erosion or deposition?

PROBLEMS and PUZZLES

Weather Watch Can you find any patterns in the weather? Keep a daily log of weather conditions. See page R18 for ideas. What conditions come just before a rainstorm?

Water Freeze Which freezes faster, salty water or fresh water? Make a prediction. Plan an experiment to find out. Discuss your plan with your teacher. Use plastic containers of water in your experiment.

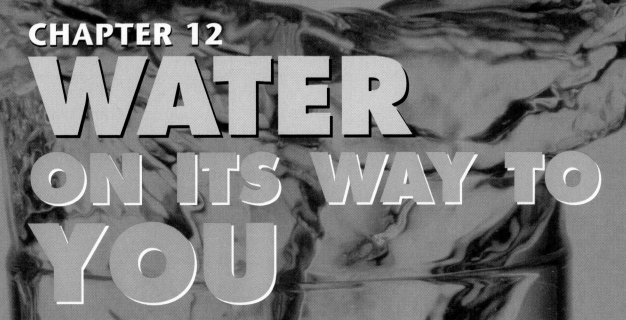

CHAPTER 12
WATER
ON ITS WAY TO
YOU

On rainy days you can see the water come pouring down. Do you know what happens to that water on and in the ground?

In this chapter you will find out how you get the water you use every day. You will also learn what happens to it after you use it.

In this chapter you will have many opportunities to read about the order in which things happen. Ordering, or sequencing, events helps you better understand a process.

Topic
EARTH SCIENCE
4

WHY IT MATTERS

More than half of Earth's fresh water is groundwater.

SCIENCE WORDS

pore space the tiny space between small rock particles in soil that allows liquids and gases to pass through

water table the upper area of groundwater

runoff the water that flows over Earth's surface that doesn't evaporate or soak into the ground

transpiration the process when plants release water vapor into the air through their leaves

drought a long period of time with little or no precipitation

Go with the Flow

What did pioneers do for water? They couldn't always settle near rivers and streams.

Many dug wells to reach groundwater, but how did they know where to dig? How deep to dig?

EXPLORE

HYPOTHESIZE How do you think water travels through soil and rocks? Write a hypothesis in your *Science Journal*. How would you test your idea?

Investigate How Fast Water Flows in Soil and Rocks

Test how fast water flows through different materials.

PROCEDURES

1. With a pencil tip, make a small hole in the bottom of one paper cup.

2. Place your finger over the hole. Fill the cup with perlite or soil. Hold the cup over a plastic container. Have your partner pour in water to cover the perlite or soil.

3. OBSERVE Take away your finger. Time how long it takes the water to drain. Record the results in your *Science Journal*.

4. REPEAT Repeat using marbles.

CONCLUDE AND APPLY

1. IDENTIFY Which material let water soak through faster?

2. EXPLAIN How does the kind of material affect how fast water flows through it?

3. INFER What happens to rainwater falling on soil?

GOING FURTHER: Apply

4. DRAW CONCLUSIONS What can you say about the type of soil that probably is found where wells are dug?

MATERIALS

- cup of perlite or soil
- cup of marbles
- two 12-oz paper cups
- pencil
- stopwatch
- plastic container
- 1 L of water
- measuring cup
- *Science Journal*

407

How Fast Does Water Flow in Soil and Rocks?

How does the way water flows underground affect the water on Earth's surface?

Soil is the top part of the ground. It is made up of mineral particles mixed with decaying plant and animal material, water, and air.

There are tiny spaces between the particles, called **pore spaces** (pôr spās'əz). These spaces allow liquids and gases to pass through. Materials with pores are said to be porous. Soil is porous, so water can soak into it because of the pull of gravity. Water in the soil is called soil water.

The Explore Activity showed how water moves quickly through soils that have large pore spaces. Sandy soils have large pore spaces. Water moves more slowly through soils with small particles and small pore spaces, such as clay.

Water passes through the soil and into porous rocks that lie below. River and lake water also soaks into these rocks. Water passes down through porous rocks until it reaches a layer of nonporous rock. When it can go no deeper, the water begins to fill the spaces in the rocks above. Water in the underground rocks is called groundwater. The upper area of groundwater is known as the **water table** (wô'tər tā'bəl).

HOW WATER TRAVELS THROUGH SOIL AND ROCKS

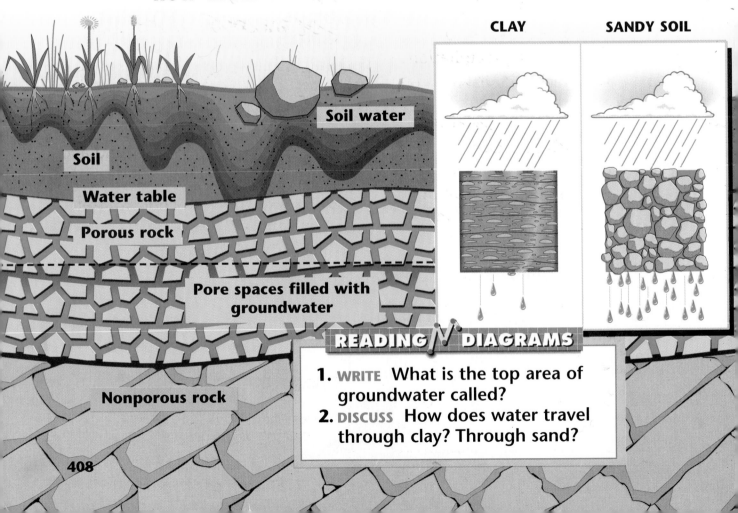

CLAY   SANDY SOIL

Soil water

Soil

Water table

Porous rock

Pore spaces filled with groundwater

Nonporous rock

READING DIAGRAMS

1. **WRITE** What is the top area of groundwater called?
2. **DISCUSS** How does water travel through clay? Through sand?

408

Runoff usually ends up in gutters, ditches, rivers, lakes, and oceans.

What Happens with Too Much Precipitation?

Have you ever seen it rain so hard that streams of water rush through streets? The precipitation that doesn't evaporate or soak into the ground becomes **runoff** (run′ôf′). Runoff is the water that flows over Earth's surface.

The amount and size of runoff is greater in some places than in others. It is also greater at some times of the year, such as during seasons of heavy rains. Soil type and *vegetation*, or plant life, affect runoff. So does the amount of rainfall and the slope of the surface.

Brain Power

How do you think a soil's pore size affects runoff?

QUICK LAB

Make Runoffs

MATH LiNK

HYPOTHESIZE How do different soils affect runoff? Write a hypothesis in your *Science Journal*.

MATERIALS

- two 1-qt milk cartons
- plastic tray with sides
- soil
- sand
- marker
- 1 L of water
- measuring cup
- scissors
- *Science Journal*

PROCEDURES

SAFETY Be careful using scissors

1. Cut the milk cartons as shown. Label one *Soil* and the other *Sand*. Place them on the tray.

2. Put an equal amount of sand and soil in the cartons.

3. Fill the measuring cup with water. Slowly pour it over the soil until the soil can hold no more water. Determine the volume of water you poured into the soil. Record it in your *Science Journal*.

4. **REPEAT** Repeat step 3 for the sand.

CONCLUDE AND APPLY

COMPARE Which absorbed the most water? Which had the most runoff?

How Do Wells Work?

Groundwater is an important source of fresh water. People use groundwater to meet their many needs, such as household cleaning, farming, and industry. Digging a well is the most common way of getting water from the ground.

For a well to produce water, its bottom must be below the water table. This allows the water to flow through the rock formations into the water table. When building a well, it is important to know how deep the water table is from the surface. The water table is closer to the surface in some places and farther away in others. Periods of heavy rain can cause the water table to rise. Lack of rain can cause it to drop.

In some wells pumps bring well water to the surface. In other wells water rises on its own because of pressure in the underground rocks.

This diagram puts together what you learned in this topic with what you learned about the water cycle. It also shows you how deep wells have to be dug to get water.

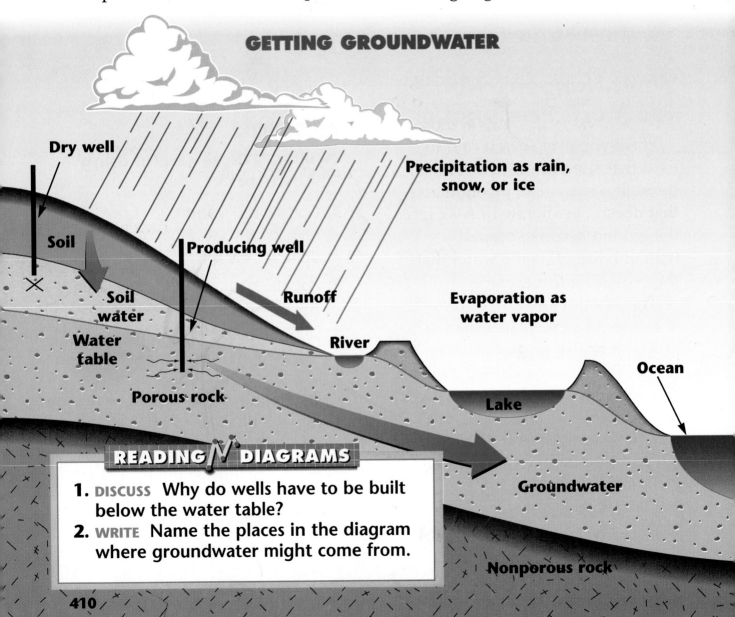

GETTING GROUNDWATER

Dry well

Soil

Producing well

Precipitation as rain, snow, or ice

Soil water

Runoff

Evaporation as water vapor

Water table

River

Porous rock

Lake

Ocean

Groundwater

Nonporous rock

READING DIAGRAMS

1. **DISCUSS** Why do wells have to be built below the water table?
2. **WRITE** Name the places in the diagram where groundwater might come from.

How Do Plants Move Water from the Ground?

Not all of the water that is on or in the ground stays there. It moves through the water cycle. Plants also help move water from the soil and the ground into the atmosphere.

You learned that plant and animal cells are largely made up of water. Both need water to survive.

Plants also contribute to the amount of water vapor in the air. Through their roots plants soak up nutrients and water from the soil. The water moves to all the plant's cells. The water combines with carbon dioxide. The green material in the cell's chloroplasts traps energy from the Sun. The energy is used to combine water and carbon dioxide to make the plant's food.

Some of the water that isn't used to make food escapes from the plant's leaves. Plants release water vapor into the air through tiny pores in their leaves. This process is called **transpiration** (tran′spə rā′shən).

READING *N* DIAGRAMS

1. **DISCUSS** Describe the process of transpiration.
2. **REPRESENT** Draw what happens to the water vapor the plant releases into the air.

PLANTS MOVE WATER FROM THE GROUND INTO THE AIR

Air

Air

Air

Pore

Plants give off water as water vapor through pores in their leaves.

Ground surface

Soil

Water movement

Plants take up soil water through their roots.

What Happens when There Is Little Rain?

What changes have you observed when it hasn't rained for a while? Water on land surfaces evaporates back into the air. If it hasn't rained in a long time, rivers and lakes may dry up. When there is no precipitation, a **drought** (drout) may occur. A drought is a long period of time with little or no precipitation. Droughts often affect crops, vegetation, and water supplies.

Droughts are even more severe when temperatures are high. In hot temperatures water particles absorb more heat energy. This causes the water particles to move and evaporate quickly.

During a drought lands that were fertile and green become dry. Wells can go dry as the water table drops. Water for human needs can become scarce if the drought continues. Some plants and animals may die from lack of water.

When it rains again, the water often cannot soak into the dry, hardened ground. As a result there is a lot of runoff, which creates streams and water holes. Once water collects, it is able to soak into the soil.

Land surfaces can crack and plants may die during a drought.

Sometimes dams cannot hold back rising floodwaters. When floodwaters rise, people must leave their homes and find shelter in a safer area.

What Causes Floods?

Can you think of ways to prevent floods? Floods are great flows of water over land that is usually dry. When this happens water accumulates more rapidly than the soil can absorb it. This causes water runoffs over the ground.

Many things can cause floods. Pore spaces may not be able to take in any more water. This happens because the pore spaces are already full of water or ice. How do pore spaces become so full? It usually happens when there are long periods of heavy rain. It can also happen when snow and ice melt in the spring.

Runoff from heavy rains or melting ice may become very great in spring. Rivers can't hold all the water pouring into them, and they overflow their banks. In cities storm drains may not be able to carry away water fast enough. In deserts very dry soil may not be able to soak up water fast enough.

When floods occur houses can be damaged. Crops can be washed away, and lives can be lost. In an effort to control floods, people build dams and raise river banks. Even so, these structures can't always hold back the water. Dams sometimes break or overflow, releasing floodwaters suddenly and without warning.

Skill: Using Variables

SURFACE AREA AND EVAPORATION

Variables are things, or factors, in an experiment that can be changed to find answers to questions. In this activity you'll answer this question: Does size or surface area of a puddle affect how fast it will evaporate? For a fair test, all of the factors in the experiment must remain the same. The only variable is surface area.

PROCEDURES

1. MAKE A MODEL Use the sponges to make models of puddles with different surface areas.

2. Place one sponge in each pan of the balance. Add paper clips to the pan with the smaller sponge until both sides of the balance are equal in mass.

3. INFER Find a way to add equal amounts of water to both sponges.

4. OBSERVE Once you have set up your models, turn on the lamp. Check the models every half-hour. Record your observations in your *Science Journal*.

CONCLUDE AND APPLY

1. INFER Which model became lighter first? What does this tell you about surface area and evaporation?

2. IDENTIFY What variables did you change? Keep the same?

3. EXPERIMENT What could you do to make water evaporate faster? Slower? Test your ideas.

MATERIALS

- water
- measuring cup
- spotlight lamp
- small box of paper clips
- whole kitchen sponge
- half kitchen sponge
- scissors
- pan balance
- *Science Journal*

Water flows through the ground and becomes a source of fresh water for plants, animals, and humans. Understanding how the water flows may help you in some of your everyday activities. If you have a garden, you will have a better idea of when to water your plants. During a rainy period, you won't have to water your plants as often as in the hotter summer months. You'll also be more aware of areas that flood, and be more prepared!

It helps to know how soil absorbs water when you have a garden.

REVIEW

1. How does soil type affect the movement of water under the ground?

2. What can cause runoff?

3. How do plants move water from the ground into the air?

4. **USE VARIABLES** How would you set up an experiment to determine how temperature affects the evaporation of water?

5. **CRITICAL THINKING** *Synthesize* How could floods affect people who don't live in a flooded area?

WHY IT MATTERS THINK ABOUT IT If your area was in danger of a flood, what could you do to help?

WHY IT MATTERS WRITE ABOUT IT Create a safety plan for your community in case of a flood.

READING SKILL Write a paragraph to describe the sequence of events of how groundwater forms.

FLOOD!

We can't live without water, but sometimes we can't live with it! Too much water, as in floods, can be very dangerous. Throughout its history the United States has had its share of floods. Here are a few.

1889: JOHNSTOWN, PENNSYLVANIA
A major dam breaks, and a wall of water rushes through Johnstown, sweeping away everything in its path. More than 2,200 people drown. Nearly 800 recovered bodies are never identified.

1972: RAPID CITY, SOUTH DAKOTA
Heavy rain leads to a flash flood along the river that flows through the city. At least 237 people drown. Damage totals more than $100 million.

A Closer Look

1972: ATLANTIC COASTLINE
Hurricane Agnes brings rains that flood land from New York to Virginia. Entire communities are ruined, and 118 people die.

1976: BIG THOMPSON CANYON, COLORADO Heavy rains, up to 20.32 centimeters (8 inches) an hour, lead to a flash flood. It kills 139 people, most of them tourists. A two-story power plant in the water's path becomes a pile of bricks. Damage is $30 million.

1993: MISSISSIPPI RIVER FLOOD
Melting snow and storms lead to months of flooding along the Mississippi and Missouri Rivers. The result is 52 deaths and about 31,080 square kilometers (12,000 square miles) of farmland ruined. The cost is about $15 to $20 billion!

DISCUSSION STARTER

1. Should people be allowed to build homes in areas that are known to have had floods?

2. Find four other important events in U.S. history that occurred between 1889–1993.

To learn more about floods, visit **www.mhschool.com/science** and enter the keyword FLOOD!

*inter*NET CONNECTION

WHY IT MATTERS

Earth has a lot of water, but only a small part is available for humans.

SCIENCE WORDS

irrigation a way to get water into the soil by artificial means

water treatment plant a place where water is made clean and pure

filtration the passing of a liquid through materials that remove impurities

sewage water mixed with waste

sewer a large pipe or channel that carries sewage to a sewage treatment plant

septic tank an underground tank in which sewage is broken down by bacteria

water conservation the use of water-saving methods

Water Please!

Why do you think Earth is known as the blue planet? From a space shuttle, astronauts see Earth as huge brown islands in a sea of blue. Most of the water they see is Earth's salty oceans and seas.

As you discovered there's also a small amount of fresh water on Earth. What can we do to make sure there's fresh water in the future?

EXPLORE

HYPOTHESIZE People use—and waste—fresh water every day. How can you find out how much water is used at your school each day? Write a hypothesis in your *Science Journal.*

EXPLORE ACTIVITY

Design Your Own Experiment

HOW MUCH FRESH WATER IS USED?

PROCEDURES

1. PLAN Determine ways to measure or estimate the amount of water used daily in school.

2. COLLECT DATA How can you figure out how much water is being used by each student? By each class? Record your results in your *Science Journal*.

3. COMMUNICATE Design a table to record all the data you gathered from your investigation.

CONCLUDE AND APPLY

1. COMPARE Which activities used the most water each day? Which used the least?

2. USE NUMBERS How can you estimate how much water is used in the whole school in a day?

3. INFER From your observations can you think of ways to save water?

GOING FURTHER: Apply

4. COMMUNICATE What is another way to record the data you collected? Think about a way to present the information clearly.

MATERIALS

- two 9-oz plastic cups
- measuring cup
- stopwatch, clock, or watch with second hand
- calculator (optional)
- *Science Journal*

How Much Fresh Water Is There?

What will happen when there isn't enough fresh water? The Explore Activity showed how much water is used in your school every day. There seems to be plenty of water around. Actually, only about $\frac{3}{100}$ of Earth's water is fresh. How much fresh water do you think is readily available for people to use?

Look at the pie chart. You will see that Earth's fresh water is a slice pulled from the rest of the graph. This shows you the small amount of fresh water there is. The slice is then broken into smaller sections. Only $\frac{1}{10}$ of Earth's fresh water supply is easily obtained for human use. This fresh water is found in rivers, lakes, and groundwater.

Fresh water found in frozen ice caps and glaciers isn't readily available. These solid water sources make up about $\frac{7}{10}$ of all the fresh water on Earth.

There is also fresh water under the ground, but the groundwater very deep down is not easy to reach. The very deep groundwater makes up about $\frac{2}{10}$ of Earth's fresh water.

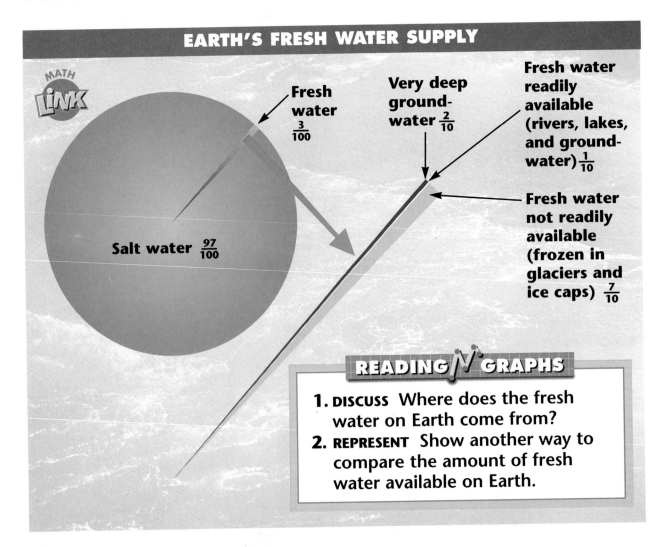

EARTH'S FRESH WATER SUPPLY

MATH LINK

Fresh water $\frac{3}{100}$

Very deep ground-water $\frac{2}{10}$

Fresh water readily available (rivers, lakes, and ground-water) $\frac{1}{10}$

Fresh water not readily available (frozen in glaciers and ice caps) $\frac{7}{10}$

Salt water $\frac{97}{100}$

READING GRAPHS

1. **DISCUSS** Where does the fresh water on Earth come from?
2. **REPRESENT** Show another way to compare the amount of fresh water available on Earth.

How Much Fresh Water Is Used?

Every day people use water at school, at home, and in office buildings, stores, restaurants, and hotels. Aside from individual water use, we all have a "share" in the water use. This includes water used in farming, in industry, and by our communities. Think about the production of goods and the services that are all a part of modern life.

Communities provide many services that require water. These services include street cleaning, firefighting, and watering trees and grass in parks. Many communities also maintain swimming pools.

A person needs only a few quarts of water a day to stay alive. In the United States, each person may directly use as much as 760 liters (200 gallons) a day. The water is

Firefighting is one community service that needs water.

used for personal and household purposes. Some everyday water uses include drinking, cooking, cleaning, flushing toilets, disposing of garbage, and watering gardens.

This pictograph shows how much water is used for some of these activities.

SOME HOUSEHOLD USES OF WATER

1 toilet flush	
1 average bath	
1 three-minute shower	
1 dishwasher load	
1 clothes washer load	

🍼 represents 2 gallons (about 8 liters) of water.

How Is Water Used in Farming and Industry?

How much water do you think farms and factories use? In places where rainfall is low or irregular, water for growing crops is supplied by **irrigation** (ir'i gā'shən). Irrigation is a way to get water into the soil by artificial means. It is used to help increase crop production.

Irrigation water is pumped from rivers, lakes, and under the ground. It is distributed to fields of growing crops by plowed ditches called *furrows*, pipes, or sprinklers.

This can has only about $\frac{1}{2}$ liter ($\frac{1}{2}$ quart) of water in it, but 10 liters (10 quarts) were used to process it.

Different types of irrigation are used to bring water to farmlands.

Factories provide us with the products we need and want. Some of the water they use becomes part of the products they make. However, most of the water is used in washing, cleaning, cooling, and carrying away waste.

How Water Produces Electricity

Power plants produce electricity that supplies us with the energy for many everyday activities. Hydro-electric power plants produce electricity from the energy of waterfalls and water flowing from dams. Other kinds of power plants use the energy of steam to make electricity. The steam comes from water heated by burning fuel.

How Does Water Get Polluted?

Wastes from industry, farming, and humans are the main sources of water pollution. Rivers and lakes become polluted when untreated wastes are dumped into them. The wastes are full of harmful bacteria and chemicals.

Many farmers use *fertilizers*, which are chemicals or animal waste, to treat soil. *Pesticides*, which are chemicals that kill insects, are also widely used. Sometimes these wastes are carried along with runoff water that moves into the ground. This polluted water may pass into rivers and lakes, or become part of groundwater. Fish that live in these waters may become sick or die.

Landfills are one way to get rid of waste, but they take up too much space.

Even wastes buried in a landfill can pollute groundwater. A landfill is a place where solid wastes are buried between layers of soil. The water table under a landfill must be at least 2 meters (6 feet) deep. A flood in a landfill could cause many problems.

Waste is often emptied into rivers.

How Does Water Get to Our Homes?

Where does the water in your home come from? First, a water supply must be located. Then, before the water can be distributed, it must be made safe for use. This means meeting safe drinking-water rules set by government.

The quality of water is different from place to place. Some water supplies need little treatment, while others need a lot. The place where water is made clean and pure is called a **water treatment plant** (wô'tər trēt'mənt plant).

At the plant water first passes through a screen to remove animals, plants, and trash. Then, various chemicals are mixed with the water in a mixing basin. The chemicals remove impurities and kill harmful bacteria.

From there the water moves to a settling basin, where most other impurities sink. Any impurities that are left are removed by **filtration** (fil trā'shən). Filtration is the passing of a liquid through materials that remove impurities.

Finally, the chemical element chlorine is added. The chlorine kills any remaining bacteria. Then, the water is stored and ready to be pumped to where it is needed.

WATER TREATMENT PLANT

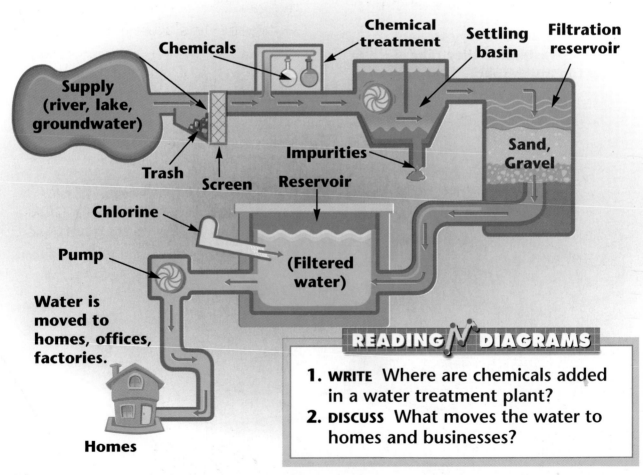

Chemicals

Chemical treatment

Settling basin

Filtration reservoir

Supply (river, lake, groundwater)

Sand, Gravel

Trash

Screen

Impurities

Reservoir

Chlorine

Pump

(Filtered water)

Water is moved to homes, offices, factories.

Homes

READING DIAGRAMS

1. **WRITE** Where are chemicals added in a water treatment plant?
2. **DISCUSS** What moves the water to homes and businesses?

What Happens to Used Water?

Most of the water used in homes and factories is used to carry off waste. Water mixed with waste is **sewage** (sü′ij). **Sewers** (sü′ərz) are large pipes or channels that carry sewage to a sewage treatment plant. This is where sewage is treated before it is returned to rivers and lakes.

At a plant large objects are removed and the *sludge*, or solid material, settles. The waste water is treated to kill germs. Then the clean water flows into rivers and lakes. The sludge is put into tanks, where it is broken down by bacteria. Leftover sludge is used as fertilizer, burned in an incinerator, or dumped out at sea.

Areas with no public sewage disposal systems have **septic tanks** (sep′tik tangks). A septic tank is an underground tank in which sewage is broken down by bacteria.

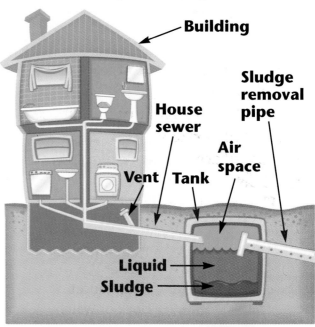

SEPTIC TANK

- Building
- Sludge removal pipe
- House sewer
- Air space
- Vent
- Tank
- Liquid
- Sludge

Sewage from a building flows through a pipe into the septic tank. Bacteria in the sewage begin to break it down into liquid, sludge, and gas. The gas escapes through a vent. Leftover sludge is pumped out every so often. The liquid drains into underground pipes that are covered with gravel. The pipes have holes that let the liquid drain out and seep into the ground.

Used water is cleaned at treatment plants like this one.

425

QUICK LAB

Wasted Water

HYPOTHESIZE Can you estimate how much water a leaky faucet might waste in a day? Write your hypothesis in your *Science Journal.*

MATERIALS

- 1,000-mL (1-L) pitcher
- water faucet
- clock or watch with second hand
- calculator (optional)
- *Science Journal*

PROCEDURES

1. Turn on the faucet until it drips slowly.

2. **COLLECT DATA** Place the pitcher under the faucet for five minutes.

3. **MEASURE** Measure the collected water. Record the amount in your *Science Journal.*

CONCLUDE AND APPLY

1. **OBSERVE** How much water was wasted in five minutes?

2. **USE NUMBERS** If the faucet dripped like this every day, how much water would be wasted in an hour? In a day? In a week? In a year?

How Can We Save Water?

Can you identify some ways to save water in school? The use of water-saving methods is called **water conservation** (wô′tər kon′sər vā′shən). It helps to reduce the amount of water needed for homes, farms, industries, and businesses. Here are some ways you and your family can conserve water:

- Fix leaky faucets.
- Run only full loads in clothes washers and dishwashers.
- Take short showers instead of baths.
- Use shower heads that conserve water.
- Place a brick in the toilet tank.
- Use water only when you need it.
- Don't run water while you are brushing your teeth!
- Don't run water to get cold water. Put drinking water in the refrigerator to keep it cold.

Brain Power

Can you think of any other ways your family can help save water? Make a list or chart that you can post in your home for family members to follow.

The Dead Sea is the saltiest body of water on Earth, nine times saltier than the oceans. Only a few kinds of plants and some bacteria can survive in it. Fish that enter from the Jordan River die. What might be done to make salt water usable by people?

WHY IT MATTERS

Only a small part of Earth's water is fresh. Since we all need fresh water, it is important that we know how to use it wisely. Think about how you use water every day. Do you keep the water running when you wash dishes? How much water could you save by using tubs of water? Try it! Just think about the amount of water that could be saved if everyone on the planet remembered to conserve.

We all count on water in many ways.

REVIEW

1. How much water do you use at school compared to at home?

2. What are the three main sources of fresh water we use?

3. How does groundwater become polluted? How can it be cleaned?

4. **COMMUNICATE** Make a table to show how water can be wasted at home. Then show how this wasted water could be conserved.

5. **CRITICAL THINKING** *Apply* Since all water is reused and can be cleaned, why is it important to conserve water?

WHY IT MATTERS THINK ABOUT IT What would happen if people did not try to conserve water? How would this affect you and your community?

WHY IT MATTERS WRITE ABOUT IT Write a public service ad to persuade people in your community to conserve water.

SURVIVING ON THE
SAVANNAS

It's the dry season on the African savannas. Hot winds blow. Water holes dry up. Animals keep moving in search of grass. Its long roots can reach water deep underground. In the dry season, its stems and leaves dry out, but its roots don't.

People of the savanna used to migrate to wetter land for the dry season. Now they store rainwater in terraces during the wet season. They plant trees to stop erosion.

The thick bark of acacia trees protects them from fire. In the dry season, some trees store water in their trunks.

After months of hot, dry weather, clouds gather. Lightning starts fires in the dry grass. The rain begins.

After a month or so, the rain stops. By then the savannas are covered with thick, green grass.

Animals of the African savannas must search for water during the dry season.

DISCUSSION STARTER

1. Why do you think there's grass on savannas, but not many trees?

2. Why would planting trees help people during the dry season?

To learn more about life on the savanna, visit **www.mhschool.com/science** and enter the keyword SAVANNA.

*inter*NET
CONNECTION

CHAPTER 12 REVIEW

SCIENCE WORDS

drought p. 412   sewer p. 425

filtration p. 424   transpiration p. 411

irrigation p. 422   water conserva-

pore space p. 408   tion p. 426

runoff p. 409   water table p. 408

septic tank p. 425   water treatment

sewage p. 425   plant p. 424

USING SCIENCE WORDS

Number a paper from 1 to 10. Fill in 1 to 5 with words from the list above.

1. The passing of a liquid through materials that remove impurities is called ___?___.

2. A place where sewage is broken down by bacteria is a(n) ___?___.

3. The upper area of groundwater is known as the ___?___.

4. A way to get water into soil for growing crops by artificial means is ___?___.

5. Water mixed with waste is ___?___.

6–10. **Pick five words from the list above that were not used in 1 to 5, and use each in a sentence.**

UNDERSTANDING SCIENCE IDEAS

11. Why is it important to find out how deep the water table is from the surface when digging a well?

12. How do floods create runoffs?

USING IDEAS AND SKILLS

13. **READING SKILL: SEQUENCE OF EVENTS** Describe how rain becomes part of the water table.

14. **USE VARIABLES** Why do you think scientists use variables in their experiments?

15. **THINKING LIKE A SCIENTIST** After you clean the dishes, how does the water you just used get back into the water cycle?

PROBLEMS and PUZZLES

"Flow" Model Pack moist soil to fill one side of a plastic shoe box. Tilt the box, soil side up. Trickle water from a pitcher over the top edge of the soil to model a stream. (Place your model in a tub or sink to catch any overflow.) How does the stream change the soil over time?

Oil Spill Place sand, water with food coloring, and vegetable oil in a jar. Seal the jar and shake. Plan a way to get the oil out of the mixture. You may use only materials that are safe. Present your plan to your teacher. Try it.

429

SCIENCE WORDS

atmosphere p. 372   runoff p. 409

current p. 396   sewer p. 425

drought p. 412   tide p. 398

freeze p. 387   water conserva-

groundwater p. 374   tion p. 426

ice cap p. 373   water table p. 408

irrigation p. 422   wave p. 399

precipitation p. 386

USING SCIENCE WORDS

Number a paper from 1 to 10. Beside each number write the word or words that best complete the sentence.

1. Water stored in the cracks of underground rocks is called __?__.

2. The thick sheets of ice at the South Pole make up a(n) __?__.

3. Rain and snow are examples of __?__.

4. Water becomes a solid when it __?__.

5. The rise and fall of ocean levels caused by the Moon's gravity is called a(n) __?__.

6. A large flow of water in the ocean is called a(n) __?__.

7. The upper area of groundwater is called the __?__.

8. A long dry period with little or no rain or snow is called a(n) __?__.

9. Watering a garden is an example of __?__.

10. Using water without wasting it is __?__.

UNDERSTANDING SCIENCE IDEAS

Write 11 to 15. For each number write the letter for the best answer. You may wish to use the hints provided.

11. To grow, many plants depend on
    a. water vapor
    b. groundwater
    c. soil water
    d. ice water
    (Hint: Read page 374.)

12. Clouds are made up of
    a. vapor
    b. water droplets
    c. electricity
    d. ice
    (Hint: Read page 385.)

13. Winds cause oceans to have
    a. tides
    b. pollution
    c. waves
    d. runoff
    (Hint: Read page 399.)

14. Water in wells comes from
    a. condensation
    b. the water table
    c. runoff
    d. irrigation
    (Hint: Read page 410.)

15. At a water treatment plant, water is
    a. cleaned with filters
    b. used to make electricity
    c. converted to steam
    d. used for irrigation
    (Hint: Read page 424.)

USING IDEAS AND SKILLS

16.  **COMMUNICATE** Survey four people about how much water they usually drink in a day. Make a pictograph to show your results.

17. Tell what water conservation means, and give examples showing why it is important.

18. How do currents often keep the eastern coast of the United States warmer than the rest of the country in winter?

19. Draw a simple picture that shows how water moves into, through, and out of a water treatment plant.

THINKING LIKE A SCIENTIST

20.  **USE VARIABLES** Does salt water or fresh water evaporate faster? How could you find out? Which variables would you change or keep the same in your experiment?

WRITING IN YOUR JOURNAL

SCIENCE IN YOUR LIFE
List five different ways you use water every day. Tell how water conservation can help you reduce the amount of water you use in one of those ways.

PRODUCT ADS
Water for drinking is sold in grocery stores. What do the labels suggest makes the bottled water better to drink than water from a faucet? Why might faucet water be better?

HOW SCIENTISTS WORK
Scientists do experiments to learn about different things. Scientists try to design experiments in which there is only one variable. Why is it important for scientists to do this?

Design your own
Experiment

Figure out a way to decide if people really like bottled water better than faucet water. Review your experiment with your teacher before you carry it out.

inter**NET** CONNECTION

For help in reviewing this unit, visit *www.mhschool.com/science*

PROBLEMS and PUZZLES

Water Force

Measure the force of water using three milk cartons with their tops cut off.

- Place the three cartons at the edge of a sink.

- Poke a round hole at the bottom of each carton. Seal the hole with tape.

- Fill carton 1 to the top with water.

- Fill carton 2 halfway with water.

- Fill carton 3 one-fourth full with water.

- Look at the taped holes you made. Which hole has the greatest weight of water pushing on it?

- Out of which hole do you think water will shoot the farthest? Take the tape off each hole, and see if your prediction is correct.

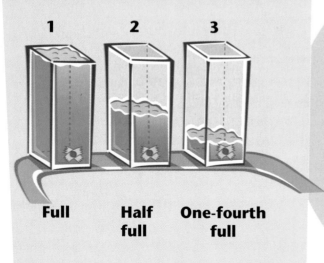

1	2	3
Full	**Half full**	**One-fourth full**

WHERE'S THE WATER?

Tape a small plastic cup to the middle of the bottom of a large bowl. Fill the bowl around the cup about 2 centimeters ($\frac{3}{4}$ inch) deep with water. Cover the bowl securely with plastic wrap held in place with a string or rubber band. Place a marble on the plastic wrap directly above the small cup. Predict what will happen when you place the bowl in sunlight for several hours. Try it.

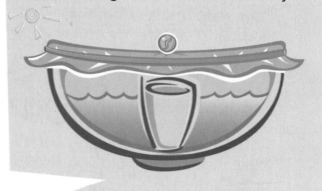

SALT OR FRESH FLOAT

Will a balloon filled with salty water float higher or lower in water than a balloon filled with fresh water? Make a prediction. Plan an experiment to test your prediction. Discuss your plan with your teacher. Try it.

UNIT 7

HUMAN BODY: A BODY IN MOTION

CHAPTER 13

MOVING ABOUT

Playing soccer. Dancing. Reading. Making model planes or boats. What do you like to do for fun? No matter what your favorite activity is, you need to move and use your body in some way. In this chapter you will learn about the structure of your body and how it moves.

As you read Chapter 13, look for details that support the main idea of each passage.

WHY IT MATTERS

It is important to know about the parts that support the body and how to take care of them.

SCIENCE WORDS

skeleton a supporting frame that gives the body its shape and protects many organs

marrow soft tissue that fills some bones

joint a place where two or more bones meet

ligament a tough band of tissue that holds two bones together where they meet

cartilage a flexible tissue that covers the ends of some bones; also found in the nose and ears

sprain a pull or tear in a muscle or ligament

fracture a break or crack in a bone

Your Skeleton

Have you ever seen an office building or house being built? Supporting the roof and walls of most buildings is a frame. A frame is a supporting network usually made of wood or metal.

Firmly squeeze your arm or leg. Under your soft skin and muscles are bones. Do you think the bones you feel are like the frame of a building?

EXPLORE

HYPOTHESIZE Do you think a supporting frame is important to a building? Why or why not? Write a hypothesis in your *Science Journal.*

Design Your Own Experiment

ART
LINK

HOW IMPORTANT IS A SUPPORTING FRAME?

PROCEDURES

SAFETY Use the scissors carefully!

1. **COMMUNICATE** Work as a class to design a model of a simple building. Copy it into your *Science Journal*.

2. **MAKE A MODEL** Work with your group to design and build a frame for it. Use any materials you like. Paper can be used for the walls and roof. Record your design.

3. **MAKE A MODEL** Build another model of the same building, but without a frame.

4. **COMMUNICATE** Work as a class to design a way to test the strength of each model.

5. **COLLECT DATA** Test the strength of your models. Record the results.

CONCLUDE AND APPLY

1. **COMPARE** Which model was stronger?

2. **COMPARE AND CONTRAST** Which model was the strongest in the entire class? What was it made of? How was it built?

3. **DRAW CONCLUSIONS** What conclusions can you draw about the importance of a strong supporting frame?

GOING FURTHER: Apply

4. **EXPERIMENT** If you could redesign the frame, how would you change it? Why? Build and test your new design. Is it stronger?

MATERIALS

- construction paper
- scissors
- glue or tape
- blocks, straws, or craft sticks
- any other building supplies you choose
- *Science Journal*

How Important Is a Supporting Frame?

As the Explore Activity showed, most structures need a supporting frame to stand firmly. You also have a supporting frame. Your frame, called a **skeleton** (skel′i tən), is made up of bones and cartilage. A skeleton has several jobs.

- It gives your body its shape.

- It protects some organs. Your ribs curve around your heart and lungs to form a protective cage. The bones of your skull protect your brain.

- It moves the body. The skeleton works together with muscles to move the body in many different ways. You will learn more about muscles in Topic 2.

Brain Power

How do you think the shape of a bone relates to its job? Each of the 206 bones of the adult skeleton is the size and shape best fitted to do its job. For example, long and strong leg bones support your weight. Each *vertebra* (vûr′tə brə) making up your spine is shaped to stack one on the other.

THE SKELETON

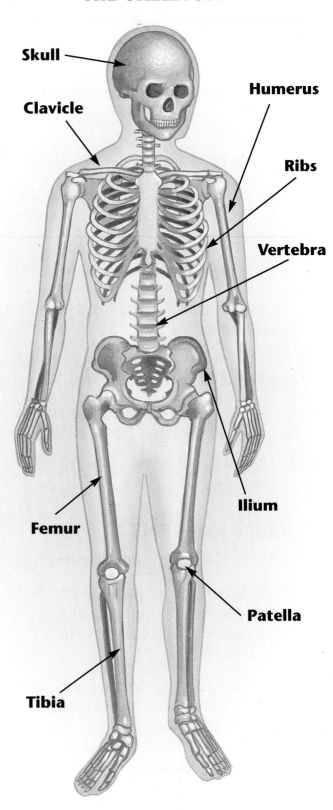

Skull
Clavicle
Humerus
Ribs
Vertebra
Ilium
Femur
Patella
Tibia

These are the major bones of the human skeleton.

WHAT ARE BONES LIKE?

1 A bone is covered with a tough but thin membrane that has many small blood vessels. The blood vessels bring nutrients and oxygen to the living parts of the bone and remove wastes.

2 Inside some bones is a soft tissue known as **marrow** (mar'ō). Yellow marrow is made mostly of fat cells and is one of the body's energy reserves. It is usually found in the long, hollow spaces of long bones.

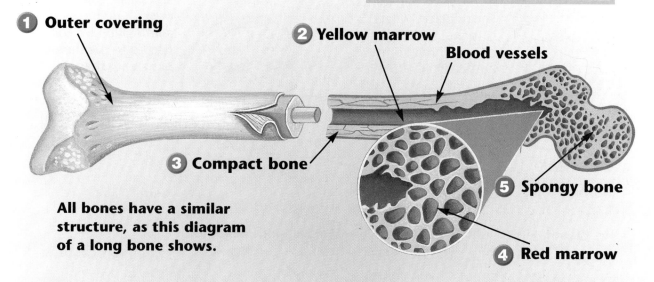

1 Outer covering

2 Yellow marrow

Blood vessels

3 Compact bone

5 Spongy bone

4 Red marrow

All bones have a similar structure, as this diagram of a long bone shows.

3 Part of the bone is compact, or solid. It is made up of living bone cells and nonliving materials. The nonliving part is made up of layers of hardened minerals such as calcium and phosphorus. In between the mineral layers are living bone cells.

4 Red marrow fills the spaces in spongy bone. Red marrow makes new red blood cells, substances that stop a cut from bleeding, and germ-fighting white blood cells.

5 Part of the bone is made of bone tissue that looks like a dry sponge. It is made of strong, hard, bony tubes. It is also full of spaces that help keep the bone light. Spongy bone is found in the ends of long bones. It is also found in the middle of short, flat bones.

READING IN DIAGRAMS

1. DISCUSS What are the differences between the bone tissue making up the long part of the bone and the bone tissue making up its ends?

2. WRITE What does red marrow do? Write a short paragraph.

Where Do Bones Meet?

The skeleton has different types of **joints** (joints). A joint is a place where two or more bones meet.

Joints can be classified into three major groups—immovable joints, partly movable joints, and movable joints. Movable joints work in different ways.

TYPES OF JOINTS

Immovable Joints

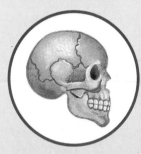

Head

Immovable joints (i mü'və bəl joints) are places where bones fit together too tightly to move. Nearly all of the 29 bones in your skull meet at immovable joints. Only the lower jaw can move.

Partly Movable Joints

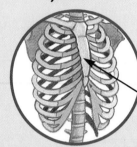

Breastbone

Ribs

Partly movable joints are places where bones can move only a little. Ribs are connected to the breastbone with these joints.

Movable Joints

Movable joints are places where bones can move easily.

Gliding joint

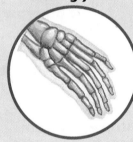

Hand and wrist

Small bones in your wrists and ankles meet at gliding joints. The bones can slide against one another. This joint allows some movement in all directions.

Ball-and-socket joint

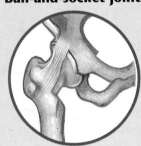

Hip

Your hips are examples of ball-and-socket joints. The ball of one bone fits into the socket, or cup, of another bone. This joint allows bones to move back and forth, in a circle, and side to side.

Hinge joint

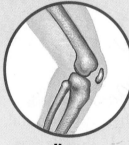

Knee

Your knees are hinge joints. A hinge joint is similar to a door hinge. It allows bones to move back and forth in one direction.

Pivot joint

Neck

The joint between your skull and neck is a pivot joint. It allows your head to move up and down, and side to side.

READING DIAGRAMS

REPRESENT Make a chart that classifies the three types of joints in your body.

Is the Skeleton Made of Just Bones?

Your skeleton is made up of more than just bones and joints. A **ligament** (lig'ə mənt) is a tough band of tissue that holds two bones together where they meet. Ligaments are tough, but they stretch when a joint bends.

Cartilage (kär'tə lij) is a flexible tissue that covers the ends of some bones. It helps protect them from grinding against one another at a joint. It also absorbs some energy from bumps, walking, and running.

Cartilage can also be found in some other places. You have it in the tip of your nose and in your outer ear. Can you feel it?

Bones, cartilage, and ligaments work together to form the *skeletal system* (skel'i təl sis'təm).

If you hurt your skeletal system, it is important to get help. For example, a sudden movement or fall may twist or overstretch a joint. This can pull or tear a muscle or ligament. That is called a **sprain** (sprān). A doctor or nurse can bandage the area and apply ice to reduce the swelling. A sudden movement or fall may **fracture** (frak'chər) a bone. A fracture is a break or crack in a bone. A doctor needs to fit the broken ends together. A cast keeps the ends in place as bone cells heal the break.

Keeping Bones Healthy

It is important to take good care of your skeletal system. Bones grow until you are 17 to 20 years old. To grow properly you need to eat foods rich in vitamins and minerals. Vitamins help your bones take in minerals. Among the minerals your bones need are phosphorus and calcium. Bone cells use minerals to build more hard bone. As you grow you need to exercise, too. This helps your bones grow thicker and stronger.

Calcium is a mineral that makes bones and teeth hard and strong. You get calcium from the foods you eat. These are some of the foods that contain calcium.

Skill: Measuring

MEASURING AND COMPARING BODY PARTS

"The length from heel to toe is equal to the length from elbow to wrist." Do you think this statement is true? How could you find out? In this activity you will use a ruler to measure the length of different body parts. You will create a bar graph of your results. Then you will use the graph to look for relationships between the lengths of different body parts.

MATERIALS

- ruler
- meter tape
- graph paper
- *Science Journal*

PROCEDURES

1. **COMMUNICATE** Copy the graph into your *Science Journal,* or create your own.

2. **COLLECT DATA/MEASURE** Take turns measuring as many different body parts as you can. Ask your partner to help you. Record the data in your *Science Journal.*

3. **COMMUNICATE** Complete your bar graphs by plotting the data you collected.

CONCLUDE AND APPLY

1. **IDENTIFY** Use your graph to identify your shortest and longest body parts.

2. **COMPARE AND CONTRAST** Is the original statement true for you? Your partner?

3. **IDENTIFY** Study both of your graphs. Can you find any patterns in the lengths of body parts? For example, are both of your middle fingers longer than your index fingers?

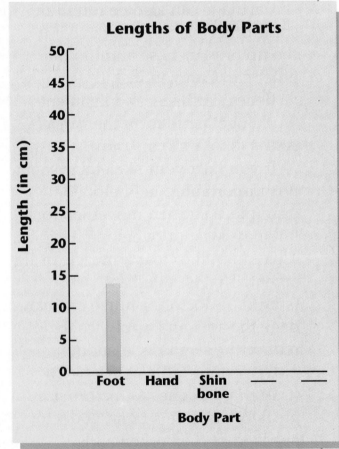

Lengths of Body Parts

Understanding what the skeletal system is made of and how it works can help you keep it strong. You know that bones need calcium. Eat calcium-rich foods. You know the limits of how joints can move. Be aware of movements during physical activities.

Your skeletal system can be injured, so treat it with care. Seek help if you need it. Knowing more about your body helps you take good care of it.

Keeping your skeletal system in good shape allows you to participate in many different activities.

REVIEW

1. What are the major functions of the skeleton?

2. Describe the parts and basic structure of a bone.

3. What are the functions of cartilage and ligaments?

4. **MEASURE** What is the average height of someone your age? How could you find out?

5. **CRITICAL THINKING** *Synthesize* Choose one type of movable joint. Describe how you would make a model of it.

WHY IT MATTERS THINK ABOUT IT What did you learn about your skeletal system that can help you take better care of it?

WHY IT MATTERS WRITE ABOUT IT Make a list of things you plan to do to take better care of your skeletal system.

READING SKILL Look at the diagram on page 437. What supporting details help you understand what bones are like?

(Don't) Gimme A BREAK!

Color has been added to this X ray of a broken arm bone. Which type of fracture does the X ray show?

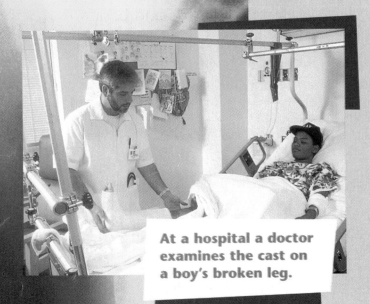

At a hospital a doctor examines the cast on a boy's broken leg.

A Closer Look

Have you ever broken a bone? A break in a bone is called a fracture.

Fractures are caused by sudden, powerful pressure against a bone. Falling can break a bone, sometimes in several places. Twisting an ankle or throwing a ball with too much force can also cause a fracture.

A broken bone is often very painful. To avoid doing more damage, don't move until emergency workers arrive. They'll wrap the bone to keep it from moving on the ride to the hospital. There X rays will show where the bone is broken and how bad the damage is.

It takes six to eight weeks for most broken bones to heal. A cast or splint can keep most broken bones from moving while they heal. However, some fractures require an operation. Screws or wires may be used to hold the pieces of bone together.

As a bone heals, new tissue fills in the cracks. Minerals in the tissue harden. Soon the bone is as good as new!

GREENSTICK

SIMPLE

COMPOUND

In a greenstick fracture, the bone cracks, but it doesn't break apart.

In a simple fracture, the bone breaks, but it doesn't tear through the skin.

In a compound fracture, the bone breaks and tears through the skin. This sometimes leads to an infection.

Discussion
Starter

1 Which type of fracture might require antibiotics? Why?

2 Why do fractures require X rays?

*inter*NET
CONNECTION To learn more about broken bones, visit
www.mhschool.com/science and enter the keyword **BREAK.**

443

WHY IT MATTERS

It is important to know about your muscles and how to take care of them.

SCIENCE WORDS

skeletal muscle a muscle that is attached to a bone and allows movement

tendon a strong band of tissue that connects a muscle to bone

cardiac muscle the type of muscle that makes up the heart

smooth muscle the type of muscle that makes up internal organs and blood vessels

involuntary muscle a muscle that causes movements you cannot control

voluntary muscle a muscle that causes movements you can control

Your Muscles

What allows your body to walk, sit, jump, smile, breathe, and move blood around? Muscle power! Muscles have many jobs in your body. The one you can observe easily is that they move your body.

In Topic 1 you learned that your skeletal system supports your body. However, bones cannot move on their own. That is the job of muscles.

EXPLORE

HYPOTHESIZE How do you think muscles work to move bones? Write a hypothesis in your *Science Journal*. How could you test your ideas?

Investigate How Muscles Move Bones

Use a model to test how muscles move bones.

PROCEDURES

⚠ **SAFETY** Use the scissors carefully!

1. **COLLECT DATA** Measure the lengths of a group member's upper and lower arm bones. Record the data in your *Science Journal*.

2. **MEASURE** Cut the cardboard pieces to the same lengths as the arm bones. Trace a hand on the paper. Cut it out.

3. **MAKE A MODEL** Assemble the model as shown.

4. **EXPERIMENT** Lay the model on a desk. Hold where indicated. Pull the top string gently in the direction shown. Then pull the bottom string. Record your observations.

CONCLUDE AND APPLY

1. **IDENTIFY** Which parts of your model represent bones? Muscles?

2. **COMMUNICATE** What happened to the "arm" when you pulled the top string? The bottom string?

3. **COMMUNICATE** What happened to the bottom string when you pulled on the top string? To the top string when you pulled on the bottom string?

GOING FURTHER: Apply

4. **EXPERIMENT** Build a model of the knee joint. How is it similar to the arm model? Different? What are its strengths and weaknesses?

MATERIALS

- 2 equal-length pieces of string
- tape
- cardboard
- scissors
- paper fastener
- ruler
- construction paper
- *Science Journal*

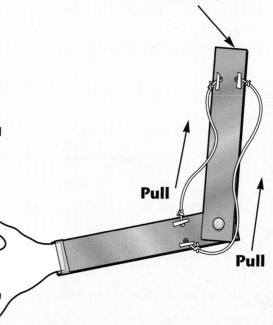

Hold here

Pull

Pull

How Do Muscles Move Bones?

The muscles that are attached to and move bones are called **skeletal muscles** (skel'i təl mus'əlz). As the model in the Explore Activity shows, skeletal muscles pull bones to move them. Muscles do not push bones. As you study this diagram, think about how the muscles in your upper arm work like the strings that pulled the cardboard bones.

1 A message from your brain causes this muscle, called the *biceps* (bī'seps), to contract. When a muscle contracts, it becomes shorter and thicker. As the biceps contracts, it pulls on the arm bone it is attached to.

1 Biceps

2 Triceps

2 Most muscles work in pairs to move bones. This muscle, called the *triceps* (trī'seps), relaxes when the biceps contracts. When a muscle relaxes, it becomes longer and thinner.

4

3

3 To straighten your arm, a message from your brain causes the triceps to contract. When the triceps contracts, it pulls on the bone it is attached to.

4 As the triceps contracts, the biceps relaxes. Your arm straightens.

A microscopic view of stained skeletal muscle cells

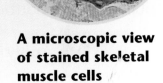

READING DIAGRAMS

1. **DISCUSS** What happens to a muscle to make it pull on a bone?
2. **WRITE** How do most muscles work together to move a bone? Write a description in your *Science Journal*.

How Do Muscles Contract and Relax?

To help you understand how a muscle contracts and relaxes, try this.

Think of your hands as a muscle. Hold your fingers as shown in the first picture. Then slide your fingers in between each other as shown in the second picture. As your hands move closer to each other, your interlocking fingers get thicker. This is a model of how a muscle contracts. Now move your hands back to where they started. This is a model of how a muscle relaxes.

How Muscles Are Attached to Bones

How were the "muscles" attached to the arm model in the Explore Activity? In real life a muscle is not attached to bones with tape! A muscle is attached to a bone by a tough cord of tissue called a **tendon** (ten′dən).

Hold up one hand, and look at the back of it. Now wiggle your fingers up and down. Do you see narrow bands running from your fingers to your arm? They are the tendons shown in the diagram. These tendons run from muscles in your arm to your fingers.

This is a model of a relaxed muscle.

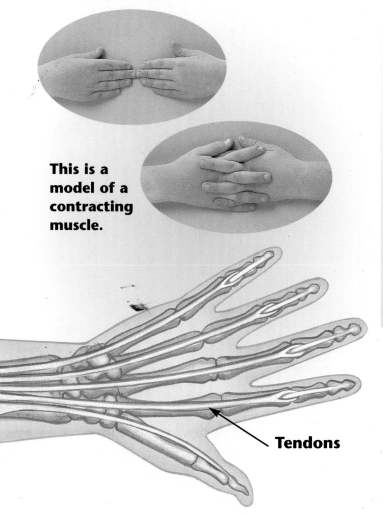

This is a model of a contracting muscle.

Tendons

NATIONAL GEOGRAPHIC

FUNtastic Facts

Humans are not the only animals that shiver when they are cold—birds do, too. When a bird senses that it's too cold, nerves stimulate muscles and make them rapidly contract and relax. The moving muscles create heat, which warms the bird's body. What are some other ways birds stay warm?

447

What Other Types of Muscles Make Up the Body?

Three types of muscles make up your body. You have learned about one type, skeletal muscle. Another type of muscle is called **cardiac muscle** (kär′dē ak′ mus′əl). Cardiac muscle is found in only one place in your body. Do you know where? Your heart.

The heart is a hollow organ made up of four parts, or chambers. The walls of the heart are made of strong cardiac muscle. When your cardiac muscle contracts, it squeezes blood out of your heart. The blood delivers oxygen and nutrients to your cells. It also picks up and carries away wastes your cells must get rid of. When your cardiac muscle relaxes, your heart fills with more blood.

Your cardiac muscle contracts in less than one second. It beats like this about 75 times a minute, or about 100,000 times every day. It will continue to beat without stopping for the rest of your life. As long as your cardiac muscle gets enough nutrients and oxygen, it will never tire.

THE HUMAN HEART

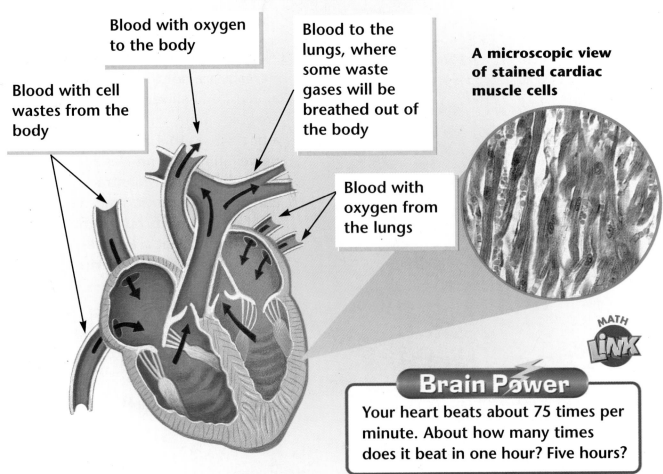

Blood with oxygen to the body

Blood to the lungs, where some waste gases will be breathed out of the body

A microscopic view of stained cardiac muscle cells

Blood with cell wastes from the body

Blood with oxygen from the lungs

MATH LINK

Brain Power
Your heart beats about 75 times per minute. About how many times does it beat in one hour? Five hours?

448

The third type of muscle is called **smooth muscle** (smüth mus'əl). Smooth muscles makes up internal organs and blood vessels. Smooth muscles are not attached to bones. Instead they help other body parts do their jobs.

For example, smooth muscles in your lungs help you breathe. Those in your blood vessels help control how your blood flows around your body. Smooth muscles in the colored parts of your eyes help let in just the right amount of light. There are also smooth muscles in your food tube, or esophagus (i sof'ə gəs), stomach, and intestines. By contracting they squeeze food along your digestive system.

Blood vessel

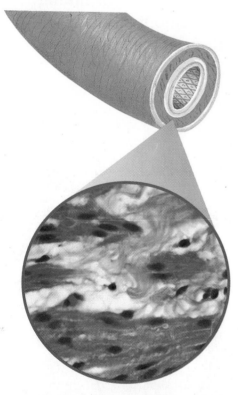

A microscopic view of stained smooth muscle cells

How Muscles Can Be Classified

Muscles can be classified by how they are controlled. Cardiac and smooth muscles are **involuntary muscles** (in vol'ən ter'ē mus'əlz). An involuntary muscle is a muscle that causes movements you cannot control by thinking about them. Imagine if you had to think about your heart beating. You wouldn't be able to do much else!

Most skeletal muscles are **voluntary muscles** (vol'ən ter'ē mus'əlz). A voluntary muscle is a muscle that causes movements you can control.

Can you think of any muscles that are both voluntary and involuntary? One example is a large, flat muscle under your lungs. As it moves down, your lungs fill with air. As it moves up, it pushes air out of your lungs. You don't have to think about moving it to breathe, but you can breathe fast or slow if you want to.

All of your muscles make up your *muscular system* (mus'kyə lər sis'təm). This table organizes the characteristics of the muscles in your muscular system.

CHARACTERISTICS OF MUSCLES

Muscle	Type	Appearance
Skeletal	voluntary	stripes
Smooth	mostly involuntary	no stripes
Cardiac	involuntary	stripes with cells that branch and spread

449

Using Muscles

HYPOTHESIZE Do you think you used more voluntary or involuntary muscles in the past half-hour? Why do you think so? Write a hypothesis in your *Science Journal.*

MATERIALS

• *Science Journal*

Muscles Used in the Last Half-Hour			
Muscles Used	**Activity**	**Voluntary Muscle**	**Involuntary Muscle**
Arm muscles	raising hand in class	✔	
Eyelids	blinking	✔	✔

PROCEDURES

1. Copy this chart into your *Science Journal.*

2. Think about all the ways you used muscles in the past half-hour. Record the information in the chart.

CONCLUDE AND APPLY

1. **INTERPRET DATA** How many different ways did you use your muscles?

2. **INTERPRET DATA** Did you use more voluntary or involuntary muscles? Did you use any muscles that are both voluntary and involuntary? What were they?

450

How Can You Take Care of Your Muscles?

• **Exercise.** As you use your muscles, they grow bigger and more powerful. This helps them work without tiring easily.

• **Eat the right foods.** Eat foods that are rich in proteins and full of vitamins and minerals. This will help your muscles grow and stay healthy.

• **Get plenty of rest.** Using a muscle too much can make it sore. Using a sore muscle may hurt or even tear it. Rest your muscles when they are tired.

• **Never take steroids unless your doctor tells you to.** Steroids are medicines used to help people with certain diseases. Taking steroids without a doctor's guidance is dangerous.

Eating these foods will help you keep your muscles healthy.

What types of things do you like to do? No matter what your favorite activities are, they all depend on strong, healthy skeletal muscles.

All physical activities depend on other muscles, too. Your body gets its energy from the foods you eat. However, you cannot digest food without your smooth muscles. You also need the oxygen and nutrients supplied by your blood. Blood cannot reach all parts of your body if you do not have a strong cardiac muscle. Exercise, eat right, and take care of your muscles and bones. You will be amazed at what you can do and how far you will go.

Keeping your skeletal system in good shape allows you to participate in many different activities.

REVIEW

1. How do muscles work to move bones?

2. What is an involuntary muscle? Give three examples.

3. What is a voluntary muscle? Give three examples.

4. **MAKE A MODEL** Describe another model you would build to show how muscles move bones. What materials would you use? What would each represent?

5. **CRITICAL THINKING** *Analyze* Which muscles relax and contract when you bend your leg? When you straighten your leg?

WHY IT MATTERS THINK ABOUT IT Your friend doesn't like to eat things like meat and cheese. What is important about these foods? What else could she eat?

WHY IT MATTERS WRITE ABOUT IT Write a short paragraph describing a plan that you developed to keep your muscles healthy.

Be a PT!

What's a PT? It's a physical therapist. That's someone who helps injured people improve their strength and coordination.

A PT sees many patients in a day. First, a PT may help an injured child learn to walk again. Next, the PT might help a football player exercise an injured knee. Then, the PT may help an elderly heart patient learn to strengthen that important muscle.

A PT often works on a team. The patient's doctor is part of the team, too. First, the PT learns what the patient can and can't do. Then, the team sets a treatment goal. For one patient, the goal might be to walk without a cane. For another, just lifting an arm is important.

The PT plans a patient's treatment. It may involve moving muscles to strengthen them. It might also include water therapy, heating pads, or ice. Sound waves or electric current may help. A cane, crutches, a walker, or a brace might help patients reach their goals.

To become a PT, you need a college degree in physical therapy. People with other degrees can earn a certificate, which may take

A Closer Look

two years more. Then if you pass a test, you get your physical therapist's license.

Many PTs work in hospitals. Others work in nursing homes, rehab centers, schools, and clinics. Some even visit patients at home.

People who want to be PTs should be outgoing and full of energy. They must also be patient and caring. Being a PT means helping people get better and feel better!

DISCUSSION STARTER

1. Why would a patient's doctor be on the treatment team?

2. Would you want to be a PT? Why or why not?

To learn more about physical therapy, visit **www.mhschool.com/science** and enter the keyword THERAPY.

*inter***NET**
CONNECTION

SCIENCE WORDS

cardiac
  muscle p. 448
cartilage p. 439
fracture p. 439
involuntary
  muscle p. 449
joint p. 438
ligament p. 439
marrow p. 437

skeletal
  muscle p. 446
skeleton p. 436
smooth
  muscle p. 449
sprain p. 439
tendon p. 447
voluntary
  muscle p. 449

USING SCIENCE WORDS

Number a paper from 1 to 10. Fill in 1 to 5 with words from the list above.

1. A tough band of tissue that holds two bones together where they meet is a(n) __?__.

2. The supporting frame that gives the body its shape and protects many organs is called the __?__.

3. A muscle that is attached to a bone and allows movement is a(n) __?__.

4. A strong band of tissue that connects a muscle to bone is a(n) __?__.

5. A smooth muscle is classified as a(n) __?__.

6–10. **Pick five words from the list above that were not used in 1 to 5, and use each in a sentence.**

UNDERSTANDING SCIENCE IDEAS

11. What are some things you can do to keep your skeletal system healthy?

12. What are some things you can do to keep your muscular system healthy?

USING IDEAS AND SKILLS

13. **READING SKILL: SUPPORTING DETAILS** Look at the diagram on page 446. What supporting details explain how muscles move bones? Use those details to draw another diagram that shows the same information.

14. **MEASURE** Which leg bone is longer, your thighbone or your shinbone? Measure to find out. What is the combined length of the bones making up your leg?

15. **THINKING LIKE A SCIENTIST** Name two different joints in your body. Identify each type of joint. How is each the right type of joint for the way it is used?

PROBLEMS and PUZZLES

Heartbeat The cardiac muscle works without your conscious control. How can you affect how quickly your heart beats? How do you know?

CHAPTER 14
ALCOHOL, TOBACCO, AND DRUGS

Good times with your friends can be a big part of your life. After school clubs, doing projects together—these things can build friendships that last a lifetime.

To be sure that the good times are healthy ones, think about the sign you see here. The circle with a slash means "Don't." "Don't smoke" for example. Smoking can cut a lifetime short. Read about why it is important to keep clear of alcohol, tobacco, and drugs.

In Chapter 14 you will practice summarizing as you read. Use your own words to restate what a page is about.

WHY IT MATTERS

It is important to understand the effects of alcohol and tobacco on the body.

SCIENCE WORDS

drug a substance other than food that changes the way a person feels, thinks, and acts

depressant a drug that slows down the activity of the body

nicotine a poisonous, oily substance found in tobacco

tar a sticky, brown substance found in tobacco

carbon monoxide a poisonous gas given off by burning tobacco

stimulant a substance that speeds up the activity of the body

passive smoke smoke that is inhaled by someone other than the smoker

Alcohol and Tobacco

Do you think a warning on a container of alcohol or a cigarette package would convince most people not to drink or smoke? Why or why not? What might convince some people not to try cigarettes or alcohol?

EXPLORE

HYPOTHESIZE How might advertisements convince someone to start using alcohol or tobacco? Write a hypothesis in your *Science Journal*. How could you test your ideas?

GOVERNMENT WARNING According To The Surgeon General, (1) Women Should Not Drink Alcoholic Beverages During Pregnancy Because Of Risk Of Birth Defects, (2) Consumption Of Alcoholic Beverages Impairs Your Ability To Drive A Car Or Operate Machinery, And May Cause Health Problems.

SURGEON GENERAL'S WARNING Smoking Causes Lung Cancer, Heart Disease, Emphysema, And May Complicate Pregnancy.

Investigate Why People Might Use Alcohol and Tobacco

Examine how ads for alcohol and tobacco try to convince people to use the products.

MATERIALS

- magazine and newspaper ads for alcohol and tobacco products
- paper
- *Science Journal*

PROCEDURES

1. CLASSIFY Sort the ads into two groups—alcohol and tobacco.

2. COLLECT DATA On separate sheets of paper, write down any television ads for beer you can remember. Also write down any alcohol and tobacco ads you remember from billboards. Add the notes to the groups.

3. OBSERVE What are people in the ads doing? How old are they? What race and gender are they? What other things do you notice? Record your observations in your *Science Journal*.

CONCLUDE AND APPLY

1. DRAW CONCLUSIONS What ad features might convince people to use the products?

2. MAKE DECISIONS Choose two ads that best represent your findings.

3. COMMUNICATE Share your group's observations with your class. Use the two ads to illustrate your findings.

4. COMMUNICATE Make a class list of ways the ads try to convince people to use the products.

GOING FURTHER: Apply

5. ASK QUESTIONS What questions do you have about how alcohol and tobacco affect the body that are not answered by the ads? Make a list. Look for answers as you continue this topic.

Why Might People Use Alcohol and Tobacco?

Ads like those in the Explore Activity can often encourage people to try alcohol and tobacco products. They usually use several approaches.

- They show people having fun.
- They show people being part of the crowd.
- The people in the ads are pretty, handsome, and healthy looking.
- They use status symbols like cars and jewelry. People might think that they will look and be successful if they use the product.
- They use a popular and well-known character to promote their products.

How Alcohol Affects the Body

What don't alcohol and tobacco ads tell you? They don't tell you about the effects alcohol and tobacco have on the body.

Alcohol (al'kə hôl') is found in beer, wine, and liquor. It is even in certain medications, like cough syrup. Alcohol is a **drug** (drug). A drug is a substance other than food that changes the way a person feels, thinks, and acts.

Alcohol can affect different people in different ways. The effect of alcohol on a 36-kilogram (80-pound) person will be much greater than the effect on a 64-kilogram (140-pound) person. The alcohol reaches the body's organ systems very quickly.

Ads for alcohol and tobacco products don't tell you how the products can affect the body. In what ways could this ad encourage people to try alcohol and tobacco products?

Alcohol passes through the walls of the stomach and small intestine and into blood vessels. Blood vessels carry the alcohol and blood through the body.

One part of the body affected by alcohol is the liver. One of its jobs is to break down alcohol. If a person drinks a lot of alcohol in a short time, the liver can't keep up. The person may pass out or even die from alcohol poisoning.

Alcohol may also slow down messages to and from the brain. That is because alcohol is a **depressant** (di pres'ənt). A depressant is a drug that slows down the activity of the body.

Alcohol can cause unclear speech and dizziness. It can cause loss of memory, muscle control, and balance. It can also slow down reaction time and the senses. That is why it is so dangerous to drink and drive.

Drinking a lot of alcohol over a long time has many harmful effects on the body. It can damage the heart and nerves, and it can even cause certain types of cancer. It also makes the liver work hard. This can cause liver disease. Liver disease can kill people who drink a lot of alcohol often.

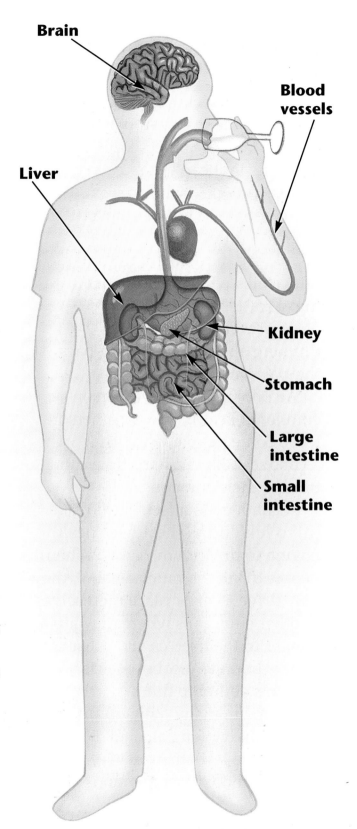

Alcohol moves into the bloodstream quickly through the digestive system. It travels through the body and can affect almost every part.

What Other Effects Does Alcohol Have?

Alcohol affects your social health, or the way you behave toward others. Some people who drink alcohol can become very loud or very quiet. Alcohol can cause some people to not be respectful to others. Studies show that some people are more likely to commit crimes when they are drinking. That is because alcohol often prevents people from thinking about and holding back their actions.

Alcohol also affects a person's emotional health, or how a person feels. Some people who drink alcohol can have a hard time controlling their emotions.

Alcohol even affects *intellectual* (in'tə lek'chü əl) health, or health having to do with thoughts. When people drink too much alcohol, they may drive a car or place themselves in other situations where they are a danger to themselves and others. That is because alcohol affects a person's ability to think clearly.

There are many dangers associated with drinking alcohol. Most states have laws that prevent the sale of alcohol to people under a certain age. Some communities don't allow the sale of alcoholic beverages at all.

Many people who are old enough to drink use alcohol safely. However, some people can begin drinking too

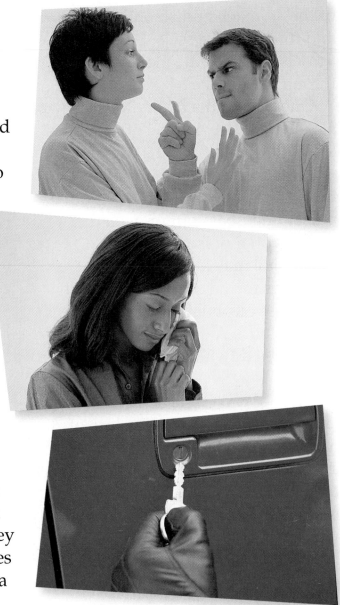

Alcohol affects your social, emotional, and intellectual health.

much or too often. Some people can start to feel a strong need for alcohol. They become dependent on it because alcohol is *addictive* (ə dik'tiv). It is very hard for them to stop drinking. People with drinking problems can get help from support organizations and their doctors to stop.

460

Why Use Tobacco?

Almost everyone has heard something about the harmful effects of tobacco on health. Still many people begin using tobacco every year. Some smoke. Others use smokeless tobacco, called chewing tobacco or snuff.

Most new smokers are not adults. They are young people. Why do young people start using tobacco? Why do you think adults continue to use tobacco?

The table below gives you some answers. The physical act of chewing or smoking tobacco becomes part of a person's behavior and actions. It becomes a habit. Tobacco also becomes addictive, and people can't stop using it.

To understand why it is hard to quit using tobacco, you need to understand what is in tobacco. You also need to know how these substances affect the body.

Just say no!

WHY USE TOBACCO?	
Young people say...	Adults say...
My friends do it.	I like it and the way it tastes.
It makes me look grown-up.	It is relaxing.
It makes me look more important than others.	It is a habit.
It makes me look "cool."	I can't stop.

READING ∕∨∖ TABLES

1. **DISCUSS** For each point in the table, think of a reason people shouldn't use tobacco.
2. **REPRESENT** Design another table or chart to show your responses.

What Is in Tobacco?

The tobacco found in cigarettes, cigars, pipe tobacco, and smokeless tobacco is made from the dried leaves of the tobacco plant. Several thousand chemical substances are found in tobacco. Among them is the harmful drug **nicotine** (nik′ə tēn′). Nicotine is a poisonnous, oily substance. **Tar** (tär) is a sticky, brown substance. The yellow-brown substance left in a used cigarette filter is tar.

When tobacco burns it produces the poisonous gas called **carbon monoxide** (kär′bən mon ok′sīd). A motor vehicle also gives off carbon monoxide in its exhaust.

How Tobacco Affects the Body

Nicotine is a **stimulant** (stim′yə lənt). It speeds up the activity of the body. It makes the heart beat faster. It affects the way the brain sends and receives messages. Nicotine also raises blood pressure and the amount of fat in the blood.

Tar damages the lungs. It also deadens taste buds, stains teeth, and causes bad breath.

With time smoking increases the risk of disease. Many smokers die of heart attacks. Many also die of lung cancer, which quickly destroys the lungs. Smoking also causes other lung diseases that make breathing very difficult.

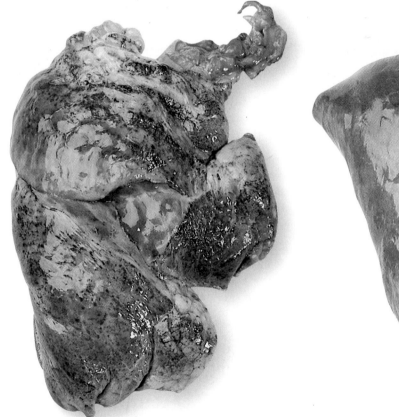

The lungs of a smoker are blackened and diseased.
The lungs of a nonsmoker are healthy and pink.

462

Carbon monoxide takes the place of some of the oxygen taken in by the lungs. Less oxygen is available for the body. The smoker feels out of breath.

Even people who don't smoke are at risk for problems from cigarette smoke. **Passive smoke** (pas'iv smōk), or secondhand smoke, is smoke that is inhaled by someone other than the smoker. People who inhale passive smoke suffer from many of the same symptoms as smokers. With time it can also cause serious health problems. That is why many states have laws that limit areas where people can smoke or don't allow smoking in public places at all. Do you agree with these laws? Why or why not?

A mother who does not smoke protects her baby from health problems caused by tobacco.

Why Is It Hard to Stop Using Tobacco?

Did you know that seven out of every ten adult smokers have tried to quit at least once? Many of them began using tobacco when they were young. They now wish they had not.

Why does it often take many tries to quit? Quitting using tobacco is difficult. People trying to quit may have trouble sleeping. They may feel dizzy, sad, and nervous. The body has these reactions when it no longer is getting nicotine. That is because nicotine is addictive, just like alcohol.

People trying to quit can find help. Support groups and doctors can help. So can family members. It may take several tries to quit for good, but it is worth the effort. After a person stops using tobacco, the risk of tobacco-related illnesses decreases.

$2.75 PER PACK

MATH LINK

Brain Power

What if someone smokes one pack of cigarettes a day? How much does he or she spend in one week? One month? One year? What would you do with that much money instead of buying cigarettes?

MATH LINK

Skill: Interpreting Data

COMPARE SMOKING NOW AND IN THE PAST

Do you think fewer people smoke now than in the past? To answer this question, you will interpret data. When you interpret data, you use information from a picture, a table, or a graph. Interpret the data in the graph to answer the question.

MATERIALS

- *Science Journal*

PROCEDURES

1. **CLASSIFY** What type of graph is used to show the data?

2. **COLLECT DATA** In the year 1979, about how many men out of every 100 smoked? In 1985? In 1995? Record the data in your *Science Journal.*

3. **USE NUMBERS** In the year 1979, about how many women out of every 100 smoked? In 1985? In 1995? Record the data in your *Science Journal.*

CONCLUDE AND APPLY

1. **COMPARE AND CONTRAST** Did more or fewer men smoke in 1995 than in 1979? Did more or fewer women smoke in 1995 than in 1979?

2. **COMPARE AND CONTRAST** About how many more men out of every 100 smoked in 1979 than in 1991? Than in 1995?

3. **IDENTIFY** What pattern do you see in the number of men and women who smoked from 1979 to 1995?

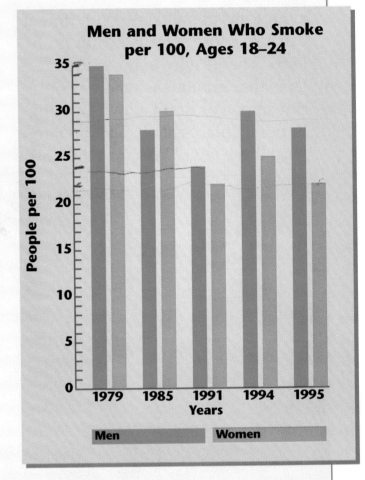

Men and Women Who Smoke per 100, Ages 18–24

People per 100

Years

Men   Women

Knowing how alcohol and tobacco affect the body should give you a very clear answer to any tempting advertisement. DON'T DRINK OR SMOKE.

Many people think, "Just one drink, cigarette, or use of chewing tobacco won't hurt me in any noticeable way." They're right. JUST ONE probably won't. However, that "just one" almost always leads to another and another. Each time people use alcohol or tobacco, they do a little bit more damage to their body. They can also become addicted. With time this adds up to big problems. Who needs problems? JUST DON'T START!

REVIEW

1. What types of messages do ads use to tempt people to use alcohol and tobacco?

2. What effects does alcohol have on a person who has a few drinks? Who drinks for many years?

3. What effects does tobacco have on a smoker? On a nonsmoker who is exposed to smoke?

4. **INTERPRET DATA** Look at the graph on page 464. Did more men or more women smoke in 1995?

5. **CRITICAL THINKING** *Synthesize* What would you do or say to convince someone to quit smoking?

WHY IT MATTERS THINK ABOUT IT How would you design a no-smoking and no-drinking campaign at your school?

WHY IT MATTERS WRITE ABOUT IT Use what you have learned about the effects of alcohol and tobacco to create another type of ad. This ad should convince people not to use alcohol and tobacco products.

Analyzing Ads

Why do some kids smoke or drink? Many people think it's because ads make smoking and drinking look "cool."

All ads are carefully designed to sell something. They try to convince you that their product will make you more grown-up. More fun to be around. Part of the "in-crowd." Slim and attractive.

"Living the good life!" an ad may say. People in the ad are drinking alcohol, a drug. You know that using drugs isn't part of a "good life." Drugs can kill!

"Low, low tar!" a cigarette ad may brag. It doesn't mention that cigarettes have nicotine, a drug.

Don't be fooled by slick ads. Analyze the words that ad makers use. Look for words that tempt your senses—how something tastes, smells, feels to the touch, looks, or sounds. Look for words that praise you, such as "You know a good thing when you see it. So buy one today!"

Look through magazine ads. Discuss with your classmates the words or images in each ad that might make people buy the product.

Choosing NOT to use alcohol or cigarettes is "cool." You don't need ads to convince you of that, do you?

This **NO SMOKING** symbol needs no words to pass on its message.

GET A LIFE   GET A CELL PHONE

STOP WATCHING LIFE
AND START LIVING IT!
BLAHMO BRAND CELL
PHONES FIT THE WAY
YOU WANT TO LIVE!

FOR A STORE LOCATION NEAR YOU,
LOG ON TO WWW.BLAHMO.COM,
FOR OUR COMPLETE LINE
OF TRENDY CELLULAR PHONES

BLAHMO
WORKS GOOD

If you DIDN'T get your Backpack at Coolmart...

You're a LOSER!

Almost too
cool for
YOU!

Look us up on the web www.coolmart.com for the store nearest you!

COOLMART
Where the cool kids shop

DISCUSSION STARTER

1. Why do you think beer and cigarette ads show healthy, active people having fun?

2. What special words do ads have to convince you to buy a product?

To learn more about ads, visit *www.mhschool.com/science* and enter the keyword ADS.

*inter*NET
CONNECTION

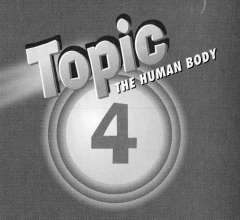
WHY IT MATTERS

It is important to understand the effects of drugs on the body.

SCIENCE WORDS

side effect an unwanted result of using a medicine

dependence a strong need or desire for a medicine or drug

cocaine an illegal stimulant made from the leaves of the coca plant

marijuana a mind-altering drug made from the leaves, flowers, and seeds of the cannabis plant

misuse to use a legal drug improperly or in an unsafe way

abuse to use legal drugs in an unsafe way on purpose or to use illegal drugs

Medicines and Other Drugs

Why might a doctor or nurse give someone medicine? What are medicines used for? They can be used to help things like a headache, cough, fever, or itchy insect bite. All medicines are not the same. That is why it is important to take only a medicine given by a doctor, nurse, or trusted adult.

EXPLORE

HYPOTHESIZE How do you think medicines are similar and different? Write a hypothesis in your *Science Journal.* How could you test your ideas?

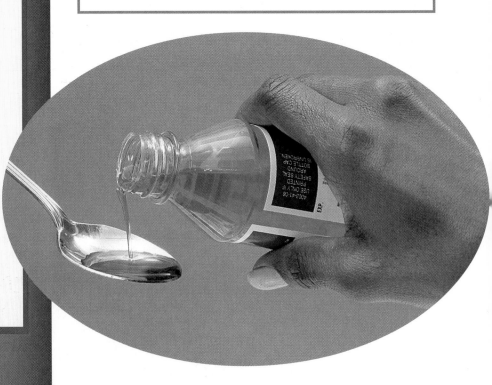

EXPLORE ACTIVITY

Investigate How Medicines Are Similar and Different

Examine medicine labels to determine a difference in how medicines can be obtained.

MATERIALS

- 4 empty medicine bottles with labels
- *Science Journal*

PROCEDURES

1. OBSERVE Carefully observe the bottles and labels. How are they similar? Different? Record your observations in your *Science Journal.*

2. OBSERVE What types of information can be found on the labels? Make a list in your *Science Journal.*

3. COMPARE How are the labels different? What seems to be the major difference?

4. CLASSIFY Use this difference to classify the bottles into two groups.

CONCLUDE AND APPLY

1. DRAW CONCLUSIONS How are the two groups similar? How are they different?

2. COMPARE AND CONTRAST Compare your observations with other groups. On what do you agree? Disagree?

3. COMMUNICATE Make a class list of information you collected from the labels in each group.

GOING FURTHER: Apply

4. INFER Why do you think it is important to carefully read all medicine labels?

WILSON'S
PHARMACY #121

Rx# 17720612

John Davis   11/10/98

Take one teaspoon twice
a day for cough.

Codex 3%   42GN ALEB

Dr. Harold Smith

NO REFILLS

Discard after 12/15/98

Cough No More

Do you think you might like to be a pharmacist? If so, you need to like science. A pharmacist must know all about chemistry and the human body.

How Are Medicines Similar and Different?

A medicine is a drug used to treat, cure, or prevent disease or injury. As the Explore Activity shows, medicines can be classified into two groups based on how they are obtained.

One group contains *over-the-counter* medicines. These medicines can be purchased off the shelves in stores. They may be used to treat certain illnesses or problems. Some examples include pain relievers, cough medicines, and lotions for insect bites.

The label on an over-the-counter medicine tells how much medicine should be taken and how often. Many labels also warn people with certain medical or health conditions that they may not be able to use the medicine. Labels also provide dates after which the medicine should not be used. This is an *expiration date* (ek'spə rā'shən dāt).

The other group contains medicines that can only be purchased with an order from a doctor. This order is called a *prescription* (pri skrip'shən). When a doctor orders a prescription, she makes the best choice for a medicine to help you.

A prescription medicine can only be purchased in a drugstore or from a pharmacy. A *pharmacist* (fär'mə sist) prepares the medication for you. A pharmacist is trained and licensed to prepare and give out medicines according to a doctor's orders. A prescription medicine's label tells many things, such as the patient's and doctor's names, and how much medicine to take.

How Can Medicines Be Used Safely?

No matter what type of medicine a person uses, it is important to use it safely. To do so everyone must understand the risks and follow some basic rules.

One risk is that almost all medicines have some sort of **side effect** (sīd i fekt'). A side effect is an unwanted result of using a medicine. For example, some cold and allergy medicines can make the user feel sleepy or dizzy. Some medicines may cause a headache or raise blood pressure.

Another risk is *allergy* (al'ər jē). An allergy is a sensitivity to a substance. Some allergies result in a rash or fever. A more serious allergy reaction is having trouble breathing. If you ever feel "funny" or different after taking a medication, tell an adult at once.

A third risk is **dependence** (di pen'dəns). Dependence is a strong need or desire for a medicine or drug. This can happen if people take certain medicines for a long time. They may feel that they can't do without it. They may need a doctor's help to stop using the medicine without feeling anxious or sick.

HOW TO USE MEDICINE SAFELY

ALWAYS . . .	NEVER . . .
use medicine only from an adult you trust to help you.	EVER take medicine without a trusted adult present.
follow directions from your doctor and on the label carefully.	EVER use medicine without reading the label. Don't take two medicines at the same time unless told to do so by a doctor or adult.
use a medicine that is only for you.	EVER use someone else's medicine.
use only the recommended amount.	EVER use more or less than the amount recommended.
tell an adult if you think you might have a side effect, have an allergy, or feel dependent.	EVER think feelings of side effects, allergy, or dependence will go away by themselves.
store all medicines away from small children.	EVER leave medicines outside of a locked cabinet.
check the expiration date.	EVER think the expiration date is not important. An old medicine can make you sick.
make sure the safety seal on a new package is not broken.	EVER take a medicine if the safety seal on a new package is broken.

How Are Drugs Classified?

Drugs can be classified into two groups. One group contains legal drugs. It is legal for adults to use them, but not children. Alcohol and nicotine are legal drugs. Over-the-counter and prescription medicines are also legal drugs. The other group contains illegal drugs. That means that it is against the law for anyone to sell, buy, and use them.

Both legal and illegal drugs can be classified further. They are classified based on how they affect the body. For example, you learned in Topic 3 that nicotine is a stimulant. Alcohol is a depressant. A third class of drugs contains mind-altering drugs, which affect how a person thinks and sees things.

How Some Other Legal Drugs Affect the Body

Caffeine (ka fēn′) is a stimulant found in tea, coffee, and many soft drinks. In large amounts it can cause a person to have trouble sleeping and to feel anxious and restless. It also raises blood pressure, heart rate, and breathing rate. Caffeine can cause dependence.

Sleeping pills are medicines that help a person relax. Some can be purchased over the counter. Some are prescribed by doctors. *Tranquilizers* (trang′kwə lī′zərz) are sometimes prescribed by doctors to treat nervousness. Sleeping pills and tranquilizers are depressants. They slow messages in the nervous system. They cause drowsiness and lower blood pressure. They also slow heartbeat and breathing rates. Both can cause dependence.

HOW SOME LEGAL AND ILLEGAL DRUGS ARE CLASSIFIED

	Legal	Illegal
Stimulants	nicotine caffeine	cocaine crack
Depressants	alcohol sleeping pills tranquilizers	heroin
Mind-altering		LSD marijuana

READING N TABLES

1. **WRITE** Make two lists—one for legal drugs and one for illegal drugs. After reading page 473, write a brief description of how each drug affects the body.
2. **REPRESENT** Design another table or chart to show this information.

How Some Illegal Drugs Affect the Body

Cocaine (kō kān') is an illegal stimulant made from the leaves of the coca plant. It is usually available as a powder, which is breathed in through the nose.

Crack (krak) is a very harmful form of cocaine. It is made into pellets, which are smoked. Heavy users of cocaine and crack become nervous, suspicious, and depressed. Heavy use also causes heart failure, seizures, brain damage, and even death. Cocaine and crack cause dependence very quickly.

Narcotics (när kot'iks) are a type of painkiller. One illegal narcotic is heroin (her'ō in). Heroin damages the heart, brain, and nerves. Since heroin is injected, users also risk getting AIDS if they share needles. Heroin causes dependence.

LSD is a mind-altering drug. It causes users to see things that are not there. It also changes how things look, smell, taste, and sound. Users suffer memory loss and are confused about time, place, and people.

Marijuana comes from the leaves, seeds, and flowers of the cannabis (kan'ə bis) plant. The dried and crushed parts are smoked as cigarettes or in pipes.

Marijuana (mar'ə wä'nə) is also a mind-altering drug. Some effects of smoking marijuana are increased heart rate, trouble remembering, nervousness, and being unable to concentrate or react quickly. Long-term effects include damage to brain cells, loss of interest in doing things, and lung damage.

Brain Power

Write a short paragraph that explains the following statement. "All medicines are drugs. Not all drugs are medicines."

473

QUICK LAB

ART
LiNK

Help Use Drugs Safely

HYPOTHESIZE People can easily misuse a drug. Maybe they did not understand the directions. Maybe they did not read the label at all. What could you do to a drug label to help people not misuse the product? Write a hypothesis in your *Science Journal.*

MATERIALS

- paper
- coloring pens or pencils
- *Science Journal*

PROCEDURES

1. PREDICT Make a list of things you think might improve a drug's label to help avoid misuse. Record it in your *Science Journal.*

2. MAKE A MODEL Create a drug label showing your ideas.

3. COLLECT DATA Present your model to other groups. Do they think your ideas might help? Record the responses.

CONCLUDE AND APPLY

1. DRAW CONCLUSIONS Make a class list of the label ideas. Which ideas seem to be most effective? Why?

2. COMPARE How do these ideas compare with your hypothesis?

When Can Medicine Hurt You?

Taking more or less of a medicine than you should and taking someone else's medicine can hurt you. To do anything like this is to **misuse** (mis ūz′) a drug. This means using a legal drug improperly or in an unsafe way. People can misuse a drug on purpose or by not reading the label.

People can also **abuse** (ə būz′) drugs. To abuse drugs is to use legal drugs in an unsafe way on purpose or to use illegal drugs.

Misused drugs can be poisonous or make you very sick. Abusing drugs can cause a person to become addicted to them. It is very hard for addicted people to stop using drugs. They usually need help from a doctor or treatment center.

People trying to end a drug addiction often get help from a drug treatment center like this one.

Some people use drugs to help them get well. Understanding the effects legal drugs have and how to use them safely can help keep people healthy.

Some people abuse legal drugs. Others use illegal drugs. Often they are trying to solve problems or feel better about themselves. Understanding the effects that drug abuse has on the body can help you see that this is not the way to solve problems. It helps you make the only right choice—don't abuse drugs. Why? It will keep you healthy and—most importantly—ALIVE.

DID YOU KNOW?

Before the 1940s people could become very sick and even die of infections caused by bacteria. During the 1940s medicines called *antibiotics* (an'tē bī ot'iks) were developed. Antibiotics kill bacteria or stop them from growing. *Penicillin* (pen'ə sil'in) is a type of antibiotic. It was developed from a mold found growing on an orange. How would our lives be different if antibiotics were never discovered?

REVIEW

1. What is the difference between over-the-counter and prescription medicines?

2. How can people use medicines safely?

3. How do caffeine and sleeping pills affect the body?

4. **COMMUNICATE** Name two illegal drugs. What effects do they have on the body?

5. **CRITICAL THINKING** *Analyze* What if someone takes a cold remedy while taking another prescription medicine without telling her doctor? Explain if this is drug misuse or abuse.

WHY IT MATTERS THINK ABOUT IT
What would you say to someone trying to sell or give you an illegal drug?

WHY IT MATTERS WRITE ABOUT IT
How could you help someone be prepared to turn down illegal drugs? Make a list of responses that you would share with a younger brother or sister.

READING SKILL Summarize the important facts about why it is important not to use illegal drugs.

Making a Difference

Helping Kids Say NO!

How can kids on drugs be helped? A court in Lancaster, Ohio, uses a new program.

When teens come to court on drug charges, the judge sentences them to a one-year program. For the first month, they're tested every week for drug use. They get counseling three times a week. They meet with the judge, their counselor, and their probation officer once a week.

Drug counselor Don Rawlins directs the Lancaster program. He says the kids need a month of "clean time." Without it, kids in trouble often continue doing drugs and end up right back in court.

After the first month, there are less counseling sessions and meetings. The parents get involved in helping their kids. Everyone hopes this new court will help teens stay out of trouble . . . and out of court!

DISCUSSION STARTER

1. Why do they call it "clean time"?
2. What do you think the kids talk about at counseling sessions?

To learn more about saying "No" to drugs, visit **www.mhschool.com/science** and enter the keyword NO.

*inter*NET CONNECTION

SCIENCE WORDS

abuse p. 474

carbon monoxide p. 462

cocaine p. 473

dependence p. 471

depressant p. 459

drug p. 458

marijuana p. 473

misuse p. 474

nicotine p. 462

passive smoke p. 463

side effect p. 471

stimulant p. 462

tar p. 462

USING SCIENCE WORDS

Number a paper from 1 to 10. Fill in 1 to 5 with words from the list above.

1. The addictive substance in tobacco is ___?___.

2. A strong need or desire for a medicine or drug is known as ___?___.

3. Alcohol is a drug that slows down the activity of the body. It is a(n) ___?___.

4. To use an illegal drug or to use a legal drug in an unsafe way is to ___?___ a drug.

5. Nicotine is a drug that speeds up the activity of the body. It is a(n) ___?___.

6–10. Pick five words from the list above that were not used in 1 to 5, and use each in a sentence.

UNDERSTANDING SCIENCE IDEAS

11. How can people who do not smoke suffer the effects of cigarette smoke?

12. How can alcohol affect your social, emotional, and intellectual health?

USING IDEAS AND SKILLS

13. **READING SKILL: SUMMARIZE** List the important facts about how alcohol affects the body. Write a short paragraph using your own words to restate the facts.

14. **INTERPRET DATA** How many more students per 100 used cocaine in 1979 than in 1990? Than in 1995?

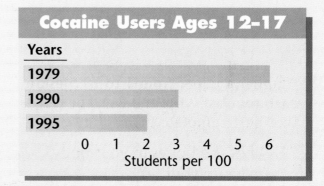

Cocaine Users Ages 12–17

Years	Students per 100
1979	(bar to ~5.5)
1990	(bar to ~3.5)
1995	(bar to ~2.5)

0 1 2 3 4 5 6
Students per 100

15. **THINKING LIKE A SCIENTIST** Your older sister has a headache. She took a pain reliever two hours ago. Now she wants to take some more. What would you tell her?

PROBLEMS and PUZZLES

Brain Drain Can breathing the fumes of household chemicals cause damage to the brain? Work with an adult. Examine the labels of some everyday household products for warnings. Make a list of the products. Include a brief description of how each product should be used safely.

WARNING
Hazardous to humans & animals

SCIENCE WORDS

carbon
  monoxide p. 462
cardiac
  muscle p. 448
cocaine p. 473
dependence p. 471
drug p. 458
fracture p. 439
ligament p. 439

marrow p. 437
nicotine p. 462
skeletal
  muscle p. 446
skeleton p. 436
stimulant p. 462
tendon p. 447
voluntary
  muscle p. 449

USING SCIENCE WORDS

Number a paper from 1 to 10. Beside each number write the word or words that best complete the sentence.

1. All of the bones in your body make up your __?__ .

2. The bands of tissue that hold bones together are called __?__ .

3. The bands of tissue that connect muscles to bones are called __?__ .

4. A muscle that you can control to cause movement is a(n) __?__ .

5. The muscles of your heart are called __?__ .

6. A substance that changes the way you think or feel is a(n) __?__ .

7. An addictive substance in tobacco is __?__ .

8. A drug that speeds up the activity of the body is a(n) __?__ .

9. A strong need or desire for a drug is called __?__ .

10. An illegal drug called __?__ is sometimes found in the form of crack.

UNDERSTANDING SCIENCE IDEAS

Write 11 to 15. For each number write the letter for the best answer. You may wish to use the hints provided.

11. Hips are examples of movable joints called
    a. pivot joints
    b. hinge joints
    c. gliding joints
    d. ball-and-socket joints
    (Hint: Read page 438.)

12. Which type of muscles are attached to bones?
    a. cardiac muscles
    b. skeletal muscles
    c. smooth muscles
    d. involuntary muscles
    (Hint: Read page 446.)

13. People who have been drinking alcohol should not drive because
    a. they get headaches
    b. they react too slowly
    c. alcohol damages the liver
    d. alcohol is addictive
    (Hint: Read page 459.)

14. Which of these is a prescription medicine?
    a. tranquilizer
    b. aspirin
    c. mouthwash
    d. insect bite lotion
    (Hint: Read page 472.)

15. Cocaine abuse may cause
 a. heart failure
 b. depression
 c. death
 d. all of these
 (Hint: Read page 473.)

USING IDEAS AND SKILLS

16. Tell what red bone marrow is and what it does.

17.  **MEASURE** Which is greater, the distance around your head just above your eyebrows or the length of your arm from your shoulder to your wrist? Describe how you would find out.

18. Which foods will help your muscles grow and stay healthy?

THINKING LIKE A SCIENTIST

19. **INTERPRET DATA** Refer to the graph on page 464. Did more young men or women smoke in 1994? 1995? What can you say about the data?

20. Even medicines can be bad for you if you misuse them. What have you learned that will help you not misuse medicine?

interNET CONNECTION

For help in reviewing this unit, visit
www.mhschool.com/science

WRITING IN YOUR JOURNAL

SCIENCE IN YOUR LIFE
List two over-the-counter medicines and two prescription medicines. Describe what each is supposed to do. How can you tell what a medicine is for? Who can help you find out?

PRODUCT ADS
Why do you think that advertisements for cigarettes and alcohol sometimes use cartoon characters? What is your opinion of such advertisements? Why do you feel this way?

HOW SCIENTISTS WORK
Scientists gather pieces of information such as survey counts and measurements, and organize the results into tables and graphs. How do tables and graphs help scientists?

Design your own Experiment

Form a hypothesis about whether thick or thin bones are stronger. Design an experiment that tests your hypothesis by using models. Think safety first. Review your experiment with your teacher before you do it.

PROBLEMS and PUZZLES

Shorter or Taller?

One hundred years ago, the average nine-year-old was 15 centimeters shorter than a nine-year-old today. Write a hypothesis to explain this. Do you think people will be smaller, bigger, or the same size in the future?

A Poster Puzzle

How could you write an advertisement to convince people not to drink or not to smoke? As a group discuss how you can explain the harms of drinking and smoking. Your group will write and design a poster to explain how alcohol and tobacco affect the body's health, as well as mental and emotional health. Your poster may target alcohol, tobacco, or both. Remember that advertisements work because they are able to attract people's attention and convince them to use a product. What can you say or show to convince people to refuse alcohol and tobacco?

Robot Design

THE PROBLEM

The owners of the Handy Dandy Robot Company need a new robot. All the designs that have been submitted so far have not been good. They have hired you to design their new, best-selling robot.

THE PLAN

Design a robot that will do a task. Explain what it does and its parts. What types of joints will it need? Write a hypothesis that outlines the types of joints your robot will need.

TEST YOUR HYPOTHESIS

Explain how you would test your hypothesis. How would you expect each joint to work? How would you change your design if it didn't work?

ANALYZE THE RESULTS

How would you judge whether or not you have chosen the right joints for your robot to complete its task?

Write a report in your *Science Journal*. Describe in detail your plan for designing the robot. Tell how you would test your ideas.

REFERENCE SECTION

DIAGRAM BUILDERS

Building a Frog

All animals carry out the same kinds of life activities. For example, they take in and digest food. **What are the organ systems that carry out these activities like?**

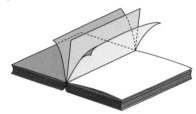

BASE

Explore three systems of a frog. Look at the diagram on the facing page. Lift up all the plastic overlays (1, 2, 3), and look at the page beneath them, the base. You see an outline of a frog.

How would you describe the shape of a frog? How do you think its systems "fit" into the shape?

OVERLAY 1

1 Now drop overlay 1 onto the base. Find the nervous system. **What parts make up this system? In what parts of the body is the system located?**

OVERLAY 2

2 Now drop overlay 2 onto overlay 1. You have added the circulatory system to the diagram. **What parts make up the circulatory system? How does this system "fit" into the shape of the frog?**

OVERLAY 3

3 Now drop overlay 3 onto overlay 2. The digestive system is added. The heart blocks your view a bit. **How does this system "fit" into the animal's shape?**

SUMMARIZE

You can see three different systems of the frog. Do the differences have anything to do with what the systems do? Explain.

BASE: Start with a frog body.

DIAGRAM BUILDERS
Activities

1 Make a Table

Set up a table to show the three systems of the frog. You want to show how the systems differ. Decide first on how many columns and rows you will need and what headings you will use.

2 Make a Model

Use modeling clay and art materials to put together a model of the frog with these three systems inside. Share your models with others. What did you do best in your model? How can you improve it?

3 Write an Explanation

How are the nerves arranged in the frog? What other animals have the nerves arranged differently? Why is there a difference?

REFERENCE SECTION

HANDBOOK

Temperature

1. The temperature is 77 degrees Fahrenheit.

2. That is the same as 25 degrees Celsius.

3. Water boils at 212 degrees Fahrenheit.

4. Water freezes at 0 degrees Celsius.

Length and Area

1. This classroom is 10 meters wide and 20 meters long.

2. That means the area is 200 square meters.

Mass and Weight

1. That baseball bat weighs 32 ounces.

2. 32 ounces is the same as 2 pounds.

3. The mass of the bat is 907 grams.

Volume of Fluids

1. This bottle of juice has a volume of 1 liter.

2. That is a little more than 1 quart.

I weigh 85 pounds. That is a force of 380.8 newtons.

Weight/Force

Rate

1. She can walk 20 meters in 5 seconds.

2. That means her speed is 4 meters per second.

Table of Measurements

SI (International System) of Units	English System of Units
Temperature Water freezes at 0 degrees Celsius (°C) and boils at 100°C.	**Temperature** Water freezes at 32 degrees Fahrenheit (°F) and boils at 212°F.
Length and Distance 10 millimeters (mm) = 1 centimeter (cm) 100 centimeters = 1 meter (m) 1,000 meters = 1 kilometer (km)	**Length and Distance** 12 inches (in.) = 1 foot (ft) 3 feet = 1 yard (yd) 5,280 feet = 1 mile (mi)
Volume 1 cubic centimeter (cm^3) = 1 milliliter (mL) 1,000 milliliters = 1 liter (L)	**Volume of Fluids** 8 fluid ounces (fl oz) = 1 cup (c) 2 cups = 1 pint (pt) 2 pints = 1 quart (qt) 4 quarts = 1 gallon (gal)
Mass 1,000 milligrams (mg) = 1 gram (g) 1,000 grams = 1 kilogram (kg)	**Weight** 16 ounces (oz) = 1 pound (lb) 2,000 pounds = 1 ton (T)
Area 1 square kilometer (km^2) = l km x l km 1 hectare = 10,000 square meters (m^2)	**Rate** mph = miles per hour
Rate m/s = meters per second km/h = kilometers per hour	
Force 1 newton (N) = 1 kg x m/s^2	

In the Classroom

The most important part of doing any experiment is doing it safely. You can be safe by paying attention to your teacher and doing your work carefully. Here are some other ways to stay safe while you do experiments.

Before the Experiment

- Read all of the directions. Make sure you understand them. When you see

  ◪, be sure to follow the safety rule.

- Listen to your teacher for special safety directions. If you don't understand something, ask for help.

During the Experiment

- Wear safety goggles when your teacher tells you to wear them and whenever you see ⬛.
- Wear a safety apron if you work with anything messy or anything that might spill.
- If you spill something, wipe it up right away or ask your teacher for help.

- Tell your teacher if something breaks. If glass breaks do not clean it up yourself.
- Keep your hair and clothes away from open flames. Tie back long hair and roll up long sleeves.

- Be careful around a hot plate. Know when it is on and when it is off. Remember that the plate stays hot for a few minutes after you turn it off.
- Keep your hands dry around electrical equipment.
- Don't eat or drink anything during the experiment.

After the Experiment

- Put equipment back the way your teacher tells you.
- Dispose of things the way your teacher tells you.
- Clean up your work area and wash your hands.

In the Field

- Always be accompanied by a trusted adult—like your teacher or a parent or guardian.
- Never touch animals or plants without the adult's approval. The animal might bite. The plant might be poison ivy or another dangerous plant.

Responsibility

Acting safely is one way to be responsible. You can also be responsible by treating animals, the environment, and each other with respect in the class and in the field.

Treat Living Things with Respect

- If you have animals in the classroom, keep their homes clean. Change the water in fish tanks and clean out cages.
- Feed classroom animals the right amounts of food.

- Give your classroom animals enough space.
- When you observe animals, don't hurt them or disturb their homes.
- Find a way to care for animals while school is on vacation.

Treat the Environment with Respect

- Do not pick flowers.
- Do not litter, including gum and food.
- If you see litter, ask your teacher if you can pick it up.

- Recycle materials used in experiments. Ask your teacher what materials can be recycled instead of thrown away. These might include plastics, aluminum, and newspapers.

Treat Each Other with Respect

- Use materials carefully around others so that people don't get hurt or get stains on their clothes.
- Be careful not to bump people when they are doing experiments. Do not disturb or damage their experiments.
- If you see that people are having trouble with an experiment, help them.

Use a Hand Lens

You use a hand lens to magnify an object, or make the object look larger. With a hand lens, you can see details that would be hard to see without the hand lens.

Magnify a Piece of Cereal

1. Place a piece of your favorite cereal on a flat surface. Look at the cereal carefully. Draw a picture of it.
2. Hold the hand lens so that it is just above the cereal. Look through the lens, and slowly move it away from the cereal. The cereal will look larger.
3. Keep moving the hand lens until the cereal begins to look blurry. Then move the lens a little closer to the cereal until you can see it clearly.
4. Draw a picture of the cereal as you see it through the hand lens. Fill in details that you did not see before.
5. Repeat this activity using objects you are studying in science. It might be a rock, some soil, a flower, a seed, or something else.

Use a Microscope

Hand lenses make objects look several times larger. A microscope, however, can magnify an object to look hundreds of times larger.

Examine Salt Grains

1. Place the microscope on a flat surface. Always carry a microscope with both hands. Hold the arm with one hand, and put your other hand beneath the base.
2. Look at the drawing to learn the different parts of the microscope.
3. Move the mirror so that it reflects light up toward the stage. Never point the mirror directly at the Sun or a bright light.
4. Place a few grains of salt on the slide. Put the slide under the stage clips on the stage. Be sure that the salt grains are over the hole in the stage.
5. Look through the eyepiece. Turn the focusing knob slowly until the salt grains come into focus.
6. Draw what the grains look like through the microscope.
7. Look at other objects through the microscope. Try a piece of leaf, a strand of human hair, or a pencil mark.

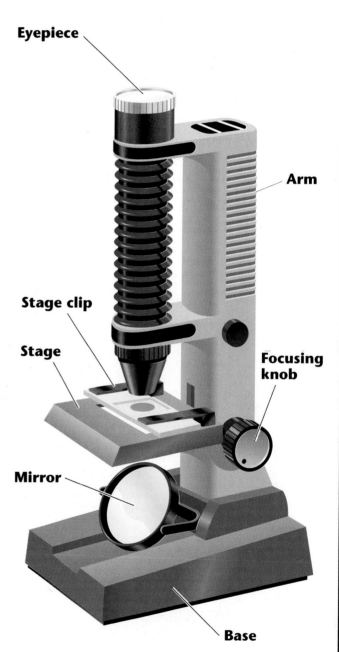

Eyepiece

Arm

Stage clip

Stage

Focusing knob

Mirror

Base

Use a Compass

HANDBOOK

You use a compass to find directions. A compass is a small, thin magnet that swings freely, like a spinner in a board game. One end of the magnet always points north. This end is the magnet's north pole. How does a compass work?

1. Place the compass on a surface that has no magnetic material such as steel. A wooden table or a sidewalk works well.
2. Find the magnet's north pole. The north pole is marked in some way, usually with a color or an arrowhead.
3. Notice the letters *N, E, S,* and *W* on the compass. These letters stand for the directions north, east, south, and west. When the magnet stops swinging, turn the compass so that the *N* lines up with the north pole of the magnet.
4. Face to the north. Then face to the east, to the south, and to the west.
5. Repeat this activity by holding the compass in your hand and then at different places indoors and outdoors.

Use a Compass to Study Shadows

A shadow is the shade that something makes when that thing blocks light. A shadow points away from the light that causes it. Find out how shadows change as the Sun moves across the sky.

1. Go outside on a sunny morning, and look at your shadow. Hold a compass flat in the palm of your hand. In which direction is your shadow pointing? In which direction is the Sun in the sky?
2. Go outside late in the afternoon with the compass. Now in which direction is your shadow pointing? In which direction is the Sun in the sky?

Use a Telescope

Have you ever seen the Moon near the horizon? A little while later, the Moon is higher in the sky. The Moon appears to move across the sky because Earth turns. Do stars appear to move across the sky, too? Make these observations on a clear night to find out.

Look at the Stars

1. Pick out a group of stars that you would be able to find again. The Big Dipper is a good choice. Choose a star in the star group.
2. Notice where the star is located compared to a treetop, a house roof, or some other point on land.
3. Find the same star an hour later. Notice that it appears to have moved in the sky. Predict how far the star will appear to move in another hour. Observe the star in an hour to check your prediction.

A telescope gathers light better than your eyes can. With a telescope you can see stars that you could not see with just your eyes.

The Moon moves around Earth. As a result of this motion, different parts of the Moon are lit by the Sun at different times. The Moon looks like it changes shape. These shapes are the Moon's phases. It takes about 30 days for the Moon to make one trip around Earth and complete all its phases. Check this out for yourself.

Look at the Moon

1. Make a calendar that shows the next 30 days.
2. Each day draw in the Moon's shape in the calendar box for that day. How many days does it take to come back to the same shape?

Use a Camera, Tape Recorder, Map, and Compass

HANDBOOK

Camera

You can use a camera to record what you observe in nature. Keep these tips in mind.

1. Hold the camera steady. Gently press the button so that you do not jerk the camera.
2. Try to take pictures with the Sun at your back. Then your pictures will be bright and clear.
3. Don't get too close to the subject. Without a special lens, the picture could turn out blurry.
4. Be patient. If you are taking a picture of an animal, you may have to wait for the animal to appear.

Tape Recorder

You can record observations on a tape recorder. This is sometimes better than writing notes because a tape recorder can record your observations at the exact time you are making them. Later you can listen to the tape and write down your observations.

Map and Compass

When you are busy observing nature, it might be easy to get lost. You can use a map of the area and a compass to find your way. Here are some tips.

1. Lightly mark on the map your starting place. It might be the place where the bus parked.
2. Always know where you are on the map compared to your starting place. Watch for landmarks on the map, such as a river, a pond, trails, or buildings.
3. Use the map and compass to find special places to observe, such as a pond. Look at the map to see which direction the place is from you. Hold the compass to see where that direction is.
4. Use your map and compass with a friend.

Length

Find Length with a Ruler

1. Look at this section of a ruler. Each centimeter is divided into 10 millimeters. How long is the paper clip?
2. The length of the paper clip is 3 centimeters plus 2 millimeters. You can write this length as 3.2 centimeters.
3. Place the ruler on your desk. Lay a pencil against the ruler so that one end of the pencil lines up with the left edge of the ruler. Record the length of the pencil.
4. Trade your pencil with a classmate. Measure and record the length of each other's pencils. Compare your answers.

Measuring Area

Area is the amount of surface something covers. To find the area of a rectangle, multiply the rectangle's length by its width. For example, the rectangle here is 3 centimeters long and 2 centimeters wide. Its area is 3 cm x 2 cm = 6 square centimeters. You write the area as 6 cm^2.

1. Find the area of your science book. Measure the book's length to the nearest centimeter. Measure its width.
2. Multiply the book's length by its width. Remember to put the answer in cm^2.

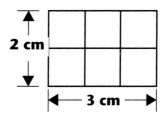

2 cm

3 cm

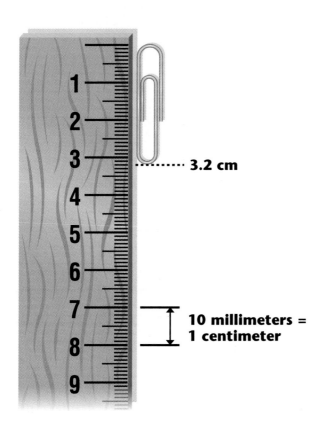

3.2 cm

10 millimeters = 1 centimeter

Time

You use timing devices to measure how long something takes to happen. Some timing devices you use in science are a clock with a second hand and a stopwatch. Which one is more accurate?

Comparing a Clock and a Stopwatch

1. Look at a clock with a second hand. The second hand is the hand that you can see moving. It measures seconds.
2. Get an egg timer with falling sand or some device like a windup toy that runs down after a certain length of time. When the second hand of the clock points to 12, tell your partner to start the egg timer. Watch the clock while the sand in the egg timer is falling.
3. When the sand stops falling, count how many seconds it took. Record this measurement. Repeat the activity, and compare the two measurements.
4. Switch roles with your partner.
5. Look at a stopwatch. Click the button on the top right. This starts the time. Click the button again. This stops the time. Click the button on the top left. This sets the stopwatch back to zero. Notice that the stopwatch tells time in hours, minutes, seconds, and hundredths of a second.
6. Repeat the activity in steps 1–3, but use the stopwatch instead of a clock. Make sure the stopwatch is set to zero. Click the top right button to start timing.

Click the button again when the sand stops falling. Make sure you and your partner time the sand twice.

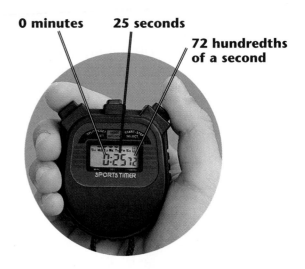

0 minutes   25 seconds

72 hundredths of a second

More About Time

1. Use the stopwatch to time how long it takes an ice cube to melt under cold running water. How long does an ice cube take to melt under warm running water?
2. Match each of these times with the action you think took that amount of time.

a.   b.   c.

1. A Little League baseball game
2. Saying the Pledge of Allegiance
3. Recess

Volume

Have you ever used a measuring cup? Measuring cups measure the volume of liquids. Volume is the amount of space something takes up. To bake a cake, you might measure the volume of water, vegetable oil, or melted butter. In science you use special measuring cups called beakers and graduated cylinders. These containers are marked in milliliters (mL).

Measure the Volume of a Liquid

1. Look at the beaker and at the graduated cylinder. The beaker has marks for each 25 mL up to 200 mL. The graduated cylinder has marks for each 1 mL up to 100 mL.

2. The surface of the water in the graduated cylinder curves up at the sides. You measure the volume by reading the height of the water at the flat part. What is the volume of water in the graduated cylinder? How much water is in the beaker? They both contain 75 mL of water.

3. Pour 50 mL of water from a pitcher into a graduated cylinder. The water should be at the 50-mL mark on the graduated cylinder. If you go over the mark, pour a little water back into the pitcher.

4. Pour the 50 mL of water into a beaker.

5. Repeat steps 3 and 4 using 30 mL, 45 mL, and 25 mL of water.

6. Measure the volume of water you have in the beaker. Do you have about the same amount of water as your classmates?

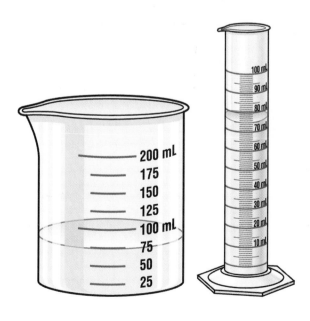

Mass

Mass is the amount of matter an object has. You use a balance to measure mass. To find the mass of an object, you balance it with objects whose masses you know. Let's find the mass of a box of crayons.

Measure the Mass of a Box of Crayons

1. Place the balance on a flat, level surface. Check that the two pans are empty and clean.
2. Make sure the empty pans are balanced with each other. The pointer should point to the middle mark. If it does not, move the slider a little to the right or left to balance the pans.
3. Gently place a box of crayons on the left pan. This pan will drop lower.
4. Add masses to the right pan until the pans are balanced.
5. Add the numbers on the masses that are in the right pan. The total is the mass of the box of crayons, in grams. Record this number. After the number, write a *g* for "grams."

Handbook

Predict the Mass of More Crayons

1. Leave the box of crayons and the masses on the balance.
2. Get two more crayons. If you put them in the pan with the box of crayons, what do you think the mass of all the crayons will be? Write down what you predict the total mass will be.
3. Check your prediction. Gently place the two crayons in the left pan. Add masses to the right pan until the pans are balanced.
4. Add the numbers on the masses as you did before. Record this number. How close is it to your prediction?

More About Mass

What was the mass of all your crayons? It was probably less than 100 grams. What would happen if you replaced the crayons with a pineapple? You may not have enough masses to balance the pineapple. It has a mass of about 1,000 grams. That's the same as 1 kilogram because *kilo* means "1,000."

1. How many kilograms do all these masses add up to?

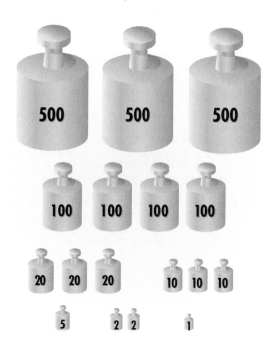

2. Which of these objects have a mass greater than 1 kilogram?
   a. large dog
   b. robin
   c. desktop computer
   d. calculator
   e. whole watermelon

Weight/Force

You use a spring scale to measure weight. An object has weight because the force of gravity pulls down on the object. Therefore, weight is a force. Like all forces weight is measured in newtons (N).

Measure the Weight of an Object

1. Look at your spring scale to see how many newtons it measures. See how the measurements are divided. The spring scale shown here measures up to 10 N. It has a mark for every 1 N.
2. Hold the spring scale by the top loop. Put the object to be measured on the bottom hook. If the object will not stay on the hook, place it in a net bag. Then hang the bag from the hook.
3. Let go of the object slowly. It will pull down on a spring inside the scale. The spring is connected to a pointer. The pointer on the spring scale shown here is a small bar.

4. Wait for the pointer to stop moving. Read the number of newtons next to the pointer. This is the object's weight. The mug in the picture weighs 3 N.

More About Spring Scales

You probably weigh yourself by standing on a bathroom scale. This is a spring scale. The force of your body stretches a spring inside the scale. The dial on the scale is probably marked in pounds—the English unit of weight. One pound is equal to about 4.5 newtons.

Here are some spring scales you may have seen.

Temperature

Temperature is how hot or cold something is. You use a thermometer to measure temperature. A thermometer is made of a thin tube with colored liquid inside. When the liquid gets warmer, it expands and moves up the tube. When the liquid gets cooler, it contracts and moves down the tube. You may have seen most temperatures measured in degrees Fahrenheit (°F). Scientists measure temperature in degrees Celsius (°C).

Read a Thermometer

1. Look at the thermometer shown here. It has two scales—a Fahrenheit scale and a Celsius scale. Every 20 degrees on each scale has a number.
2. What is the temperature shown on the thermometer? At what temperature does water freeze? Give your answers in °F and in °C.

How Is Temperature Measured?

1. Fill a large beaker about one-half full of cool water. Find the temperature of the water by holding a thermometer in the water. Do not let the bulb at the bottom of the thermometer touch the sides or bottom of the beaker.
2. Keep the thermometer in the water until the liquid in the tube stops moving—about a minute. Read and record the temperature on the Celsius scale.
3. Fill another large beaker one-half full of warm water from a faucet. Be careful not to burn yourself by using hot water.
4. Find and record the temperature of the warm water just as you did in steps 1 and 2.

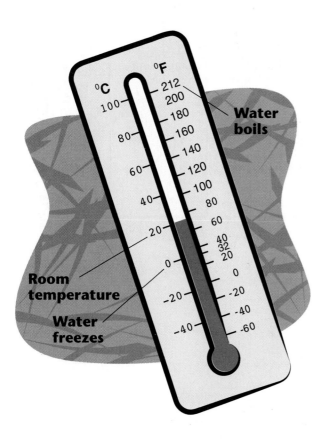

Weather

What was the weather like yesterday? What is it like today? The weather changes from day to day. You can observe different parts of the weather to find out how it changes.

Measure Temperature

1. Use a thermometer to find the air temperature outside. Look at page R17 to review thermometers.
2. Hold a thermometer outside for two minutes. Then read and record the temperature.
3. Take the temperature at the same time each day for a week. Record it in a chart.

Observe Wind Speed and Direction

1. Observe how the wind is affecting things around you. Look at a flag or the branches of a tree. How hard is the wind blowing the flag or branches? Observe for about five minutes. Write down your observations.
2. Hold a compass to see which direction the wind is coming from. Write down this direction.
3. Observe the wind each day for a week. Record your observations in your chart.

Observe Clouds, Rain, and Snow

1. Observe how much of the sky is covered by clouds. Use these symbols to record the cloud cover in your chart each day.

Clear skies; no clouds   **Partly cloudy**   **Cloudy**

2. Record in your chart if it is raining or snowing.
3. At the end of the week, how has the weather changed from day to day?

Systems

What do a toy car, a tomato plant, and a yo-yo have in common? They are all systems. A system is a set of parts that work together to form a whole. Look at the three systems below. Think of how each part helps the system work.

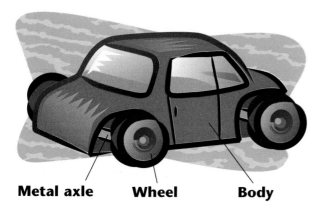

Metal axle   **Wheel**   **Body**

This system has three main parts—the body, the axles, and the wheels. Would the system work well if the axles could not turn?

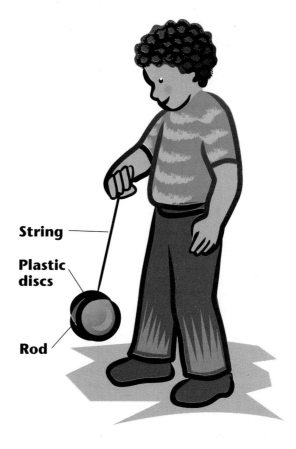

String

Plastic discs

Rod

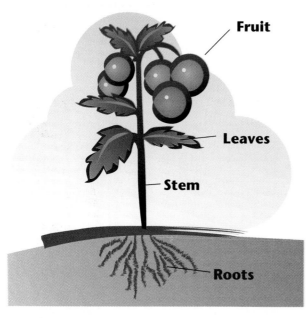

Fruit

Leaves

Stem

Roots

In this system roots take in water, and leaves make food. The stem carries water and food to different parts of the plant. What would happen if you cut off all the leaves?

Even simple things can be systems. How do all the parts of the yo-yo work together to make the toy go up and down?

Look for some other systems at school, at home, and outside. Remember to look for things that are made of parts. List the parts. Then describe how you think each part helps the system work.

Make Graphs to Organize Data

When you do an experiment in science, you collect information. To find out what your information means, you can organize it into graphs. There are many kinds of graphs.

Bar Graphs

A bar graph uses bars to show information. For example, suppose you are growing a plant. Every week you measure how high the plant has grown. Here is what you find.

Week	Height (cm)
1	1
2	3
3	6
4	10
5	17
6	20
7	22
8	23

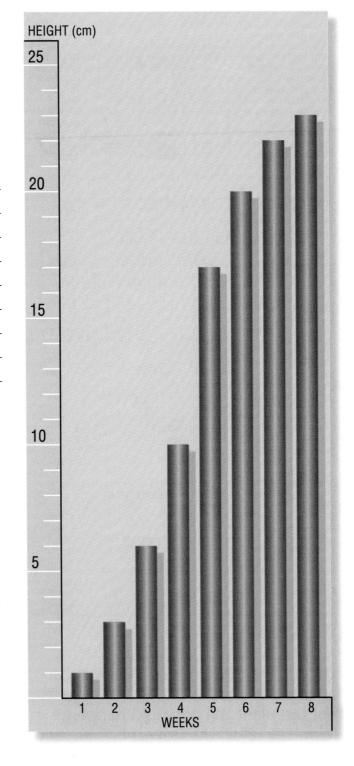

The bar graph at right organizes the measurements you collected so that you can easily compare them.

1. Look at the bar for week 2. Put your finger at the top of the bar. Move your finger straight over to the left to find how many centimeters the plant grew by the end of week 2.
2. Between which two weeks did the plant grow most?
3. When did plant growth begin to level off?

Pictographs

A pictograph uses symbols, or pictures, to show information. What if you collect information about how much water your family uses each day? Here is what you find.

Activity	Water Used Each Day (L)
Drinking	10
Showering	180
Bathing	240
Brushing teeth	80
Washing dishes	140
Washing hands	30
Washing clothes	280
Flushing toilet	90

You can organize this information into the pictograph shown here. The pictograph has to explain what the symbol on the graph means. In this case each bottle means 20 liters of water. A half bottle means half of 20, or 10 liters of water.

1. Which activity uses the most water?
2. Which activity uses the least water?

Line Graphs

A line graph shows information by connecting dots plotted on the graph.

It shows change over time. For example, what if you measure the temperature out of doors every hour starting at 6 A.M.? Here is what you find.

Time	Temperature (°C)
6 A.M.	10
7 A.M.	12
8 A.M.	14
9 A.M.	16
10 A.M.	18
11 A.M.	20

You can organize this information into a line graph. Follow these steps.

1. Make a scale along the bottom and side of the graph. The scales should include all the numbers in the chart. Label the scales.
2. Plot points on the graph. For example, place your finger at the "6 A.M." on the bottom line. Place a finger from your other hand on the "10" on the left line. Move your "6 A.M." finger up and your "10" finger to the right until they meet, and make a pencil point. Plot the other points in this way.
3. Connect the points with a line.

A Family's Daily Use of Water

= 20 liters of water

| Drinking |
| Showering |
| Bathing |
| Brushing teeth |
| Washing dishes |
| Washing hands |
| Washing clothes |
| Flushing toilet |

Make Maps to Show Information

Locate Places

A map is a drawing that shows an area from above. Most maps have numbers and letters along the top and side. They help you find places easily. For example, what if you wanted to find the library on the map below. It is located at D7. Place a finger on the letter D along the side of the map and another finger on the number 7 at the top. Then move your fingers straight across and down the map until they meet. The library is located where D and 7 meet, or very nearby.

1. What building is located at G3?
2. The hospital is located three blocks south and three blocks east of the library. What is its number and letter?
3. Make a map of an area in your community. It might be a park or the area between your home and school. Include numbers and letters along the top and side. Use a compass to find north, and mark north on your map. Exchange maps with classmates.

Idea Maps

The map below left shows how places are connected to each other. Idea maps, on the other hand, show how ideas are connected to each other. Idea maps help you organize information about a topic.

Look at the idea map below. It connects ideas about water. This map shows that Earth's water is either fresh water or salt water. The map also shows four sources of fresh water. You can see that there is no connection between "rivers" and "salt water" on the map. This reminds you that salt water does not flow in rivers.

Make an idea map about a topic you are learning in science. Your map can include words, phrases, or even sentences. Arrange your map in a way that makes sense to you and helps you understand the ideas.

North

	1	2	3	4	5	6	7	8	9	10
A										
B										
C										
D							Library			
E										
F			Store							Hospital
G										

West   East

South

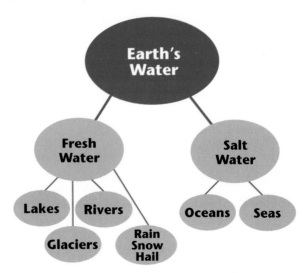

Make Tables and Charts to Organize Data

Tables help you organize data during experiments. Most tables have columns that run up and down, and rows that run across. The columns and rows have headings that tell you what kind of data goes in each part of the table.

A Sample Table

What if you are going to do an experiment to find out how long different kinds of seeds take to sprout? Before you begin the experiment, you should set up your table. Follow these steps.

1. In this experiment you will plant 20 radish seeds, 20 bean seeds, and 20 corn seeds. Your table must show how many of each kind of seed sprouted on days 1, 2, 3, 4, and 5.
2. Make your table with columns, rows, and headings. You might use a computer. Some computer programs let you build a table with just the click of a mouse. You can delete or add columns and rows if you need to.
3. Give your table a title. Your table could look like the one here.

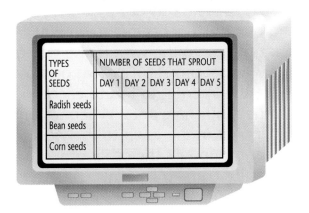

TYPES OF SEEDS	NUMBER OF SEEDS THAT SPROUT				
	DAY 1	DAY 2	DAY 3	DAY 4	DAY 5
Radish seeds					
Bean seeds					
Corn seeds					

Make a Table

Now what if you are going to do an experiment to find out how temperature affects the sprouting of seeds? You will plant 20 bean seeds in each of two trays. You will keep each tray at a different temperature, as shown below, and observe the trays for seven days. Make a table that you can use for this experiment.

Make a Chart

A chart is simply a table with pictures as well as words to label the rows or columns.

Computer

A computer has many uses. The Internet connects your computer to many other computers around the world, so you can collect all kinds of information. You can use a computer to show this information and write reports. Best of all you can use a computer to explore, discover, and learn.

You can also get information from CD-ROMs. They are computer disks that can hold large amounts of information. You can fit a whole encyclopedia on one CD-ROM.

Use Computers for a Project

Here is how one group of students uses computers as they work on a weather project.

1. The students use instruments to measure temperature, wind speed, wind direction, and other parts of the weather. They input this information, or data, into the computer. The students keep the data in a table. This helps them compare the data from one day to the next.

weather data

2. The teacher finds out that another group of students in a town 200 kilometers to the west is also doing a weather project. The two groups use the Internet to talk to each other and share data. When a storm happens in the town to the west, that group tells the other group that it's coming its way.

email: It's going to storm here. The sky is turning dark gray. The winds are sometimes 65 km per hour from the northwest.

4. Meanwhile some students go to the library to gather more information from a CD-ROM disk. The CD-ROM has an encyclopedia that includes movie clips with sound. The clips give examples of different kinds of storms.

5. The students have kept all their information in a folder called Weather Project. Now they use that information to write a report about the weather. On the computer they can move paragraphs, add words, take out words, put in diagrams, and draw their own weather maps. Then they print the report in color.

3. The students want to find out more. They decide to stay on the Internet and send questions to a local TV weather forecaster. She has a Web site and answers questions from students every day.

Calculator

Sometimes after you make measurements, you have to multiply or divide your measurements to get other information. A calculator helps you multiply and divide, especially if the numbers have decimal points.

Multiply Decimals

What if you are measuring the width of your classroom? You discover that the floor is covered with tiles and the room is exactly 32 tiles wide. You measure a tile, and it is 22.7 centimeters wide. To find the width of the room, you can multiply 32 by 22.7. You can use your calculator.

1. Make sure the calculator is on. Press the **ON** key.

2. Press **3** and **2**.

3. Press **×**.

4. Press **2**, **2**, **.**, and **7**.

5. Press **=**. Your total should be 726.4. That is how wide the room is in centimeters.

Divide Decimals

Now what if you wanted to find out how many desks placed side by side would be needed to reach across the room? You measure one desk, and it is 60 centimeters wide. To find the number of desks needed, divide 726.4 by 60.

1. Turn the calculator on.

2. Press **7**, **2**, **6**, **.**, and **4**.

3. Press **÷**.

4. Press **6** and **0**.

5. Press **=**. Your total should be about 12.1. This means you can fit 12 desks across the room with a little space left over.

What if the room was 35 tiles wide? How wide would the room be? How many desks would fit across it?

GLOSSARY

This Glossary will help you to pronounce and understand the meanings of the Science Words introduced in this book. The page number at the end of the definition tells where the word appears.

A

abuse (*v.*, ə būz′; *n.*, ə būs′) To use legal drugs in an unsafe way on purpose or to use illegal drugs. (p. 474)

adaptation (ad′əp tā′shən) A special trait that helps an organism survive. (p. 276)

addictive (ə dik′tiv) Causing dependence, or a strong need to have a particular substance. (p. 460)

alcohol (al′kə hôl′) A drug found in beer, wine, liquor, and even some medications. (p. 458)

allergy (al′ər jē) A sensitivity to a substance that can cause a rash, fever, or trouble breathing. (p. 471)

alloy (al′oi) A mixture of two or more metals. (p. 96)

alternating current (ôl′tər nā ting kûr′ənt) Current that flows in a circuit first in one direction, then in the opposite direction. (p. 342)

amber (am′bər) Hardened tree sap, yellow to brown in color, often a source of insect fossils. (p. 164)

amphibian (am fib′ē ən) A cold-blooded vertebrate that spends part of its life in water and part of its life on land. (p. 239)

antibiotic (an′tē bī ot′ik) A type of medicine that kills bacteria or stops them from growing. (p. 470)

area (âr′ē ə) The number of unit squares that fit inside a surface. (p. 81)

arthropod (är′thrə pod′) An invertebrate with jointed legs and a body that is divided into sections. (p. 227)

asexual reproduction (a sek′shü əl rē′prə duk′shən) Producing offspring with only one parent. (p. 268)

atmosphere (at′məs fîr′) Gases that surround Earth. (p. 372)

B

bacteria (bak tîr′ē ə) *pl., sing.* **bacterium** (bak tîr′ē əm) One-celled organisms that have cell walls but no nuclei. (p. 19)

balance (bal′əns) An instrument used to measure mass. (p. 70)

biceps (bī′seps) A muscle in the upper arm that bends the arm by contracting. (p. 446)

bilateral symmetry (bī lat′ər əl sim′ə trē) A form of symmetry in which an animal has only two sides, which are mirror images. (p. 215)

bladder (blad′ər) The body structure that stores urine until it is removed from the body. (p. 254)

PRONUNCIATION KEY

a	at	e	end	o	hot	u	up	hw	white	ə	about
ā	ape	ē	me	ō	old	ū	use	ng	song		taken
ä	far	i	it	ô	fork	ü	rule	th	thin		pencil
âr	care	ī	ice	oi	oil	ù	pull	th	this		lemon
		îr	pierce	ou	out	ûr	turn	zh	measure		circus

′ = *primary accent; shows which syllable takes the main stress, such as* **kil** *in* **kilogram** (kil′ə gram′)
′ = *secondary accent; shows which syllables take lighter stresses, such as* **gram** *in* **kilogram**

budding (bud'ing) A form of asexual reproduction in simple invertebrates where a bud forms on the adult's body and slowly develops into a new animal before breaking off. (p. 268)

buoyancy (boi'ən sē) The upward force of a liquid or gas. (p. 69)

C

caffeine (ka fēn') A stimulant found in tea, coffee, and many soft drinks. (p. 472)

camouflage (kam'ə fläzh') An adaptation by which an animal can hide by blending in with its surroundings. (p. 276)

carbon monoxide (kär'bən mon ok'sīd) A poisonous gas given off by burning tobacco. (p. 462)

cardiac muscle (kär'dē ak' mus'əl) The type of muscle that makes up the heart. (p. 448)

cartilage (kär'tə lij) A flexible tissue that covers the ends of some bones; found in the nose and ears. (p. 439)

cartilaginous (kär'tə laj'ə nəs) Said of a fish with a skeleton made of cartilage. (p. 237)

cast (kast) A fossil formed or shaped within a mold. (p. 163)

cell (sel) The smallest unit of living matter. (p. 5)

cell membrane (sel mem'brān) An animal cell's thin outer covering. It is found beneath the cell wall in plants. (p. 15)

cell wall (sel wôl) A thick, stiff structure that protects and supports a plant cell. (p. 14)

chemical change (kem'i kəl chānj) A change that produces new matter with different properties from the original matter. *See* **physical change**. (p. 104)

chitin (kī'tin) A light but tough material that makes up the exoskeletons of certain invertebrates. (p. 228)

chlorophyll (klôr'ə fil') A material (usually green) found in plant cells that makes food for the plant when sunlight strikes it. (p. 5)

chloroplast (klôr'ə plast') A plant cell's food factory. Chloroplasts contain a substance (usually green) that uses the Sun's energy to make food. (p. 14)

chromosome (krō'mə sōm') One of the threadlike structures inside a cell nucleus that determine an organism's traits. (p. 16)

circuit (sûr'kit) A complete path that electricity can move through. (p. 304)

circuit breaker (sûr'kit brā'kər) A reusable switch that protects circuits from dangerously high currents. (p. 322)

circulatory system (sûr'kyə lə tôr'ē sis'təm) The organ system that moves blood through the body. (p. 252)

class (klas) A smaller group within a phylum, such as all those animals that produce milk for their young. Classes are made up of smaller groups called *orders*. (p. 30)

clone (klōn) An exact copy of its parent formed by asexual reproduction. (p. 268)

closed circuit (klōzd sûr'kit) A clear and complete path that electricity can flow through. (p. 305)

cloud (kloud) Tiny drops of condensed water that gather in the atmosphere. (p. 385)

cnidarian (nī dâr'ē ən) An invertebrate with poison stingers on tentacles. (p. 223)

cocaine (kō kān') An illegal stimulant made from the leaves of the coca plant. (p. 473)

cold-blooded (kōld'blud'id) Said of an animal that cannot control its body temperature. (p. 236)

community (kə mū'ni tē) The living part of an ecosystem. (p. 50)

compound (kom'pound) A substance made when two or more elements are joined and lose their own properties. (p. 94)

compound machine (kom′pound mə shēn′) A combination of two or more machines. (p. 139)

condensation (kon′den sā′shən) When water particles change from a gas to a liquid. (p. 385)

conduction (kən duk′shən) The transfer of energy caused by one particle of matter hitting into another. (p. 118)

conductor (kən duk′tər) 1. A material that transfers heat well. (p. 116) 2. Said of a material through which electricity flows easily. (p. 295)

consumer (kən sü′mər) Any organism that eats the food producers make. (p. 54)

continental glacier (kon′tə nen′təl glā′shər) A glacier covering large sections of land in Earth's polar regions. (p. 177)

contract (v., kən trakt′) To decrease in size, or shrink, as most matter does when it cools. (p. 120)

convection (kən′vek′shən) The transfer of energy by the flow of liquids or gases, such as water boiling in a pot or warm air rising in a room. (p. 118)

crack (krak) A very harmful form of cocaine. (p. 473)

crust (krust) Solid rock that makes up Earth's outermost layer. (p. 202)

crystal (kris′təl) The clear and shiny particle of frozen water that makes up a snowflake. (p. 390)

current (kûr′ənt) An ocean movement; a large stream of water that flows in the ocean. (p. 396)

current electricity (kûr′ənt i lek tris′i tē) A moving electrical charge. (p. 304)

cytoplasm (sī′tə plaz′əm) A jellylike substance that fills a cell. (p. 15)

D

decomposer (dē′kəm pō′zər) An organism that breaks down wastes and the remains of other organisms. (p. 54)

deep ocean current (dēp ō′shən kûr′ənt) A stream of water that flows more than 200 meters (650 feet) beneath the sea. (p. 396)

density (den′si tē) The amount of matter in a given space. In scientific terms density is the mass per unit of volume. (p. 84)

dependence (di pen′dəns) A strong need or desire for a medicine or drug. (p. 471)

depressant (di pres′ənt) A drug that slows down the activity of the body. (p. 459)

diaphragm (dī′ə fram′) A muscle below the lungs. When relaxed the diaphragm pushes up. Air leaves the lungs. When the diaphragm flattens and pulls down, the lungs fill with air. (p. 253)

digestive system (di jes′tiv sis′təm) The organ system that breaks down food for fuel. (p. 255)

direct current (di rekt′ kûr′ənt) Current that flows in one direction through a circuit. (p. 342)

discharge (v., dis chärj′; n., dis′chärj) When a buildup of electrical charge empties into something. (p. 295)

drought (drout) A long period of time with little or no precipitation. (p. 412)

drug (drug) A substance other than food that changes the way a person feels, thinks, and acts. (p. 458)

drumlin (drum′lin) An oval mound of glacial till. (p. 177)

PRONUNCIATION KEY

a **at**; ā **ape**; ä **far**; âr **care**; e **end**; ē **me**; i **it**; ī **ice**; îr **pierce**; o **hot**; ō **old**; ô **fork**; oi **oil**; ou **out**; u **up**; ū **use**; ü **rule**; ủ **pull**; ûr **turn**; hw **white**; ng **song**; th **thin**; <u>th</u> **this**; zh **measure**; ə **about, taken, pencil, lemon, circus**

GLOSSARY

dry cell (drī sel) A battery that changes chemical energy into electrical energy. It is made of a carbon rod and a moist chemical paste. (p. 306)

E

earthquake (ûrth′kwāk′) Movement or vibration in the rocks that make up Earth's crust. (p. 198)

echinoderm (i kĭ′nə dûrm′) A spiny-skinned invertebrate. (p. 226)

ecology (ē kol′ə jē) The study of how living and nonliving things interact. (p. 50)

ecosystem (ek′ō sis′təm) The living and nonliving things in an environment and all their interactions. (p. 50)

effort force (ef′ərt fôrs) The force applied to a machine. (p. 132)

egg (eg) The female sex cell. (p. 269)

electrical charge (i lek′tri kəl chärj) The positive or negative property of the particles that make up matter. (p. 292)

electricity (i lek tris′i tē) The energy caused by the flow of particles with negative electrical charges. (p. 292)

electrode (i lek′trōd) The negative or positive terminal of a wet cell. (p. 344)

electromagnet (i lek′trō mag′nit) A temporary magnet created when current flows through wire wrapped in coils around an iron bar. (p. 333)

element (el′ə mənt) A substance that is made up of only one type of matter. (p. 90)

embryo (em′brē ō′) A developing organism that results from fertilization; an undeveloped animal or plant. (pp. 43, 269)

endoskeleton (en′dō skel′i tən) An internal supporting structure. (p. 226)

energy (en′ər jē) The ability to do work. (p. 129)

energy transformation (en′ər jē trans′fər mā′shən) A change of energy from one form to another. (p. 354)

erosion (i rō′zhən) The wearing away of rocks and rock materials, as when glaciers leave distinctive features on Earth's surface. (p. 155)

erratic (i rat′ik) An isolated boulder left behind by a glacier. (p. 179)

evaporation (i vap′ə rā′shən) The change of a liquid to a gas. (pp. 93, 384)

evolution (ev′ə lü′shən) The change in living things over time. (p. 40)

excretory system (ek′skri tôr′ē sis′təm) The organ system that removes liquid wastes. (p. 254)

exoskeleton (ek′sō skel′i tən) A hard covering that protects the body of certain invertebrates. (p. 227)

expand (ek spand′) To swell or get larger, as most matter does when it is heated. (p. 120)

expiration date (ek′spə rā′shən dāt) The date on a medicine label after which the medicine should not be used. (p. 470)

extinct (ek stingkt′) Said of an organism no longer alive on Earth. (p. 43)

F

family (fam′ə lē) A smaller group of organisms within a class. Families are made up of still smaller groups of very similar organisms called *genuses*. (p. 30)

fault (fôlt) A break in Earth's outer layer caused by the movement of rocks. (p. 200)

fertilization (fûr′tə lə zā′shən) Occurs during sexual reproduction when an egg and a sperm join. (p. 269)

fertilizer (fûr′tə li′zər) Chemicals or animal waste used to treat the soil so that plants grow stronger. (p. 423)

filter (fil′tər) A tool used to separate things by size. It works by means of an interwoven material that retains the bigger pieces but allows smaller pieces to fall through the holes of the filter. (p. 93)

filtration (fil trā′shən) The passing of a liquid through materials that remove solid impurities. (p. 424)

fixed pulley (fikst pùl′ē) A pulley that does not increase the effort force needed to move an object but does change the direction of that force. The pulley wheel is attached to one place so that the object moves, not the wheel. *See* **pulley**. (p. 134)

food chain (füd chān) The set of steps in which organisms get the food they need to survive. (p. 213)

food web (füd web) The pattern that shows how food chains are related. (p. 213)

force (fôrs) The push or pull needed to make an object move. (p. 128)

fossil (fos′əl) Any evidence of an organism that lived in the past. (pp. 40, 156)

fracture (frak′chər) A break or crack in a bone. (p. 439)

freeze (frēz) When moving particles in water slow down, lose heat, and change from a liquid to a solid. (p. 387)

fungi (fun′jī) *pl., sing.* **fungus** (fung′gəs) One- or many-celled organisms that lack true roots, stems, and leaves, and absorb food from dead organisms. (p. 19)

fuse (fūz) A device that melts to keep too much electric current from flowing through wires. Once melted a fuse cannot be reused. (p. 322)

G

gas (gas) A form of matter that does not take up a definite amount of space and has no definite shape. (p. 71)

gears (gîrz) Wheels with teeth that transfer motion and force from one source to another. (pp. 138, 358)

generator (jen′ər rā′tər) A device that creates alternating current by spinning an electric coil between the poles of a powerful magnet. (p. 343)

genus (jē′nəs) A group made up of two or more very similar species, like dogs and wolves. (p. 33)

geologist (jē ol′ə jist) A scientist who studies the physical properties of rocks to tell how the rocks may have formed. (p. 148)

gizzard (giz′ərd) A muscular organ in birds that breaks down food by grinding it with stored pebbles. (p. 255)

glacial till (glā′shəl til) An unsorted mixture of rock materials deposited as a glacier melts. (p. 177)

glacier (glā′shər) A large mass of ice and snow that moves over land. (pp. 176, 373)

grounded (ground′əd) Said of an electric charge that flows into the ground, or surface of Earth. (p. 297)

groundwater (ground wô′tər) Water stored in the cracks of underground rocks. (p. 374)

H

habitat (hab′i tat′) The home of an organism. (p. 50)

heat (hēt) The movement of energy from warmer to cooler objects. (p. 116)

PRONUNCIATION KEY

a **at**; ā **ape**; ä **far**; âr **care**; e **end**; ē **me**; i **it**; ī **ice**; îr **pierce**; o **hot**; ō **old**; ô **fork**; oi **oil**; ou **out**; u **up**; ū **use**; ü **rule**; ù **pull**; ûr **turn**; hw **white**; ng **song**; th **thin**; <u>th</u> **this**; zh **measure**; ə **about, taken, pencil, lemon, circus**

GLOSSARY

heredity (hə red′i tē) The passing of traits from parent to offspring. (p. 270)

hibernate (hī′bər nāt′) An instinct that causes some animals to sleep through the winter; all body processes slow down, and body temperature can drop to a few degrees above freezing. (p. 280)

horizon (hə rī′zən) A layer of soil differing from the layers above and below it. (p. 187)

humus (hū′məs) Leftover decomposed plant and animal matter in the soil. (p. 186)

I

ice cap (īs kap) A thick sheet of ice covering a large area of land. (p. 373)

igneous rock (ig′nē əs rok) "Fire-made" rock formed from melted rock material. (p. 151)

immovable joint (i mü′və bəl joint) A place where bones fit together too tightly to move. (p. 438)

imprint (*n.*, im′print′) A fossil created by a print or impression. (p. 162)

inclined plane (in klīnd′ plān) A straight, slanted surface that is not moved when it is used. (p. 136)

inherited behavior (in her′i təd bi hāv′yər) A behavior that is inborn, not learned. (p. 280)

inner core (in′ər kôr) A sphere of solid material at Earth's center. (p. 202)

instinct (in′stingkt′) A pattern of behavior that requires no thinking because it is programmed into an animal's brain. (p. 280)

insulator (in′sə lā′tər) **1.** A material that does not transfer heat very well. (p. 116) **2.** Said of a material through which electricity does not flow easily. (p. 295)

invertebrate (in vûr′tə brit′) An animal without a backbone. (p. 214)

involuntary muscle (in vol′ən ter′ē mus′əl) A muscle that causes movements you cannot control. (p. 449)

irrigation (ir′i gā′shən) A way to get water into the soil by artificial means. (p. 422)

J

joint (joint) A place where two or more bones meet. (p. 438)

K

kidney (kid′nē) One of two main waste-removal organs in vertebrates that filters wastes from the blood. (p. 254)

kilogram (kil′ə gram′) The metric unit used to measure mass. (p. 70)

kingdom (king′dəm) One of the largest groups of organisms into which an organism can be classified. (p. 28)

L

larva (lär′və) A wormlike stage of some organisms that hatches from an egg during complete metamorphosis; a young organism with a form different from its parents. (p. 266)

lava (lä′və) Magma that reaches Earth's surface through volcanoes or cracks. (p. 151)

learned behavior (lûrnd bi hāv′yər) Behavior that is not inborn. (p. 281)

length (lengkth) The number of units that fit along one edge of something. (p. 80)

lever (lev′ər) A simple machine made of a rigid bar on a pivot point. (p. 132)

life cycle (līf sī′kəl) The stages of growth and change of an organism's life. (p. 266)

life span (līf span) How long an organism can be expected to live. (p. 267)

ligament (lig′ə mənt) A tough band of tissue that holds two bones together where they meet. (p. 439)

liquid (lik′wid) A form of matter that takes up a definite amount of space and has no definite shape. (p. 71)

load (lōd) The object being lifted or moved. (p. 132)

LSD (el es dē) A mind-altering drug. (p. 473)

luster (lus′tər) The way a mineral reflects light. (p. 149)

M

magma (mag′mə) Melted rock material. (p. 151)

magnetic field (mag net′ik fēld) A region of magnetic force around a magnet. (p. 332)

mammal (mam′əl) A warm-blooded vertebrate with hair or fur that feeds milk to its young; most are born live. (p. 242)

mantle (man′təl) The layer of rock lying below the crust. (p. 202)

marijuana (mar′ə wä′nə) An illegal drug made from the crushed leaves, flowers, and seeds of the cannabis plant. (p. 473)

marrow (mar′ō) Soft tissue that fills some bones. (p. 437)

mass (mas) The amount of matter making up an object. (p. 70)

mass extinction (mas ek stingk′shən) The dying out at the same time of many different species. (p. 44)

matter (ma′tər) Anything that takes up space and has properties that you can observe and describe. (p. 68)

melt (melt) When water particles absorb heat energy and change from a solid to a liquid. (p. 387)

metamorphic rock (met′ə môr′fik rok) Rock whose form has been changed by heat and/or pressure. (p. 154)

metamorphosis (met′ə môr′fə sis) A process of changes during certain animals' development. (p. 264)

metric system (met′rik sis′təm) A system of measurement based on units of ten. (p. 80)

microorganism (mī′krō ôr′gə niz′əm) An organism that is so small you need a microscope to see it. (p. 8)

migrate (mī′grāt) An instinct that causes some animals to move to a different area to either avoid cold weather, find new food supplies, or find a safe place to breed and raise their young. (p. 280)

mimicry (mim′i krē) When one organism imitates the traits of another. (p. 278)

mineral (min′ər əl) A naturally occurring substance, neither plant nor animal. (p. 148)

misuse (v., mis ūz′) To use a legal drug improperly or in an unsafe way. (p. 474)

mixture (miks′chər) Two or more types of matter that are mixed together and keep their own properties. (p. 92)

mold (mōld) n., A fossil clearly showing the outside features of the organism. (p. 163)

mollusk (mol′əsk) A soft-bodied invertebrate. (p. 226)

molting (mōl′ting) A process by which an arthropod sheds its exoskeleton. (p. 228)

moraine (mə rān′) Rock debris carried and deposited as a glacier melts. (p. 177)

PRONUNCIATION KEY

a **at**; ā **ape**; ä **far**; âr **care**; e **end**; ē **me**; i **it**; ī **ice**; îr **pierce**; o **hot**; ō **old**; ô **fork**; oi **oil**; ou **out**; u **up**; ū **use**; ü **rule**; u̇ **pull**; ûr **turn**; hw **white**; ng **song**; th **thin**; <u>th</u> **this**; zh **measure**; ə **about, taken, pencil, lemon, circus**

GLOSSARY

movable joint (mü′və bəl joint) A place where bones meet and can move easily. (p. 438)

movable pulley (mü′və bəl pül′ē) A pulley that increases the effort force needed to move an object. The pulley wheel can change position, but the direction of the force remains unchanged. *See* **pulley**. (p. 134)

muscular system (mus′kyə lər sis′təm) The organ system made up of muscles that move bones. (pp. 256, 449)

N

narcotic (när kot′ik) A type of medicine that is used as a painkiller. (p. 473)

nervous system (nûr′vəs sis′təm) The organ system that controls all other body systems. (p. 257)

newton (nü′tən) A metric unit for weight, measuring the amount of pull or push a force such as gravity produces between two masses. (p. 83)

nicotine (nik′ə tēn′) A poisonous, oily substance found in tobacco. (p. 462)

nucleus (nü′klē əs) A cell's central control station. (p. 15)

nymph (nimf) A stage of some organisms that hatch from an egg during incomplete metamorphosis; a nymph is a young insect that looks like an adult. (p. 267)

O

open circuit (ō′pən sûr′kit) A broken or incomplete path that electricity cannot flow through. (p. 305)

order (ôr′dər) A smaller group within a class. Orders are made up of still smaller groups of similar organisms called *families*. (p. 30)

organ (ôr′gən) A group of tissues that work together to do a certain job. (p. 6)

organ system (ôr′gən sis′təm) A group of organs that work together to carry on life functions. (p. 6)

organism (ôr′gə niz′əm) A living thing that carries out five basic life functions on its own. (p. 4)

outer core (ou′tər kôr) A liquid layer of Earth lying below the mantle. (p. 202)

outwash plain (out′wôsh plān) Gravel, sand, and clay carried from glaciers by melting water and streams. (p. 179)

over-the-counter (ō′vər <u>th</u>ə koun′tər) Said of a medicine that can be purchased off the shelves in stores. (p. 470)

oxygen (ok′sə jən) A part of the air that is needed by most organisms to live. (p. 4)

P

parallel circuit (par′ə lel′ sûr′kit) A circuit in which each energy-using device is connected to the cell separately. (p. 317)

partly immovable joint (pärt′lē i mü′və bəl joint) A place where bones meet and can move only a little. (p. 438)

passive smoke (pas′iv smōk) Smoke that is inhaled by someone other than the smoker. (p. 463)

penicillin (pen′ə sil′in) A type of antibiotic first developed from a type of mold. (p. 470)

periodic (pîr′ē od′ik) Repeating in a pattern, like the *periodic* table of the elements. (p. 90)

permeability (pûr′mē ə bil′i tē) The rate at which water can pass through a material. Water passes quickly through porous soils with a high permeability. (p. 191)

pesticide (pes′tə sīd′) A chemical that kills insects. (p. 423)

petrified (pet′rə fīd′) Said of parts of plants or animals, especially wood and bone, that have been preserved by being "turned to stone." (p. 165)

pharmacist (fär′mə sist) A person trained and licensed to prepare and give out medicines according to a doctor's orders. (p. 470)

phylum (fī′ləm), *pl.* **phyla** (fī′lə) A smaller group into which members of a kingdom are further classified. Members share at least one major characteristic, like having a backbone. (pp. 30, 222)

physical change (fiz′i kəl chānj) A change that begins and ends with the same type of matter. *See* **chemical change**. (p. 107)

plasma (plaz′mə) The liquid part of blood. (p. 252)

pole (pōl) One of two ends of a magnet; where a magnet's pull is strongest. (p. 330)

population (pop′yə lā′shən) One type of organism living in an area. (p. 50)

pore space (pôr spās) Any of the gaps between soil particles, usually filled with water and air. *Porous* soils have large, well-connected pore spaces. (pp. 190, 408)

precipitation (pri sip′i tā′shən) Water in the atmosphere that falls to Earth as rain, snow, hail, or sleet. (p. 386)

prescription (pri skrip′shən) An order from a doctor, usually for medicine. (p. 470)

producer (prə dü′sər) An organism, such as a plant, that makes food. (p. 54)

property (prop′ər tē) A characteristic of something that you can observe, such as mass, volume, weight, and density. (p. 68)

protective resemblance (prə tek′tiv ri zem′bləns) A type of adaptation in which an animal resembles something in its environment. (p. 276)

protist (prō′tist) Any of a variety of one-celled organisms that live in pond water. (p. 19)

pulley (pul′ē) A grooved wheel that turns by the action of a rope in the groove. *See* **fixed pulley** and **movable pulley**. (p. 134)

pupa (pū′pə) A stage of some organisms that follows the larva stage in complete metamorphosis; many changes take place as adult tissues and organs form. (p. 266)

R

radial symmetry (rā′dē əl sim′ə trē) A form of symmetry in which an animal has matching body parts that extend outward from a central point. (p. 215)

radiate (rā′dē āt′) To send energy traveling in all directions through space. (p. 354)

radiation (rā′dē ā′shən) The transfer of heat through space. (p. 119)

rechargeable battery (rē charj′ə bəl bat′ə rē) A battery in which the chemical reactions can be reversed by a recharger, allowing these batteries to be used again and again. (p. 357)

reflex (rē′fleks′) The simplest inherited behavior, which is automatic, like an animal scratching an itch. (p. 280)

regeneration (rē jen′ə rā′shən) A form of asexual reproduction in simple animals in which a whole animal develops from just a part of the original animal. (p. 268)

relative age (rel′ə tiv āj) The age of something compared to the age of another thing. (p. 153)

PRONUNCIATION KEY

a **at**; ā **ape**; ä **far**; âr **care**; e **end**; ē **me**; i **it**; ī **ice**; îr **pierce**; o **hot**; ō **old**; ô **fork**; oi **oil**; ou **out**; u **up**; ū **use**; ü **rule**; ú **pull**; ûr **turn**; hw **white**; ng **song**; th **thin**; th **this**; zh **measure**; ə **about, taken, pencil, lemon, circus**

reptile (rep′təl) A cold-blooded vertebrate that lives on land and has a backbone, an endoskeleton, and waterproof skin with scales or plates. (p. 240)

resistor (ri zis′tər) A material through which electricity has difficulty flowing. (p. 307)

respiratory system (res′pər ə tôr′ē sis′təm) The organ system that brings oxygen to body cells and removes waste gas. (p. 253)

rock cycle (rok sī′kəl) A never-ending process by which rocks are changed from one type to another. (p. 155)

rock debris (rok də brē′) Boulders, rock fragments, gravel, sand, and soil that are picked up by a glacier as it moves. (p. 176)

runoff (run′ôf′) The water that flows over Earth's surface but does not evaporate or soak into the ground. (p. 409)

S

scale (skāl) An instrument used to measure weight. (p. 83)

screw (skrü) An inclined plane that is wrapped around a pole. (p. 137)

sediment (sed′ə mənt) Deposited rock particles and other materials that settle in a liquid. (p. 152)

sedimentary rock (sed′ə men′tə rē rok) Rock formed from bits or layers of rocks cemented together. (p. 152)

seismic wave (sīz′mik wāv) A vibration caused by rocks moving and breaking along faults. (p. 200)

seismogram (sīz′mə gram′) The record of seismic waves made by a seismograph. (p. 201)

seismograph (sīz′mə graf′) An instrument that detects, measures, and records the energy of earthquake vibrations. (p. 198)

septic tank (sep′tik tangk) An underground tank in which sewage is broken down by bacteria. (p. 425)

series circuit (sîr′ēz sûr′kit) A circuit in which the current must flow through one energy-using device in order to flow through the other. (p. 316)

sewage (sü′ij) Water mixed with waste. (p. 425)

sewer (sü′ər) A large pipe or channel that carries sewage to a sewage treatment plant. (p. 425)

sexual reproduction (sek′shü əl rē′prə duk′shən) Producing offspring with two parents. (p. 268)

short circuit (shôrt sûr′kit) When too much current flows through a conductor. (p. 308)

side effect (sīd i fekt′) An unwanted result of using a medicine. (p. 471)

simple machine (sim′pəl mə shēn′) A machine with few moving parts that makes it easier to do work. (p. 130)

skeletal muscle (skel′i təl mus′əl) A muscle that is attached to a bone and allows movement. (p. 446)

skeletal system (skel′i təl sis′təm) The organ system made up of bones, cartilage, and ligaments. (pp. 256, 439)

skeleton (skel′i tən) An internal supporting frame that gives the body its shape and protects many organs. (p. 436)

smooth muscle (smü<u>th</u> mus′əl) The type of muscle that makes up internal organs and blood vessels. (p. 449)

soil profile (soil prō′fil) A vertical section of soil from the surface down to bedrock. (p. 187)

soil water (soil wô′tər) Water that soaks into the ground. (p. 374)

solid (sol′id) A form of matter that has a definite shape and takes up a definite amount of space. (p. 70)

species (spē′shēz) The smallest classification group, made up of only one type of organism that can reproduce with others of the same species; for example, all dogs belong to the same species. (p. 30)

sperm (spûrm) The male sex cell. (p. 269)

spherical symmetry (sfer′i kəl sim′ə trē) A form of symmetry in which the parts of an animal with a round body match up when it is folded through its center. (p. 215)

sponge (spunj) The simplest kind of invertebrate. (p. 214)

sprain (sprān) A pull or tear in a muscle or ligament. (p. 439)

standard unit (stan′dərd ū′nit) A unit of measure that people all understand and agree to use. (p. 80)

state (stāt) A form of matter, such as a solid, liquid, or gas; how quickly the particles of matter vibrate, how much heat energy they have, and how they are arranged determine the state of matter. (p. 70)

static electricity (stat′ik i lek tris′i tē) A buildup of an electrical charge. (p. 294)

stimulant (stim′yə lənt) A substance that speeds up the activity of the body. (p. 462)

streak plate (strēk plāt) A glass plate that a mineral can be rubbed against to find out the color of the streak it leaves. (p. 149)

subsoil (sub′soil′) A hard layer of clay and minerals that lies beneath topsoil. (p. 187)

surface current (sûr′fis kûr′ənt) The movement of the ocean caused by steady winds blowing over the ocean. (p. 397)

switch (swich) A device that can open or close an electric circuit. (p. 309)

symmetry (sim′ə trē) The way an animal's body parts match up around a point or central line. (p. 214)

system (sis′təm) A group of parts that work together. (p. 6)

T

tar (tär) A sticky, brown substance found in tobacco. (p. 462)

temperature (tem′pər ə chər) A measure of how hot or cold something is. (p. 121)

tendon (ten′dən) A strong band of tissue that connects a muscle to bone. (p. 447)

terminal (tûr′mə nəl) One of two places where wires can be attached to a cell or battery. (p. 306)

terminus (tûr′mə nəs) The end, or outer margin, of a glacier where rock debris accumulates. (p. 177)

thermometer (thər mom′i tər) An instrument used to measure temperature. (p. 121)

tide (tīd) The rise and fall of ocean water levels. (p. 398)

tissue (tish′ü) A group of similar cells that work together to carry out a job. (p. 5)

topsoil (top′soil′) The dark, top layer of soil, rich in humus and minerals, in which many tiny organisms live and most plants grow. (p. 187)

trait (trāt) A characteristic of an organism. (p. 28)

tranquilizer (trang′kwə lī′zər) A type of medicine used to calm a person. (p. 472)

PRONUNCIATION KEY

a **at**; ā **ape**; ä **far**; âr **care**; e **end**; ē **me**; i **it**; ī **ice**; îr **pierce**; o **hot**; ō **old**; ô **fork**; oi **oil**; ou **out**; u **up**; ū **use**; ü **rule**; u̇ **pull**; ûr **turn**; hw **white**; ng **song**; th **thin**; <u>th</u> **this**; zh **measure**; ə **about, taken, pencil, lemon, circus**

transformer (trans fôr′mər) A device in which alternating current in one coil produces current in a second coil. (p. 346)

transpiration (tran′spə rā′shən) The process whereby plants release water vapor into the air through their leaves. (p. 411)

triceps (trī′seps) A muscle on the outside of the upper arm that straightens the arm by contracting. (p. 446)

U

urine (yür′in) The concentrated wastes filtered by the kidneys. (p. 254)

V

vacuole (vak′ū ōl′) A holding bin for food, water, and waste. (p. 15)

vertebrate (vûr′tə brāt′) An animal with a backbone. (p. 214)

virus (vī′rəs) Nonliving particles smaller than cells that are able to reproduce inside living cells. (p. 20)

volt (vōlt) A unit for measuring the force that makes negative charges flow. (p. 345)

volume (vol′ūm) How much space an object takes up. (p. 81)

voluntary muscle (vol′ən ter′ē mus′əl) A muscle that causes movements you can control. (p. 449)

W

warm-blooded (wôrm′blud′id) Said of an animal with a constant body temperature. (p. 236)

water conservation (wôtər kon′sər vā′shən) The use of water-saving methods. (p. 426)

water cycle (wô′tər sī′kəl) The continuous movement of water between Earth's surface and the air, changing from liquid to gas to liquid. (p. 388)

water table (wô′tər tā′bəl) The upper area of groundwater. (p. 408)

water treatment plant (wô′tər trēt′mənt plant) A place where water is made clean and pure. (p. 424)

water vapor (wô′tər vā′pər) Water as a gas in Earth's atmosphere. (p. 372)

wave (wāv) An up-and-down movement of water. (p. 399)

weathering (weth′ər ing) The process of breaking down rocks into smaller pieces that create sediment. (p. 155)

wedge (wej) A simple machine made by combining two inclined planes. It translates a downward force into two outward forces in opposite directions. (p. 137)

weight (wāt) The measure of the pull of gravity between an object and Earth. (p. 83)

wet cell (wet sel) A device that produces electricity using two different metal bars placed in an acid solution. (p. 344)

wheel and axle (hwēl and ak′səl) A simple machine made of a handle or axis attached to the center of a wheel. (p. 135)

work (wûrk) To apply a force that makes an object move. An object must move some distance to call what happens work. (p. 128)

INDEX

W

INDEX

CREDITS

Design & Production: Kirchoff/Wohlberg, Inc.

Maps: Geosystems.

Transvision: Stephen Ogilvy (photography); Guy Porfirio (illustration).

Illustrations: Kenneth Batelman: pp. 74, 105, 121; Dan Brown: pp. 376, 384, 385, 388-389, 389, 398, 399, 400, 408, 410; Elizabeth Callen: pp. 284, 368; Barbara Cousins: pp. 252, 253, 254, 255, 256, 257, 266; Steven Cowden: pp. 296, 297, 298, 318-319, 348, 354; Michael DiGiorgio: pp. 215, 222, 236; Jeff Fagan: pp. 132, 133, 137; Howard S. Friedman: p. 54; Colin Hayes: pp. 127, 134, 135, 310, 333, 343, 346, 347, 445, R7, R11, R13, R15, R20-R23; Tom Leonard: pp. 4, 5, 6, 16, 42, 43, 44, 51, 213, 225, 237, 264, 265, 268, 271, 332, 335, 344, 356, 362, 370, 436, 437, 438, 446, 447, 448, 449, 459; Olivia: pp. 24, 61, 64, 100, 141, 172, 205, 248, 285, 294, 326, 365, 404, 429, 454, 477, R2-R4, R9, R10, R13, R16-R19, R23-R25; Sharron O'Neil: pp. 14, 15, 20, 28, 31, 40, 41, 153, 176, 186, 190, 191, 374, 411; Vilma Ortiz-Dillon: pp. 144, 208, 386, 396, 397, 421, 424, 425, 432; Rob Schuster: pp. 84, 108, 117, 118, 120, 179, 307, 322, 342, 355, 358, 359; Matt Straub: pp. 7, 33, 58, 243, 458, 461, 480; Ted Williams: pp. 69, 92, 93, 95, 119, 154, 155, 198, 200, 201, 202, 338-339, 392-393, 456, 457, 463, 465, 469; Craig Zolman: pp. 303, 304, 305, 306, 308, 309, 316, 317, 318, 319, 320, 321, 368.

Photography Credits:

Contents: iii: Jim Battles/Debinsky Photo Associates. iv: inset, Corbis; Richard Price/FPG. v: E.R. Degginger/Bruce Coleman, Inc. vi: R. Williams/Bruce Coleman, Inc. vii: Jim Foster/The Stock Market. viii: Steve Wilkings/The Stock Market. ix: Mehau Kulyk/Science Photo Library.

National Geographic Invitation to Science: S2: t. Michael Nichols/National Geographic; b. Vanne Goodall. S3: t., b. Michael Nichols/National Geographic.

Be a Scientist: S4: bkgrd. Paul S. Howell/Liaison Agency; inset, Stuart Westmorland/Tony Stone Images. S5: David Mager. S6: t. Steven M. Barnett; m. The Granger Collection, New York; b. Corbis. S7: t. Bruce Avera Hunter/National Geographic Society-Image Collection; b. Michael Justice/Liaison. S8: Eric Neurath/Stock, Boston. S10: Robert Halstead-TPI/Masterfile. S11: l. Stuart Westmorland/Tony Stone Images; r. Steinhart Aquarium/Tom McHugh/Photo Researchers, Inc. S12: James Stanfield. S13: l. Tom Tracy/Tony Stone Images; r. Steven M. Barnett; r. Andrew Wood/Photo Researchers, Inc. S14: The Granger Collection, New York. S15: t. National Geographic Society Photographic Laboratory; b. David Mager. S16: t., b. David Doubilet. S17: Jeff Rotman/Tony Stone Images. S19: Stephen Ogilvy.

Unit 1: 1: F.C. Millington/TCL Masterfile; John Lythgoe/TCL Masterfile. 2: Stephen Ogilvy. 3: t., b. Stephen Ogilvy. 7: Stephen Ogilvy. 8: l. David M. Philipps/Photo Researchers, Inc.; r. Astrid & Hanns-Frieder/Photo Researchers, Inc.; b.l. Michael Abbey/Photo Researchers, Inc; b.r. Edward R. Degginger/Bruce Coleman, Inc. 9: Ann & Carl Purcell/Words & Pictures/PNI. 10: l. Enrico Ferorelli; r. Phyllis Picardi/Stock, Boston/PNI. 11: Dan McCoy/Rainbow/PNI. 12: Stephen Ogilvy. 13: Nigel Cattlin/Photo Researchers, Inc. 17: Stephen Ogilvy. 18: l. & r. PhotoDisc; inset t.l. & inset t.r. Biophoto Associates/Photo Researchers, Inc.; inset b.l. Ken Edward/Photo Researchers, Inc.; inset b.r. J.F. Gennaro/Photo Researchers, Inc. 19: t.l. M.I. Walker/Photo Researchers, Inc.; m.l. Biophoto Associates/Photo Researchers, Inc.; b.l. Eric V. Grave/Photo Researchers, Inc.; inset r. CNRI/Science Photo/Photo Researchers, Inc.; r. Joy Spur/Bruce Coleman, Inc. 21: Doctor Dennis Kunkel/Phototake/PNI. 22-23: David Scharf/Peter Arnold, Inc. 23: R. Maisonneuvre/Photo Researchers, Inc.; V.I. LAB E.R.I.C./FPG. 25: Tom & Pat Leeson. 26: Stephen Ogilvy. 27: t.l. Gregory Ochocki/Photo Researchers, Inc.; t.r. J. Foott/Tom Stack & Associates; m.l. Kjell B. Sandved; m.r. Charlie Heidecker/Visuals Unlimited; m.l. Carl R. Sams II/Peter Arnold, Inc.; m.r. Richard Schiell/Animals Animals; b.l. Hans Pfletschinger/Peter Arnold, Inc.; b.r. Mike Bacon/Tom Stack & Associates. 29: M.I. Walker/Photo Researchers, Inc. 30: Margaret Miller/Photo Researchers, Inc. 32: Stephen Ogilvy. 33: PhotoDisc. 34: l. Richard R. Hansen/Photo Researchers, Inc.; r. Jany Sauvanet/Photo Researchers, Inc.; b. Kevin Schafer/Corbis. 35: l. Adam Jones/Photo Researchers, Inc.; m. Stephen Dalton/Photo Researchers, Inc.; r. Scott Camazine/Photo Researchers, Inc. 36: Dieter & Mary Plage/Bruce Coleman, Inc. 37: Edward R. Degginger/Bruce Coleman, Inc. 38: Francois Gohier/Photo Researchers, Inc. 39: l. Biophoto Associates/Photo Researchers, Inc.; r. Edward R. Degginger/Photo Researchers, Inc. 41: Stephen Ogilvy. 43: Charles E. Mohr/Photo Researchers, Inc. 45: Tom McHugh/Photo Researchers, Inc. 46: Project Lokahi. 46-47: Ken Lucas/Visuals Unlimited. 48: Stephen J. Krasemann/Photo Researchers, Inc. 49: Stephen Ogilvy. 50: Stephen Ogilvy. 51: Stephen Ogilvy. 52: l. Stephen Krasemann/Photo Researchers, Inc.; m. Jim Steinberg/Photo Researchers, Inc.; r. Renee Lynn/Photo Researchers, Inc. 53: b.l. C.K. Lorenz/Photo Researchers, Inc.; m. Leonide Principe/Photo Researchers, Inc.; r. F. Stuart Westmorland/Photo Researchers, Inc. 55: t. Microfield Scientific/Photo Researchers, Inc.; b. Andrew J. Martinez/Photo Researchers, Inc. 56: inset, Charlie Ott/Photo Researchers, Inc. 56-57: Stephen Dalton/Photo Researchers, Inc. 57: r. Stephen Ogilvy. 59: Arthur Tilley/FPG. 60: Chinch Gryniewicz/Ecoscene/Corbis.

Unit 2: 65: Picture Perfect; Phil Degginger/Bruce Coleman, Inc. 66: PhotoDisc. 67: Stephen Ogilvy. 68: Stephen Ogilvy. 70: Stephen Ogilvy. 71: r. PhotoDisc; l. Stephen Ogilvy. 72: r. Charles Gupton/AllStock/PNI; l. Stephen Ogilvy. 73: all Stephen Ogilvy. 74: Stephen Ogilvy. 75: Stephen Ogilvy. 76: l. James A. Sugar/Black Star/PNI; r. Lisa Quinones/Black Star/PNI. 77: James A. Sugar/Black Star/PNI. 78: Stephen Ogilvy. 79: Stephen Ogilvy. 80: PhotoDisc. 82: Stephen Ogilvy. 83: Stephen Ogilvy. 84: Stephen Ogilvy. 85: Craig Tuttle/The Stock Market. 86: Stephen Ogilvy. 87: t. BIPM; b. Stockbyte. 88: PhotoDisc. 89: Stephen Ogilvy. 91: Corbis/Bettmann. 92: Stephen Ogilvy. 94: Stephen Ogilvy. 95: Stephen Ogilvy. 96: PhotoDisc; (soda can) Steven Needham/Envision. 97: Stephen Ogilvy. 98: t. Science Photo Library/Photo Researchers. 98-99: b. Chris Collins/The Stock Market. 99: Corbis/Bettmann. 101: Stock Imagery, Inc.; E.J. West/Stock Imagery, Inc. 102: l. Jean Higgins/Envision; r. Rafael Macia/Photo Researchers, Inc. 103: Stephen Ogilvy. 104: col 1: l. Michael Keller/FPG; r. Charles Winters/Photo Researchers, Inc.; col 2: t. Ron Rovtar/FPG; b. James L. Amos/Photo Researchers, Inc. 106: l. Stephen Ogilvy; r.t. R.B. Smith/Dembinsky Photo; r.b. Charles Winters/Photo Researchers, Inc. 109: Stephen Ogilvy. 110: col 1: t. Gerald Zanetti/The Stock Market; m. Biophoto Associates/Photo Researchers, Inc.; b. Philip James Corwin/Corbis; col 2: t. Robert Jonathan Kligge/The Stock Market; m. Brownie Harris/The Stock Market; b. Adam Hart-Davis/Photo Researchers, Inc. 111: Stephen Ogilvy. 112: t. Joel Arrington/Visuals Unlimited; m. David McGlynn/FPG; b. Paul Bierman/Visuals Unlimited. 112-113: PhotoDisc. 113: Sylvan Wittwer/Visuals Unlimited. 114: Richard Ellis/Photo Researchers, Inc. 115: Stephen Ogilvy. 116: Stephen Ogilvy. 117: Stephen Ogilvy. 119: Stephen Ogilvy. 122: t. Edward R. Degginger/Bruce Coleman, Inc.; m. Tim Davis/Photo Researchers, Inc.; b. Hans Reinhard/Bruce Coleman, Inc. 124: PhotoDisc; Ken Karp. 125: Jade Albert/FPG. 126: Debra P. Hershkowitz. 128: l. Idaho Ketchum/The Stock Market; r. Dollarhide Monkmeyer. 129: Hank Morgan/Photo Researchers, Inc. 130: l. Steve Elmore/Bruce Coleman, Inc.; b. Edward R. Degginger/Bruce Coleman, Inc.; r. J. Fennell/Bruce Coleman, Inc. 131: l. Tony Freeman/PhotoEdit; c. Kenneth H. Thomas/Photo Researchers, Inc.; t.r. Tony Freeman/PhotoEdit; b.r. Science VU/Visuals Unlimited. 133: David Mager. 135: Alan Schein/The Stock Market. 136: David Young-Wolff/PhotoEdit. 138: Michal Newman/PhotoEdit. 139: PhotoDisc. 140: l. Culver Pictures, Inc.; m. www.artoday.com.

Unit 3: 145: Carr Clifton; Tom Bean. 146: Sinclair Stammers/Photo Researchers, Inc. 147: Stephen Ogilvy. 148: l. & m. Ken Karp; r. Stephen Ogilvy; b. Joyce Photographics/Photo Researchers, Inc. 149: t.r. Corbis; t.l., b.r. Stephen Ogilvy; b.l. Mark A. Schneider/VU. 150: PhotoDisc. 151: l. Ken Karp; m. & r. E.R. Degginger/Photo Researchers, Inc. 152: t.l. Charles Winters/Photo Researchers, Inc.; t.r. A.J. Copley/VU; b.l. Stephen Ogilvy; b.r. Ken Karp. 153: Stephen Ogilvy. 154: Corbis. 156: t. J C Carton/Bruce Coleman, Inc.; b. Edward R. Degginger/Bruce Coleman, Inc. 157: Stephen Ogilvy. 158: t. David Burnett/Contract Press Images/PNI; b. E.R. Degginger/Photo Researchers, Inc. 159: NASA. 160: l. Weststock; m. PhotoDisc. 162: Francois Gohier/Photo Researchers, Inc.; 163: l. Charles R. Belinky/Photo Researchers, Inc.; r. Stephen Ogilvy. 164: l. Edward R. Degginger/Bruce Coleman, Inc.; r. Novosti/Photo Researchers, Inc. 165: l. A.J. Copley/Visuals Unlimited; r. Ed Bohon/The Stock Market. 166: Carlos Goldin/Photo Researchers, Inc. 167: A.J. Copley/Visuals Unlimited. 168: l. Tom McHugh/Photo Researchers, Inc.; r. A.J. Copley/Visuals Unlimited. 169: l. Phototake/PNI; r. Phil Degginger/Bruce Coleman, Inc. 170: Richard Lydekker/Linda Hall Library. 171: courtesy Lisa White. 173: N.&M. Freeman/Bruce Coleman, Inc. 174: Lee Foster/Bruce Coleman, Inc. 175: Stephen Ogilvy. 177: Charlie

Heidecker/Visuals Unlimited. 178: Stephen Ogilvy. 180: John Serrao/ Photo Researchers, Inc. 181: Joyce Photographics/Photo Researchers, Inc. 182-183: Ron Sanford/The Stock Market. 183: Photo Researchers, Inc. 184: Stephen Ogilvy. 185: Stephen Ogilvy. 187: Black/Bruce Coleman, Inc. 188: Stephen Ogilvy. 188-189: Janis Burger/Bruce Coleman, Inc. 190: Stephen Ogilvy. 192: Kazuyoshi Nomachi/Photo Researchers, Inc. 193: Richard T. Nowitz/Photo Researchers, Inc. 195: t.r. Barry Hennings/Photo Researchers, Inc.; b.l. Franco Sal- Moiragni/The Stock Market; t.l. Gary S. Withey/Bruce Coleman, Inc.; bkgrd. Lynette Cook/Science Photo Library/Photo Researchers, Inc. 196: Stephen Ogilvy. 197: Stephen Ogilvy. 199: l. PhotoDisc; r. Stephen Ogilvy. 203: Russell D. Curtis/Photo Researchers, Inc. 204: Corbis.

Unit 4: 209: Art Wolf/Tony Stone Images. 210: Hans Reinhard/Bruce Coleman, Inc. 211: Stephen Ogilvy. 212: l. Maryann Frazier/Photo Researchers, Inc.; r. Scott Smith/Animals Animals. 214: l. Stephen Ogilvy; r. Charles V. Angelo/Photo Researchers, Inc. 216: t.r. Joe McDonald/Bruce Coleman, Inc.; m.r. James R. McCullagh/Visuals Unlimited; b.l. Neil S. McDaniel/Photo Researchers, Inc.; b.c. Ron & Valerie Taylor/Bruce Coleman, Inc.; b.r. John Chellman/Animals Animals. 217: l. David Doubilet; r. Andrew J. Martinez/Photo Researchers, Inc. 218: Sisse Brimberg/National Geographic Image Collection. 219: t. Fran Coleman/Animals Animals; b. Joel Sartore. 220: l. & r. Chip Clark. 221: t. Kim Taylor/Bruce Coleman, Inc; b. Ray Coleman/Photo Researchers, Inc. 223: inset, Marian Bacon/Animals Animals; t. Sefton/Bruce Coleman, Inc. 224: t. Carol Geake/Animals Animals; b. J.H. Robinson/ Photo Researchers, Inc. 226: l. Joyce & Frank Burek/Animals Animals; b.r. Zig Leszczynski/Animals Animals. 227: Doug Sokell/Visuals Unlimited. 228: l. Jane Burton/Bruce Coleman, Inc.; r. Tom McHugh/ Photo Researchers, Inc. 229: col 1: L. West/Photo Researchers, Inc.; insets l. & r. Dwight Kuhn; col 2 clockwise from top: L. West/Bruce Coleman, Inc.; John D. Cunningham/Visuals Unlimited; Mary Beth Angelo/Photo Researchers, Inc.; Cabisco/Visuals Unlimited; Fabio Colombini/Animals Animals; Mary Snyderman/Visuals Unlimited. 230-231: L. Newman A./Photo Researchers, Inc. 231: William J. Pohley/ Visuals Unlimited. 232: t.l. Richard Hamilton Smith/Dembinsky Photo Assoc. 232-233: PhotoDisc. 233: t. Richard T. Nowitz/Photo Researchers,Inc.; David Young-Wolf/PhotoEdit. 234: Stephen Ogilvy. 235: Norman Owen Tomalin/Bruce Coleman, Inc. 237: Hans Reinhard/ Bruce Coleman, Inc. 238: Dave B. Fleetham/Visuals Unlimited; inset, Jane Burton/Bruce Coleman, Inc. 239: t. G.I. Bernard/OSF Animals Animals; b. L. West/Bruce Coleman, Inc. 240: Tom McHugh/Photo Researchers, Inc. 241: Roy David Farris/Visuals Unlimited. 242: Jean Phillipe Varin/Photo Researchers, Inc. 243: clockwise from t.l.: Dan Guravich/Photo Researchers, Inc.; Ron & Valerie Taylor/Bruce Coleman, Inc.; Jeff Lepore/Photo Researchers, Inc.; Dwight R. Kuhn; Wally Eberhart/Visuals Unlimited; Zig Leszczynski/Animals Animals. 244: Stephen Ogilvy. 245: t. Eric & David Hosking/Corbis; b. W. Perry Conway/Corbis. 246: Douglas Faulkner/Photo Researchers, Inc. 247: inset, Kennan Ward/Bruce Coleman, Inc.; bkgrd. Peter B. Kaplan/Photo Researchers, Inc. 249: Charles Krebs/Tony Stone Images; L.L. Rue III/Bruce Coleman, Inc. 250: PhotoDisc. 251: Stephen Ogilvy. 258: Kjell B. Sandved/Photo Researchers, Inc. 259: Stephen Spotte/Photo Researchers, Inc. 260: PhotoDisc. 261: b.r. PhotoDisc; t.l. Larry Cameron/Photo Researchers, Inc.; t.r. Norman Owen Tomalin/Bruce Coleman, Inc. 262: Gerard Lacz/Animals Animals. 263: Stephen Ogilvy. 270: Stephen Ogilvy. 271: AP/Wide World Photos. 272: Stephen Ogilvy. 273: b.r. D. Long/Visuals Unlimited; bkgrd. G. Buttner/Okapia/Photo Researchers, Inc.; r. Wally Eberhart/Visuals Unlimited. 274: Michael Fogden/Bruce Coleman, Inc. 276: Breck P. Kent/Animals Animals; Michael Fogden/Bruce Coleman, Inc. 277: K & K Ammann/Bruce Coleman, Inc. 278: John Shaw/Bruce Coleman, Inc. 280: l. Maria Zorn/Animals Animals; r. W.J.C. Murray/Bruce Coleman, Inc. 282: Rita Nannini/Photo Researchers, Inc. 283: A. Ramey/PhotoEdit. 284: PhotoDisc; b.r. Thomas C. Boyden/Dembinsky Photo Assoc.

Unit 5: 289: PhotoDisc. 290: Tim Davis/Photo Researchers, Inc. 291: Stephen Ogilvy. 292: Stockbyte. 293: PhotoDisc. 294: PhotoDisc. 295: Stephen Ogilvy. 297: Kent Wood/Photo Researchers, Inc. 299: PhotoDisc. 300: l. The Granger Collection, New York; r. Dale Camera Graphics/Phototake/PNI. 301: The Granger Collection, New York. 302: Stephen Ogilvy. 305: Stephen Ogilvy. 308: Stephen Ogilvy. 309: Norbert Wu. 311: Stephen Ogilvy. 312: b.l. Culver Pictures, Inc.; m. Stock Montage, Inc.; b.r. PhotoDisc; t.r. Rich Treptow/Photo Researchers, Inc. 313: m. Norman Owen Tomalin/Bruce Coleman, Inc.; b.r. Will & Deni McIntyre/Photo Researchers, Inc. 314: PhotoDisc. 315: Stephen Ogilvy. 322: l. PhotoDisc; r. Norman Owen Tomalin/Bruce Coleman, Inc. 323: Stephen Ogilvy. 324: Don Mason/The Stock Market. 324-325: Michael

W. Davidson/Photo Researchers, Inc. 325: David Parker/Seagate/Photo Researchers, Inc. 327: PhotoDisc. 328: Stephen Ogilvy. 329: Stephen Ogilvy. 330: Stephen Ogilvy. 331: Stephen Ogilvy. 332: Stephen Ogilvy. 334: l. Stephen Ogilvy; r. David R. Frazier/Photo Researchers, Inc. 336: l. Stephen Ogilvy; r. Science Photo Library/Photo Researchers, Inc. 337: Stephen Ogilvy. 340: AP/Wide World Photos. 341: Stephen Ogilvy. 345: Stephen Ogilvy. 346: Ken Sherman/Bruce Coleman, Inc. 349: Historical Picture Archive/Corbis. 350: Stephen Ogilvy. 351: t. Elena Rooraid/PhotoEdit. b. Dennis Hallinan/FPG. 352: Stephen Ogilvy. 353: Stephen Ogilvy. 355: Stephen Ogilvy. 357: Stephen Ogilvy. 358: Stephen Ogilvy. 359: Stephen Ogilvy. 360: l. Martin Withers/Dembinsky Photo & PhotoDisc; c. Gelfan/Monkmeyer; r. Andrew/Photo Researchers, Inc. 360-361: PhotoDisc. 361: l. Charles D. Winters/Photo Researchers, Inc.; b. Stockbyte; r. Aaron Haupt/Photo Researchers, Inc. 363: Stephen Ogilvy. 364: bkgrd. Arthur Tilley/FPG; b.l. Robert Pettit/Dembinsky Photo; t.r. Schneider Studio/The Stock Market; b.r. Simon Fraser/Photo Researchers, Inc.; t.l. Werner Bertsch/Bruce Coleman, Inc.

Unit 6: 369: Picture Perfect; John Turner/Tony Stone Images. 371: Stephen Ogilvy. 372: Planet Earth Pictures/FPG. 373: l. PhotoDisc; r. Courtesy of Lake Michigan. 374: Roy Morsch/The Stock Market. 375: Joe McDonald/Bruce Coleman, Inc.; inset, Ron & Valerie Taylor. 377: Stephen Ogilvy. 378: Stephen Ogilvy. 379: Wendell Metzen/Bruce Coleman, Inc. 380-381: L.A. Frank, The University of Iowa & NASA/ Goddard Space Flight Center; Michael Freeman/Bruce Coleman, Inc./PNI; Chad Ehlers/Photo Network/PNI. 382: Stephen Ogilvy. 383: Stephen Ogilvy. 386: Stephen Ogilvy. 387: inset, Joe DiMaggio/The Stock Market; Lee Rentz/Bruce Coleman, Inc. 390: t. John Shaw/Bruce Coleman, Inc.; b. Howard B. Bluestein/Photo Researchers, Inc. 391: Steve Smith/FPG. 392: Library of Congress/Corbis. 393: l. Barry L. Runk/Grant Heilman; r. Charles D. Winters/Photo Researchers, Inc. 394: Stephen Ogilvy. 395: Stephen Ogilvy. 398: t. & b. Andrew J. Martinez/Photo Researchers, Inc. 399: Stephen Ogilvy. 401: bkgrd. & inset, Courtesy of Bruce M. Richmond/USGS. 402: Wendell Metzen/Bruce Coleman, Inc. 403: bkgrd. PhotoDisc; b. Gary Randall/ FPG; m. Martin Bond/Science Photo Library/Photo Researchers, Inc. 405: Superstock; Chris Vincent/The Stock Market. 406: Culver Pictures, Inc. 407: Stephen Ogilvy. 409: l. Michael S. Renner/Bruce Coleman, Inc.; r. Stephen Ogilvy. 412: l. PhotoDisc; inset, J. Dermid/Bruce Coleman, Inc. 413: Richard & Susan Day/Animals Animals. 414: Stephen Ogilvy. 415: PhotoDisc. 416: l. Corbis/Bettmann; r. AP/Wide World Photos. 416-417: Black/Bruce Coleman, Inc. 417: t.l. AP/Wide World Photos; t.r. Corbis/UPI/Bettman; b. AP/Wide World Photos. 418: PhotoDisc. 419: Stephen Ogilvy. 420: PhotoDisc. 421: Richard Hutchings/Photo Researchers, Inc. 422: all PhotoDisc. 423: b. PhotoDisc; r. Blackstone R. Millbury/Bruce Coleman, Inc. 425: Norman Owen Tomalin/Bruce Coleman, Inc. 426: John Elk III/Bruce Coleman, Inc. 427: Stephen Ogilvy. 428: m. David L. Pearson/Visuals Unlimited; bkgrd. John Shaw/Bruce Coleman; t. John Gerlach/Dembinsky Photo Assoc.

Unit 7: 433: Ken Chernus/FPG; J.Y. Mallet/PhotoEdit. 434: Adam Jones/ Dembinsky Photo. 435: Stephen Ogilvy. 439: Stephen Ogilvy. 441: Stephen Ogilvy. 442: l. Billy E. Barnes/PhotoEdit/PNI; r. Dept. of Clinical Radiology, Salisbury District Hospital/SPL/Photo Researchers, Inc. 444: Michael Krasowitz/FPG. 446: Dwight R. Kuhn. 447: l. & c. Stephen Ogilvy; r. Rob Curtis/VIREO. 448: CNRI/Photo Researchers, Inc. 449: Marshall Sklar/Photo Researchers, Inc. 450: Stephen Ogilvy. 451: Stephen Ogilvy. 452: b. Corbis; t. Mark E. Gibson/Dembinsky Photo. 453: t. Blair Seitz/Photo Researchers, Inc.; b. Mark Gibson/Visuals Unlimited. 455: Bill Losh/FPG. 458: Michael A. Keller/The Stock Market. 460: Stephen Ogilvy. 462: Matt Meadows/Peter Arnold, Inc. 463: Arthur Tilley/FPG. 466: PhotoDisc. 467: Mark C. Burnett/ Photo Researchers, Inc. 468: Stephen Ogilvy. 470: José Pelaez/The Stock Market. 473: Bill Beatty/Visuals Unlimited. 474: l. Stephen Ogilvy; r. Jeff Greenberg/PhotoEdit. 476: m. Barros & Barros/The Image Bank; t. Bill Bachmann/Photo Researchers, Inc.; bkgrd. Ed Gallucci/The Stock Market.

Handbook: Steven Ogilvy: pp. R6, R8, R12, R14, R15, R26.

PERIODIC TABLE OF THE ELEMENTS

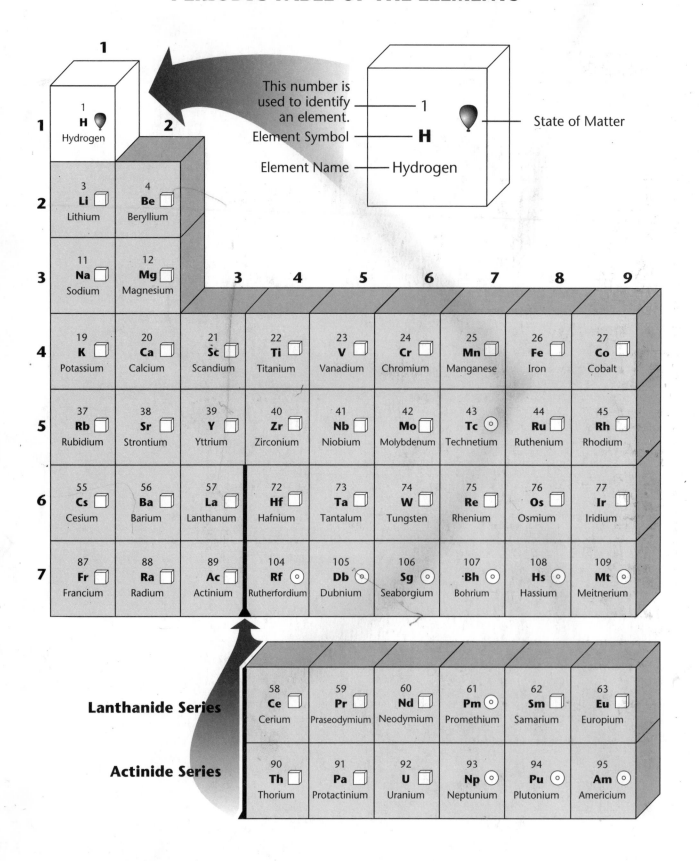